Accession no.
36136965

KT-231-895

The Pattern
of the Chinese Past

WITHDRAWN

The Pattern of the Chinese Past

A Social and Economic Interpretation

MARK ELVIN

LIS - LIBRARY

| Date | Fund |
| 12/05/14 | p-Che |

Order No.

2495296

University of Chester

STANFORD UNIVERSITY PRESS

STANFORD, CALIFORNIA

To my colleagues, past and present,
in the Department of Economic History
of the University of Glasgow

Stanford University Press
Stanford, California
© 1973 by Mark Elvin
Originating publisher: Eyre Methuen Ltd, London, 1973
First published in the U.S.A. by
Stanford University Press in 1973
Printed in the United States of America
Cloth ISBN 0-8047-0826-6   Paper ISBN 0-8047-0876-2
Last figure below indicates year of this printing:
07   06   05   04   03   02   01   00   99   98

Contents

Part Three · Economic development without technological change

Preface

A satisfactory comprehensive history of the social and economic development of pre-modern China, the largest country in the world in terms of population, and with a documentary record covering three millennia, is still far from possible. The present work is only an attempt to disengage the major themes that seem to be of relevance to our understanding of China today. In particular, I have studied three questions. Why did the Chinese Empire stay together when the Roman Empire, and every other empire of antiquity or the middle ages, ultimately collapsed? What were the causes of the medieval revolution which made the Chinese economy after about 1100 the most advanced in the world? And why did China after about 1350 fail to maintain her earlier pace of technological advance while still, in many respects, advancing economically? The three sections of the book deal with these problems in turn; but the division of subject-matter is to some extent only one of convenience. These topics are so interrelated that, in the last analysis, none of them can be considered in isolation from the others.

The chief stimulus for this enterprise was provided by the Department of Economic History at Glasgow University. When I left the seclusion of the Institute of Oriental Studies at Cambridge to join the Department early in 1968, I found myself faced with the need to compare the Chinese experience of social and economic development (and non-development) in a systematic fashion with what had happened in Europe and elsewhere. The ideas set forth here are in large measure the results of that comparison, whether this always appears overtly or not; and it therefore seems appropriate that I should respectfully dedicate this work to my colleagues.

MARK ELVIN

Acknowledgements

The number of friends and colleagues whose ideas I have drawn upon for this book is so great that I shall not attempt to thank them all individually. Let me simply say that I am very conscious of the immensity of my debt, and perpetually grateful to them. Special mention should, however, be made of a few: Piet van der Loon, who first made me conscious of the importance of regionality and the popular tradition in China; Ted Pulleyblank, who drove home the analytical problems raised by the vigour of early Chinese achievements in the scientific and economic spheres and the later relative stagnation; Joseph Needham, for his inspiring insight into scientific and technological history; Radha Sinha, in conversations with whom the conception of the high-level equilibrium trap emerged; Bill Skinner, for a sense of the structural changes in late traditional China which can be brought to light by local systems analysis; Yoshinobu Shiba, on whose writings I have relied so heavily in Part II; Rhoads Murphey, for insight into the effects of the vast size of the late traditional economy, and much other help; and Tom Metzger, for a deepened understanding of Chinese bureaucracy and the position of merchants in Ch'ing society. They should not be held responsible for my views, but they have helped me very greatly.

Thanks are due to Stanford University Press and to the Social Science Research Council (USA) for permission to use substantial portions of conference papers on market towns and water control in Shang-hai county, and on the pre-modern Chinese cotton industry; to the editor of *Modern Asian Studies* for permission to use material which first appeared in an article on land tenure in the issue of April 1970; and to Michigan University Center for Chinese Studies for permission to use material from my translations of works by Ayao Hoshi and Yoshinobu Shiba, published under their auspices. Gratitude is due to John Fairbank, Director of the East Asian Research Center at Harvard, for generously allowing me time to finish the last draft of the manuscript at the Center when I should have been pursuing another project.

I should also like to record my appreciation of advice given to me about farming by Michael Harvey, and about spinning machinery by David Holm, John Grant, and Douglas Steen and Partners of Dundee. Ed North of the University of Strathclyde provided two stimulating suggestions about Chinese hydraulic machinery; chapter 4 was much improved as the result of comments by Bill Jenner of the University of Leeds. Conversations with Charles Hucker, Tom Smith and George Moseley have enabled me to tighten my argument at several important places; and I should like to thank the Center for Chinese Studies at Michigan University, the Program on East Asian Local Systems at Stanford University and the Department of History at Tufts University for extending to me the invitations to lecture which made these conversations possible.

Simple justice dictates the breaking of a long-standing convention regarding publishers in order to put on record the contribution made by Richard Newnham as midwife of this book. His help has been indispensable. Finally, I should like to acknowledge a debt so basic as to be unrepayable: that which I owe to Philip Whitting, my former teacher at St Paul's School, London, from whom I learned most of what I know about the nature and study of history.

Maps

by John Flower

Figures and diagrams

The principal Chinese dynasties

(Dates are in some cases only approximate)

Early Empire	Ch'in	BC 221–207
	Former Han	BC 206–AD 8
	Later Han	AD 25–220
	Three Kingdoms	AD 221–64
	Western Chin	AD 265–311
	Northern and Southern Dynasties (Toba AD 386–533)	AD 311–580
Middle Empire	Sui	AD 589–617
	T'ang	AD 618–906
	Five Dynasties and Ten Kingdoms	AD 907–59
Later Empire	Northern Sung	AD 960–1126
	Chin/Mongol rule in north, Southern Sung in south	AD 1127–1275
	Mongols (Yuan)	AD 1276–1367
	Ming	AD 1368–1644
	Manchus (Ch'ing)	AD 1645–1911

The term 'late traditional China' is frequently used in the text to refer to China under the last two of the above dynasties only.

Part One · The formation of the world's largest enduring state

1 · Empires and their size

The question of the size of political units seems never to attract among historians and sociologists the attention which it deserves.[1] What determines why states and empires have expanded to the limits which they have historically achieved ? What are the conditions under which it has been possible to maintain these frontiers ? Why have the larger states normally broken up into fragments after a certain period of time ? As a general problem – distinct from the specific question of why particular units have disintegrated – this is still largely unexplored territory.

To the historian of China at least, it is also a matter of some moment. In the broadest of perspectives, the Chinese Empire is the major exception in the pre-modern world to what would appear to be the rule that units of territorial and demographic extent comparable to that of China are not stable entities over long periods of time. It would obviously be interesting to know why. The more so because the survival of the Chinese Empire was a close-run thing. Formed in the middle of the third century BC, it endured until the early fourth AD, when it was temporarily broken up by barbarian conquests. In other words, it did not at this time have the staying power of the Roman Empire in the East after the Western Roman Empire had collapsed. On the other hand, the Chinese Empire was reunited in the later part of the sixth century AD; and, except during the first half of the tenth century, China Proper (that is, excluding Manchuria, Mongolia, Chinese Turkestan and Tibet) was never thereafter under more than two administrations. After 1275 it was never for long under more than one. The Eastern Roman or Byzantine Empire per contra declined and was ultimately destroyed. Is it possible to identify the variables which account for these differing fates ?

I believe it is possible to do so to a first level of approximation in terms of three main elements and their relationships. These are the size of a political unit (of which a more precise definition in a moment), the productivity of its economy, and the proportion of total output which has to be spent on defence and administration. Intimately related to all three of these is the state of technology, understood in its widest sense: organizational, economic and military. The initial expansion of a political unit is usually due to some form of superiority over its neighbours in one or more of these respects. It may organize its people more effectively; and the reasons for this can include widespread literacy or a particular kind of ideology. Its labour force may, per worker, produce a bigger surplus above subsistence, permitting the maintenance of a larger nonproductive military and administrative establishment. Or again its soldiers may have better weapons, tighter discipline or more skilful tactics, which enable them to defeat enemies more numerous than themselves. Obviously, superiority in any one of these forms can to a considerable extent be used to compensate for weakness in others. A state with better soldiers needs fewer of them, and can so relieve some of the pressure on its productive resources. Organizing skill in the form of logistic capacity can to some degree substitute for military prowess; and so forth.

If the size of political units is to a great extent determined by the above factors, it is clearly likely to be unstable. Any improvement in the skills of an empire's neighbours, whether in political combination (as when Chinghis Khan combined the previously fragmented Mongol tribes), or in economic production, or in weaponry, will tend to imperil its territorial integrity. And the diffusion of techniques across the frontiers is, in the long run, virtually impossible to prevent. Thus Sir Charles Oman interestingly observes of the military techniques of the Germans at the time of Constantine that 'three hundred years of close contact with the [Roman] empire had taught them much', with the consequence that 'the ascendancy of the Roman infantry . . . was no longer so marked as in earlier ages'.[2] It will be shown later that one of the causes of the dramatic expansion of the Mongol Empire in the thirteenth century was its acquisition of Chinese ironmaking techniques and ironworkers. Recent European empires in Africa and Asia have found it virtually impossible to resist quite modest improvements in the political and organizational skills of their native subjects, in spite of retaining a clear economic and military superiority on a man-for-man basis. In order simply to maintain itself intact, then, an empire must be continually improving its technology at a pace sufficient to counterbalance the improvements made by its neighbours, or by subjected but still hostile populations.

It may be supposed that, in general, empires tend to expand to the point at which their technological superiority over their neighbours is approximately counterbalanced by the burdens of size. 'Size' prior to modern times must be conceived mainly in terms of the time and cost of communications over the vast distances involved, rather than just in terms of these distances themselves. In this sense, of course, the Chinese and the Roman empires were both much larger than any political unit existing at the present time. The burdens of size consist mainly in the need to maintain a more extended bureaucracy with more intermediate layers, the growing difficulties of effective co-ordination as territorial area increases, and the heavier cost of maintaining troops on longer frontier lines further removed from the main sources of trustworthy manpower and supplies. Size obviously has its advantages too, in the possession of greater and more varied resources, for example; and the acquisition of some territories (as of Egypt by Rome) may bring with it an important increase in imperial wealth. Roughly speaking, however, the larger the unit the more it has to excel its neighbours if it is to survive for long.

In so far as the assumption in the foregoing paragraphs holds true (namely that empires tend to expand to an equilibrium point at which they can just maintain their full extent), it follows that, internally, their social institutions are likely to be under a continual strain. The critical factor, particularly evident in the Roman and the early Chinese empires, is usually the heavy cost, relative to the total output of food and goods, of maintaining the administrative superstructure, and of providing the soldiers and supplies necessary for imperial security. Inevitably there is harsh taxation; and this in turn tends to induce social and political changes that undermine the fiscal soundness of the state. Typically, the peasant cultivator is impoverished and forced to sell his land. The need to find a haven from the tax-collector leads him to seek for patronage or protection from the powerful, evading public exactions at what is often the cost of his personal independence. As wealth, especially landed wealth, accumulates in the hands of a few persons, the government's revenues fall. Against this statesmen employ such policies as confiscating the possessions of the rich, imposing limitations on land-holdings (both the acquisition of land and the sale of land), and distributing public land to small farmers, soldiers and veterans. On the relative success or failure of these attempts, well exemplified in the seventh century AD by the Byzantine Themes and the T'ang 'equitable fields' and divisional militia, the political cohesion of empires and even their survival often depend.

The social changes which lead to a decline in the number of free subjects also make the recruitment of an imperial army difficult. Both the Roman and the Chinese empires were initially conquered by citizensoldiers. In both, these were replaced, though in rather different fashions, by professionals as the empire grew too large for a citizen-soldiery. In both, the cost of this army led to dangerous and ultimately fatal expedients. Barbarian troops were increasingly relied upon as auxiliaries, or even as the main fighting force. An active defence policy was too frequently rejected on the grounds of its expense; and attempts were made to subdue hostile barbarians by diplomacy, bribery and settlement on imperial lands. The outcome was a weakened internal structure, a barbarization from within, finally a total or partial collapse.

*

At this point we may return to our initial question. Why should the Chinese Empire, after its reunification in the sixth century AD, have remained essentially immune to these disruptive forces? Why did it not at some point break up permanently into separate states like those of Europe, but remain an empire with provinces the size of European states? The analytical framework just set up suggests the core of the answer: the Chinese must on the whole have managed to keep one step ahead of their neighbours in the relevant technical skills, military, economic and organizational; or more precisely, since strength in one of these sectors could at least partially offset weakness in another, in the complex of such skills considered as a whole. The first and second parts of this book will be devoted to showing that, on the whole, this bald simplification is empirically true.

This is not to say, of course, that China was immune from external *conquest*. She was not. But she was in the last resort immune from political *fragmentation*. It is here that an assumption only implicit in the argument so far must be brought out and made explicit. This is that the *cost* of the best military techniques tends to increase with time. In so far as a state has static revenues, or revenues rising more slowly than the cost of warfare, it will tend to fragment.* A similar effect arises if, for some reason such as the institutional changes outlined earlier, state revenues are falling while the cost of warfare stays constant. Why are there such consequences? Because, other things being equal, a reduction in the size of political units reduces the financial burdens of large geographical scale, and enables the resources so saved to be put into weaponry.†

Now, manifestly, there is something absurd about this argument if it is applied indiscriminately to all historic periods, and thus to all states of technology. In contemporary terms, it amounts to saying that Switzerland or Mauretania should be better able to afford atomic bombs and missiles than the USA or USSR. The argument is rescued from such an unhappy conclusion by the all-important qualification that it must be limited to periods or areas where the financial burdens of scale are still significantly large relative to the cost of the best armaments. In modern times this is no longer the case; and this fact is, indeed, one of the ways in which 'modernity' may be partially defined.

In traditional China the complex of factors making for fragmentation, as described above, never operated strongly over a long enough period of time to create enduring disunity. Two other causes also contributed to this. One was what may be loosely termed the 'geographical unity' of China and its relative isolation from the rest of the Eurasian landmass. The other was what may be characterized, equally loosely, as the 'cultural unity' of China. Both, however, were established in the course of imperial history; they were not simply present ready-made at the birth of the empire. For 'geographic unity' to be political and economic reality, rather than just latter-day cartographic fancy, there had first to be the revolution in transport and communications described in chapter 10. Cultural unity also had to be created. It began, perhaps, in 213 BC with the destruction of local records by the first emperor, a deliberate act

---

* A familiar case of this is the Ottoman Empire after the later sixteenth century. In order to keep up with the Europeans, it was necessary to increase the use of firearms and artillery. This meant that the cavalry, accustomed to a campaigning season and rewarded with fiefs, had to be progressively replaced with full-time paid professionals. The resulting pressures, at a time of financial crisis brought about by the inflow of New World silver, were disastrous.

† A related question is that of the effects of the spread of advanced military technology among an empire's subjects, as opposed to its soldiers. An example of this, described in chapter 8, is the diffusion of muskets among the Chinese population after about 1700. Such a diffusion lowers the relative effectiveness of soldiers vis-à-vis civilians, and leads to increased social strain, either in the form of reduced internal control, or heavier taxes to pay for more soldiers.

of policy aimed at extinguishing local loyalties. It continued for more than a millennium with the Han Chinese colonization of the south; and included the re-sinification of the north on two occasions: the first after the barbarian invasions of the fourth century AD, and the second after the Chin Tartar and Mongol conquests of the twelfth and thirteenth centuries. Nonetheless by about 1400 or 1500 both geographical and cultural unity had clearly acquired significance, even if less fundamental than the technological factors which had made them possible. Anyone, moreover, who is tempted to ascribe more than a modest part in ensuring imperial survival to the myth of Chinese imperial unity – although the myth existed and was sedulously fostered – can see the limited applicability of this line of argument by reflecting on the ultimate impotency of the alluring and almost inextinguishable myth of the Roman Empire to realize any enduring imperial resurrection in the West.

Obviously the consequences of unity for Chinese history were immense. The state retained a near-monopoly over the means of force and so a true feudalism (as opposed to a version of manorial agrarian organization) could never take hold. The great cities, so much larger than their European counterparts, never developed the distinctive institutions and autonomy only possible within the looser feudal matrix. The cultural diversity, and the competition between a multitude of states still sharing an overarching community of values and ideas, so important a force in Europe's later progress, was absent. Tracing the underlying reason for these differences is one of the keys to an understanding of China, then and now.

2 · The early Chinese empire

For the purposes of practical analysis, Chinese imperial history must be taken as starting in the third century BC with the Ch'in dynasty. In a sense, however, it began much earlier with the kingdom of the Western Chou, which is conventionally dated from 1122 to 771 BC. At its greatest extent this empire before the imperial age probably controlled the central and lower valley of the Yellow River, or in other words the modern provinces of Shensi, Honan, Shansi, Shantung and Hopei. By the ninth century the power of its rulers had been reduced to a formally acknowledged but increasingly empty sovereignty; and their descendants maintained a shadowy existence as High Kings until 256 BC. A considerable amount is known about the economic, organizational and military foundations of Chou hegemony, but it is not yet sufficient to permit any confident generalization about the changing distribution of technical skills (in the broadest sense) associated with its rise and subsequent disintegration. We shall therefore begin a little later, when the picture is clearer: in the seventh century BC.

Before this time the peasants of the Yellow River valley, the cradle of Chinese culture, practised a primitive system of burn and clear agriculture. Village communities, acting collectively, would open up and farm an area for several years; then they would move on, using neither crop rotation nor the fallow field. They were governed by local lords to whom they paid part of their harvest as tax. The lords were the chief subjects of a number of principalities, the rulers of which were regarded as owing a nominal allegiance to the Chou High King. The lords' estates, in contrast to the independent peasant collectivities, were worked by slaves or other persons placed in some form of dependent status.

After the seventh century BC, permanent fields began to take the place of the temporary clearances. In 594 BC the state of Lu levied the first land tax of which there is a record. By the later part of the millennium both fallowing and manures were in fairly widespread use. So too were iron agricultural tools, which were sometimes described as 'a matter of life and death to the peasantry'. They permitted the effective working of the land by smaller groups of people than previously; and so probably helped to dissolve the old communal structures. Systematic agricultural science appeared in the late first century BC with the *Book of Fan Sheng-chih*, a treatise which might be compared to the roughly contemporary writings of Varro and Columella in the West. The outcome of permanent cultivation was the institution of landed property; and by the fourth century BC large quantities of land were being bought and sold. This development was encouraged by the states of Wei and Ch'in in the north-west of China; and later idealists sometimes accused them of having destroyed the communal-feudal system of high antiquity.

Rostovtzeff remarks of Rome that 'How and when those who had probably once been serfs of the aristocracy became free peasants, owners of small plots of land and members of the plebeian class, we do not know.'[1] There is something of a similar problem for early imperial China. The first empire, formally proclaimed in 221 BC, was characterized by a free peasantry. Clearly their existence had much to do with the process by which the empire had been put together: systematic conquest by the state of Ch'in (see map I). The Ch'in rulers attempted to attract the population of rival kingdoms by offering in-migrants land, houses and exemption from the obligation to bear arms. They rewarded their own subjects for valour in battle by granting them rank, land and servants. In the regions which they had conquered they deliberately broke the power of the indigenous aristocracies by removing the peasants from their communities and setting them up as individual farmers who owed taxes and military service to the state. Those on whom they bestowed titles did not live off fiefs in the old manner, but simply enjoyed the right to revenues from a designated section of the population. There are distant resemblances in these processes to the liberating influences exerted on Roman social structure by the military crises facing the Republic during the conquest of the Italian peninsula in the fourth century BC and after. In slightly later times, the colonization of newly conquered lands, especially in the north-west, also helped to create a Chinese free smallholding class.

There were, of course, other causes lying behind the creation of a united empire. Transport and communications had improved steadily in

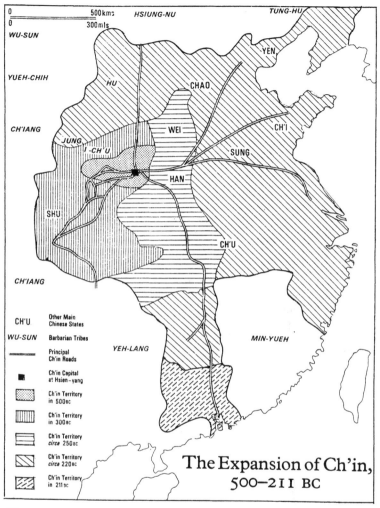

The Expansion of Ch'in, 500–211 BC

Map 1

the preceding centuries. This may be seen, for example, in the manner in which the average mileage covered by the diplomatic missions sent out by the state of Lu increased from 112 miles per mission in the late eighth century to 454 miles per mission in the late sixth century. There is also evidence of a good deal of road-building. In the various states, government had become more bureaucratic, although still very simple in its structures; and power had been more effectively centralized. Military techniques had been improved. In particular, iron weapons were beginning to displace bronze. Military institutions had been rendered more effective. Thus the temporary ascendancy of the state of Ch'i in present-day Hopei and Shantung during the middle part of the seventh century BC is commonly attributed to its new militia system, whose main features were soon copied by its rivals. With the passing of time, the number of separate states in north China had diminished and the emotion of patriotism had been extended to progressively larger units, thus strengthening their capacity for cohesion. Even so, prior to the third century BC, states which had grown beyond a certain size sometimes split up because of the lack of the economic and technical means to hold them together. This was notably the fate of Chin which in 403 BC fragmented into Han, Wei and Chao.[2] The importance of virtually all the factors stressed in the theoretical analysis of the preceding chapter is thus already conspicuous in this late pre-imperial period.

The warfare of this age was marked by a sharp divide. In the course of the fourth century BC there appeared two innovations which were to influence Chinese military history for the next two thousand years. These were the crossbow and mounted archery. The former was a Chinese invention; the latter was introduced by the non-Chinese peoples of the north-western frontier and probably came from the Near East. Prior to this time, battles had been infantry engagements in which the only use made of horses had been to pull the chariots of the élite. The military differences between Chinese and the barbarians had not been in terms of weapons so much as in terms of organization and discipline, in both of which the Chinese of course excelled. Mounted archery posed a new problem. Although the Chinese were quick to make use of the technique themselves, they could never hope to equal the tribes of the steppe, for whom riding was now becoming a way of life, and who had access to almost unlimited pasturage for their horses. They had also to depend on defensive walls and on the crossbow, the range of which was greater than that of the light bow carried by an archer on horseback. Warfare consequently grew more complicated and more costly. The crossbow trigger was an intricate bronze mechanism whose manufacture demanded great skill. The construction of the long defensive fortifications which began to appear in the north and west at this time, and which were the precursors of the Ch'in Great Wall, meant heavy demands on the population in the form of conscripted labour. Getting horses large enough for use in battle became a constant and expensive problem.

As was to be expected, the maintenance of the new empire imposed a heavy financial strain. The cost of the campaigns waged in the north against the Hsiung-nu barbarians (commonly identified with the Huns) and against the Yueh barbarians in the south emerges plainly from the *Han History*, even when allowance is made for its hostile attitude:

> The first emperor of Ch'in sent forth the men of the empire to guard the northern loop of the Yellow River. For more than ten years they were exposed to the rigours of military life, and countless numbers died . . . He also made the empire transport fodder and grain, beginning with the coastal commanderies of Huang, Ch'ui and Lang-yeh, whose inhabitants had to take these commodities to the northern loop of the Yellow River at a cost of 30 *chung* of grain for one *shih* delivered [a ratio of 192 : 1]. Although the men toiled at farming, there was not enough grain for rations; and the women could not spin enough yarn for the tents. The common people were ruined . . . This was the origin of rebellion in the empire.[3]

There followed some years of peasant revolts and civil war. Understandably the Han dynasty, which then succeeded the Ch'in, was conciliatory in its dealings with the barbarians, being fearful of provoking a new social crisis. Emperor Wen of the Han (who ruled from 179 to 159 BC) refused to listen to his generals' pleas for a punitive expedition against the Hsiung-nu when the latter had broken a treaty of friendship and invaded China yet again. 'Although we may gain what we desire by the cruel weapons of war,' he told them, 'to mobilize them would also exhaust our strength. How can we contemplate sending the common people off to remote regions?'[4] He preferred passive defence and diplomacy.

The main military system of the Ch'in and the Han was the *keng-i*, the conscription of peasants in rotation for training and service. This system was not well adapted to dealing with the frontier defences of a huge empire, except by unfairly retaining some conscripts long beyond their nominal term of obligation. It was therefore necessary to establish military colonies as well, and to make use of barbarian auxiliaries. One advantage of the system, however, was the creation of a trained reserve army which comprised in effect most of the adult male population.

Both the *keng-i* conscription system and the financing of the imperial administration depended on the efficient levy of recruits and taxes. The collection of revenue and the enlistment of soldiers were both imperilled by the growth of latifundia, huge properties owned by officials or merchants, worked by tenants or slaves, and able to resist most of the demands made on them by local government authorities. A primary reason for their spread was the pressure of taxation on the independent peasants. Early in the second century BC, Chao Ts'o submitted a famous memorial on this subject:

> These days a family of five peasants will have at least two persons who are liable for labour-services and conscription, while they will only be able to farm a hundred *mou* of land, the yield from which will not exceed a hundred *shih*.* What with their ploughing in the spring and hoeing in the summer, harvesting in the autumn and storing in the winter, with felling firewood, repairing government offices and rendering labour-services, they will be unable to escape the windblown dust of spring, the heat of summer, the heavy rains of autumn or the chill of winter. In none of the four seasons will they have a day of rest. What is more, in their private lives they will have to meet people and see them off, to mourn for the dead and ask after the sick. They will have to care for the orphaned and to bring up the young amongst them. And, in spite of all this painful toil, they will still have to endure such natural disasters as flood and drought, and also the cruelty of an impatient government which imposes taxes at inconvenient times, and gives orders in the morning and rescinds them in the evening. When the time comes that the levy must be met, those who own something sell it off at half price; and those who own nothing borrow at doubled rates of interest. It is for this reason that some dispose of their lands and houses, and sell their children and grandchildren to redeem their debts.[5]

*

Action thus became necessary to preserve the free peasantry as the source of the state's money and manpower. It was also desirable to weaken both the merchants, many of whom had acquired estates rather after the manner of the Italian businessmen in and after the second

* One *mou* in Han times was approximately 0·1236 of an acre (or 0·1139 according to Loewe), and one *shih* was about 16·7 litres (Loewe says 'almost 20'). Both measures varied with time and place, and in the case of the *shih* also with the commodity measured.

century BC, and the regional aristocracy, some of who had rebelled. Emperor Wu of the Han (140–85 BC) therefore took a series of drastic measures. Of the 197 Han princes and marquises, some 127 were declared guilty of some crime or to be without proper heirs; and their land was confiscated on an enormous scale. New taxes were imposed upon business, and on the strings of copper cash held by the merchants. Violators were thrown into prison or had their property impounded. The government commissioners 'obtained the wealth of the people to the tune of hundreds of thousands of cash, and their slaves in thousands and in tens of thousands. As far as agricultural land was concerned, they took several hundred *ch'ing* [100 *mou*, i.e. 12·36 acres] in the larger counties, and over a hundred *ch'ing* in the smaller ones. They did likewise for houses. In this way most of the merchants of the middle grade and above were ruined.'6 By the end of the second century BC the state itself had become the largest landowner – something which probably did not occur in Rome until the confiscations of the Julio-Claudian emperors in the middle of the first century AD.

At the same time a tradition was started of slaughtering politically suspect families and all their dependents. Bureaucrats were now often chosen from among persons of low social status, the object being to ensure their exclusive devotion to the emperor. State monopolies were introduced in salt, iron and wine, with the intention of debarring the merchant class from some of the main avenues to wealth.*

Emperor Wu also felt compelled (like Marcus Aurelius when he faced the Quadi and the Marcomanni) to take vigorous steps against the Hsiung-nu although (again like Marcus) he was aware of the economic dangers of so doing. In 91 BC he is said to have made the following observations to Wei Ch'ing, a general who had led several expeditions against these barbarians:

> In the early years of the Han dynasty there was an increasing number of incursions into China by the four kinds of barbarians. If I had not

---

* The monopolies in salt and iron only meant government control of distribution and sale, not of production. In particular, the formation of a nation-wide iron industry run by the state would have been impossibly difficult. The general level of technique was extremely high, as is attested by archaeological finds of steel saws, planes and axes as well as a wealth of cast-iron farm tools; and the majority of the artisans were independent men who jealously guarded their professional secrets. See Fujii Hiroshi, 'Kandai entetsu sembai no jittai' (The Reality behind the Han Monopolies of Salt and Iron), *Shigaku zasshi* LXXIX.ii (Feb. 1970).

changed this, later generations would have been helpless. If I had not sent armies out on punitive expeditions, the empire would not now be at peace. But, if one does these things, one cannot avoid placing a heavy burden on the people. If later generations repeat what I have done, they will be following in the footsteps of the ruined dynasty of Ch'in.[7]

The emperor's fears were well founded. Even during his reign, the pressure of taxation levied for military purposes was driving peasants to seek the protection of patrons. According to the *Discourses on Salt and Iron* written during his son's reign:

The army was mobilized several times. Supplies were not adequate. Services were also exacted from the common people. The farmers suffered from these toilsome duties and did not go out to work in their fields but fled in large numbers to the great households. The officials and the village heads were fearful, and did not dare impose responsibilities upon the latter, but instead harassed the humbler folk; and these, being unable to pay, absconded to distant parts. [Landlord] families of moderate means were able on this account to do uncommonly well for themselves. Those who fled later were those who had been held responsible for the services due from those who had fled earlier . . . Ever more people thus followed the example of the fugitives.[8]

The costly barbarian policy of emperor Wu thus provoked some of the developments that his domestic policy had been designed to prevent.

The abundance of state-owned land introduced a new element into the situation. That the *Han History* says 'when commoners reach twenty years of age they receive land, and when they are sixty return it' should not be taken as indicating the existence of a regular system of land allocation; but the distribution of shares of land (*fen-ti*) to poor persons did enable the government to counterbalance the growth of great estates. Public lands were also a useful source of rewards for officials. When the emperor Ai came to the throne in 7 BC he imposed a limit on landholdings, and also on the number of slaves whom anyone might own; but broke the rules himself not long afterwards with an enormous gift of land to a favourite.

The efforts made by the early Chinese imperial state to prevent the growth of large estates culminated under the rule of Wang Mang, a high official who had usurped the throne in AD 9. Wang was under the spell of the *Ritual of the Chou Dynasty*, an idealized account of the institutions of high antiquity; and he endeavoured to restore the 'well-field system', so-called because the fields were laid out in 3 × 3 grids like a noughts-and-crosses matrix or the Chinese character for 'well', and ascribed by this work to the communal-feudal period. He also tried to abolish the buying and selling of land, and the traffic in slaves. In spite of its archaic flavour his policy was in many ways a logical extension of that adopted more than a century earlier by emperor Wu, and amounted to no more than had been advocated by several respected statesmen of the Han dynasty. Wang's programme is described as follows by the *Han History*:

> Wang Mang said: The Ch'in dynasty was without the True Way. It increased taxation to supply itself with services. It exhausted the people's strength in order to take its desires to the extreme. It destroyed the system of the sages, and abolished the well-fields. In consequence the accumulation of property began. Greed and vice came into being. The powerful counted their fields in thousands, while the weak had not even the space in which to insert the point of an awl . . . The Han dynasty reduced the land tax to one-thirtieth, but did not exempt the infirm from conscription and poll tax. Powerful commoners encroached and took forcible possession of the allocated land (*fen-t'ien*) in order to rent it out. Thus although the tax was nominally one-thirtieth it in fact amounted to one-half [because of tenant sharecropping]. Fathers and sons, husbands and wives, worked all the year long at ploughing and hoeing without gaining enough to live on. So the rich had dogs and horses fed on more grain and vegetables than they could eat, and acted in a manner that was haughty and depraved. The poor could not get their fill of dregs, and were driven by poverty to crime . . . Henceforth the land of the empire shall be designated 'The King's Land'. Slaves shall be styled 'private dependents'. Neither may be bought or sold. Families with less than eight male members, but with more than a hundred *mou* of farmland each, shall divide up the surplus and give it to rural groups of nine neighbouring families. Thus, in the accordance with this system, those without land are now to receive it. Anyone who dares to criticize the sages' institution of the well-fields, or who deludes the masses in violation of the law, shall be banished to the frontiers, there to ward off the demons of the mountains and the swamps.[9]

These measures proved impossible to enforce; and after a mere two years the attempt to do so was largely abandoned.

A word is in order here about the probable extent of slavery in early imperial China. The institution was in no sense the foundation of the rural economy, any more than it was in the greater part of the Roman Empire;[10] but the percentage of the population enslaved is not easy to determine. Plausible estimates for the Former Han dynasty (206 BC–AD 8) range from one to ten per cent; and wooden documents from the second century BC show that the slave-owning class contained commoner landlords who owned no more than fifty to sixty acres of land.[11] Since slaves were expensive they were probably mostly used as personal servants, bodyguards and agents. They were also occasionally employed in manufacturing. The *Han History* says of Chang An-shih, who flourished at the end of the second century BC:

> Although he was a member of the high nobility and enjoyed as his stipend the revenue of ten thousand families, yet he dressed in black silk and his wife spun thread. He had seven hundred slaves, all of whom possessed technical skills. He directed their production, and made a fortune by the accumulation of small profits.[12]

It seems reasonable to conclude that it was a society in which slavery played a significant part, but which was not a 'slave society'.

To return to Wang Mang. Like emperor Wu, he also engaged in an aggressive policy towards the Hsiung-nu, and is said to have sent an army of over 300,000 men against them. The famines that broke out towards the end of his reign were in part the result of this diversion of manpower from production. The still relatively primitive economy was overstrained by the demands which this energetic ruler placed upon it; and rebellion, swollen by the migrations of peasants driven from their homes as the result of a disastrous change in the course of the Yellow River at this time, broke out both among the ordinary people and the landlord class. In AD 25 the Han dynasty was restored by a coalition of magnates under a collateral member of the imperial house who had formerly been a landowner.

The debt which the renewed Han dynasty owed to the proprietors of the great estates made it all but impossible for the state any longer to attempt forced reductions in the holdings of these powerful persons. Most of the formerly free peasantry thus gradually fell into a state of dependency; and a quasi-feudal system emerged in which a number of local strongmen drew most of the economic and military power firmly into their own hands. The classic description of this new social order is that given by Chung-ch'ang Tung at the beginning of the third century AD:

The houses of the powerful are compounds where several hundreds of ridgebeams are linked together. Their fertile fields fill the countryside. Their slaves throng in thousands, and their military dependents can be counted in tens of thousands. Their boats, carts and merchants are spread throughout the four quarters. Their stocks of goods held back for speculation fill up the principal cities. Their great mansions cannot contain their precious stones and treasure. The upland valleys cannot hold their horses, cattle, sheep and swine. Their elegant apartments are full of seductive lads and lovely concubines. Singing-girls and courtesans are lined up in their deep halls.[13]

There is an obvious and important parallel here with the roughly contemporary appearance of the class of dependent tenants (*coloni*) in Rome.

The effect on defence of these social developments, depriving the central government of money and manpower, was predictably serious. The system of rotational conscription collapsed around AD 46, with consequences vividly described by the historian Ying Shao writing about a century later:

Ever since the abolition of the conscript footsoldiers and cavalry in the commanderies and principates, the officials have been unprepared for emergencies. This has encouraged bandits. When there is trouble somewhere, adjacent areas come to help; there is a great deal of commotion, rough and ready measures are improvised, and the common people are afflicted. They have not been instructed in the military skills; and so to make use of them to meet a crisis, driving them forth all of a sudden to confront powerful enemies, is like having pigeons and magpies arrest eagles and sparrow-hawks, or pigs and sheep take aim at wolves and tigers. For this reason they are always beaten whenever there is any fighting; and the imperial cohorts are thrown into disarray.[14]

A corollary of weakening internal control was that pounded earth and brick fortifications, which had previously been found only along the frontiers, became common in the interior. Typical of the time of disorders which characterized the end of Wang Mang's reign was Chao Kang, the head of an important family in what is now Hopei province. 'He built a fortified camp on the county boundary, put into good repair his armour and weapons of offence, and was the scourge of the locality.'[15] During the second century AD, the persistent attacks of the Ch'iang barbarians led to a second wave of camp building, much of it at government command, and reminiscent of the *castella* and *emporia* of

Roman Africa and Thrace. Even more of these fortresses were built during the anarchy which followed the peasant uprising of the Yellow Turbans in AD 184. Some of them were great and impressive strongholds, like Camp Mei of Tung Cho, a general who for a time controlled the imperial government.

With the breakdown of the conscription system, the Later Han dynasty had to rely on more or less voluntary recruited troops, on soldiers levied locally by magnates through personal influence rather than through governmental authority, on amnestied convicts, and above all on barbarian auxiliaries, the Chinese counterpart of the 'federates' under their own commanders who became the mainstay of the Roman Empire after the third century AD. Barbarian horsemen were sometimes even imported to crush internal revolts, as during the uprising of Chou Chien and Su Mao in AD 27. Their normal role was of course frontier defence. Thus the decisive compaign led by General Tu Hsien against the northern Hsiung-nu depended almost entirely on non-Chinese cavalry. According to the *History of the Later Han* compiled in the fifth century by Fan Yeh:

> [In AD 88] he sent the five regiments of the Northern Army forth out of the passes, and also the mixed battalions of Li-yang, the cavalrymen from the twelve frontier commanderies and warriors from the Ch'iang and Hu barbarians. The next year, Tu Hsien and Keng Ping each took 4,000 cavalry and together with 10,000 horsemen under Shih-tzu, the southern Hsiung-nu Prince of Tso Ku-li, went north out of the Chi-lu Pass. T'un-tu-ho, the ruler of the southern Hsiung-nu, led over ten thousand horsemen out of the Man-i Valley. Teng Hung, general of the Trans-Liao Region, came forth from the Ku-yang Pass together with 8,000 Ch'iang and Hu horsemen who were frontier dependents, and 10,000 horsemen under An-kuo, the Hsiung-nu Prince of Tso Hsien. All of them gathered at Mount Cho-hsieh. Tu Hsien despatched Lieutenant General Yen P'an and adjutants Keng K'uei and Keng T'an to lead over ten thousand picked horsemen under Shih-tzu, Prince of Tso Ku-li, and Hsu-tzu, Prince of Yu Hu-yen, to fight with the ruler of the northern Hsiung-nu at Mount Chi-lo. They won a great victory.[16]

Thus the security of the Later Han Empire came to depend on the goodwill of those who had been its enemies – an ominous portent for the future, as was to be a similar state of dependency for Imperial Rome.

3 · The crisis of the third century AD

In the course of the second century discontent among the peasantry had interacted with the confusion and financial strain engendered by the attacks made along the north-western frontier by the Ch'iang barbarians to create a social crisis. The Ch'iang seem to have become a major threat about the same time that they took up settled agriculture, a recurring theme in the history of barbarian tribes on the periphery of China. Peasant uprisings also became increasingly common and culminated in AD 184 with the Yellow Turbans, religious sectaries who organized themselves on communal lines hoping for an age of 'Great Well-being'. The country was torn apart by wars between the rebels and a number of contending military leaders; and the powers of the Han imperial house from this point until its formal demise in AD 220 existed in little but name. Out of the flux three rival kingdoms eventually emerged, Wei in the north, Wu south of the Yangtze and Shu in landlocked Szechwan; and it is tempting to compare this time with the period when the Roman Empire too was divided into three, with independent states in Gaul and Palmyra. In the course of the re-establishment of peace, the structure of Later Han land tenure and military organization were changed almost out of recognition.

The greatest innovator of this age was Ts'ao Ts'ao, the soldier-poet who was the actual founder of the state of Wei, though he maintained until his death the often useful fiction that he was still the servant of the Han. His main creations were a system of state colonies and a system of hereditary military households. The state colony lands, farmed by government tenants, provided the taxes (or rents) which served as the financial underpinning of his government. The military households, who derived originally from his personal retainers, constituted the core of the Wei army. The government tenants and the military households together amounted to nearly half of the population of his state; and they were registered separately from the ordinary commoners.

These innovations must be seen in the context of the anarchic conditions. Independent local centres of power had sprung up everywhere. One such was that of the magnate Hsu Chu, described in the *Record of the Three Kingdoms* compiled by Ch'en Shou in the later part of the third century:

> In the last years of the [Han] dynasty, he gathered together young men and several thousand families of his clansmen, and together they built strong walls with which to resist the [Yellow Turban] bandits.[1]

Whenever possible the new Wei officials tried to break up such concentrations. Thus, when Ts'ang Tz'u arrived in Tun-huang as its magistrate in AD 227:

> The old powerful families had excessive land, and the humble folk not soil enough on which to stick an awl. He ordered it all to be divided up and allocated on a per person basis.[2]

Similar treatment was given to local militarists who had acquired large numbers of private retainers (*pu-ch'ü*), men-at-arms not unlike the *bucellarii* or armed servants of the great proprietors of the later Roman Empire. Thus Liu Chieh, the commandery archivist of Chi-nan, had 'over a thousand *clientes* who practised robbery and disorganized the administration'. When he refused to allow his men to be enlisted in the military household system, the governor appointed by Ts'ao Ts'ao forcibly conscripted the magnate himself to show others that such behaviour would not be tolerated.[3]

In one sense the state colony system is best understood as a public version of the private system used by the magnates. The colonists were called 'clientes', and there were cases where Wei officials turned their former retainers into state colonists. Conversely, the agricultural officials set over the state colonists to some extent turned the latter into their personal dependents, doing their best to increase their own revenue by concealing from the central government the full number of colonists they administered. In another sense the state colonies and the system of military households may be seen as an attempt to guarantee the services essential to the state by imposing on a large part of the population an ascribed hereditary status with concomitant obligations. There are suggestive parallels here with the creation of what Rostovtzeff calls 'a caste society' in the Roman state in the later third century. This is especially so as regards the restriction placed on the movements of many tenants (the *coloni adscripticii*) in order to ensure regular tax-payments;

and the formation of a military caste as the result of Septimius Severus' decision to recognize the validity of the marriages of Roman soldiers, and the imposition of compulsory army service on the sons of veterans.

Ts'ao Ts'ao founded his first state colonies in AD 196, or possibly a few years earlier. According to the *Record of the Three Kingdoms*:

> After the onset of famine and rebellion there was a universal lack of grain. Opposing armies arose but had no plans that would enable them to survive to the year's end. When they were hungry, they robbed. When they were full, they tossed away what was left. Countless numbers were fragmented and dispersed, destroyed by their own actions without ever having encountered an enemy . . . People ate each other. The countryside was desolate. Ts'ao Ts'ao said: 'It is by strong soldiers and a sufficiency of food that a state is established. The men of Ch'in took possession of the empire by giving urgent attention to farming. Hsiao-wu made use of military colonies to bring order to the western regions. This is a good method used by former generations.' In this year he recruited commoners to farm state colonies around Hsu [in central Honan] and obtained a million measures of grain. Then he instituted land officials in the provinces and commanderies, and marched out on campaign in every direction. There was no need to expend effort on the transport of grain. In consequence he destroyed the swarms of bandits and brought peace to the empire.[4]

In the frontier areas soldier-farmers usually manned the colonies. The *Record of the Three Kingdoms* makes it clear how they functioned:

> At this time [AD 243], it was desired to extend the area under cultivation and to amass a supply of grain that would make it possible to destroy the 'bandits' [that is, the other rival states]. Teng Ai [a high official who had begun life as a state colonist] . . . was of the opinion that, although the land was good, there was an insufficiency of water for the fullest use to be made of the productive power of the soil. It would also be necessary to excavate canals to provide water for irrigation, to make possible the accumulation of large supplies of grain for the troops, and to serve as routes for the transport of the government grain . . . Three-quarters of the empire had now been stabilized. The trouble lay south of the river Huai. For every large military expedition more than half the soldiers had to be used for transportation work, which was very expensive and a heavy burden . . . Twenty thousand colonists should be stationed north of the Huai, and 30,000 south of it. At any one time twenty per cent of these men would be detailed to rest, and so there would be a regular force of 40,000 persons

who would simultaneously farm and serve as soldiers . . . Within six or seven years thirty million measures of grain would be stockpiled on the Huai. This would be enough to feed 100,000 men for five years. Wu would thus be conquered and [Wei] arms prevail everywhere. Ssu-ma [the de facto ruler of Wei] gave his approval.[5]

These passages demonstrate very clearly the determining effect of the state's military needs upon the new patterns of land tenure.

There is little detailed evidence on the operation of the military household system in Wei; but a decree issued by its successor state of Chin in AD 279, on the eve of the final campaign of conquest which was to extend its hegemony over the south, may be taken as representative:

There shall now be conscripted from the military families one person in cases where they contain two or three grown males, two persons if they have four grown males, and three persons if they have six or more grown males. The age limits are to be seventeen years of age for entry into service, and fifty years of age for retirement from service. Families of military officers on the reserve list shall be subject to selection in the same way. Officers will be appointed in accordance with ability. Those of them who wish to buy horses and serve as cavalrymen shall be appointed [cavalry] commanders.[6]

In a few campaigns, such as that of Wei against Shu in AD 263, quite substantial numbers of non-professional troops are also known to have been used.

Ts'ao Ts'ao's system did not last for long. The state colonists, often with the connivance of the agricultural officials, kept evading their obligations, either by engaging in commerce or avoiding registration. The Wei minister of agriculture, Ssu-ma Chih, insisted that 'they should concentrate solely on farming and sericulture, for the sake of the national finances';[7] but his measures had little effect. After AD 280, when the Ssu-ma family had taken over the state of Wei, assumed the dynastic title of Chin and unified the empire, the state colonies were dismantled. Their influence however lived on. Former colony land was treated as state land and 'allocated' (k'o) to the former colonists as individuals. The standard 'allotment' was fifty mou (about 6·2 acres) for an adult male, the same as in the colonies. There were further provisions for assigning land to adult women and to adolescent and elderly males. Private land in the hands of commoners was subject to a statutory limitation on the amount that might be 'possessed' (chan) by a household. This was seventy *mou* if the head was a male, and thirty *mou* if the head was a woman, for households headed by women paid tax at half the usual rate. There were separate schedules of taxation for land held in 'allocation' and land held in 'possession'. In the first case, the annual grain levy was four measures for fifty *mou*; in the second case 2·8 measures for seventy *mou*. Large holdings were only tolerated in the form of service-tenure fiefs, not as purely private property. It was decreed that 'officials from the first to the ninth rank should hold land in accordance with their status'. This was defined as fifty *ch'ing* for those of the first rank, and lesser amounts down to ten *ch'ing* for the ninth rank.

What little evidence there is suggests that the Chin land system did not work well. The *Chin History* (compiled between AD 644 and 646 by the emperor T'ai-tsung of the T'ang and an imperially appointed committee) reproduces a memorial written by Shu Hsi some time between AD 296 and 305:

> I have read the edict which states that the government granaries are empty, that there is starvation and penury in Kuan-yu [Shensi], and that it is desirable to promote agriculture in a large way so as to bring about an abundance of grain . . . In the thousand counties of the empire there are many people today wandering about in search of food. Having abandoned their calling, they are without any property or the substance of allocated land . . . Strict orders should be issued prohibiting this and the provincial authorities told to make a careful inspection. If anyone fails to be assigned land, the responsibility for this shall be placed on the local officials . . . Furthermore, in the ten commanderies of Ssu-chou [around Lo-yang] the land is constricted and the population dense. The situation is especially bad in the San-Wei, and yet grazing lands for pigs, sheep and horses are spread throughout this region. All of these should be done away with, so that provision may be made for those with no or little land . . . All the pasturages should be removed, so that the horses, cattle, pigs and sheep feed on the grass of the empty plains,* while the men who roam about in search of a living may receive land from the bounty of the state . . . Furthermore, there are several thousand *ch'ing* of good land in the Wu marshes in the commandery of Chi [in Honan], but the water is stagnant, and the people have not opened them up for cultivation. I have heard that the men of this region all say: 'It would

---

* The importance of livestock in the farm economy of north-eastern China at this time is in marked contrast with the predominance of cereal crop cultivation, brought about by intense population pressure, in the late traditional period and at the present.

not be difficult to drain these salt marshes and turn them into leve land, and highly profitable; but the great and powerful families begrudge the abundance of fish which they can catch there, and have used their persuasion upon the officials to such effect that no beginning has ever been made.[8]

It would seem reasonable to suppose that the opposition of the powerful often made a dead letter of the allocation laws. The situation described by Fu Hsien in AD 279 probably only grew worse with the passing of time:

The army and the administration are still not well off for funds; and the common people do not have a sufficiency. If any year there is a bad harvest, there are persons who look like corpses. The true reason for this is that there are numerous officials and a plethora of troubles. There are too many exemptions, *too many who live at the expense of others, and but few who farm for themselves* . . . We ought to begin by amalgamating official posts and cutting down on commitments. Corvées and military service should be eased. Superiors and inferiors should concentrate especially on agriculture.[9] [Emphasis supplied by the present author, as in other quotations throughout this book.]

The Roman Empire of a century or so later shows the sapping effect of the growth of great and privileged estates. There were many more of them in the western half of the empire, which collapsed, than in the eastern half, which did not.[10]

The barbarization of the Chinese Empire continued apace. A constant influx of in-migrants sought to settle in the north and, as in the case of the Goths who settled within the Roman frontiers in the reign of Theodosius I, it was usually impolitic to refuse them. More significantly still, the civilization of the barbarians outside the empire also advanced. During the anarchy of the third century many Chinese had fled northwards to seek the protection of barbarian rulers. Once there, they had instructed their hosts in Chinese military skills and organization, and the arts of literacy. By the opening years of the fourth century, barbarian monarchs were not only welcoming Chinese literati at their courts but also acquiring an interest in Chinese philosophy, literature and astronomy. Liu Yuan, the Hsiung-nu founder of a short-lived dynasty, knew by heart such Confucian scriptures as *The Book of Odes* and *The Book of Changes*, as well as Chinese historical chronicles. His favourite saying is reputed to have been, 'The True Way derives from the enlarging of a man's capacities. To be ignorant of even one thing is a cause of shame

to the gentleman.'[11] It is a mistake to believe that it was simply unsoftened native vigour that made the barbarians a menace. They became
really dangerous to the extent that they became civilized, and versed in
the arts of organization, production and war. In AD 311 Liu Yuan's son
sacked the Chin capital at Lo-yang, and brought the age of the early
empire to its close.

4 · Sino-barbarian synthesis in north China

After Chin power had been broken in the north, the central administration migrated to its territories south of the Yangtze, and there set up
the successor state of Eastern Chin. North China was overrun with competing barbarian armies. Some were invaders; others were composed of
non-Han peoples long settled in or indigenous to China. The leading
Chinese families who stayed on gathered together their retainers and
built entrenched camps and strongholds for self-defence. The resulting
fragmented feudalism was somewhat comparable to that in fifth-century
Gaul. The *Chin History* describes one of the marcher lords of this time,
who lived on the northern Chin frontier:

> After the outbreak of rebellion in the Yung-chia reign-period [AD
> 307–12], the common people fled from their homes and everywhere
> gathered in camps, in groups of up to several thousand families.
> Within a given county these camps would be allied together. At this
> time, all those with any power had gathered people into such camps,
> and of them Su Chün was the strongest. He sent Hsu Wei, his senior
> aide-de-camp, to proclaim his orders to these camps, and extended
> over them the civilizing influence of government. He also had the dry
> bones of those who had died collected and given burial. From far
> and near people responded to his favour and to his sense of justice,
> and chose him to be their chief.[1]

For some years Su was thus able to preserve a zone of relative security
in his home area in the south-east portion of the north China plain,
and to provide a protective barrier for the Chin state in the south.

Some of the camps were well organized. They had their own improvised codes of law, and rough and ready systems of ceremonial and
education. A good example of this is Yü Kun's fortress on Mount Yü:

> At that time the common people were peaceable, having as yet no
> knowledge of warfare and self-defence. Yü Kun declared: 'Confucius

said: "To make the people fight without having given them instruction amounts to abandoning them." ' He therefore called together all the men of some social standing and conferred with them. 'When two or three men of superior quality are placed in a situation of peril,' he told them, 'they will find the means to keep life and honour intact, and to safeguard their wives and children. The men of old had a saying: "When a thousand people assemble, but do not choose one of their number to be their leader, they will either scatter or fall into disorder unless they disperse." What shall we do about it ?' They all answered: 'Excellent. Who should be our leader now but you?' Yü Kun was silent for a while. Then he said to them: 'My friends, in this acute crisis, you have laid ease aside. You have not dared to shirk difficulties. Yet, when men set up a leader, what matters most is that they should obey his orders.' They thereupon swore an oath to him, saying: 'We shall not take advantage of these troubled times to molest our neighbours or to pillage houses. We shall not burn or carry off the crops which others have grown. We shall not plot immoral acts nor commit injustice. With our united efforts and a singleness of purpose, we shall meet the dangers that face us in a spirit of mutual sympathy.' Everyone else followed their lead. They at once narrowed the defiles, barricaded the footpaths, repaired the walls and entrenchments, and set up stockades. They examined each person's achievements, calculated requirements, and shared out work and rest in equitable fashion. They supplied each other's needs. They perfected their military equipment, gauged their strength and trusted to their abilities. Once everything was in good order, Yü had the large districts select senior persons and the smaller districts select men of worth, and he led them in person. Once social divisions had been made clear, and there was no ambiguity in the structure of command, superiors and inferiors observed the proper etiquette, and young and old the proper ceremonials.[2]

This passage is interesting not only for the picture which it gives of the times, but also for what it reveals about Chinese reactions under stress and their view of what made a properly ordered society. This might be summarized as follows: the overall leadership of a superior person based on his acceptance by senior persons who are in turn accepted by their communities, a precisely delineated hierarchy infused with a pervading sense of moral unity, and equity in the allocation of resources and responsibilities. In terms of historical fact, of course, it is almost certainly an idealized portrait. Many of the fortresses were little more than the lairs of robber barons. They fought among themselves, and often sought safety by placing themselves under the protection of one of the barbarian armies who were now disputing the mastery of north China. These non-Han proved surprisingly willing to accept their aristocratic pretensions; and this acceptance was in some respects the beginning of the process which led, in the later Toba empire, to official rank being largely allocated on the basis of birth.

For most of the fourth century the northern plain was the arena of a struggle between shifting confederations of Ch'iang, Hu, Ti, Hsiung-nu and Hsien-pi, the last being a tribe ethnically related to the Mongols. Towards its end, the Hsien-pi, and those Hsiung-nu who had allied with them, emerged victorious. The Hsien-pi Mu-jung clan held the north-east, the Hsien-pi Toba clan held the centre, and the Hsien-pi T'u-fa clan held the north-west. The attitude at first adopted by these largely nomadic conquerors to their subjugated territories had probably been similar to that attributed by Chinese historians to general Yü-wu-lun. He is said to have given the T'u-fa leader Li-lu-ku the following piece of advice:

Our former rulers in ancient times . . . lacked any ceremonial clothing, and moved hither and thither in irregular fashion, being without the institution of cities. By these means they were able to split the empire down the middle and to overawe the other regions. You have now assumed the imperial dignity and are acting in sincere conformity with the wishes of Heaven. But living in a paradise such as this is not a system which can endure from generation to generation. Our storehouses bursting with grain and silks will arouse the cupidity of enemies . . . We ought to install the Chinese in the walled cities, and assign them to agriculture and sericulture, so that they may supply us with the resources which we need for our army and administration. We should ourselves practise the arts of war, so as to be able to kill those who do not submit to us. We shall suppress any rebellions to the east or the west with our well-prepared plans. If there is an enemy who is stronger than we are, we can escape from his onslaught by running away. Is this not a suitable course to take?[3]

By this time, the Toba branch of the Hsien-pi was already urbanized, but perhaps an echo of the rough attitudes of general Yü-wu-lun (who belonged to a less developed branch) may be found in the policy of forced agricultural settlement adopted by the early Toba rulers as they moved from being tribal chiefs to the emperors of an administratively complex state. The emperor Tao-wu (AD 386–406) set up his capital at P'ing-ch'eng in the arable lands along the present frontier between

Shansi province and Inner Mongolia; dissolved the old Hsien-pi tribal organization; and carried out a series of raids against neighbouring barbarians from which he brought back large numbers of human beings, horses, cattle and sheep as loot. The animals were mostly distributed to his followers, and the (involuntary) in-migrants were assigned land on a per capita basis and provided with plough-oxen and sometimes tools.

These forcible removals of populations, which sometimes affected upwards of a hundred thousand people at one time, were continued by Tao-wu's successors until AD 469, by which time the long process of Toba subjugation of north China was more or less complete. After this there was no longer any need to use such techniques to break up the financial basis of hostile local concentrations of power, or to promote agricultural output in the immediate neighbourhood of the Toba capital, in any case a difficult matter in view of the climate and soils.

Chinese officials who had entered the service of the Toba repeatedly stressed the need to develop agriculture as a means of paying for administrative and military expenses. Under the emperor T'ai-wu (AD 424–52), a policy of accelerating the cultivation of government-owned land was energetically pursued. During his reign, according to the *Wei History*:*

The authorities assigned work to the commoners of the metropolitan area. They made families which did not own oxen exchange their own labour for the loan of oxen, and open up land for farming. Families with oxen, who provided oxen for the cultivation of 22 *mou* by a member of a family without oxen, were recompensed with his labour on 7 *mou* of their own land. Such was the ratio established. As to those who lent their oxen for the cultivation of 7 *mou* belonging to the adolescent and to the elderly of families without oxen, they were recompensed with the labour of the adolescent and the elderly on 2 *mou* of their own land . . . Families were listed and distinguished according to the number of their members. The area which they had been told to farm was clearly recorded. Their names were written up at the place where they worked, so that it was possible to distinguish between their varying degrees of success. They were also forbidden to drink wine, to attend theatrical entertainments, or to abandon agriculture for wine-making or trade.[4]

This policy was later extended to other areas besides that around the

* Compiled in the sixth century by Wei Shou. The Toba state is often known to history as the (Northern) Wei, a title not used here in order to avoid confusion with the other states of this name.

LIBRARY UNIVERSITY OF CHESTER

capital; and it seems to have resulted in a substantial increase in the cultivated acreage.

As the Toba empire became increasingly based upon agriculture, members of the imperial family and the Hsien-pi nobility, besides of course the more important Chinese families among their subjects, were drawn into large-scale farming and handicraft operations, often for the market. Early evidence of this is the magisterial Confucian rebuke said to have been delivered by the Chinese statesman Kao Yun to Kung-tsung, heir-apparent of the emperor T'ai-wu:

When Kung-tsung was young . . . he engaged in the management of fields and gardens so as to make a profit from them. Kao Yun said to him: 'Neither heaven nor earth has private possessions. Thus they are able to arch above and to give support from below. The true king has no private possessions. Thus he is able to embrace and nourish his people. The holy kings of ancient times governed with the utmost public spirit. They left gold undisturbed in the mountains and pearls in the deeps. Their lack of selfishness was an example to the world, their frugality a lesson. Therefore, though a thousand years have passed, their fame has not perished. Now the reserves in Your Highness' state have doubled. All within the four seas are loyal to you. Everywhere what you do and say is taken as establishing a rule. Yet you engage in the management of private lands; you rear chickens and dogs; you sell your produce in the market place, competing for profits with the common people. The news of this has spread about and cannot be concealed. Now the empire, which is Your Highness' empire, has as its riches everything within the four seas. You can obtain whatever you desire. You can gratify any wish. Yet you strive with peddler-men and peddler-women for trifling profits . . . Distribute your fields and orchards to the poor. Sell off your livestock . . .' Kung-tsung did not agree.[5]

The heir-apparent is also known to have had slaves who wove silks and who made wine for sale.

The provinces were dominated by local magnates, many of whom were not just large landowners but also hereditary officials. One such was Ch'üan Ch'i, whom a later history described as follows:

Ch'üan Ch'i was the scion of a great family of Feng-yang in Shang-lo [in present-day Shensi province]. From his great-grandfather onwards they had been hereditary county magistrates of Feng-yang. When Ch'üan Ch'i succeeded his father he was only eleven years old; but as the result of a request made by over three hundred of the local people, the court gave its permission that in spite of his youth he might, as a special exception, succeed to the magistracy. At the beginning of the Hsiao-ch'ang reign-period [AD 525–7] he held the positions of major-general defending Lo-chou and prefect of Shang-lo. When Hsiao Pao-yin, who had been sent to put down a rebellion in the Kuan-hsi region, in his turn raised the banner of revolt, Ch'üan Ch'i led three thousand local soldiers to the defence . . .[6]

Later on, Ch'üan Ch'i's son was appointed hereditary governor of Lo-chou, though in view of his premature death in battle he was in his turn succeeded by his younger brother, and not a son. The control exercised by the central government over such local notables must usually have been very limited. This was all the more so because, prior to AD 484, Toba officials were not paid any salaries. They met their expenses from their landholdings if they were local residents; and if not, from commerce and from lending out at interest to merchants money which they had forcibly levied from the people.

★

As the Toba state came to meet the challenge of transition from a dynasty of conquest to a bureaucratic empire, such a situation was intolerable. The chief problem was how to assert some measure of control over the powerful landowners. They not only dominated their localities but shielded more and more protected dependents from the obligation to pay taxes. In AD 458 the emperor Wen-ch'eng complained that 'in recent years, the levies in kind have been made lighter, but there are cases of defaulting and arrears in every province and commandery'.[7] Until this fiscal system was improved (and such incidental Toba expedients as military plunder, and the dissolution of Buddhist monasteries, abandoned) there was little hope of consolidating imperial authority. Conversely, until there was greater imperial authority an improvement of the fiscal position, which depended above all on a more equitable distribution of the tax burden, was hardly possible. Between AD 484 and 486, a group of Chinese statesmen under the patronage of the astute empress-dowager Wen-ming therefore designed an interlocking series of measures, drawing to a great extent upon traditional Chinese practices and ideals, which aimed at solving both problems simultaneously.

These innovations led to some of the key institutions of the middle empire which was to emerge about a century later. They consisted of a new system of household registration and taxation, the state-supervised allocation of fixed quantities of land to commoners, the conversion of large private landholdings to service-tenure fiefs contingent upon the holding of an official post, and the payment of salaries to officials. The underlying conception was a co-ordinated programme which would strengthen the central government. Two remarks made around this time by Kao Lü, a leading official, show this clearly:

> We have made equitable the taxes on the common people in order to develop their loyalty to the sovereign. The sovereign amasses the resources taken from them in order to pay for the tasks which he has to undertake. He pays official salaries so that his favour may descend generously, and that when the officials receive them they may feel deep gratitude.

And:

> We fear knavery among the common people, and so we have set up 'neighbourhoods' and 'groups' as a means of filling them with a proper respect. We pay the officials salaries in recognition of their hard and painful work. We share out the commoners' land equitably among them, knowing how hard it is to assign toil and leisure in a fair fashion.[8]

The registration system was based on deliberately artificial units: five-family groups called 'neighbourhoods', and multiples of these called 'cantons' and 'groups'. The intention was to end the widely prevalent situation of thirty to fifty related households under the rule of a powerful clan head enrolling for taxation purposes as a single household. To this end also the taxable unit was changed from the household to the married couple, or as it was delicately called, 'the bed'.

Once the size of the population had been accurately established, it was possible to move on immediately to the second stage, which was the fairer distribution of lands. The statesman Li An-shih argued in a famous memorial that:

> We want to ensure that no land lies neglected, that none of our people are vagrants, that powerful families do not monopolize the fertile fields, and that humble persons also have their share of the acreage. These are the means by which we may show pity for poverty, repress greed, equalize wealth and want, and ensure that all the commoners are enrolled in the population registers.[9]

The imperial decree that followed Li's suggestion reiterated his aims:

> We are now sending commissioners to the provinces and commanderies who will, in co-operation with the local officials, allot the land of the

empire in an equitable fashion. The reversion and allocation of the land will be on a lifetime basis.[10]

More precisely, commoners were to be assigned twenty *mou* as hereditary property, forty *mou* as a lifetime holding, and thirty *mou* for every ox up to a maximum of four oxen. Masters received a lifelong holding for each of their slaves. Various detailed regulations met such special problems as densely settled areas, rights to land which had been newly opened up for cultivation, and the sale and purchase of hereditary land so as to bring holdings in line with the prescribed size.

The first surviving document attesting a systematic wholesale distribution of land only dates from AD 547, under the Western Wei dynasty, which ruled an area comprising the modern provinces of Shensi, Kansu and Ningsia; and it refers to the somewhat untypical frontier area of Tun-huang.[11] But there is no doubt that these regulations were at least to some extent put into effect. In so far as underdeveloped regions were concerned, they were merely a continuation of the traditions established by Ts'ao Ts'ao's state colonies, and by the forcible settlement of migrants in the early years of Toba rule. One vexed question was obviously the quality of the land assigned. According to one Toba official:

> Ever since the Ching-ming reign-period [AD 500–3] there have been disastrous droughts for successive years along the northern frontier. It has not been possible to cultivate the steppe or the dry lands. Only irrigated fields have been to some small degree cultivable. The rich land has however been monopolized by the generals and their subordinate officers. The barren soils and waste acres have been given to the commoners, whose difficulties in consequence grow ever worse. I would request that all the irrigated fields belonging to these garrison areas should be shared out among the humble folk in accordance with the land regulations, the poor taking precedence over the rich.[12]

The emperor is said to have agreed. The *History of the Northern Ch'i*, describing conditions in AD 534 at the beginning of the Eastern Wei dynasty (which ruled over what are now the provinces of Shansi, Hopei, Honan and Shantung), tells of the same policy being carried out, but again in somewhat special circumstances. The area around the new capital at Yeh had been cleared of its population to make room for those forced to move from around the region around the former capital at Lo-yang:

> Land was first given to the people at this time. The titled and the powerful all occupied fertile fields, while the poor and the weak all received

lands of poor quality. Kao Lung-chih spoke of this to the emperor Kao-tsu, and the allocation was entirely changed and equity achieved.[13]

How much land was actually taken away from the large landowners, the reduction of whose estates was one of the avowed objects of the new laws? Our answer here must consider in detail what may be called the 'upper level' of the equitable field system. The edict issued at Li An-shih's request stated:

> The officials who rule over the people shall be given public land in the locality in which they serve. Provincial governors are to have fifteen *ch'ing*, grand administrators ten *ch'ing*, deputy provincial officials eight *ch'ing*, and county magistrates and sub-prefects six *ch'ing*. When officials change office these shall be handed over to their successors. Those who sell their land will be punished according to the law.[14]

In so far as the officials were, like Ch'üan Ch'i (on whom see page 46), *locally based and hereditary*, these regulations were simply a paper revolution. The Toba dynasty gave official position to magnates in their own localities as a reward for, or an inducement to, loyalty to the government. The initial object of the new rules was to find some way of asserting the principle of state control over a large number of semi-independent magnates; it would certainly have been foolish, and probably fatal, to have deliberately provoked a head-on conflict with the most powerful class in the realm. The result was a proliferation of administrative units. The numbers in which these were created may be judged by the suppression in AD 556 by Northern Ch'i (which even so only ruled over part of the former Toba realm) of three provinces, 153 commanderies, and 589 counties as superfluous.

Smaller landowners probably found legal cover for their holdings in the provisions assigning land to slaves. Perhaps representative of such persons was Hsiao Ta-huan, a member of a southern dynasty who had fled north and found service under the Western Wei. 'I have,' he wrote of himself, 'two hundred *mou* of land which provide me with my rice gruel, and ten which provide me with [mulberry trees for] silk and with hemp. I have a few serving-maids to look after the weaving, and four slaves who suffice to plough and hoe for me.' With this he felt 'self-sufficient and content'.[15] Two hundred *mou*, it may be noted, amounted to four lifetime holdings for the slaves and one for the owner.*

★ He was of course entitled to a further ten *mou* to bring his hereditary property (for mulberry trees and hemp) up to the maximum permitted.

The foregoing considerations suggest that confiscation of the estates of the rich were rare, though some must have owned more than the 185 acres or so allotted to provincial governors. The new laws were significant, however, as a reassertion of state power over the peasantry, and as an attempt to link the right to hold large quantities of land with services to the state. As such, they went well beyond the mere distribution of public lands to the poor which was found at this time under the Chinese dynasties in the southern part of the country.

*

The increasing sinification of the Toba administrative system – a process typified by the institutional innovations of the empress-dowager and her Chinese advisers, and symbolized by the removal of the capital in AD 494 from P'ing-ch'eng on the frontier between grazing land and arable to Lo-yang in the heartland of ancient China – demoralized the garrisons of northern tribesmen who were the military foundation of the dynasty's power. In AD 524 they revolted. Although they were quickly put down, a decade of civil warfare ensued between rival militarists, ending with the division of the northern empire in AD 534 into eastern and western successor states.

During the intermittent wars of the next fifty years, the military institutions later to be characteristic of the middle empire were first given shape in the north-west. Most troops in northern China at the beginning of this period were hereditary professionals, either tribesmen or else conscripted Chinese. They were often referred to as 'castle people'; and their status was if anything below that of ordinary commoners. There were also a number of volunteers called 'local soldiers' under local leaders. These had to be paid, or otherwise rewarded; and the position of a leader who did not maintain good relations with them could become precarious. A new style of military organization arose in the years following AD 542 when Yü-wen T'ai, generalissimo and de facto ruler of Western Wei, lost most of his old-style forces in a defeat at the hands of the Eastern Wei, and had thereafter to make such 'local soldiers' the mainstay of his army.

The main problems he faced were how to extend central control over heterogeneous and quasi-feudal forces of this type, with their particularist loyalties, how to supply and equip them given only limited central financial resources, and how to train them adequately. These were solved step by step until an institution emerged known as the 'divisional militia', distinguished by the combination of farmwork and military service, strong central control but geographical and organizational dispersion, with only intermittent or periodic assembly of large units for training and manoeuvres.

In AD 543 Yü-wen T'ai recruited 'powerful persons from the Kuanlung [Shensi] area'. These were clearly notables with their personal troops; and this practice continued for some decades thereafter. In AD 574, for example, emperor Wu of the Northern Chou, the state which had by this time succeeded the Western Wei in the north-west, issued a decree which stated that: 'Those who are able to lead the soldiers who follow them in the five provinces of Ching, Hsiang, An, Yen and Hsia [that is to say, the frontier areas in northern Hupei and the part of Shensi just south of the Ordos] should be given an official rank and commissioned.'[16] The first measures to establish a co-ordinated system were taken by the Western Wei in AD 550. According to the *Family Biography of the Marquis of Yeh*, a work written in the ninth century:

> When the divisional militia were first established, they selected one stalwart man from every six households of the three middle ranks and above in which there were three taxable adult males, and exempted him personally from taxation. The commandery prefect would have him trained and inspected during the agricultural off-season. His weapons, his uniform, his beast of burden, grain and vegetables were jointly provided by the six families.* They cared for him and trained him as if he were a son or a younger brother. In this way it was possible for a few of such men to overcome superior numbers.[17]

There are said to have been a hundred divisional units in all, each of them under a colonel. Presumably the majority of the 'local soldiers' were incorporated into them. Interestingly, for a while the later Roman Empire also had the institution of financial support of an individual recruit by small groups of taxpayers, Diocletian's *temones* and *capitula*.

To some extent the divisional militia bore the imprint of earlier Toba practices. In the early years of the Toba empire, troops levied from other tribes had campaigned under their own leaders bringing their own provisions. Rather later, a system of 'rota soldiers' had been introduced to supplement the regular army, every fifteen families being

---

* A possible alternative translation makes 'six families' (*liu chia*) refer to the 'Six Pillars of State' (*liu chu kuo chia*), that is, the generals at the head of the army, or in other words the state.

obliged to provide each year one soldier and twelve lengths of silk for his expenses. There had also been a horse levy, by which every sixty families, or sometimes fewer, had had to provide the government with a horse. On the other hand, in early times, the traditional Toba warrior had tended not to engage in farming or stockraising in person. His slaves had done this for him. Later on he had been maintained out of the revenue from taxes. In the context of Toba institutions, the formal combination of farming and fighting was a new departure. It was also a reversion to the methods of Ts'ao Ts'ao.

Personal loyalties among the militiamen persisted strongly for a while, as sons or other relatives normally succeeded to the command left vacant when a general died. Little by little, however, these loyalties were whittled away by fragmenting the command structure, and shifting upper personnel around. Under emperor Wu of the Northern Chou (AD 561–77), the divisional militia were expanded to about 200,000 men. When the commander of the Northern Chou palace guards usurped the throne in AD 581, and not long afterwards proclaimed himself emperor Wen of the Sui dynasty, he had at his disposal a force fit for the conquest and reunification of the empire.

The restoration of the unity of the Chinese Empire which took place under the new Sui dynasty thus mainly resulted from improvements in organization. A new land system in the north as a whole, and a new military system in the north-west, had placed a greater concentration of resources and power in the hands of the rulers of the state of Western Wei/Northern Chou. The actual reunification was the work of a small group of north-western militarists, from whom the dynasties of the Northern Chou, the Sui and the succeeding T'ang (AD 618–906) all sprang. Although deeply versed in Chinese culture, they were not ethnically or spiritually fully Chinese. Hsien-pi influence was still strong, even as compared with the north-east, which was dominated in the sixth century by the Chinese aristocrats of Shantung. An illustration of this influence at a personal level may be seen in the marriages made by three of the daughters of Tu-ku Hsin, a leading Hsien-pi general of the Western Wei. The eldest was the empress of emperor Ming of the Northern Chou; the fourth was the mother of Li Yuan, founder of the T'ang dynasty; and the seventh was the wife of Yang Chien, founder of the Sui. In both its institutions and the composition of its ruling class, the early middle empire was a sino-barbarian synthesis.

5 · The middle empire

The middle empire was established in AD 589 when the first emperor of the new Sui dynasty brought China under a single administration for the first time in two-and-a-half centuries. The long period of sino-barbarian synthesis had brought it institutions in the equitable field system and the divisional militia which were well designed to defeudalize society, in the sense of ending the fragmentation of authority, controlling the aristocracy and replacing the great estates with communities of free peasant smallholders. In these respects it may well be likened to Byzantium under the Heraclian dynasty, whose policies aimed at making the soldier-farmer and the independent peasant the backbone of the empire. In logistic capacity, and in the art of warfare, the Chinese middle empire was also markedly superior to its predecessor; and to this superiority its survival through various vicissitudes until the early years of the tenth century must be mainly attributed.

During the period of barbarian rule in the north, the Chinese dynasties in the Yangtze valley had developed agricultural production in this potentially rich but hitherto little exploited region. More and more it became the granary of the empire, acquiring a significance somewhat like that which Egypt had had, up to this period, in the Romano-Byzantine Empire. In contrasting the subsequent historical evolution of the two imperial areas it is necessary to remember that the Yangtze valley was economically acquired, if one may put it that way, at about the same time that the Islamic conquest of AD 642 permanently removed Egypt from Byzantium's grasp. A major technological innovation, the Grand Canal, performing artificially what the Mediterranean did naturally for Egypt and Constantinople, brought the riches of the south within easy reach of an administration and an army based, both in accordance with tradition and the imperatives of defence, in the north.*

* See map 2. As is pointed out on p. 65, the new long-distance supply system gradually made the self-supply system of the militia obsolete.

Canals for the transport of military supplies had been built since at least the Ch'in dynasty, but the integrated nationwide system created by the Sui was new. The main routes, constructed at breakneck speed during the first decade of the seventh century by enormous levies of conscripted labourers, including many women, ran for about twelve hundred miles at a width of forty paces. In terms of scale, it was probably an engineering feat without parallel in the world of its time.

Emperor Wen of the Sui (AD 581†–604) assimilated the militia to the status of commoners, and incorporated them into the equitable field system. In AD 590 he decreed:

> All soldiers are to be attached to a prefecture and a county. They are to open up lands for cultivation, and are to be placed on the registers exactly like the enrolled households of commoners.[1]

Although the Sui divisional militia system partially collapsed when the dynasty succumbed to the revolts caused by the harsh exactions of emperor Yang (AD 605–16), the practice of settling troops on the land was followed by the succeeding T'ang dynasty. According to the *New T'ang History*, compiled in the eleventh century by Ou-yang Hsiu and Sung Ch'i:

> The emperor Kao-tsu [AD 618–26] began his uprising in T'ai-yuan with volunteer troops [actually the local units of the divisional militia under his command]. After he had subdued the empire he dismissed them all, so that they could return home. Thirty thousand of them still wished to continue as guards, and to them he distributed the rich land north of the Wei River along the Pai-chü [an irrigation canal near Ching-yang in Shensi] which had been abandoned by the common people. He bestowed upon them the title 'Original Imperial Bodyguard'. Later, as they grew old and were no longer fit for service, they were replaced by their sons and younger brothers. They were called the 'Army of Fathers and Sons'.[2]

The fully matured divisional militia system, as it appeared a few decades later, was described in the following somewhat idealized terms by the ninth-century writer Tu Mu:

> In the Chen-kuan reign-period [AD 627–49], when the wars were over and the government pursued the arts of peace, the sixteen Guards at the capital were used to train the military officers, and in the provinces

---

† The date of his successful usurpation. The Sui dynasty is usually regarded as beginning in AD 589.

the 574 units of the divisional militia were used to provide the rank and file. If, by some mischance, two or three thousand square *li* of our territory fell into enemy hands, enemy forces reached serious proportions, or barbarian depredations occurred on all sides, then the military officers would summon them to take up their posts at the frontiers. When the empire was once again at peace, authority reunited, orders everywhere carried out, and everyone trustworthy and obedient, then the military officers would summon them to take up their posts in the interior. When they resided in the interior, civil officials acted as their generals [an oversimplification – there was joint civilian/military control] . . . and they were dispersed in divisional units, the largest of which did not contain more than 1,200 men. For three out of the four seasons they worked at farming, flailing [harrowing?] and ploughing with their raincoats on. For one season they perfected themselves in the military skills of riding, swordsmanship and archery, being examined by their lieutenant colonels. Fathers and elder brothers gave instruction, and were allowed to have no other profession. Although the muster-rolls were stored in the generals' headquarters, the troops were scattered across the countryside. Their power was so dispersed, and the men so full of self-respect, that even if the legendary rebel Chih Yu had been at their head he could not have induced them to rise in revolt.[3]

The points of resemblance between the divisional militia and the Byzantine Themes are remarkably numerous. Viewed organizationally, both were based on soldier-farmers working military smallholdings, exempted from most taxes in consideration of their army service, and obliged to provide some part of their own equipment. Ostrogorsky has written of Byzantium during the seventh century, when the Theme system was in the process of formation, that there was 'a very close connection between the rise in status of the land-owning peasant-soldier (*stratiotes*) and the strengthening of the free peasant smallholders'.[4] The T'ang divisional militia likewise depended upon the functioning of the equitable field system to maintain a large and well-off peasant class as a reservoir for recruits.

From a military viewpoint, both were highly trained corps d'élite, relatively restricted in numbers, and most frequently used as the central component of armies also containing other elements. In both, a heavy emphasis was placed on archery, for foot soldiers and cavalry alike. The T'ang crossbow was a formidable weapon. Its most powerful type, mainly used in siege warfare, could shoot 700 paces of five Chinese feet each. The lighter variety normally carried by an infantryman shot 300 paces, and that of a cavalryman 200 paces. The standard required of the first of these in training sessions was two hits in every four shots at a range of 230 paces. Both T'ang China and Byzantium saw a marked increase in the use of body armour. In both, prolonged drilling and manoeuvring allowed commanders to use elaborate and flexible formations without running the risk of confusion. During the winter training sessions of the divisional militia, great stress was placed on conditioning the men to respond precisely to horn, drum and flag signals; and they were reputedly able to advance and retire in battle under perfect control. The first century of T'ang rule saw in consequence some extraordinary successes against superior numbers. The divisional militia cavalry are said sometimes to have scattered enemy mounted forces of up to ten times their own number. Bréhier has remarked that Byzantium 'owed its supremacy above all to a methodical conception of war, considered as an art',[5] and the same spirit was abroad in early T'ang times. Emperor T'ai-tsung (AD 627–49) insisted on personally instructing his militia soldiers in the finer points of archery. Above all, in both empires, the new institutions were an attempt to end reliance upon barbarian auxiliaries and mercenaries, to base the military structure in inexpensive fashion upon the empire's own subjects, and to compensate for relative lack of numbers with a hardened professionalism.

The most dangerous enemies of the Sui and the early T'ang were the Turks. In the fifth century they had been subordinated to the Jou-jan tribe, whose empire stretched across what is now Mongolia, and whom they served as ironworkers. In the middle of the sixth century they overthrew the Jou-jan and created a loosely-knit empire reaching to the edges of the Mediterranean world, much of this success being due to their mastery of iron. They lacked the political cohesion to make the most of their military potential. After threatening to overrun the Chinese middle empire in the early years of the seventh century they disintegrated, mainly as a result of their own internal instability skilfully exacerbated by Chinese diplomacy. The Koreans were also formidable foes, though of a very different type, being skilled in the construction of defensive fortifications. The kingdom of Kao-li, with its capital at Pyong-yang, controlled much of what is today southern Manchuria and was attacked both by emperor Yang of Sui and emperor T'ai-tsung of T'ang. The outcome of the Chinese campaigns was a demonstration of the limits placed by technology on imperial expansion. The carts used

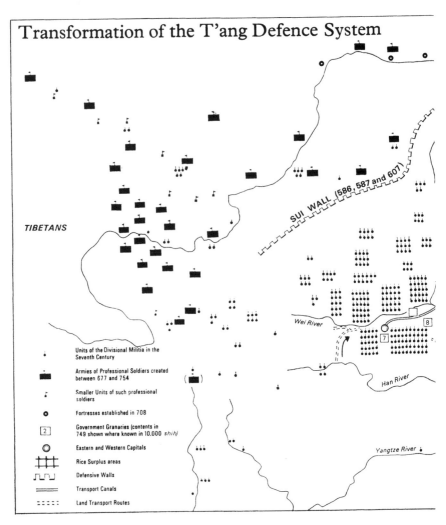

Transformation of the T'ang Defence System

TIBETANS

SUI WALL (586, 587 and 607)

Wei River

Han River

Yangtze River

	Units of the Divisional Militia in the Seventh Century
	Armies of Professional Soldiers created between 677 and 754
	Smaller Units of such professional soldiers
○	Fortresses established in 708
2	Government Granaries (contents in 749 shown where known in 10,000 *shih*)
◎	Eastern and Western Capitals
╫╫	Rice Surplus areas
⌐⌐	Defensive Walls
═══	Transport Canals
‒‒‒	Land Transport Routes

Map 2

by the Chinese in the country north-east of the terminus of the Yung-chi Canal (see map 2) required two carters to move about five bushels of grain, and sea transport was still far below the level it was to reach in early Ming times. As a result the Korean walled cities, though vulnerable to Chinese techniques of siege warfare were able to hold up the invading

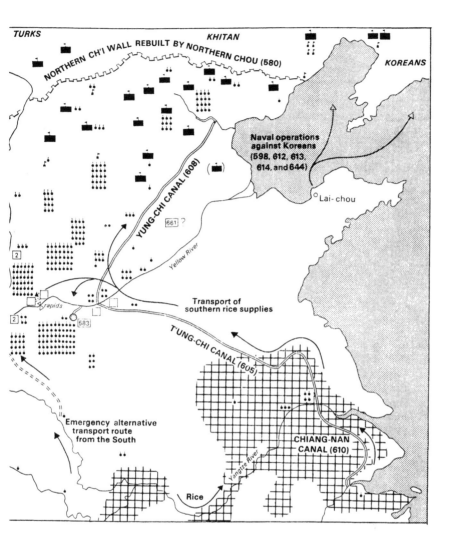

forces until they ran short of food and had to retire. Logistics was thus the ultimately decisive factor.

★

The Sui and T'ang dynasties made a resolute attempt to enforce the equitable field system of land tenure. Chinese officials of this time *did* confiscate the properties of the rich in accordance with the laws. Thus, when Chia Tun-i was made prefect of Lo-chou in AD 654:

> Many of the powerful families of Lo were occupying lands in excess of those which they were permitted under the system. Chia Tun-i confiscated over three thousand *ch'ing* in all, and gave them to the poor.[6]

Resettlement was also used to make landholding more equitable. It is said that when emperor T'ai-tsung of the T'ang was staying at Ling-k'uo near the capital in AD 644:

> The villages were closely packed together. When he asked how much land the people were receiving, he learnt that each grown male had thirty *mou*. He retired to bed at midnight, but was unable to sleep with worry that they were not allocated [the full fifty *mou* due to persons in densely populated areas, one hundred *mou* being the normal allotment]. He issued a decree that in Yung-chou [the area immediately around the capital] they should select those who had especially small holdings of land, exempt them [from services], and move them to areas where labour was abundant.[7]

In bad years tax exemptions might be granted on the basis of the amount of land actually held. In AD 734, for example, a decree was issued to the effect that:

> We have heard that around the capital and in the metropolitan area there are commoners who have reduced holdings of land . . . This year, households of the eighth rank and below ought as an exceptional measure to be excused payment of the land tax; and those who have received less than one hundred *mou* ought also to be exempted.[8]

Passages like this, taken together with the land registers and comparable documents which have survived in the dry climate of the far north-west of China, show that during the Sui and early T'ang the lower-level sytsem of land allotments did function more or less as it was supposed to, even if the parcels of land were often less than they were legally intended to be.

At the same time, the upper level of the equitable field system attained its most elaborate form. Detailed regulations specified the amounts of land to which the holders of civil and military ranks were entitled. Thus a prince of the blood had a right to one hundred *ch'ing*, and the lowest cavalry commander to a mere sixty *mou*. The object of the system was to make service in the state bureaucracy and the divisional militia the general aspiration of the well-to-do, and the promotion which such service offered the one acceptable avenue of social and economic advancement. This was done by making state service the only legal way to acquire any substantial amount of landed property. Later, when the equitable field system had broken down, the state had to turn to the development of a centrally controlled system of civil service examinations in order to exert a comparable control over the élite. Initially, however, the allocation of lands for services worked quite well. Thus in AD 631 Tai Chou could report on the effect of offering 'merit land' to those possessing army rank:

> I have recently seen the area within the passes and beyond the Yellow River, in all of which military units have been established. The strong adult males of rich families have all joined the ranks! In the most extreme cases, nine-tenths of them are doing military service; and the adult males who have been left behind are exhausted.[9]

Simple lack of land made it hard for the government always to keep its promises; and by the end of the seventh century it was the opinion of general Wei Yuan-chung that:

> For the recent campaigns, honorific grades without any substance to them have been bestowed . . . Since the promised rewards have not been made good, the honours likewise have lost their value. With the passing of time, genuine and counterfeit have become entangled and confused.[10]

But the theoretical obligations were not denied; and land registers survive which carefully record both the land in fact held by the possessor of a military rank and the deficit, often enormous, still in principle owing to him.

The Sui and T'ang equitable field system was also unstable for deeper reasons. When emperor Wen of the Sui decreed that, in order to strengthen the powers of the central government, the prefectural and county officials were to *move* every three years, and did away with the grants of land to slaves, the provisions of the land laws instantly came into clearcut opposition with the interests of the large landowners. In contrast to those of the Toba, the officials of the Sui and T'ang were not usually local magnates holding titles of office, and hence the right to large estates, in a more or less hereditary fashion, but genuine bureaucratic appointees. Although provided with 'office land' during their period of tenure, they had to relinquish this on dismissal or retirement.

Under such conditions they naturally sought to consolidate their own and their families' positions by putting together substantial personal holdings. Often they acquired 'manors away from home' in the area where they held office; and one sign of the growing importance of this practice was a decree issued in AD 752 forbidding any further increases. Some large estates, such as those which had originated with imperial gifts, were perfectly lawful; but the majority were put together by illegal purchase from the peasantry:

> Princes, dukes, officials, and rich and powerful families have recently been establishing manor lands and accumulating property without restraint, having no fear of the regulations. The 'waste land' which they have borrowed is in fact all well-prepared tilth. [It was permissible to open up hitherto untilled public land in addition to one's equitable field allotment, a practice known under the Toba empire as 'borrowing for cultivation'.] The name is but a cover under which they make their encroachments. Their 'setting up of pasturages' refers entirely to valley lands, and there are no limitations on their size. [Important persons often had large herds of cattle, sheep and horses, for which they were allowed pasturage. This gave rise to what the decree later refers to as 'having no horses, but recklessly asking for pasture lands' as a cover for landgrabbing.] Personal allocation land and permanent property are illegally bought and sold. Either the registration of ownership is changed or a mortgage is effected. In consequence, the common people have nowhere to settle. Furthermore, tenants are retained and caused to earn their bread as sharecroppers. The manor fields of princes, dukes, officials, and families with honorary rank or hereditary privilege [the right of the son of a high official to enter officialdom] should not be allowed to exceed the statutory limits on account of their appropriation of the inhabitants' property.[11]

The pressure of taxation and the hardship of bad years meant that the ordinary peasant, from his side, was frequently being tempted to sell off his allotment, even though this was illegal except in certain circumstances such as the need to pay for a funeral. After selling his land he often wandered away; and the problem of vagrants seeking to avoid taxation and military service was an administrative headache for the T'ang government.

The equitable field system was also unsuited to areas of sophisticated rice cultivation, such as the Yangtze valley. Periodic repartition of holdings discourages a farmer from improving his land, since he has no certainty of continuing to enjoy the fruits of his hard work or of bequeathing them to his family. Once rice growing advances beyond the most rudimentary stage, it demands a heavy investment of labour in the levelling of terrain, and in building and maintaining irrigation ditches. The need for such investment was ill matched to a system originating in the millet- and wheat-growing areas of the north, in which a man's land might revert to the government. The equitable field system never became firmly established in the Yangtze region; and presumably for this reason. Kiangnan, as the region was commonly called, came to play an ever more important part in the imperial economy, exerting a powerful attraction on vagrants from the north in search of better conditions. It would seem likely that in consequence the hold of the equitable field system elsewhere was in some measure undermined.

Unlike Toba law, T'ang law did not give extra arable land to the owners of slaves, but only small plots for houses and gardens. Slavery continued, however, to be important in agriculture. A pleasing illustration of what was at best a degrading institution may be found in the biography of a ninth-century worthy in the *Old T'ang History*:

> Ts'ui Chin came from Ch'eng-ku in Liang-chou [in present-day Shensi]. He was a Confucian scholar, but had no taste for an official career. He therefore made his living by farming. Having grown old without having had a son, he distributed his lands, his houses and his family's wealth among his slaves, so that they could each earn a livelihood. He and his wife then retired to the hills south of Ch'eng-ku, and concerned themselves no further with domestic affairs. They made an agreement with their slaves that these would take it in turns to pass by their hut and bring them food and wine. So husband and wife lived contentedly, chanting poems amidst the woods and springs.[12]

Such slaves formed a distinct caste. The law regarded them as 'on a par with livestock and property'. In most cases they had only personal names, but not surnames. They were not allowed to intermarry with free persons. They could be pawned, or rented out for hire like horses. Their masters branded them on the face if they committed an offence; and the penalty for a master who murdered a guiltless slave was a mere year's banishment. Although no hard and fast lines can be drawn, they were clearly different from the relatively more privileged serfs and tenant-serfs of Sung times, described in the next chapter.

★

During the eighth century the two key institutions of the middle empire collapsed – in part for the reasons already outlined. But the collapse was also no less due to the military problems brought on by increasing size. Mounting expeditions beyond the frontiers remained a heavy burden for the middle empire, just as it had been for the early empire. Thus it seems probable that the mobilization of 1,132,800 men by emperor Yang of the Sui for his campaign against Korea in AD 612 was a primary cause of the uprisings which began the year after and continued until his dynasty fell. The T'ang divisional militia were, however, initially conceived as a defensive force. Units were established across north China in a highly irregular fashion, the pattern suggesting that the main objectives were to safeguard the capitals at Ch'ang-an and Lo-yang, to block the route through Shansi usually taken by the Turks when they attacked, and to control any threat from the Hopei area where, experience had shown, revolts most frequently arose (see map 2). Only a handful of units were stationed south of the Huai River. So long as defence retained its primacy, the system of dispersion and self-supply under which the militia worked came under no great strain.* But, with the expansion of the T'ang empire to the north-west, this picture changed. The *Family Biography of the Marquis of Yeh* makes this clear:

When the divisional militia were first established, the Western Wei, the Northern Chou, and the Sui all profited from them. In the time of T'ai-tsung [AD 627–49], when each unit went on its tour of guard duty at the capital, the emperor would summon the men to the palace, give them personal instruction in archery, and load them with presents. In consequence, when he made use of them, they had no equals anywhere . . . Campaigns at that time were not excessively frequent, nor so distant as to take the soldiers away for more than a year before the victory had been won. It was under the emperor Kao-tsung [AD 650–683], who made Liu Jen-kuei the garrison commander of T'ao-ho [near Lan-chou in Kansu province] in order to prepare for the advance on Turfan, that soldiers were first encamped on the frontiers, and the army became worn out with fighting.[13]

The long campaigns undertaken during the reign of the empress Wu (AD 684–704) disrupted the schedules of guard duty on which the militiamen's service was based. Fighting and farming became harder to combine; and long-term professionals began to be recruited or conscripted. This was easier perhaps in China than in Byzantium after the

---

* The unequal geographical distribution of the units of the divisional militia did mean, however, that the requirements of defence overtaxed the resources of some areas while leaving them underutilized in others.

loss of Egypt. Both the divisional militia and the Themes were based on the assumption that it was hard for the central government to mobilize large quantities of supplies, but once Kiangnan had been developed and the canal system improved, the logic for China of a dispersed and self-sufficient defence establishment at least partly disappeared. The Themes, to which no such considerations applied, long outlasted the Chinese militia, only in the eleventh century succumbing to the pressures of feudalism.

Another reason for the rapid decline of the divisional militia was that its social status began to fall. After about AD 660, honours of a purely nominal kind were given out in such profusion as to debase their value; and the rich lost their earlier enthusiasm for militia service. The creation of new forces of palace guards diminished its importance as a ladder of promotion. Some time around AD 674, the militiamen also lost their immunity from taxation. In consequence, important persons who were liable for enrolment acquired forged ordination certificates and passed themselves off as Buddhist monks or Taoist priests. They sometimes also mutilated themselves or paid heavily for substitutes to take their place. The poor ran away, often in considerable numbers.

The fall in the quality of recruits had repercussions on the stability of the entire system. Soldiers were supposed to provide their own food by paying in grain to local state granaries. When they went off on campaign, or a tour of guard duty, they were issued with 'food tickets' equivalent in amount to the deposits of grain which they had made. On arrival at their destination, they could exchange these tickets for food from government stocks. Equally, they were supposed to supply their own pack-horse and light weapons. By the beginning of the eighth century, however, it is clear that the militiamen were so poor that they had to beg supplies from relatives and friends, or else rely upon government assistance. The distinctive characteristics of the militia as an élite force inevitably disappeared; and not long afterwards most militiamen were being enlisted as mercenaries. The whole system was formally wound up in AD 749.

Thus T'ang ambitions in Central Asia led to the disappearance of the divisional militia and to the rapid growth of frontier armies under permanent commanders (see map 2). This placed the central government in a vulnerable position, as was pitilessly revealed in AD 755 when a frontier general of Sogdian-Turkish descent called An Lu-shan rebelled, having despaired of attaining a pre-eminent position by peaceful means.

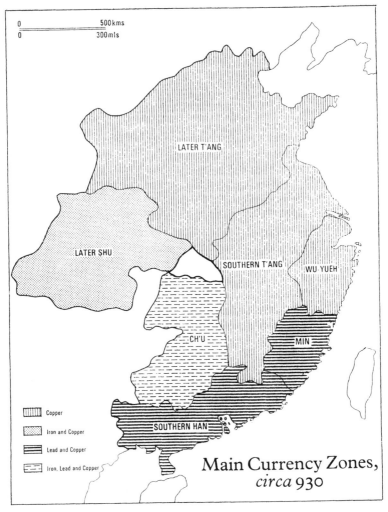

0   500 kms

0   300 mls

LATER T'ANG

LATER SHU

SOUTHERN T'ANG

WU-YUEH

CH'U

MIN

▦ Copper

▧ Iron and Copper

▤ Lead and Copper

▥ Iron, Lead and Copper

SOUTHERN HAN

Main Currency Zones,
circa 930

Map 3

The revolt which he started was suppressed in AD 763, but only by relying upon independent-minded generals who in many ways resembled him. They subsequently became established in the provinces as semi-autonomous military governors with their own private armies. Central control was weakened. The household registration system, upon which the equitable field system depended, broke down. China was given over to a struggle for revenue between the state and its more powerful subjects. The situation was in many respects comparable to what Ostrogorsky has described as 'the struggle between the central power and the great landed proprietors in the tenth century, which was the great turning-point in the economic and social evolution of the Byzantine Empire'.[14] China too fell prey to the *seigneurialisation croissante*, to use Marc Bloch's phrase, which was characteristic of all of Europe at this time.

Towards the end of the eighth century, the famous stateman Lu Chih wrote:

> Our institutions have now become ineffective and confused. The drawing of boundaries between landholdings has fallen into decay. Men devour each other without restraint. There are no longer limits placed on the holding of land. The rich accumulate tens of thousands of *mou*. The poor do not have land enough to stand on, but depend on the powerful, serving them as their private dependents. They borrow seed and provisions, rent from them their fields and huts, and toil all the year round without a day of rest. When they have paid back all that they have borrowed, they are always afflicted with want.[15]

The philosopher and essayist Liu Tsung-yuan echoed his sentiments:

> Rich persons these days pay ever less tax; but the poor do not escape the levies which have to be paid to the county authorities. It is most inequitable. This is not the only cause for concern, however. The rich always make the poor perform services and act like their slaves. In most cases, they provide them with land and take half the crop, getting a double or triple return for what they have contributed.[16]

Peasants who became the dependents of a magnate were likely to escape the payment of taxes entirely. Yang K'uei, writing late in the ninth century, explained the mechanisms by which this happened:

> Those upper-class persons who live in prefectures or counties in which they are not registered are either called 'retired officials' or 'aristocrats'. Since they are living away from home, they have by law no labour-service obligations. What is more, the entire household of anyone who has won the metropolitan doctorate [in the examinations] is free from selective labour-service, while the degree-holder himself is also personally exempt from miscellaneous labour-services. There is as a result a class of self-seeking persons who, having once held some

petty office or other, will claim that when they formerly lived in their native places they used to serve as officials. These insatiable people not only establish manorial lands of their own but take possession of others' property on a wide scale. The ordinary folk are terrified of the labour-services, and desire to present them [with their own land] in the hope of receiving their protection . . .

In times past, a limit was placed on holdings of land. There were maxima for personal shares. Nowadays, aristocratic households have countless acres and sly rogues commend themselves to them. Limits should therefore be placed on holdings of land in accordance with official rank. If large-scale possessions are forbidden, the rich will not try to avoid the corvées and the poor will not be worn out by having to do labour-services when it is not their turn . . .[17]

Yang's analysis was sound, his proposals unrealistic. Under the pressure of internal fragmentation, and repeated attacks from the Khitan and other barbarian tribes in the north, the T'ang empire split up in AD 906. North of the Yangtze the next fifty years saw five dynasties come and go. South of the great river separate states were formed in what are now the modern provinces of Szechwan, Hunan, Kiangsi-Anhwei, Kiangsu-Chekiang, Fukien and Kwangtung (see map 3). For a moment it appeared that China was tending in the direction taken by western Europe after the fall of Rome.

6 · Manorialism without feudalism

In 960 the Chinese empire was largely reunited by T'ai-tsu, the founder of the Sung dynasty, the final touches being added after his death by his younger brother T'ai-tsung. The conditions which made this later empire both possible and permanent are dealt with fully in the second part of this book. In brief, what happened was that an economic and technological revolution reduced the burden of the imperial administrative superstructure, increased the efficiency of the Chinese war machine, and created enough economic integration to be a real obstacle to renewed political fragmentation. At this point, therefore, Chinese historical evolution began to diverge significantly from that of Europe, to which in one way or another it had run nearly parallel for over a millennium. It is the purpose of this chapter to show how slight this divergence was at first, and to pinpoint the continued existence of imperial unity as the primary immediate cause of the differences. To anticipate the conclusion: Chinese society, like that of Europe at this time, developed in the direction of manorialism (*régime seigneuriale*); but since the state retained control over defence functions, as it did not in Europe, there was no feudal superstructure (*régime féodale*), in the sense of a dominant specialist military class disposing of fiefs granted in return for military service and ruling these as more or less unquestioned lords.

In the last part of chapter 5 we traced the growth of large private estates or manors. By the tenth century, these had become the foundation of a new and distinctive social order based on the enserfment of much of the peasant population and exerting a dominant influence over most of the rest. The manorial regime of Sung times was so protean in its forms and regional variations as to make simple description extremely difficult. Perhaps our clearest guide to the class structure is an official form issued in 1180 by Chu Hsi in connection with famine relief in Nan-k'ang prefecture:

Total number of families in the borough: ......

Number of rich families with rice available for sale: ......

Number of piculs of rice available for sale excluding that needed for the supply of family members and their tenant-serfs: ......
(Enter surnames and personal names of household members, and the quantity of rice. Also enter surnames and personal names of their tenant-serfs.)

Number of rich families without surplus rice available for sale, and only able to supply themselves and to keep their tenant-serfs from want: ......
(As before, enter the surnames and personal names of household members, and also the surnames and personal names of their tenant-serfs.)

Number of families owning a moderate amount of property and able to provide for themselves, but not to provide in full for their tenant-serfs: ......
(Enter names of households, surnames and personal names of their tenant-serfs, and the amount by which they are short.)

Number of [registered] households of the lowest rank who need to buy rice: ......

Number of farming families: ......
(Enter names of households, numbers of adults and children, and also what subsidiary occupations are pursued.)

Number of non-farming families: ......
(Enter names of households, numbers of adults and children, and what occupations are followed.)

Number of *families cultivating land belonging to others*: ......
(Enter the names of households, names of owners of land which they farm, numbers of adults and children, and any other occupation concurrently pursued.)[1]

There was thus a society consisting of a manorial sector and of a free sector containing smallholders, artisans and ordinary tenants, the line of demarcation between the two being neatly pointed up by the distinction between 'tenant-serfs' and 'families cultivating land belonging to others'. Unfortunately, the social realities behind the rather vague terms used in most Chinese texts are much less immediately apparent than they are here, and have to be inferred from context.

Bondage to the soil

Tenant-serfs may be defined as those tenants who were bound to the soil. There is no record of this practice in T'ang times, and it seems to have been an innovation of the tenth century. In 1027 the Sung government tried to relax it by decree:

> According to the *old regulations* for the prefectures of the provinces of Chiang-nan, Huai-nan, Liang-che, Fu-chien, Ching-hu and Kuang-nan, the agricultural tenants of private persons may not move away at an untimely moment. They are only allowed to live elsewhere if their masters send them, and furnish them with permits. Many of them are maltreated by their masters and prevented from moving. *Henceforth,* tenants shall no longer need a permit from their masters if they are to move; but they must give notice of their intention to move only after they have gathered in the harvest from every field. Thus the master will obtain certainty, and the tenants their convenience. That is to say, they may not untimely move away in accordance with their personal whims. If this system is used, then their masters will not obstruct them, or force them to stay.[2]

It is doubtful if this law had much impact. If it had been respected there would have been little point in a decree in 1153 which conferred on tenants the much more restricted right to leave when the land which they worked passed by sale from one master to another. It is also known to have been common in Liang-che province for proprietors to record the names of the tenants on the deeds of sale of land, along with the fields and the cottages. The significance of this practice is brought out by a report cited in the statutes of the Yuan dynasty (1276–1367):

> The wealthy families of Kiangnan place their reliance exclusively on the possession of land, for when they buy the land they acquire the tenants with it. These so-called tenants are free commoners, but their masters impose services on them to such an extent that great damage is done to the official assignment of corvées. If a tenant has a son, then he serves as a servant. If he has a daughter then she becomes a servant-girl, or else a wife or concubine.[3]

State measures aimed at a partial liberation of the tenant-serfs in other areas were probably equally ineffective. Thus, when the prefect of O-chou, now Wu-ch'ang in Hupei province, persuaded the court to decree that 'When fields are being bought and sold, it is impermissible for the tenants to be included in the contract, and these latter shall be allowed to do as they please,' there was a storm of landlord protest.[4] This was early in the twelfth century. About a hundred and fifty years later the judge of Hsia-chou, now I-ch'ang in western Hupei, could write:

Commoners who come under the jurisdiction of this province have the audacity to pawn and sell their tenant-serfs, drawing up contracts which specify the number of persons. No period of years is laid down; and the transactions are no different from the sale and purchase of enslaved prisoners of war. There are some of them who show a certain fear of the law, and so sell a small patch of remote agricultural land along with the tenant-serfs, styling this 'tenant-serfs going along with the fields'; but in addition to the public contract they also draw up a private contract . . . This practice dates from the time of the late Sung dynasty.[5]

This passage suggests that the subjection of tenant-serfs grew harsher with the course of time, and in part changed from bondage to the soil to bondage to the master's person. This latter point is confirmed by cases in twelfth-century Hupei in which the tenant-serfs of landowners whose lands had been confiscated by the government as a punishment left their fields and followed their masters.

In parts of western China, at least, the state could also act to enforce bondage to the soil, and buttress the manorial order. This may be seen from a letter written around the middle of the twelfth century by the scholar Hu Hung to the general Liu Ch'i about the conditions in his native central Hunan:

There is a chain of obedience stretching down from masters to tenants; and it is by means of this that the state is supplied. It cannot be dispensed with for a single day. Since this is so, how can tenants be allowed to do as they please? This would result in their masters being unable to control them! Tenants depend on their masters for their livelihood, and so they have to provide them with services and submit to their discipline. Officials should inflict a vigorous punishment on tenants, and forbid them to act in accordance with their own pleasure, in the event that a master lays a plaint on any of the following grounds: (1) that his tenants are behaving perversely and refusing to recognize the distinction between superior and inferior; (2) that they are practising commerce and not working hard at farming and sericulture; (3) that they are drinking or gambling without restraint, and are unamenable to discipline; (4) that, being unmarried, they are enticing other men's wives away; or (5) that, having many adult males in their families and more than enough food and clothing, they have been able to buy half an acre or an acre of farmland and a house, have set up a tax-paying household of their own and wish to leave their master.[6]

Cruel masters, however, deserved no help from the state (see the continuation of this passage given on pages 241–2). In the under-developed area which is now eastern Szechwan, southern Hupei and north-western Hunan, special laws saw to the recovery of fugitive tenant-serfs. In 1052, tenants absconding from official manors, and from private manors in two particular prefectures, were made liable to arrest and return. Then in 1184 the Ministry of Finance issued a more comprehensive ruling:

> If, in the future, any household lays a plaint that its tenant-serfs have been pilfered, this should be dealt with in accordance with the special law [of 1052]. Henceforth, in dealing with tenant-serfs who have absconded and gone to live elsewhere: (1) those who have done so within the past three years shall be compelled to return, with all their relatives, to their former masters. Notices will be posted up throughout the prefecture that if runaway families return to their lands within two months, they shall not be recklessly seized because of their failure to fulfil their obligations; and (2) those who have done so more than three years ago, and are living peaceably and do not wish to return, shall be allowed to do as they please. If, in the future, any families are made to move, then the authorities shall pursue them and bring them back, regardless of any question of a three-year limit. If violence has been used to effect the forcible removal of tenant-serfs, this shall be judged in accordance with the laws on kidnapping.[7]

It seems clear from the last few sentences that the primary motive behind this law was the desire to stop the quarrels which arose when manor lords poached each other's tenantry, a great temptation in an area where labour was still something of a precious commodity.

The origins of tenant-serfdom

This class of tenant-serfs was brought into being by a combination of processes. The first of these which calls for attention is the conditional freeing of slaves, because it seems likely that, as in Europe, it was this practice which established the institutional framework of serfdom although only contributing a modest percentage of the total tenant-serf population.* The freeing slaves began to become common in the eighth century. Here is a translation of the earliest known document laying down a standard form for this act, dating from the first part of this century:

Document Establishing Free Status

With regard to such-and-such male slaves and such-and-such female slaves, there being several persons of both sexes –

We have heard that when slaves are released to be free persons the mountains of felicity rise up high, and that when free persons are crushed down into servile status there is hatred deep as hell. The foregoing slaves have long endured bitter toil in servile bondage. When they have risen in the morning, they have been deeply respectful. At night, they have not been able to be at their ease. We, too, have long sighed with regret at this, and borne the burden of such feelings in our hearts. We have sacrificed to the spirits of our ancestors and now release the foregoing persons to be freemen. When the fish who has been in captivity sees the open sea, he skims upon the waves. When the breath of spring touches the sleeping willow tree, it stretches aloft. Let what should be done now be done without further discussion. The sons and grandsons shall likewise not be begrudged their liberation. The officials have just laws, while [ordinary] men have one-sided judgments. If anyone acts contrary to this deed, then appeal may be freely made to the government.

Signed (relatives, neighbours and officials).[8]

Like other extant documents of manumission, this speaks of unconditional freeing.† Since conditions (assuming that they existed) must have differed from case to case, they would obviously have had no place

---

* On the importance of slaves in agriculture in Toba and T'ang times, see pp. 49, 50 and 63. In 845, when 4,600 Buddhist monasteries were abolished, and over a quarter of a million monks and nuns returned to lay life, several tens of millions of *mou* of land were confiscated, and 150,000 slaves turned into tax-paying households. There were also brokers dealing in slaves, both in the T'ang and the Northern Sung. But it does not seem that slaves represented more than a modest percentage of the total population.

†Several T'ang forms of manumission in fact emphasize that once a slave has been set at liberty, he is 'free to go north, south, east or west as he desires, following the dictates of his own will', and even to become a high official. On the other hand, the penalties for re-enslaving manumitted slaves laid down in the T'ang code suggest that the danger of the reimposition of servitude was a real one. See Hiraoka Takeo, 'Hōjūryō – Po chü-i no dohi kaihō' (Manumission – The Liberation of his Slaves by Po chü-i), *Tōhō gakuhō* XXXVIII (Mar. 1967), pp. 226–7, 234–5.

in a standardized form of this kind. It may also have been felt inappropriate to include them along with such fine sentiments about the beauties of freedom.* In any event, at least one case is known of Sung tenants who were the direct descendants of the late T'ang slaves who had farmed the same land; and it is tempting to imagine that this was quite common. The imposition of conditions on liberated slaves, particularly that they should continue to farm their former owner's land, is the most plausible reason for the greater harshness of manorial tenancy in Sung than in T'ang times, above all bondage to the soil.

This is admittedly speculation.† Other forms of enserfment are much easier to document. Free peasants who sold their land because of poverty were often compelled to stay on as tenant-serfs on their former holdings. This is apparent from a memorial written in 1205 by Fan Sun, then chief judge of K'uei-chou province:

> In the remote border areas of Shih-chou and Ch'ien-chou, which form part of this province, there is a succession of mountainous valleys where the land is uncultivated and the inhabitants are sparse. Large proprietors need men for cultivation and clearing. Rich and powerful families struggle with each other for the use of local persons as tenants and entice others from elsewhere, sometimes leading the removal of

---

* It is not clear why such sentiments first became prevalent in T'ang times. The Buddhist doctrines of Karma and reincarnation, introduced some centuries earlier, provided a convenient explanation and justification of the difference between free men and slaves: slavery was a punishment for sins committed in a former existence. On the other hand, Buddhism also regarded the release of slaves as a meritorious act, which would help the benefactor and his family both in this and in the other world; and the acquisition of such merit was the motive for many acts of manumission. Hiraoka Takeo has, however, pointed to a spirit of humanism pervading the documents which cannot be attributed to Buddhism. [Hiraoka (1967), pp. 233 et seq.]

† Changes in Chinese law may offer some slight support. In 1003, for example, the Sung emperor Chen-tsung observed that 'the serfs of the present time are basically free persons who have been hired'. He ordered an end to 'the old system' by which masters branded or tattooed the faces of serfs guilty of some crime. Does this indicate the assimilation of substantial numbers of free persons to a servile status? In T'ang times the punishment for flogging a slave or a retainer to death was banishment for a year. The early Sung government per contra tried to enforce a death penalty for killing a serf or a tenant by scourging; but by the twelfth century the penalty for flogging a tenant-serf to death had become merely a mild form of local banishment. Obviously the status of tenant-serfs had worsened by this time; and it may also be that what this meant was that many tenants were now being treated in the way thought 'normal' by masters for slaves or serfs. See Miyazaki Ichisada, *Ajia-shi kenkyū* (Studies in Asian History), I (Kyoto: 1962), pp. 455-7.

crowds of persons with their entire households. I would request that the law of the Huang-yu reign-period [1049–53] regarding tenants who abscond from official manors should be applied with a few additional provisions, namely: tenants shall be personally liable to perform services [for their masters], but this obligation shall not be extended to any of their family, or their womenfolk. When [a peasant] has mortgaged or sold his fields and house, he shall be free in due order to leave the property, and may not be made to act as a tenant paying rent. Nor may he be made to serve as a field-hand, even if he does not pay rent. All those [peasants] who have borrowed either money or goods may only be required to return these as specified in their contract. It is forbidden to coerce them into becoming tenants. When a tenant dies and his widow wishes to marry again, she should be allowed to do as she pleases; and the daughters of tenants ought to be freely betrothed and married. In this way, the people of the deep hills and barren valleys may live contented.[9]

One may infer that the banned practices were fairly frequent. Straightforward coercion was another common means. Yeh Shih, writing in the thirteenth century, had this to say about the manor lords of the T'ai-hu region:

The common people cannot face the officials for a single day, just as sheep cannot consort with tigers. And why should this be true only of the relationships between officials and common people? A family that is fairly well-off for food and clothing will make the people who live in its neighbourhood till its fields as tenant-serfs. The management will be in the hands of no more than one or two trusted and experienced slaves; but the people from the neighbourhood will be unable to endure the exactions of their landlord and the trickery practised on them by the slaves. Furthermore, families who have accumulated considerable holdings, and attained wealth and high status, make the people of their whole community till their fields as tenant-serfs. Their exactions and criminal frauds may be so cruel as to be unbearable; and entire families will sometimes run away, or throw away their lives in resisting.[10]

Sometimes there may have been inducements. The censor Wang Yen-sou made the following interesting remark in 1087:

Rich commoners invite in-migrants to be their tenants. Each year before the harvest has been gathered in, they go to any lengths to lend them everything they need. If they once fail to show them gentle treatment, they are certain to go somewhere else the following year.[11]

These persons were clearly not bound to the soil; but it appears that peasants were at times ensnared into debt and dependence by the offer of seemingly attractive terms.

There was also a limited reverse flow from the ranks of the tenant-serfs back into the free peasantry. This may be seen from the observations of Hu Hung already quoted, and from the warning issued by Yuan Ts'ai in the twelfth century in his book on the domestic affairs of well-to-do families. Speaking of tenants, he wrote: 'One should not allow them to have fields and gardens of their own, for if one does, they immediately become filled with greedy schemes.'[12] Cases are known of masters taking legal action to prevent their tenant-serfs farming on their own account land abandoned by other peasants, presumably for fear that this would enable them to break away from their control.

Serfs, tenants and manorial power

The question of what percentage of the peasantry held the status of tenant-serfs, and what percentage was more or less free, is an extremely difficult one to answer. There were marked regional variations, for the manorial regime did not spread to every part of China any more than it did to every part of medieval Europe. Thus, according to Yü Ch'üeh, a scholar-general of the fourteenth century:

> Che-tung [the southern, mountainous part of present-day Chekiang] lay in ancient times within the kingdom of Yueh. Its land is divided into small units. There are no very rich or poor persons. In its hilly valleys there live people whose dwelling-houses occupy a sixth of an acre of land, and whose fields amount to one and two-thirds of an acre, the property having been handed down intact from one generation to the next. The land is not fertile; and these humble folk have to toil for their living. Even persons of quality are modest and frugal, being imbued with respect for the *Book of Odes* and the *Book of Documents*. They are unlike the men of Wu [southern Kiangsu and northern Chekiang], with their high-handed land-grabbing great families whose harvests each year amount to several million measures, while none of the poor have anything at all to store away.[13]

These regional variations do not fit, so far as we can tell, with the varying regional proportions of so-called 'local/landowning households' (*chu-hu*) and 'in-migrant/tenant households' (*k'o-hu*) which appear in the official population registers. These are therefore no guide, as is sometimes supposed, to the proportions of free and unfree peasants. Nor is this really surprising, because (at least under the Northern Sung) if a household's existence was to be recorded at all, it had in principle to own some land.[14] Strictly speaking, tenant-serfs could only have appeared as members of their masters' households; and the very low ratio of persons to registered households (even on the assumption that only males were listed) shows that this did not in fact happen. The function, so far as there was one, of the division into *chu-hu* and *k'o-hu* was to share out the tax burden more equitably. The *k'o-hu*, being historically derived from recent settlers mostly farming new or inferior land, were charged at a lower rate than the *chu-hu*. In time they were meant to be re-registered as *chu-hu*; but this seems rarely to have happened.

In fact, it seems clear that the registration laws were systematically ignored, and that neither the 'local/landowning households', nor the 'in-migrant/tenant households', should be thought of as classes of independent smallholding peasants. Most of them were nearly or wholly landless, as witness an account written in 1167 by Lü Tsu-ch'ien about Yen-chou:

> I have carefully put in order the population registers of this prefecture. For a total of six counties there are only 10,718 adult males belonging to households of the first to fourth ranks. There are 71,479 adult males belonging to households of the fifth rank owning taxable property. Although nominally they own taxable property, most of them only pay in fractional amounts, and it is as if they owned nothing. They are not capable of being self-sufficient. There are altogether 40,198 adult males belonging to households without taxable property. They possess not a scrap of land, not one foot of a rafter of a house. They turn from this occupation to that in hunger and cold, unable to make plans in the morning for the selfsame evening. This prefecture has charge of 122,393 adult males, and of these those in the fifth rank of household owning taxable property and without property amount to 111,675 adult males.[15]*

It is not clear if Lü was including the 'in-migrant/tenant households' in the landless households of the fifth rank or not. Some of the latter may well have been farm labourers paid by the day, a class commonly regarded as the worst off of all, as they did not even have the security of

---

* For arithmetical consistency, it is necessary to assume that there are two errors in this text: 71,479 for 71,477, and 111,675 for 111,575.

the tenant-serf. In any case, something like seventy per cent of the *registered* households here must have depended on a landlord to rent them at least some land, thus falling into Chu Hsi's category of 'families cultivating land belonging to others'. There must in addition have been a substantial number of *unregistered* tenant-serfs attached to the manors of the powerful.

It is certain, moreover, that many of those who were nominally free tenants came under manorial jurisdiction. We learn of Fan Ch'üan, a Kiangsi landowner who held a subordinate post in local government, and later became a supervisor of customs, that:

> He brazenly assumed an air of authority, and bought up rich lands which extended into neighbouring areas. Not even the aristocrats had manors and gardens on the scale that he did. He lent out money at interest, and told his retainers to seize any who defaulted, bind them, string them up and lash them. It was worse than official justice.[16]

Sometimes the large landed interests took over local administration and made it their creature. According to Huang Chen, an official of the thirteenth century:

> In the fertile lands of northern Chekiang, rich and titled persons have established numerous manors. It is the custom of their managers to order the chiefs of the county police to use their constables to arrest their tenants. Although the pretext is supervising the rents, they do not collect the rents outstanding but privily devise means of imprisoning and murdering them, in order to establish their authority over the villages. It is impossible to tell to how many persons this happens every year. The relatives have been accustomed to this practice for so long that they do not regard it as murder. They simply weep at the punishment, burn the corpse and depart. Thus it is that, although many have died, no plaint has ever been lodged with the officials. Sometimes, never having seen anyone arrested return alive, the villagers join their families and villages together, and resist arrest to the death. There are frequently affrays in which people are killed or wounded. The [manor] managers presume upon the power of the rich and titled families, and denounce them for compounding their crimes by resisting arrest. Thus, even though the tenants die, they cannot obtain redress from the officials.[17]

It is no exaggeration to say that, even though the extent of tenant-serfdom cannot at present be estimated, the manor was the dominant institution in most of the Chinese countryside. A further confirmation of this may be found in the decision of the Sung government in the eleventh century to entrust local administrative duties to groups of five, twenty-five and 250 households led by their wealthiest members. This system used the existing hierarchical structure in the countryside and lasted until the seventeenth century, when the manorial order finally collapsed.

Structure and management of the manor

What, then, was the nature of the manor? Geographically it might be compact or scattered. The manor outside Ch'eng-tu owned by T'ien Ch'in-ch'üan in the tenth century, which is known to have consisted of 10,000 *mou* in a single bloc, perhaps two to three thousand of these being plough-land, may have been exceptional. But where, as in this area, vigorous day-by-day supervision was often exercised over the manorial labour force, a high degree of geographical dispersion cannot have been common. Su Hsun, who was a native of the Ch'eng-tu region, wrote about it in the eleventh century as follows:

> Rich commoners have vast properties, the fields of which stretch out in unbroken lines. They recruit migrants, and assign the cultivation to them. They drive them to work under the lash of the whip, treating them as serfs. They sit at their ease, keeping a watch on everything and giving the orders, while their subordinates hoe weeds for them in the summer, and harvest for them in the autumn. It is their delight that not one man disobeys his instructions.[18]

But there were limits to the extent to which direct management made good economic sense. The most frequent system was probably the combination of a compact demesne farm at the centre, worked by a labour force under the personal control of the proprietor or his manager, and outlying allotments farmed by tenants who owed rents and services but were free from day-to-day interference. In the eleventh century, according to Ou-yang Hsiu:

> These days, when a family owns as much as a hundred *ch'ing* of land, they will support several tens of families of dependents. Not more than ten or a dozen of these will either work as simple labourers with the landowner's oxen, or use their own oxen on the landlord's land on a profit-sharing basis. The remainder will all pay rent for their land and live apart from him.[19]

Some confirmation is provided from a later period by observations
on manor owners in a Ming dynasty gazetteer for Chiang-shan county in
Chekiang:

> They hire men to cultivate their fields, sharing the harvest with them
> once it has ripened. These are the tenants. There is another class of
> persons called 'supernumeraries'. Most of them are derived from
> family serfs. They order them to reside at the manor to watch over it.
> Sometimes, too, they give lodging in the manor buildings to single
> males from other rural communities, and furnish them with wives
> after the fashion of slaves.[20]

The social and geographical structure of manors was thus often fairly
complex.

Even where the tenant-serfs might otherwise have been independent
in the conduct of their daily work, the advantages of working together
and sharing expensive equipment, imposed a measure of organization.
The clearest illustration of this is the rules for official manors set up in
1136 in what is now the northern part of Kiangsu province:

> Every two farmers will be given one plough-ox, one plough and one
> seed-rake; also one hoe, one spade, one mattock and one reaping-hook.
> For every three head of oxen there will be used one blade for the
> opening up of waste ground; and for every tithing of five households
> one treadle-operated water-pump, two stone rollers and a wooden
> roller. Each family will have a thatched cottage of two units in area,
> and every two oxen a thatched byre of one unit of area. Each farmer
> will be lent seed worth eleven strings of copper cash.[21]

It was also laid down that 'Every five tenant farmers shall mutually guarantee each other as a tithing, and cultivate together.' Similar groups are
known to have existed on private manors, and no doubt served very
similar functions. It seems likely that this kind of sub-manorial unit lay
behind the co-operative activities described by Kao Ssu-te in early
thirteenth-century Szechwan:

> In the fourth month, when the weeds have grown tall, those who farm
> adjoining fields co-operate in removing them with the hoe. They set
> up a water clock* to determine the time-periods, and strike a drum

---

* This was probably the simple water clock shown in a Ming encyclopedia,
the *San-ts'ai t'u-hui* (*Ch'i-yung* section, ch. 10, 51a). An arrow marked with
Chinese double hours and one-hundredths of a day floated in a container, rising
as water from a reservoir dripped into the container. The accompanying text
observes that, 'Farming families install this clock in order to measure the time

to mark the intervals. The lazy are fined and the diligent rewarded. At the height of the summer, when the sun blazes like fire and the water in the fields is like hot soup, hoeing weeds is particularly arduous work; but the peasants set to it with a will, and such is their diligence that they regularly reap twice the harvest that might be expected.[22]

Many of the new irrigation projects undertaken in Sung times were the work of manors, or combines of manor-owners; and the control of the permanent staff who ran these gave them enormous influence in their localities. The state was always trying to supervise the allocation of water and the levy of labour for repairs, but those in immediate charge were invariably the wealthiest landowners, and water-control organizations of this period were often simply a further aspect of manorial power.

★

The co-operative aspects of the manor did not extend much beyond agriculture. Here is an account, written towards the end of the thirteenth century by Fang Hui, of how tenant-serfs traded their surplus rice at the local markets:

> Formerly, when I was visiting Wang Wen-cheng's family in Wei-t'ang [in Chia-shan in Chekiang province], I saw the countryside where the men of Wu live. The smoke from the thatched houses stretched away as far as one could see. All of them belonged to tenant-serfs. A farmer can cultivate thirty *mou* of today's fields; so, if a harvest of two to three piculs is obtained per *mou* (and we may for the moment take two piculs as the average), and if one picul per *mou* is paid to the master, with the addition of five [pints?] for himself by the manager of the manor when he measures out each picul, then one can say that the tenant-serf pays his master thirty piculs and obtains thirty piculs for himself. Assuming that the daily consumption of one person is a hundredth of a picul [or over one pound of rice a day], a family of five will eat eighteen piculs a year. This will leave them with a surplus

and calculate [the hours of] work. It is quite indispensable. In farming it is necessary to wait for the season for ploughing, planting, weeding, and hoeing up earth around plants; but when the season comes there is only a short time in which to do the work. If one delays, the time will not come again. This is what is meant by saying "struggle to use each moment, begrudge each instant". This is what the field clepsydra is made for.' From this passage and others quoted (for example, the poem on p. 273), it is clear that Chinese peasants were highly conscious of time and the importance of using it economically.

of twelve piculs. I saw tenant-serfs taking rice, sometimes one pint and sometimes several pints at a time, to their market-place to exchange for incense, candles, paper, horse-oil [?], salt, bean sauce, pickles, starch powder, bran, pepper, ginger, medicines or rice cakes. All of these are valued in terms of rice.[23]

So far as its consumption was concerned, the tenant-serf household was thus normally an independent economic unit.

This picture of the countryside in Sung China has had to be brief and impressionistic. In particular, less than full justice has been done to the not inconsiderable number of peasants who lived outside of the manorial order. It is clear, however, that the resemblances to conditions in medieval Europe are as striking as the differences. Manorial justice, though we have seen that it might exist in practice, was not legally recognized. Land was (for the most part) freely bought and sold in a fashion common in the ancient and the modern but not the medieval West. Nor was land held (as it had been when the upper level of the equitable field system had been in force) only upon condition of services rendered to the state. The landowners were not mainly members of a specialist military class, though during the Five Dynasties this had come close to being the case in some areas. But it would have taken only a small shift in the course of Chinese history for a true feudal super-structure to emerge. How small a shift is suggested by a proposal made in 1052 by Li Kou, a leading educational official:

> These days there are more displaced dependents who farm other men's fields as tenants, and live in areas other than their own, than there are landowning households. We should permit the rich to establish these persons as their military retainers, and to train them privately them-selves. Official rank should be bestowed [upon the master] whenever a certain number have been shown by examination to be adequate soldiers, or a certain number of robbers have been captured.[24]

This suggestion was rejected, the reason probably being that the central government had enough resources to keep the provision of defence in its own hands. Yet it seems likely that, even so, manorialism siphoned off such wealth as seriously to weaken the imperial administration. If this was the case, then we have a partial explanation of the paradox treated at length in the next chapter: the astonishing power of the Sung state, and its equally astonishing incapacity to survive unconquered.

7 · Iron, gunpowder and the Mongols

The economic revolution which underpinned the Sung empire allowed it to maintain the most formidable military machine that the world had yet seen. By 1040 the regular army amounted to 1·25 million men; and the state armaments industry set up to equip it was one of the earliest examples of standardized mass production. Even at the beginning of the dynasty, the Bow and Crossbow Department at the capital was turning out 16·5 million arrowheads a year. By 1160 the yearly output of the Imperial Armaments Office, *not* including provincial production, came to 3·24 million weapons. Body armour was manufactured in three regulation styles to the extent of several tens of thousands of sets annually. The supply system, based on canals, was superlative. In some years six million piculs or more of grain were brought from the south to the capital, and on this basis a central army of over 300,000 men was supported in the immediate vicinity of the capital. The main forces on the northern frontiers were equally enormous: 300,000 soldiers in Hopei to face the Khitan, and 450,000 in Shensi to counter the Hsi-hsia. By Han standards, any one of these three armies would have been enough to bring the empire to financial ruin. The contrast with the penny-pinching and dispersed system of the divisional militia of early T'ang times is also striking. Yet in 1127 the Chin Tartars took K'ai-feng and conquered northern China; and in 1275 the Mongols, after having previously disposed of the Chin, captured the southern Sung capital at Hang-chou, and became the masters of the entire country. How did these disasters happen?

The answer lies pre-eminently in the transfer of technology across the imperial frontiers to the less civilized peoples beyond. As in the case of the barbarians who destroyed the Chin empire in north China in the fourth century AD, the acquisition of certain Chinese skills in political and social organization was vital to the creation of the strength of

China's conquerors in the twelfth and thirteenth centuries. The founder of the Khitan empire, which immediately preceded that of the Chin Tartars in Manchuria, not only spoke the Chinese language but based his power mainly on the Chinese section of his subjects, and began to transform a tribal structure into an elaborate Chinese-style administration. The blueprint for Mongol government was the work of Yeh-lü Ch'u-ts'ai, a scion of the former Khitan ruling house brought up under the Chin Tartar empire in north China, and completely familiar with every aspect of Chinese civilization. The most dramatic effects of technical borrowings, however, changing the balance of power across half a continent, appeared in the economic and military spheres.

Recent research suggests that the output of pig iron per person in China multiplied several times between late T'ang and early Sung. The size of the increase is the subject of a sharp controversy that turns upon fine technical points, and need not detain us here. Total production per year in the later eleventh century lay between 35,000 to 40,000 tons and 125,000 tons. My personal preference is for the higher of these two estimates,[1] though if Ming practice may be taken as a guide to Sung times government output at least must have varied greatly from year to year depending on the size of reserve stocks.

North China had become deforested in the course of the T'ang dynasty; and the revolution in pig iron production was made possible by the use of coal as a fuel. Su Tung-p'o's famous remark on P'eng-ch'eng, a town in what is today northern Kiangsu, refers to what must have been quite a common occurrence:

> From times past P'eng-ch'eng had lacked coal. In the first month of 1079 men were first sent out to look for it. They found it to the south-west of the prefectural city [Hsu-chou], and to the north of Pai-tu town. It was used for smelting iron ore, and for making extraordinarily fine sharp-edged weapons.[2]

The usual practice was to use the coal to heat clay crucibles containing iron ore, anthracite dust and a 'black earth' whose nature is not certain. Possibly, too, coke or 'refined coal', which had been used for cooking since later T'ang times, was employed in a blast furnace in direct contact with the ore. If such a development did take place, it would have been greatly helped by the powerful continuous draught given by the Chinese box-bellows, in which an arrangement of valves caused a continuous flow of air to be maintained as a single piston was alternately pushed and pulled. For many centuries the Chinese had been, and still were, masters at casting iron in a fully liquid form; and they produced steel either by means of the co-fusion of pig iron and wrought iron, or by direct decarbonization in a cold oxidizing blast. Siderurgical techniques were thus well in advance of Europe at this time. The iron and steel so produced were used for many purposes: for nails in ships, for pans and vats in the salt industry, for chain suspension bridges, even for pagodas; but farm tools, currency and armaments took by far the greater part. Iron was prodigally used in warfare. The armoured cars devised in 1127 by Li Kang, as a counter to the Chin Tartar cavalry, were cased in iron plates. When they stopped, they were linked into laagers with iron chains. Sometimes besieged soldiers even poured the metal in molten form onto the heads of their attackers.

Unfortunately for the Sung, the mastery of iron working crossed the north-eastern frontier to their enemies the Khitan, and a little later to the Chin Tartars. It was not iron alone, though, that made these barbarians so formidable. It was the combination of abundant iron with cavalry warfare, in which they had long excelled. The Sung statesman Li Kang ruefully remarked that 'The men of Chin rely above all on armoured horsemen to obtain the victory. We use foot-soldiers to oppose them and are invariably defeated.'[3] In fact there was slightly more to it than this. The Khitan, who never conquered the Sung, relied almost solely on mounted archery, dividing their soldiers into three categories of skill with the bow. The best were given complete suits of protective armour and placed at the rear. The next best were given half armour and placed in the middle. The least expert were pushed to the front and had to fight without armour, and since the Khitan bows were little use above fifty paces, they were thus very vulnerable to Chinese crossbows effective at between 120 and 300 paces. The Chin saw a way to use armour to counter this superiority in firepower. They attacked by sending in first their so-called 'hard troops' armed with halberds and consisting of men *and horses* in full armour, as a cover behind which their bowmen could advance in safety. The latter only fired when they were within easy range, using arrows with fearsome barbed heads that stuck fast in a wound. The Chinese thus found themselves out-classed; and they lacked the supplies of horses to answer in kind, perhaps because their increasing population had led to a conversion of pasture to arable.

In 1055 Kuo Ku, head of the Fen-chou militia in Shansi, used carts with pointed fronts and square sterns, equipped with long spears, as a counter to the northern cavalry. These were soon improved into primitive armoured cars whose superstructures were covered with rawhide or felt, and armed with a powerful crossbow set on a platform. Han Ch'i, an eminent eleventh-century official with long experience of military command, observed of them that 'because they could be used on the level lands of Hopei, it was possible to stem the headlong rush of the enemy on the battlefield, and by forming them into an array to create a strongpoint'.[4] Even when clad with iron sheeting, however, these war-carts so strangely reminiscent of the 'moving towns' of wagons used in Europe against horsemen by both the Russians and the Hussites were inadequate to prevent the loss of northern China. The south had a surer protection against mounted enemies in its myriad lakes and waterways.

The Chin Tartar conquest of northern China in 1127 deprived the Sung of their most important sources of iron and coal, thus seriously impairing their long-term capacity for resistance. The most immediately dangerous aspect of Chin rule however was that, unlike the prudent Khitan whom they had displaced early in the twelfth century as the rulers of Manchuria, they let iron flow freely through commercial channels into Mongolia. The Mongols, who had previously had to tip their arrows with horn and bone and lacked adequate armour and swords, now became formidable foes. In 1234 they in their turn wrested north China from the Chin and, showing a keen appreciation of the military importance of iron, immediately took steps to expand production there. It was Chinese iron that, in good measure, made possible the success of the western expedition of the Mongol leader Batu which led to the destruction of Kievan Russia in 1240.

To conquer the north, the Chin Tartars had also to make themselves masters of siege warfare. The fortifications of Chinese cities at this time were mainly rammed earth and wood, with stone strengthening. There was nothing comparable to the superb masonry defences of Byzantine Constantinople. Even so, their capture demanded much ingenuity and effort. To take T'ai-yuan, a relatively modest provincial capital, the Chin had to maintain a constant fire from over thirty stone-throwing engines, excavate protective earthworks and trenches, and build more than fifty carts covered with rawhide and iron sheeting, by means of which their men could come in close enough to fill in the moat. The capture of K'ai-feng, the capital, defended by 48,000 troops, was an even more arduous undertaking. The first attack in 1126 was repulsed by the heavy Chinese crossbows and stone-throwers, together with firebrands and piston flame-throwers which emitted a continuous jet of burning naphtha. The Chin returned to the assault towards the end of the year with every variety of siege engine, including iron-tipped rams, and towers higher than the city walls from which incendiary bombs could be fired down at the defenders. Even so, K'ai-feng only capitulated when intense starvation had led to cannibalism among the inhabitants.

The transfer of the techniques of iron working and siege warfare from China to the Khitan and the Chin Tartars took place through the migration of Chinese experts in these fields, or else their capture. Thus the father and uncle of A-pao-chi, founder of the Khitan empire in what is now Manchuria, set up their first iron smelteries early in the tenth century, using the skills of Chinese border settlers who were looking for a protector in the chaos following the collapse of the T'ang rule. Later on, iron workers and other highly-valued artisans were imported as a deliberate act of government policy. In like fashion, by employing Chinese auxiliaries as engineers, catapultiers and crossbowmen, the Khitan armies evolved from simple cavalry forces to the composite forces needed to reduce fortified Chinese cities. The Chin inherited Khitan expertise, and continued to seek out and use Chinese specialists in the military arts with such good effect that, for a short period, they even achieved an overall technological lead in this area.

Thus the Sung Chinese had long made use of a relatively mild variety of gunpowder in the form of what might be called 'military fireworks'. Sometimes the 'fire drug', as it was known, would be packed in paper or bamboo and go off with a great deal of noise and smoke, but little real damage. A 'poison drug smoke ball' emitting a gas that caused bleeding from the mouth and nose, and a 'lime projectile' giving off a smoky mist, were also used. But it was artisans, presumably Chinese, working under the Chin who were responsible for improving the fire drug into a true explosive. The first use of the shattering, rather than just the incendiary properties of gunpowder in war occurred in 1221, when the Chin took Ch'i-chou in Hupei with 'iron fire bombs'. According to Chao Yü-ch'ien they were 'shaped like gourds, with small mouths, and cast in iron two inches thick. They shattered the city walls.'[5] An improved model known as the 'Heaven-shaking thunder' played a decisive role in the successful defence of K'ai-feng by the Chin against the Mongols in 1232. The Mongols also used projectiles containing gunpowder in this siege, but only as fire-bombs.

In the field of battle the Mongols used essentially the same technique as the Chin, but with one improvement that may have been significant. While they too protected their lightly armoured bowmen behind a wall of heavily armoured horsemen carrying lances, this front line of cavalry was not a solid shield but divided into sections, so that there were gaps through which the archers could advance or retreat. The crucial initial victories of 1211 and 1212, by which Chinghis Khan permanently impaired Chin military strength, seem to have turned largely on the superior manoeuvrability which this brought. For the final defeat of the Chin, however, Chinghis's successors had to undergo a long apprenticeship in the arts of siege warfare; and for the conquest of the Southern Sung they had to make themselves the masters of naval warfare as well.

The stone-throwers used in twelfth- and thirteenth-century sieges, both by the Chinese and their northern enemies, were merely improved versions of the device shaped like a well-sweep first introduced around the time of Ts'ao Ts'ao. A wooden beam with arms of unequal length was pivoted on a stand, not unlike a large asymmetrical seesaw, with the projectile in a receptacle at the end of the long arm, and a number of ropes attached to the short arm. To fire it, a large number of men all pulled the ropes together, and the rock was hurled in a high curving trajectory like the bomb from a modern mortar. No use was made of a counterweight on the short arm. It was in fact the Mongols, around 1272 or 1273, who introduced this latter important refinement which reduced manpower requirements and allowed more accurate ranging. The new device, copied almost instantly by the Southern Sung, was known as the 'Moslem stone-thrower' and, like the European trebuchet which it resembled, presumably had an Islamic origin.

The early explosive projectiles described above were hurled by these stone-throwers just as if they had been rocks. The gun proper developed out of another Chin invention, the 'flying fire lance'. This was a rolled paper tube filled with a mixture of charcoal, iron filings, scraps of porcelain, arsenic and gunpowder, and fixed to a long handle. It burned anyone who came within ten paces of it. In 1259 the Southern Sung, now face to face with the Mongols, invented the 'fire-spurting lance'. This used a large bamboo for a barrel, and shot out pellets with a sharp report. Finally, in the fourteenth century, the Mongols substituted a barrel made of metal. Surviving specimens of firearms from the first half of this century show them to have been typically about forty centimetres long, with barrel apertures of two to three centimetres, sometimes more.

Another example of how the Mongols took over Chinese military technology, to the ultimate destruction of Chinese power, is provided by naval warfare. Waterways were among the most effective barriers to cavalry; and the Northern Sung had not only built fortresses and planted millions of trees along the Khitan frontier but had dug canals, ditches and artificial lakes to this end. The Southern Sung relied on the expanses of the Yangtze River to protect them from the Chin and the Mongols. Their mastery of this river, and of the coastal seas, was the by-product of the advances in shipbuilding and water transportation described in chapter 10. So long as it endured, they were virtually impregnable. The paddle-wheel boat, powered by men working windlasses or treadmills and first invented in T'ang times or possibly earlier, was improved and used with great effect, being both fast, independent of the direction of the wind and easy to manoeuvre. The Mongols, in contrast, were still using inflated skins and rafts to cross rivers as late as the middle of the thirteenth century. Only in 1270, on the advice of Liu Cheng, a former Sung commander, did they take the decisive step by building an adequate river fleet of their own. Five years later Hang-chou fell. Then in 1279 the first Mongol seagoing fleet destroyed the Southern Sung naval forces at the battle of Yai-shan; and in the course of the next fifteen years the Mongols made use of the vessels and sailors which they had captured to launch expeditions against Japan, Champa and Java. Once again, it was by acquiring the techniques of civilization that the barbarian had become truly formidable.

8 · The supremacy of logistics under the Ming

In the course of the fourteenth century the Mongol empire in China disintegrated. It was replaced by a number of independent Chinese states. The strongest of these, that centred upon Nanking and ruled by a former monk called Chu Yuan-chang, gradually absorbed the others; and in 1368 it became the nucleus of a new dynasty, the Ming. After the expulsion of the remnants of the Mongol forces from the north and the north-east, there followed two-and-a-half centuries of relatively stable rule. No serious external threats appeared. In the middle of the fifteenth century, it is true, the Oirats or western Mongols succeeded in largely reconstituting the unity of the Mongolian tribes and, gaining Ming armour, swords, bows and guns through the activities of their tributary missions and clandestine trading agents, briefly challenged the superiority which firearms had given the Chinese over the peoples beyond the Great Wall. In 1449 the Oirat leader Yesen even captured the emperor Ying-tsung. But Oirat policy was never aimed at the conquest of China but rather at the extraction from China by trade, and in the case of the captured Ying-tsung by ransom, of the metal goods, textiles, food and luxury articles which they desired. It was the Ming policy of limiting trade, undertaken in part to stop the outflow of firearms and other weapons, and Ming rejection of Yesen's proposals for a marriage alliance which led to the Oirat raid upon the empire.[1] Equally the 'Japanese pirates', who occasionally ravaged the coasts in the fourteenth, fifteenth and sixteenth centuries, were no threat to Ming rule. In the later period, at least, they were in fact mostly Chinese whose main interest was in the overseas trade which the Ming government had made illegal, until a change of policy occurred in 1567.[2]

Seen in contrast with the early and middle Chinese empires, the Ming empire (like the Ch'ing empire under the Manchus which succeeded it in 1645) was characterized by the relatively *low* amount of the total national product which it used for administration and defence. A recent study estimates that in 1400 the land tax took about ten per cent of the total national output of grain.[3] Since no allowance is made for the substantial amount paid over and above the regular tax at every point of transfer from the peasant to the government granaries, this is too low.* In 1426 an official inspector reported about the grain administrators of Su-chou, Sung-chiang and Hu-chou that 'They take about five times as much from the common people [as they are entitled to].' In 1447 it was estimated for the county of Ch'ang-shu in Su-chou prefecture that for a taxpayer to pay in one nominal picul of tax grain he had to hand in 2·2 to 2·3 piculs.[4] These are somewhat exceptional examples; but they suggest that a more accurate figure might be fifteen to twenty per cent. Nonetheless there is no longer any evidence of the kind quoted for the early period of the Chinese Empire that the financial burdens of government and warfare were still causing serious social problems. The pattern of Chinese history had thus undergone a major change – and one which has not hitherto been remarked upon. According to Wang Yeh-chien's calculations, moreover, the proportion of total grain output represented by the land tax in the middle of the eighteenth century was even lower, perhaps only five or six per cent.[5] His figures may be subject to the same qualification as the Ming estimate given above, but they do suggest that the trend continued across several centuries.

What were the reasons for this change? As the following chapters will show, the higher economic productivity achieved in Sung times had reduced the financial strain of imperial government. To this we may add the perfection of new techniques of political control, such as the civil service examination system which first came into generalized regular use in Sung times, serving to reduce the costs of control per head of population. By making both high office and local privileges accessible almost exclusively to those with official academic degrees, a way was found to absorb the energies and the ambitions of the able and condition them ideologically through the curriculum at their own expense and wish. Further, the high level of military technology fostered by the wars between the Sung, the Chin Tartars and the Mongols was bequeathed

* An even less justifiable burden on the farmers was the stipends paid to the members of the proliferating Ming imperial family. By the middle of the sixteenth century these amounted to over 8·5 million piculs, or about *twice* the amount brought to Peking each year by the tribute grain system. See Shimizu Taiji, *Mindai tochi seido shi kenkyū* (The Ming Land Tenure System) (Tokyo: 1968), p. 73.

to the Ming empire, leaving it, on the disintegration of Mongol power, without serious rivals in eastern Asia. Only in a few respects did the Ming improve upon what they had inherited. The building of heavy masonry fortifications is one; the present Great Wall dates from Ming times. Some companies of bombardiers (*ch'ung-shou*) also seem to have been formed, if a reference in the *Ming Veritable Records* for the eighth month of 1429 is trustworthy. Lastly, the extensive internal migrations and the improvement of communications which had taken place in T'ang and Sung times, together with long centuries of unity or near unity, had made for an internal homogenization of culture, a sense of unity and a degree of interdependence unique at this time in the world over so large a population. These phenomena will be described in some detail in chapters 10 and 14.

The use of firearms was characteristic of Ming warfare, but they were essentially auxiliary weapons. They caused no major change in tactics or strategy. The descriptions of the battles of this period in Ku Ying-t'ai's history of the Ming, published in 1658, would seem to indicate that they had two main functions. First of all they served to weaken an opposing force at long range before the fighting came to close quarters. An example of this is the battle on the P'o-yang Lake in 1363 between Ch'en Yu-liang (the ruler of the short-lived state of Han) and Chu Yuan-chang, the founder of the Ming dynasty. Chu told his generals that 'as they approached the rebel ships they were first to discharge their firearms, next their bows and crossbows, and then, when they reached the ships, to attack with their swords'. When the Ming commander Fu Yu-te was laying siege to Ch'eng-tu in the course of the Szechwan campaign of 1371, the defenders sent out 'elephants carrying men in armour'. Fu 'told his front line to smash them with firearms, and the elephants were routed'. The same technique was used by the Yung-lo emperor against the Oirat cavalry in his northern campaigns in the early fifteenth century. Thus in 1414 he had general Liao Sheng stem their onslaught with 'supernatural mechanism cannon', which 'killed several hundred of their mounted men'. Later in this same expedition the emperor told his officers that when the enemy attacked 'the "supernatural mechanism guns" should first be used to attack them, being followed by the longbows and crossbows'.

The second main use of firearms was to attack and defend fortified places. In 1371 the Ming naval forces broke through the iron chains and the bridge of boats that barred the gorge of Ch'ü-t'ang, the gateway to

Szechwan, by 'sheathing the prows of their ships with iron, and installing firearms on them'. In 1363, after Ch'en Yu-liang's soldiers had opened a breach of over two hundred feet in the walls of Fu-chou (in Kiangsi), the Ming general Teng Yü used guns to hold the attackers at bay while he rebuilt the fortifications.

The most detailed account of the uses of firearms and explosives in the later Ming period is Wang Ming-hao's *Answers to Questions on Pyrotechnical Warfare*, which has survived in the *Imperial Ming Handbook of Practical Statesmanship* compiled by Feng Ying-cheng in 1603. He begins by stressing the danger to China caused by the spread of gun-making and gunpowder technique to the barbarians. Even the Burmese chieftains in Yunnan had mastered it. The policies formulated by the founder of the dynasty were going unobserved. He had intended that 'no one should dare lightly to use these matchless weapons, and that the population at large should not be allowed to know how they worked, or spread the knowledge about privately among themselves'. The embargo on trade in saltpeter and sulphur had been flouted; and shortsighted generals had even allowed assimilated Miao tribesmen to learn about firearms in order to remedy a temporary shortage of Han Chinese troops.

He then describes the various weapons and the efforts made to improve them. The heaviest cannons, which 'when they smash the enemy can make a road of blood, and when they strike a city wall can reduce it instantly to rubble', were now forged out of wrought iron instead of being cast (as previously). The anti-cavalry bombards, with their sighting-devices so accurate that one 'might pick off a general or remove a prince', were now made of hard wood rather than of copper or iron; this made them light enough for one man to haul. The 'bird's-beak musket' was not suitable for use against the swiftly-advancing horsemen of the steppes, partly because of the cold climate and the difficulty of working the matchlock firing mechanism in the fierce winds, and partly because the rate of fire was too low. Recent attempts to overcome these problems had resulted in a 'bamboo bird musket' and a 'musket with an automatically closing firing mechanism'. Wang dismissed these, however, as 'novelties of the moment' and of little real use compared to the triple-barrelled gun normally used against horsemen at point-blank range. The more accurate musket was useful in the warmer south, where the enemy usually fought on foot and often behind natural cover. Its chief defect was a tendency to overheat, and a cloth dipped in cold water had to be used to cool it after every three shots. The charge of the foe was broken by the use of halberds and barricades set in front of the musketeers. A steady rate of fire could be maintained by soldiers shooting in relays, and also by using the so-called 'quick guns' which could fire five or ten shots before reloading. These 'quick guns' had long barrels along which a series of touch-holes had been bored, and were loaded with charges of rammed shot and powder separated from each other by about an inch of earth. The charges were each level with a touch-hole, and were fired in succession.

Wang also describes many incendiary and explosive devices, stressing the care needed if the soldier was not to hurt himself more than the enemy. Most of these were essentially of ancient vintage, though often with new names; but some, such as the underwater mines and land-mines with tripwire triggers, suggest a considerable refinement of manu-facture. One item, explicitly singled out as a novelty, was the 'bamboo general'. This is said to have been easy to make, cheap, portable, readily usable, and to have required only easily accessible materials. What it was is not clear from the text; but we know that it could be made of bamboo or wood, could be used only once, and needed a slightly different sort of powder from other weapons. Perhaps it was a sort of rough and ready mortar?

The foregoing account gives an impression of technological vitality in the military field, but this is to a considerable extent illusory. None of these innovations was based on a fundamental breakthrough in technique; and Wang's praise for the move away from the casting of metal ordnance towards the use of wrought iron and wood, which was presumably well-based coming as it did from a military commander, suggests an under-lying weakness in metallurgy. Indigenous Chinese cannon did not improve after early Ming times, and when in the seventeenth century the Jesuit fathers did cast guns of a superior quality both for the Ming and the Manchu emperors these were much appreciated. As regards handguns, the picture is different. They were either introduced or, more probably, introduced in a more advanced form by the Portuguese and their widespread use in warfare was the major innovation of the later sixteenth century. It was probably the Japanese who first showed the Chinese their real military potential. When Toyotomi Hideyoshi in-vaded Korea in the 1590s the Japanese 'fowling-pieces' (*niao-ch'ung*) are said to have 'poured down shot like rain'. Chinese writers of the early seventeenth century (such as Ch'en Jen-hsi) commented on Japanese skill with these weapons; and we know that by 1643 the troops of the rebel Li Tzu-ch'eng had bullet-proof vests 'of several tens of layers of stitched soft silk, sometimes even of a hundred layers'. These were 'light and pliable, but such that no arrow's barb *or lead shot* could pierce them'. This passage suggests that muskets were being widely used by this time. Yet their manufacture seems to have remained primitive, though Du Halde's comment on this, made early in the eighteenth century, is intriguing:

> It is true that their invention is not so good as that of our mechanicks, but the tools they make use of are more simple, and they can imitate exactly enough any pattern that is brought them out of Europe; so that at present they are able to make watches, clocks, glass, *muskets*, and several other things, of which they had no notion, or made but very imperfectly.[6]

Nor was there any of that experimenting in new methods of using handguns on the battlefield that characterized, for example, the Thirty Years War in Europe.

The somewhat arrested development of firearms in Ming China needs explaining. Some light is perhaps thrown on it by a comparison with Japan between about 1550 and 1650, that is during and just after the last phase in her period of civil wars. Within a few years of the matchlock being introduced by Portuguese in 1543, the new weapon was in full production by swordsmiths turned gunsmiths and widely used in civil wars. Between about 1560 and 1575, Oda Nobunaga demonstrated that matchlock men firing in co-ordinated sequence from behind a screen of pointed stakes could decimate a cavalry charge, and therewith altered the nature of Japanese warfare. What had been, apart perhaps from pikemen, a matter of conflict between individuals now became a contest between organized bodies of men. Victory in battle henceforth meant greater concentrations of political and economic power; the small emergency mountain strongholds of the past were abandoned, and fortress and peacetime dwellings merged into a new kind of city, the so-called 'castle-town', large, low-lying, and serving both as symbol and as means of the increased control which feudal lords exerted over their followers. The pacification of Japan by Nobunaga's two great successors, Toyotomi Hideyoshi and Tokugawa Ieyasu, was chiefly on the basis of their superior mastery of firearms. Cannon, introduced some time after 1573, were Ieyasu's speciality; and he used them to great effect to shatter rebel strongholds. Once he had achieved political hegemony early in the seventeenth century, however, the rapid pace of advance in military technology came to a full stop. The shogunate, as the governmental system which he set up in 1603 is generally known, ran its own high-security arms factory for matchlocks and cannon at Kunitomo; banned the spread of technical information about gunpowder and gunmaking; and forbade feudal lords to own firearms. At the same time a mystique was deliberately and successfully inculcated in the warrior class, so that they came to think of the gun as a demeaning weapon, fit only for the lowest class of samurai. Apart from one or two remarkable gunsmiths, such as Kunitomo Tōbē (1778–1840), who also made airguns and telescopes, initiative disappeared entirely for the next two-and-a-half centuries.[7] The conclusion is banal but important. Competition between equals, whether the Southern Sung and the Mongols, or the contestants in the Japanese civil wars, or the states of early modern Europe, is an indispensable condition of progress in military technology.

The Ming empire was not without challenges, even if they hardly came from equals; but it met these challenges chiefly by improvements in logistics. Against barbarian enemies, the vastly superior resources of the Chinese Empire in manpower and material (created by the economic revolution described in the second part of this book) were mobilized with a greater expertise than ever before. When the Yung-lo emperor campaigned in Mongolia in 1409, his army was supplied with 200,000 piculs of grain carried in 30,000 covered carts. His lines of communication were secured by a series of specially built forts ten days' march from each other. Logistic skill, rather than firearms, was the hallmark of Ming supremacy.* Against rebels, the reserves of loyal areas were swiftly mobilized. In 1592, to give but one example, not much more than a month was needed to move four hundred pieces of field artillery across three hundred miles of difficult country between Kan-chou and Ling-chou (Ling-wu in Ningsia) to help put down the rebellion of Po-pai. Good logistics removed any urgent need to discover better weapons. It became a substitute for invention.

This logistical capacity was reflected in the size of the early Ming army: over three million men, who consumed about 37·2 million piculs of grain a year. Approximately three-quarters of a million were stationed at the capital and almost wholly dependent on imported food.[8] The rest

* The capture of the emperor Ying-tsung by Yesen in 1449 was due simply to the incompetence of the former in allowing himself to be manoeuvred into a position in which he did not have an adequate supply of water.

lived mainly on the food produced by the lands assigned to their military units. At first sight, therefore, it would appear that the defence establishment of the early Ming was more than double that of the Northern Sung, with a population that was much less than double. In fact the appearance is illusory. The armies mobilized by T'ai-tsu for the conquest of the empire were indeed enormous, far greater than were needed after victory for defence and internal security. The costs and dangers of demobilizing most of this vast body of men were awesome. Instead T'ai-tsu turned them into a hereditary military caste and settled them in so-called 'military colonies'. They were then separated into two groups: genuine soldiers with military duties, and soldier-farmers whose duty it was to till the colony lands and support the others with half their annual grain output. Seeds, animals and tools were either given or loaned without interest by the government, and the state also promoted agricultural improvements, as with its campaign to have suitable fruit-trees planted on colony lands.

Earlier dynasties, including the Mongols, had had broadly comparable institutions but none approaching the Ming system in sheer size or paralleling its extensive coverage of the interior of the country. In early times the nominal total of the colony lands was close to 900,000 *mou*, but the actual total was much greater because in addition to the standard per-person allotments on which they had to pay the fifty per cent tax the colonists often opened up two, three or even ten times the minimum area. The ratio of soldiers to military farmers also varied greatly from place to place. The principles governing this variation were succinctly stated in the *Veritable Records* for 1404: fighting men were to be relatively more numerous on the frontiers and in places of strategic importance, less so inland. But 'if a locality is strategically vital but transport to it is difficult, then the colonists shall likewise outnumber the soldiers'. In fact it seems to have been usual for about thirty per cent of those registered as 'soldiers' to be assigned to military work along the frontiers, and about twenty per cent inland; but in some places, such as major cities, the number of warriors rose to as high as fifty per cent. After the fifteenth century troops were also recruited outside the formal military system, and determining the true size of Ming military forces is thus impossible without detailed study.

The colony system was a remarkable solution to the problem of furnishing military supplies. It meant significantly lighter taxes on the civilian population, and to some extent severed the link between the financial strains of defence and the social pressures created by the resulting fiscal exactions. It also provided food on the spot against emergencies, besides being an effective way of reclaiming large tracts of devastated land, especially in the north. The farmers were under the direct control of the military authorities, to whom they paid in their entire harvest, receiving back their share in monthly instalments. Each colony centred round a fortified stronghold, provided with granaries and storehouses, where livestock could be protected in times of danger. The crucial nature of the supply question for the Ming military system may be illustrated by the case of the guard at Sung-chou. This is today the town of Sung-p'an just south of the Kansu-Szechwan border and astride the cultural frontier between Han China and Tibet. In 1385 Hsu Mu, an official in the Messenger Office of the Ministry of Rites, reported: 'The land in Sung-chou is barren and not fit for colony farming. There are three thousand soldiers without adequate food. Although we have augmented their supply with salt and grain, the gallery road is long and dangerous, and the transport extremely burdensome. I would request that the soldiers be moved to Mao-chou [about eighty miles south along the Min river], so that they may open up colony lands in its neighbourhood and there be no toil of transporting provisions. They will thereby be able to control the Ch'iang [Tibetans].' The emperor answered that for strategic reasons the Sung-chou guard could not be moved and that the civilians from the nearby counties would have to do the transport. By 1392, however, this had caused so many of them to run away that he had to order seventy per cent of the Sung-chou soldiers to engage in colony farming and two-thirds of the guard assigned to the local imperial prince to do likewise. The provincial authorities were told to find some other means of storing and moving supplies, absconding peasants being informed that if they returned to the fields they would be troubled no longer.[9]

Grain needed for frontier troops that could not be grown locally was either transported by soldiers, or by paid transport, or else provided by merchants. The government initially paid the latter in certificates entitling them to sell a certain quantity of government monopoly salt, the quantity of grain needed for a unit salt certificate being varied according to how inaccessible the military post was to which the supplies were delivered. Since it was often cheaper to grow grain on the spot than to transport it, many wealthy merchants, attracted by the profits of the salt trade, financed tenants to open up lands in the frontier areas. These became known as 'merchant colonies'. In 1492, however, the system of payment for frontier grain was changed entirely to silver, and the cultivation of frontier lands by merchants rapidly disappeared.[10] The partial return to a grain-salt barter system in the later sixteenth century does not seem to have revived them.

During the fifteenth century the military colonies decayed. There were a number of reasons for this. Frontier colonies were exposed to barbarian attack. It was even argued that farming and pasturing animals 'beyond the frontiers' tended to provoke these attacks. In any event, it seems that Yesen's onslaught in the mid fifteenth century led to a reduction in frontier colony lands. Other causes of decline were that the state no longer supplied the colony farmers with seeds and animals, and burdened them with compulsory services, of which transport was the most detested. Many ran away. More serious still was the tendency of the military officers, effectively a hereditary élite, to engross colony and other lands and to set up manors using soldiers as their private labourforce. In 1431 the Marquis of Ning-yang was denounced for using soldiers to work his estate of 50,000 acres. Shang Lu, an eminent fifteenth-century official, wrote a memorial on frontier affairs in which he stated:

> I have also investigated the situation beyond the passes. The arable land there is extremely extensive; but apart from the fixed quota of acreage held by the colony soldiers, most of the soldiers who guard the walls and passes have no land to till. The reason is that the families of meritorious metropolitan officials have taken the fields near the fortified camps beyond the passes to be their manor fields. The remaining vacant land has been occupied by the military officers of those places as their property. Every year they compel the soldiers to farm them, and grow fat on the profits. The soldiers who guard the walls and do other tasks are not only impoverished – they cannot even serve as soldiers beyond the passes. Yet the manor lands are still there . . .[11]

After Yesen, it became official policy to encourage manors on the marches so as to ensure an adequate grain supply; and many former military colonists became tenants.

Official efforts to save the system by reducing the colonists' tax obligations, and by doing away with the rule that they had to pay in their entire harvest to the military authorities, who would then return it in instalments, only hastened its dissolution. The soldier-farmers lost the sense of being soldiers, and discipline evaporated. There was no longer any way for officers to limit wasteful expenditure by troops, or to damp out the seasonal fluctuations in grain prices. The harvests became the colonists' as of right; and their fields turned into private property which could be mortgaged or sold. Before long they had become all but indistinguishable from civilians.

During the fifteenth century the northern frontier was withdrawn in several strategic places. The most serious loss was that of the so-called 'outer frontier' which ran in an arc north of Peking, with Ta-ning, deep into Mongol territory, as its coping-stone. This fallback was not the result of military weakness. It was the payment of a political debt by the Yung-lo emperor to the Urianghai Mongols who had supported his usurpation in 1402. The other major withdrawal was from Tung-sheng, which guarded the northern half of the loop of the Yellow River. This was, if anything, the reflection of military strength, or at least over-confidence. At this time the Yung-lo emperor was leading repeated expeditions far into Mongol territory, and to hold permanently onto advanced strongpoints probably seemed of little importance and a burden on the supply system. However, the subsequent weakening of the Ming military organization showed that giving up Ta-ning and Tung-sheng was a major strategic blunder. Apart from a brief reoccupation of Tung-sheng in 1438, they could not be retaken; and this led to the second, and defensive, phase of Ming frontier operations, which centred on the Great Wall.

The rebuilding and improvement of the Wall, most of which had long since fallen in ruins, occurred in two stages. The first followed the on-slaught of Yesen in the middle of the fifteenth century; the second followed the attacks of Anda in the middle of the sixteenth. By about 1600 the Wall had taken on the form in which it can now be seen: a much more sophisticated and formidable defensive fortification than its Han and T'ang predecessors. For one thing it was higher, and strengthened with an integrated network of literally thousands of watchtowers, beacons and fortified camps – with cannon too, of course. These were fired from embrasures in the tops of towers thirty to forty feet high, and set from forty to two hundred paces apart, depending on the degree of probable exposure to attack. In the most vulnerable area, across the north of Shansi, there was a double line of wall. For the first time, proper accommodation for men, weapons and munitions was built directly into the Wall; and this greatly improved mobilization in emergencies and operations in bad weather. Towards the end of the sixteenth century,

Logistics of the Ming Grand Canal

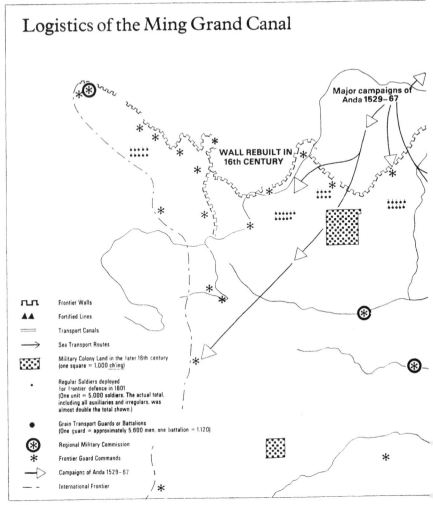

Major campaigns of Anda 1529–67

WALL REBUILT IN 16th CENTURY

⊓⊔	Frontier Walls
▲▲	Fortified Lines
══	Transport Canals
→	Sea Transport Routes
▨	Military Colony Land in the later 16th century (one square = 1,000 ch'ing)
.	Regular Soldiers deployed for frontier defence in 1601 (One unit = 5,000 soldiers. The actual total, including all auxiliaries and irregulars, was almost double the total shown.)
●	Grain Transport Guards or Battalions (One guard = approximately 5,600 men, one battalion = 1,120)
✸	Regional Military Commission
*	Frontier Guard Commands
▷	Campaigns of Anda 1529–67
— -	International Frontier

Map 4

soldiers' families were also quartered in the towers, as this was found to be the most effective way of stopping desertions.[12] Thus for almost two centuries technical skill helped to offset the ill effects of institutional decay.

★

The Ming was also the first Chinese dynasty able to fight a prolonged war on the basis of supply lines stretching across five hundred miles of

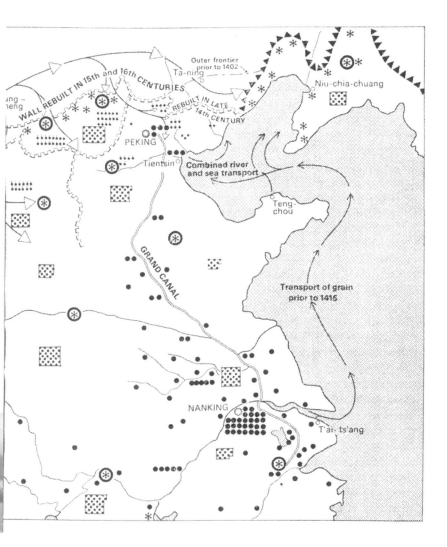

Outer frontier prior to 1402

WALL REBUILT IN 15th and 16th CENTURIES

Ta-ning

Niu-chia-chuang

REBUILT IN LATE 14th CENTURY

ang-neng

PEKING

Tientsin

Combined river and sea transport

Teng-chou

GRAND CANAL

Transport of grain prior to 1415

NANKING

T'ai-ts'ang

open sea. In the years following 1370, the food and cloth required by the armies engaged in reconquering southern Manchuria from the northern Mongols were brought by naval forces from the mouth of the Yangtze to the Liao-tung peninsula. After the surrender of the Mongol leader Na-ha-ch'u in 1387 sea transport continued as a peacetime measure; and by 1396 more than 80,000 officers and men were engaged almost full time in this work. The sea was too dangerous, however, for the system to be attractive as a permanent arrangement. Military colonies were therefore developed to supply the northern garrisons locally. By the early fifteenth century military colony land was producing over 700,000 piculs of grain a year. The long sea route from the Yangtze was closed down, and the rest of Liao-tung's requirements brought either overland or from Teng-chou in Shantung. In 1597 sea transport came briefly into prominence again as the means of supply for the Chinese forces resisting Toyotomi Hideyoshi's second invasion of Korea from Japan. It also played some part in provisioning the Ming armies fighting the new state created in Manchuria by Nurhaci and his successors in the late sixteenth and early seventeenth centuries.[13]

The greatest triumph of Ming logistics, however, was the new Grand Canal. Its terminal point was Peking, the former capital of the Mongol emperor Kubilai and substantially further north than the capital cities of any previous Chinese dynasty, being practically on the edge of the steppe. Together with the garrison cities of Mi-yun, Chi-chou and Yung-p'ing, which ringed it to the north and were themselves supplied by a specially developed system of water transport, it served as a massive defensive shield for the rest of the country. The sea transport utilized in the early fifteenth century could only guarantee about one million piculs a year, though the Mongols had sometimes managed to transport three times this amount, whereas to maintain a major centre of this nature about four times this amount was needed. The security of Ming Peking therefore depended on an advance in the art of canal-building, to hold adequate water in the steps of a watercourse crossing over the western spur of the Shantung hills. The Mongols had tried to do this, but their engineers had not been fully successful. The breakthrough only came in 1411 when Sung Li, the president of the ministry of works, and his colleagues carefully split the flow of the combined Wen and Ssu rivers at Chi-ning by means of a 'Heaven Well Lock' and set up a chain of fifteen locks between Chi-ning and Lin-ch'ing, at each of which officials 'controlled the water by opening and shutting the gates as seasonally appropriate'.[14] The new waterway was thirteen Chinese feet deep and thirty-two wide. A memorial written by Ch'iu Chün later in the fifteenth century summed up the progress this represented:

> The Han and the T'ang dynasties located their capital within the passes [that is, in Shensi]. The Sung had theirs at K'ai-feng. The waterways used by them for the transportation of tax grain all followed the natural lie of the land. Although some artifice was used, they were

not like the Hui-t'ung Canal [the section over the hills], *which has no parallel in former dynasties*. The men of Yuan undertook it, but without great success. They made use of it, but did not derive the full benefit from it. Under the present dynasty, it has been extensively repaired and widened. The former Yuan dynasty merely transported some hundreds of thousands of piculs along it. Today the highest totals have exceeded four million piculs, that is to say ten times as much.[15]

The 15,000 boats and 160,000 soldiers of the transport army thus became the dynasty's lifeline.

The potentially precarious situation of the northern capital was not lost on contemporary observers. Thus Ch'iu Chün submitted the following memorial in 1487:

The nation's capital is now at Peking, that is to say at the extreme north, while the inflow of taxes comes entirely from the south-east. The Hui-t'ung Canal may be likened to a man's throat. If food cannot be swallowed for a single day, death ensues at once. Out-of-date scholar that I am, this causes me anxiety. I would request that a sea route be opened, following the old Yuan dynasty route, and that it be operated in parallel with the transport of inland waterway in the autumn season when agricultural work is slack. The grain of Kiangsi, Hukwang and Kiangtung should be transported by inland waterway as before, but that of Che-hsi and the eastern coastal region should go by the sea route, so that there are men who are familiar with navigation. If it ever happens that there is some slight obstruction in the grain transport canal, the latter grain would come through even though the former did not. This is a plan to forestall future disaster.[16]

In fact Ch'iu was too pessimistic. Apart from 1571 and 1572, when there were floods in the Yellow River valley and the sea transport had to be partially resumed, the Grand Canal was not cut until the end of the dynasty. More serious was the decline in the Ming military and supply systems by the later part of the fifteenth century. The soldiers, who were meant to serve on a hereditary basis, were deserting in great numbers, a development which should probably be linked to the decline of serfdom and serflike tenancy, which began around this time. By 1500, in some areas such as Hsuan-fu on the northern frontier, they were down to about a third of their strength at the beginning of the dynasty; the deficit was only partly made good by new volunteers. The quantity of grain transported to the capital, at a maximum of 6·2 million piculs in 1432, was down to 3·4 millions by 1464 because of defaulting, malpractice and theft. In the course of the following century, the enforcement of discipline in the transport system grew increasingly more savage and less effective.

★

The dynasty did not collapse, however, but survived for another century and a half. It fell in 1644, in a sense by accident. There was a shortage of military manpower, partly as a result of the epidemics described in chapter 17; and internal rebellion and the external menace of the Manchus, either of which could have been dealt with on their own, happened to coincide. There were also deeper causes at work, connected with the social revolution to be described in chapter 15.

The Manchus did not conquer China. It was conquered for them by Chinese generals, such as Wu San-kuei and Hung Ch'eng-chou, who had defected to their side. Up to this time, the Manchus had followed the typical pattern of barbarian dynasties of conquest. They had grown in strength by learning settled agriculture and ironworking from the Chinese (and, in this case, also from the Koreans). They had reorganized their administration in imitation of the Chinese bureaucratic pattern. But even in the 1640s their method of fighting was really no match for the Chinese. They divided their armies into three sections. The vanguard was formed of heavily armoured men on foot, the front line equipped with long spears and the second line with long swords. The rearguard consisted of archers, wearing a light armour made of cloth, and firing over the defensive screen of their comrades. The third section was a body of élite troops, the only ones who fought mounted as opposed to travelling mounted, kept in reserve to strike the decisive blow where needed. This approach was a modification of those used long before by the Khitan and the Chin Tartars (to whom the Manchus were closely related). It was vulnerable to firearms, as the defeat of Nurhaci, the founder of the Manchu kingdom, outside the walls of Ning-yuan in 1626 quite clearly shows.

Not only did the Manchu 'conquest' largely depend upon Chinese, but not long after the establishment of the new dynasty the rebellion of Wu San-kuei almost succeeded in bringing it down. The revolt lasted from 1673 to 1683, and its suppression was mostly the work of loyalist Chinese generals, such as Chao Liang-tung. Even in the early eighteenth century the outstanding commander in the service of the Manchus was a Chinese, Yueh Chung-ch'i. Only in the reign of the Ch'ien-lung emperor (1736–95) did Manchu and Mongol generals begin to monopolize the chief military posts.

The logistic strength created under the Ming dynasty was the foundation on which the Chinese Empire in the seventeenth and eighteenth centuries expanded under the Manchu emperors. This expansion was roughly contemporaneous with the growth of two other empires: Russia and Great Britain. The frontiers of 1800 marked a rough equilibrium between these three systems; and with slight modifications, namely the loss of parts of Manchuria and Sungaria to Russia, and the separation of Outer Mongolia to form a separate state, they are those of China today. The Chinese Empire ceased to be approximately coterminous with China Proper, as the economic resources of the Chinese heartland and the mastery of firearms gave the government at Peking enduring dominion over the people of Mongolia, eastern Turkestan and Tibet.

This last point is above all true of artillery. The attitude of the Manchu government towards the musket was rightly ambivalent. The Ch'ien-lung emperor turned down a proposal to replace sword-play in the military examinations with shooting.[17] He feared damage to the traditional social order, but there were sound military reasons for not emphasizing the musket too much. In its eighteenth-century Chinese form it was by no means always a match for the expertly handled bow. This is illustrated in one of the copperplate engravings which the emperor had cut in Paris to commemorate his victories in the north-west over the Eleuths and Moslems. It shows the battle of Altshur (1759), in which the mounted archers of general Fu-te are routing the mounted musketeers of the Hodjas, who have had to come in close to make their primitive weapons effective.[18] The musket had greater penetrating power than the composite bow at pointblank range to set against its lower rate of fire and shorter range; but the quality of archery depended to a far greater extent on continuous training than did that of musketry. It is easy to see why a decree of 1789 expressed fear that the use of muskets by Manchus would lead to the neglect of archery. As in Europe, it seems that the bow was replaced by firearms while the former was still a superior weapon. An edict of 1822 takes it for granted that Manchus in Kirin are by this time using guns. They are told to hunt to keep up their prowess.[19]

Furthermore, the spread of handguns among the Chinese populace during the eighteenth century weakened the control of the central authority. This can be dated from official regulations on the carrying of firearms by the ships of the government grain transport. In 1724 a decree stated that 'It is forbidden for the grain transport ships to contract to carry the goods of others, to take smuggled salt on board, or to secrete firearms in illegal fashion.' This ban was repeated in more detail in the following year:

> Some of the grain transport ships carry cannon, muskets and gunpowder. They all proceed on their way in groups as members of a convoy. They should have no fear of bandits. What use can they have for cannon and muskets? Let the order be given that this is strictly prohibited.[20]

In 1726, persons who broke this rule were ordered to be punished like offenders against the ban on the private possession of muskets. In 1757, a slight but significant modification was introduced:

> It has been stated in a memorial to Us that: 'Bandits are very frightened of muskets; the ships of the grain transport are forbidden to carry weapons. The lieutenants in charge of both empty and loaded squadrons should perhaps be allowed to carry muskets in readiness for self-defence.' This request is to be granted. They should each be allowed to carry one musket.[21]

This concession was necessary because bandits now commonly had firearms. According to a decree of 1814 regarding the salt smugglers of Shantung:

> They may number as many as a hundred and several tens of men. *They carry muskets.* Whenever there is a periodic market they load up their illegal salt and openly display it for sale.[22]

A slightly later decree, from 1835, tells a similar story:

> Many of the Moslem folk who live along the seacoasts in Tientsin, Ts'ang-chou and Yen-shan in the province of Chihli [Hopei] make a business of selling illegal salt . . . They assemble criminal elements into bands for its sale; and these have recently been growing larger and more numerous, ranging from three or four hundred up to six or seven hundred men . . . They all use donkeys to carry their salt, calling them 'salt donkeys' and moving them about in hundreds. *They also carry muskets* to prevent the soldiers from capturing them.[23]

Chinese bandits now disposed of a large and varied arsenal. In 1836 Huang Chüeh-tzu reported a group in northern Kiangsu which had 'several portable guns which weigh over 260 pounds and need five men to fire them, but which can hit targets several hundred paces away'. Three years later he was dealing with Honanese bandits who manufactured their own firearms. In Fukien in 1840 he found the countryside dotted with so-called 'gun-towers', about ten feet high and used in local clan battles. The same year also saw an attempt to stop the unauthorized manufacture and ownership of firearms in Chang-chou and Ch'üan-chou. People here, said Huang, were 'highly skilled in the use of muskets, with the result that murders are frequent, for their guns kill eight or nine times out of ten'.[24]

Bandits would have had too great an advantage over the law-abiding population if ordinary people had not been allowed to have firearms. The previous ban on private ownership of muskets was first lifted in Fukien in 1749; and the general prohibition was removed in 1760. The spread of handguns, and the relative ease with which they could be mastered in comparison with archery, reduced the effectiveness of professional soldiers relative to civilians. In this way, to use an analogy with Marxist theory, the social relationships of destruction had begun to change in China as the late traditional period drew to its close.

It is easy to understand why the victory of the British and French in the Opium War (1839–42) was so swift. Since they were not aiming at the conquest of China but at the imposition of a certain form of peace, it was a matter of common sense for the Chinese government to come to terms. The alternative was the risk, virtually the certainty, that a pro-longed conflict would lead to strains that undermined a now precarious imperial control. The closest parallel is the Crimean War. The British and the French could not have conquered Russia, any more than they could have China, but their successes threatened to exacerbate to an unacceptable degree already existing weaknesses. In China, the key pressure point was the lower Yangtze. The Chinese government's supply of grain up the Grand Canal, foundation of the empire's logistic system since Ming times, was vulnerable to Western naval supremacy. So was the economy of the advanced south-east. The governor-general of the lower Yangtze provinces put it this way:

If the [British and French] rebels occupy for any extended period of time the area that constitutes our throat, our grainships will be unable to return to the granaries where they load. How then will it be possible for the rice to be delivered? . . . The Kiangsu region is continuously dependent upon Szechwan and Hunan for its supply of rice. If the route is blocked and merchants cannot proceed, the depth of the disaster will be unimaginable.[25]

As it turned out, capitulation proved a blessing in disguise. The importation and later the manufacture of foreign weapons by the Chinese government forces was the crucial factor which enabled them to put down the great rebellions of the mid nineteenth century, and to hold on to Chinese Turkestan.

*

The theory set out in chapter 1 that the varying balance between the burdens of scale and technological capacity has been the chief determinant of the varying sizes of pre-modern empires is thus well borne out by the Chinese historical record, although the simple manner in which it has been formulated obviously make it no more than a useful guide to analysis. In particular, one must also ask how and why technological capacity changed; and it is to this question that Part Two of the book is devoted.

Part Two · The medieval economic revolution

9 · The revolution in farming

Between the eighth and the twelfth centuries Chinese agriculture was transformed. Some improvements came in the north; thus it was early in this period that better milling machinery led to the widespread cultivation of wheat in place of millet.[1] The main arena of progress, however, was the south. Mastery of the techniques of wet-field rice cultivation allowed a great southward migration into this previously little developed area that became, as chapter 14 shows, the dynamic driving force behind an era of economic revolution.

Geographically, the trend of agricultural development in China was thus the reverse of that in medieval Europe, where the clearing and the cultivation of the northern forest lands was slowly swinging the economic centre of gravity away from the Mediterranean. The technological foundations of the two movements also differed. The symbols of European advance in the twelfth and thirteenth centuries were the axe, the improved plough and efficient horse harness. Those of the Chinese were the dam, the sluice-gate, the noria (peripheral pot-wheel) and the treadle water-pump. In both cases, an enormous input of hard work was required: in the one to cut the trees and prepare the heavy soils; in the other to level and wall the paddy-fields, and to dig and maintain the ditches needed for irrigation. The historical significance of the manor, both in China and in Europe, was that often it alone had the resources for such undertakings.

The existence of a unified empire seems to have helped the spread of advanced practices. The chief centre of agricultural invention was Liang-che province, comprising what are now southern Kiangsu and Chekiang. The superior techniques of this area spread throughout the rice-growing region as the result of the circulation around the empire of officials drawn from the landlord class and therefore often intensely interested in farming and active in promoting its improvement. After the loss of northern China to the Chin Tartars in 1127, the Southern Sung government sought to strengthen its economic position by a policy of official encouragement for more skilful husbandry.

Woodblock printing, invented in the ninth century, also contributed greatly to the spread of new methods. Practical agricultural treatises were published, written in simple language and often illustrated with woodcut pictures of tools and appliances. It was, of course, the educated and well-to-do class owning manors who primarily benefited from contact with officials and read the instructions which they promulgated as well as the fuller technical manuals. Presumably they then gave appropriate orders to their managers and bailiffs, and the new ideas were disseminated more rapidly than they would have been in a society of smallholders.

Officials familiar with the sophisticated farming of the lower Yangtze valley were sometimes shocked at the backwardness which they found elsewhere. The remarks which Chou Ch'ü-fei made in 1178 about Ch'in-chou in Kuang-nan-hsi may be taken as representative:

> The farmers of Ch'in-chou are careless. When they work the soil with an ox they merely break up the clods; and when the time comes for sowing they go to the fields and broadcast the grain. They do not transplant seedlings. There is no more wasteful use of seed than this. After they have planted it, they neither hoe it nor irrigate it, but place their reliance on the forces of nature.[2]

Similar comments were made by another bureaucrat about the province of Ching-hu-pei.

Moving around the provinces in the course of their official duties aroused a sense of critical comparison in the minds of many government servants. Thus Huang Chen observed in 1272 in a proclamation which he issued to encourage agriculture:

> In Liang-che they plough their fields after the autumn harvest has been gathered and work them over again in the second month of spring. This is called 'deep-tooth harrowing'. In Fu-chou [in Chiang-nan-hsi], however, the fields are allowed to grow wild after the rice harvest. Last year, I saw people ploughing such waste fields in the fifth month. They were all overgrown with weeds, and the productive power of the soil had been drained away.[3]

Kao Ssu-te in the thirteenth century wrote in a similar vein about Liang-che and Szechwan, more than eight hundred miles apart:

The men of Che look after their fields in a much more sophisticated way than do those of Szechwan. They bring out the richness of the soil so that there is a surplus of productive power in the land. They work it deeply with the plough until it is mature and the tilth as fine as flour. Therefore, when their seeds are planted, they are embedded firmly and close together.[4]

In less advanced areas, officials had pictures showing how to farm painted on government office walls; they had books printed and proclamations issued. The following passage comes from one such local announcement put up in 1180:

After the autumn harvest has been gathered and before the cold months set in, it is necessary for a household to turn over with the plough all the land that it possesses, so that in the cold season it will be friable. After the first month of the new year, it should be opened up again several times and ploughed repeatedly. Then sow the seeds. The mud in the fields will naturally be deep and mature. The soil will have a rich and substantial body. Thus the grain will grow in it easily, water will be retained, and it will not easily dry out.

When the sprouts are high there will also be weeds. At this point, it will be necessary to drain out the water in the field and, carefully distinguishing [between the weeds and the grain], to pull out the weeds one by one and trample them into the mud to nourish and bank up the grain. Any reeds and grasses which grow aslant along the dykes between the fields should be repeatedly cut and at harvest time removed entirely, so as to avoid wasting the powers of the soil.[5]

Some officials wrote verses and essays on agriculture, which may have helped spread useful practices. The best-known instance of this is Su Tung-p'o's lines on the 'rice-planting horse':

Formerly, when I was travelling in Wu-ch'ang [O-chou], I saw the farmers all sitting astride 'horses for the transplanting of rice shoots'. The bellies were made of elm or buckthorn so that they should be smooth. The backs were fashioned from catalpa or t'ung wood so that they should be light. The belly was shaped like a small boat, rising up at the front and the rear. The back was like an overturned tile – for the ease of the two buttocks. Hopping like sparrows in the mud, with straw mats tied to their heads to hold the rice sprouts, they covered a thousand plots a day. As compared to working with one's back doubled over, it made all the difference between toil and leisure.[6]

Books on farming found a ready welcome in such an atmosphere. Older works, above all the classic *Essential Techniques for the Common*

People written by Chia Ssu-hsieh in the sixth century, were now printed, and sometimes annotated or excerpted to make them clearer. New books were composed. Outstanding among them were Lou Shou's *Pictures and Poems on Husbandry and Weaving*, the first such text to be illustrated, and Ch'en Fu's *Treatise on Agriculture*. These authors had personal experience of what they described. Lou Shou's grandsons recalled that their grandfather had 'made enquiries from farmers and from their wives who practised the rearing of silkworms'. His pictures were 'so perfect in their delicate detail that it was as if one were in the countryside watching the peasants in person'. Ch'en Fu declared in the preface to his treatise:

> I have myself farmed in the Western Hills [near Lake T'ai], and am acquainted with the principles of farming. I have gathered these into a *Treatise on Agriculture* in three chapters, sub-divided by sections, with a systematic discussion item by item. My book contains more than mere abstract knowledge. Only if one has really trod the ground, and is capable of doing something oneself, should one dare to write explanations for the instruction of others.[7]

Both writers described the techniques used in the northern part of Liang-che.

The climax of the Sung tradition of agricultural writing came in two great works of the early Mongol period. The first of these was a compilation sponsored by the state, *The Essentials of Farming and Sericulture*, and was reprinted several times before the fall of the dynasty. The second was Wang Chen's *Treatise on Agriculture*. This was printed in 1313 at the request of the Kiangsi educational authorities. 'Although the bookstores have previously printed such works as the *Essential Techniques for the Common People* and the *Essentials of Agriculture*,' they declared, 'no book has gathered matters together so completely as the present one. If it is not printed and distributed it is to be feared that it may not survive.'[8] The *Treatise* as we now have it contains a text of over 136,000 characters and almost three hundred illustrations showing tools and machinery with such exactness that in most cases they are an adequate guide to construction, as was the author's intention. Wang Chen's friend Tai Piao-yuan described his style as one which 'avoided elegance and amassed facts'. It is a just assessment; and it is a sad, if eloquent, testimony to the decline of interest in farming technology in later centuries that this astonishing work was only saved for posterity by the reprinting in 1530 of the last surviving copy of the 1313 edition when it turned up .n the library of the provincial government of Shantung.

The growing market for grain* was one of the reasons for the consolidation of the manorial regime in Sung times; and historical parallels from Europe come to mind, notably perhaps the intensified exploitation of serfs in black-soil Russia during the first half of the nineteenth century. It is unlikely that the manor owners would have been as interested as they were in better techniques if it had not been possible for them to sell the surplus. The more efficient transport system which arose at this time (the subject of the next chapter) and the more integrated market network (chapter 12) were therefore in part the *causes* of the upswing in agricultural productivity as well as its consequences. In any event, the evidence shows that many manors produced either regularly or intermittently for the market. Suggestive is the advice given by Yuan Ts'ai in 1178:

> One's managers will include someone to have charge of the storehouse [for money and silk]. He must keep reliable accounts and watch carefully over the balances that remain. Another manager will have charge of the grain. He must keep strict accounts and look after the keys conscientiously. One should also select scrupulous men to serve as watchmen. Another manager will be in charge of making loans and undertaking sales. One ought to entrust these tasks to someone who is honest and shows compassion towards families who are in difficulties.[9]

An unambiguous illustration, also from the twelfth century, is given by Hung Mai:

> When Hsu Te-ho of Ming-k'ou in Lo-p'ing [in Chiang-nan-hsi] heard that wheat and rice were fetching high prices in the county capital, he ordered his manager Tung Te to charter a boat and go and sell [his stocks there]. When Tung Te arrived, he found that the price had risen still further. He therefore offered his grain mixed with sand and gravel, and every picul five pints under the full weight. It only took him a few days to dispose of the produce and return home with the cash.[10]

Landlords usually took either a fixed percentage of the harvest or else a fixed quantity of grain as their rent; but there is some evidence that

* This is established in great detail in my translation of Shiba Yoshinobu, *Commerce and Society in Sung China* (Ann Arbor: University of Michigan Center for Chinese Studies, 1970), chapter III. See also pp. 173 et seq.

money rents were not uncommon during this period. Some tenants would therefore have been subject to the inducements of commerce.

*

The agricultural revolution called into being by the means outlined above had four aspects. (1) Farmers learned to prepare their soil more effectively as the result of new knowledge, improved or new tools, and the more extensive use of manure, river mud and lime as fertilizers. (2) Strains of seed were introduced which either gave heavier yields, or resisted drought better, or else by ripening more rapidly made it possible to grow two crops a year on the same land. (3) A new level of proficiency was reached in hydraulic techniques, and irrigation networks of unprecedented intricacy constructed. (4) Commerce made possible more specialization in crops other than the basic foodgrains, and so a more efficient exploitation of varying resource endowments. Much of the evidence given below deals with more than one of these aspects at a time. So far as is possible, however, they will be considered in turn.

Preparation of the soil, planting, and weeding
According to the best practice, rice seeds were steeped in a decoction made by boiling bones, then sown in special seedbeds. These beds had been previously deep-ploughed two or three times in the course of the autumn and the winter until the soil was crumbly. They were then covered with wood ash, then turned over again several times with the plough at the beginning of spring before being fertilized with well matured manure and rotted hemp stalks. After the seeds had been planted they were watered with 'live', that is to say running rather than stagnant, water.*

The transition from the scratch plough to one capable of turning over the sod to form a furrow had been made in the north by the third century AD, and possibly earlier. Much later, probably in the eighth or early ninth century, this plough was modified in Kiangnan for use in wet-field rice farming. Ploughing mud requires less pulling power than for dry soil, and so only one ox or water-buffalo was needed, rather than the three or four oxen customary in the north. If animal power was not

---

* Why, apart from the obvious element of verbal magic, is not clear to me. Well water might often have contained more salts in solution than canal water, and its use have had the effect of a manure.

available, four or five men would drag the less efficient 'foot-plough' instead. Lu Kuei-meng, who lived in Sung-chiang prefecture at the end of the T'ang dynasty, has left us a description of the Kiangnan plough in his *Classic of the Plough*. It consisted of eleven parts, two of which, the ploughshare and mouldboard, were made of iron. He observed that:

> The soil that is being ploughed is called the sod, and takes the form of clods. It is the ploughshare which raises the sod and the mouldboard which turns it over. Weeds are always growing on the sod, and if it is not turned over there is no way of cutting off their roots. Therefore the ploughshare is drawn beneath them and the mouldboard presses them down from on top.[11]

There was also a device for the ploughman to alter the depth of the furrow as he desired. After ploughing, the fields were prepared with harrows, particularly the improved deep-tooth harrow invented in the Yangtze delta around this time. Stone rollers were also used, and wooden rollers with and without spikes. According to a proclamation issued by Ch'en Fu-liang to the people of Kuei-yang, in present-day Kweichow province:

> The soil in Min and Che [the south-eastern coastal region] is exceedingly poor. It therefore needs to be hoed and harrowed several times, and to receive applications of manure and irrigation water, before good fields can be obtained. In this area, however, no one expects to have to put on manure, and hoeing and harrowing are perfunctorily done.[12]

For dry farming in the north, where there was no need for transplanting, the Han plough combined with a seed-drill was employed. In late Sung or Yuan times this tool was widened to cut and sow four furrows at the same time; and a container was fixed behind the hopper holding the seeds from which sieved manure, often mixed with silkworm dung, fell down and covered the seeds in the furrows.

Organic manure was the usual fertilizer. According to Ch'en Fu:

> A manure house is always built by the side of a farmer's dwelling. To prevent the wind and rain from entering, the eaves are set low over pillars. Under the manure house a deep pit is excavated and lined with bricks or glazed tiles so that the manure cannot seep away. Sweepings, clinker, winnowed husks, broken stalks and fallen leaves are gathered and burnt, after which they are enriched with liquid manure and made into a compost heap.[13]

Providing farmers with manure became an important business. According to Wu Tzu-mu's description of thirteenth-century Hang-chou, there were 'swarms of boats carrying away rubbish and night soil'. Further on he explains:

> There is a dense population in the city of Hang-chou; and many families of humble folk who live in the streets and alleys do not have pit-privies. They can only use tubs, which they put outside their doors every day to be emptied by ordure-carriers. These latter are known as 'pouring porters'. Each of them has his boss, and they do not dare to poach each other's clientèle. If there is any poaching, the boss affected will start a quarrel which may not end until victory has been obtained before the Prefect's tribunal.[14]

Mud was also valued as a fertilizer. The poet Mao Hsu left the following lines on Su-chou under the Southern Sung:

> The scoopnets with their bamboo arms
> Lift mud from the river.
> The richest mud
> Comes from the creeks around the city.
> Fully laden, the boats return
> To where the sowing's done,
> Like traders back
> From commerce in the south.[15]

Lime was also much used on fields in the northern part of the province of Liang-che, and gave owners of quarries a useful income.

Optimum utilization of the surface of the fields was achieved by planting out the rice seedlings in clumps of six, set five or six inches apart in straight rows. P'eng Kuei-nien, writing in the twelfth century, mentions how Hupei farmers suffered from their failure to do this:

> The land is thinly populated, and they are slipshod in their methods of cultivation. When they sow, they do not plant out, a practice which is popularly known as 'diffuse scattering'. Even if they obtain a harvest it is an extremely meagre one. Whenever there is a year of abundance it is still only enough to satisfy local needs.[16]

The thoroughness of weeding also affected yields. The peasants of Hupei were criticized for their inadequacy here too. According to Wang Yen, who lived in the twelfth century:

> For the most part, the fields in Hupei are different from those in Chiang, Che and Min [the east and south-east] . . . The land is so

sparsely peopled that they do not have to bestow any great effort on their farming. They sow without planting out or weeding. If perchance they have weeded they do not apply manure, so seeds and other sprouts grow up together. They cultivate vast areas, but have poor harvests.[17]

The invention of a weeding-rake in Kiangnan during the Mongol dynasty eased this painful and time-consuming task.

New seeds and multiple cropping

In the later T'ang dynasty, and in the Sung dynasty, there was an impressive increase in the range of rice seeds available to the farmer. The most famous of these was the Champa rice from central Vietnam. It was introduced through the province of Fukien and in the eleventh century widely adopted on the orders of emperor Chen-tsung. It was an unusually drought-resistant rice of exceptionally low gluten content, which ripened faster than the older Chinese varieties and could be grown on poorer soils than rices with a higher gluten content. Its defects were that it was tough to eat and did not last as long in storage as other rices. The government therefore normally continued to demand rice of moderate gluten content for tax payments and state purchases. Other new strains were created by selective breeding; and by Sung times almost all of the types in use before the middle of the T'ang had disappeared and been replaced by a bewildering array of new ones. Thus a southern Sung gazetteer for the county of Ch'ang-shu in the lower Yangtze delta lists twenty-one kinds of moderate gluten rice, eight of high gluten rice, four of low gluten rice and ten miscellaneous varieties as being cultivated there.

In this way the southern part of the country was covered with a complex variegated pattern of cropping finely adjusted to differing soils, climatic conditions and particular economic circumstances. Chu Ch'ang-wen remarked of Su-chou prefecture in the eleventh century:

> There are early and late species of rice, and innumerable varieties of both. The peasants cultivate them in accordance with their own capabilities and the nature of their land.[18]

Combining early ripening and late ripening rice allowed the work of cultivation to be spread more evenly over the year. According to a work cited in the early Ming gazetteer for Su-chou prefecture:

> It is the custom of Wu [that is, Su-chou] to call 'early' the rice that is planted after the spring equinox [in the last third of the second lunar

month], and harvested at the time of 'Great Heat' [in the last third of the sixth lunar month]. 'Intermediate rice' is that planted between the time of 'Grain in Ear' [in the first third of the fifth lunar month] and the summer solstice [at the end of the fifth lunar month], and reaped after the time of 'White Dew' [in the first third of the eighth lunar month]. 'Late rice' is that sown within ten days after the summer solstice, and harvested after the time of 'Cold Dew' [in the first third of the ninth lunar month].[19]

This spread also reduced the risks from bad weather. Thus when Chu Hsi, the twelfth-century philosopher-official, visited Hsin-ch'ang county in present-day Chekiang after a severe drought, he could report that:

> In this county, too, there has been a severe drought. The early rice harvest was entirely lost. The fields of intermediate and late rice had already become cracked and parched when, in the middle of the seventh month, there was rain for several days in succession. As a result it has been possible to have water in all the fields; and there is hope that there will be a harvest of the intermediate and the late rice.[20]

In the most advanced areas, seasonal rural unemployment was wiped out. An admirably clear description of this is in a rather self-congratulatory poem by Ts'ao Hsun on his manor in T'ai-chou:

> Before the new year, wheat is sown.
> When the wheat has risen, we plant the sprouts of paddy.
> When the latest-ripening rice is done,
> The winter vegetables are already green.
> After the harvest there are no idle hands,
> No empty acres in the dyked fields.
> My family's hundred tenants have learned
> What it is to reap in every season.[21]

This was in Liang-che. In those other areas where cropping was not spread seasonally, the adoption of quick-ripening rice probably intensified the imbalance between the seasons. Chu Hsi observed of T'an-chou in Ching-hu-nan:

> Most of the fields in this prefecture at the present time are dyked fields, and grow only early-ripening rice. After the harvest the peasant families have nothing to do and move around as they please.[22]

This was also true in parts of Kiangsi.

Another way in which drier land was brought into production in the south, giving less seasonal unemployment and more security against natural disasters, was by growing wheat and other northern grains like millet and barley. The southwards migration of wheat into the rice region may have started before the T'ang dynasty; it only became of real economic significance under the Northern Sung. At the end of the tenth century, Yang I wrote of Ch'u-chou in the Liang-che:

> Prices rose sharply last year when the autumn harvest was a poor one; but the population avoided vagrancy. There have now been good spring rains and a doubled harvest of millet and wheat, while the silkworms have been spinning well. Provisions have gradually become adequate and the ashen pallor in people's faces has grown less. It is however the custom of Shan-yueh [that is, Ch'u-chou] to cultivate very few dry fields, to rely on irrigated agriculture, and to eat rice.[23]

When wheat was a subsidiary crop it seems to have been common for the landlord to charge no rent for it. In 1226 Fang Ta-tsung wrote of Fukien:

> The wheat harvest comes when the previous year's grain is running low. It is a relief comparable to removing a burden from one's shoulders and drinking rice-water after a journey of a thousand *li*. Therefore, where rice is concerned, the landlord and the tenant divide it between them; but where wheat is concerned, the farmer takes all the profit.[24]

Sometimes, however, landlords were against their tenants growing wheat, for fear it might divert their energies from the more important rice.

The new early-ripening rice meant that double cropping, both of rice with rice and of rice with wheat, could be extended. In the far south double and even triple cropping of rice was almost universal. Chou Ch'ü-fei remarked of Ch'in-chou: 'The land is so warm that there is no month in which they do not sow and no month in which they do not harvest.'[25] Double cropping of rice was usual along the south-east coast at least as far north as Fukien. Wei Ching, an official who flourished at the turn of the twelfth century, wrote of this province:

> It has twelve counties, one-third of them along the coast and more than half with their backs up against the mountains. Fields up against the mountains give one crop a year; but paddy along the coast gives two harvests a year.[26]

Some observers were sceptical of the value of the two-crop system here. It was Chen Te-hsiu's opinion that: 'Some fields give two harvests, which is called "having a second autumn", but in point of fact the yield is meagre and it is not as good as a single harvest.'[27] There was probably some double cropping of rice with wheat in southern Liang-che. Since peasants would hardly go to a great deal of work just to be able to abandon rice cultivation, this may be deduced from a proclamation issued by Wu Yung in Wen-chou during the thirteenth century:

> In former times, it was customary for everyone in Tung-ou [that is, Wen-chou] to turn towards fishing or the manufacture of salt. People worked but little at farming. The lands along the sea-coast have now been extensively opened up, and all the marshes have been drained and cultivated. Previously, the muddy lands were only suitable for growing moderate-gluten rice. Barley and wheat were rarely planted. Nowadays, the streams have been dammed and dykes installed. Everywhere there is an abundance of sprouting wheat.[28]

And double cropping was quite common in the lower Yangtze valley. To quote Wu Yung once again:

> The soil is rich in Wu, and can give two harvests in one year. Silk-worms can be brought to maturity eight times in one year. But in Yü-chang [that is, Nan-ch'ang in what is now Kiangsi province], girdled with streams and lakes, with many lake-fields and few hill-fields, there is only one rice harvest and silkworms mature but twice.[29]

Wheat and rice were double cropped around Su-chou from at least the eleventh century; and the double cropping of beans and wheat in dry fields was to be found throughout the south-east.

Water control

The Sung and Mongol dynasties also saw significant improvements in hydraulic techniques vital for the extension of the area of rice cultivation. As Chu Hsi put it, 'the basis of farming is using dams and dykes'.

The problems to be solved varied from one place to another, but there was an unmistakable rise in the level of skill with which they were solved. The low-lying lands near the south-eastern coast were the scene of many reclamation projects. It was in Sung times that the Sang-yuan polder at the junction of the West and North rivers in present-day Kwangtung was started. So too was the main work of opening up the P'u-t'ien plain in Fukien and the Ning-po plain in the Liang-che, with dams to prevent the tidal influx of salt water from damaging the soil, and up-country storage reservoirs to catch and store the rapid seasonal flows of water off the hills. Mastery of the drainage of the fertile basin around Lake T'ai by dredging and re-routing the Wu-sung river also dates from about this period.

Of particular importance was the rapid growth in the number of polders in Kiangnan during the Five Dynasties and the Sung. Yang Wan-li described them in the twelfth century:

> In the watery regions of Chiang-nan-tung the embankments and the ditches form a double boundary in the middle of which lie the cultivated fields. These are called 'polders'. The peasants say that 'polder' indicates an encircling dyke within which are the dyked fields, and outside of which are the encircling streams. The reason for these works is that the water level is high and the fields, on the contrary, below the level of the water. Sluice gates are pierced in the length of the embankments, and channels cut by means of which the fields may be irrigated. There are rich harvests and no floods.[30]

Some of these polders were opened up by the government and reached twenty-eight miles in circumference, being managed as official manors. Others were smaller and belonged to private manors. The state sometimes assisted their upkeep with loans.

In more mountainous areas, such as Hui-chou in Chiang-nan-tung, tanks were used to store rainwater, and streams were diverted laterally. According to Cheng Yü, who wrote during the Mongol period:

> The rustics throw shrubbery and logs into the streams that run off the hills, cementing them together with sand and mud so that they block the flow with a barrage. They excavate channels along which they lead the water to irrigate their fields.[31]

Stone dams were used in the mountain gorges of Fukien. In the upland areas of T'ung-ch'uan (that is, Tzu-chou), in present-day Szechwan, yet another technique was common. Yeh T'ing-kuei describes it in 1149:

> In Kuo-chou and Ho-chou they have no level fields. The peasants use the depressions in the hills to hold pools of rainwater, which they use for the cultivation of rice of moderate and of high gluten content.[32]

As with other agricultural techniques, some regions were backward in irrigation. Chan T'i-jen, the prefect of Ching-chiang in Kuang-nan-hsi during the reign of the emperor Ning-tsung (1195–1224), is said to have had to teach hydraulic techniques to the ignorant locals. In 1273 Huang

Chen issued this stinging proclamation to the people of Fu-chou in Chiang-nan-hsi:

> When fields are near to mountain torrents, you ought to build embankments section by section. When irrigated fields are not near to water, wells should always be dug to store water. At present, Fu-chou relies entirely on nature. If there are five days without rain, you are instantly helpless. If there are ten days of continuous rain, you likewise cannot retain it. Why don't you peasants display a little competence![33]

Various devices were used for moving water, whether for drainage or irrigation. The simplest of these, such as the counterbalanced bucket or 'well-sweep', were found almost universally, and went back long before Sung times. The more complicated, above all the square-pallet chain pump and the noria, had been known for at least some centuries, but not much used for farming. They became much more common around the end of the first millennium AD, their distribution depending mainly on whether or not there were swiftly moving streams. Where there were, as in Szechwan and up-country Hunan, the ponderous but effective noria was preferred. Elsewhere, such as the delta land around Su-chou, the treadle pallet pump predominated – mobile, adaptable, but requiring a prolonged input of hard labour. Pallet pumps were sometimes worked by animals or by water wheels linked to them by wooden gearing, but this was exceptional. Perhaps the best brief description of the main techniques available to the Sung farmer is that by the Szechwanese Buddhist monk Chü Chien in the first half of the thirteenth century:

> The hub [of the noria] is set at right angles to the stream, with the axle laid across the banks. Bamboo tubes are attached to the ends of the spokes and move around [with the wheel] when the machine is set in motion. [The tubes filled with water from the stream at the lowest point in their rotation, spilling it into an aqueduct when they reached the top.] It will not work unless it is placed in a strong current. The well-sweep is different from the noria in that it is counterbalanced, is made to rise and fall by the operator as he desires, and can be installed at wells. The 'water-shuttle' is suspended in the air from a frame. [This sounds like a pivoted beam with a channel cut in it along which the water could run from a scoop at one end.] Placed at the junction of irrigation ditches, it can be used to drain excess water and to bring water to parched land. These three devices are used in Szechwan. The machine found in Wu is called the 'dragon's backbone [pump]'. It consists of a trough of square cross section, and an axle set at right

angles at the end of this trough. Pallets, measuring over a foot and a half each way, are set in the trough and drawn through it laterally, being linked to form a continuous chain, and of dimensions slightly smaller than the trough. Pieces of wood called 'apes' heads' are nailed to the axle, and people tread on these to set the machine in motion. It is useful for any stream or pond. The only device for which it will not substitute is the well-sweep. The sweep and the water-shuttle are worked by one man, the dragon's backbone pump by several persons.[34]

The contribution of these pumps and norias was even extolled by poets. Here are lines composed in the twelfth century by Li Ch'u-ch'üan in praise of the norias of P'iao-yang county near Nanking:

> In Wu your feet grow callused treadling pumps,
> Toiling away with little to show for it.
> Kiangnan waterwheels need no human power,
> Being built by craftsmen of true skill.
> Ten tubes upon each wheel both drain and irrigate,
> Rising and falling in a circle without cease.
> Rich lands have been opened up in the surrounding hills,
> Along ten thousand acres wind rice-sprouts like green clouds –
> Clouds that before your eyes turn from green to gold,
> And fill all stomachs with the year's rich harvest.[35]

The government tried to introduce pumping equipment into areas still unfamiliar with it. Ch'en Tsao gave this advice to the people of Fang-chou in Ching-hu-pei during Southern Sung times:

> The water fields of Fang-chou are irrigated from mountain springs and have the reputation of being good fields; but for the most part you have no idea how to make [hydraulic] machinery. If you will now apply manure wherever possible, and [even] where this is not possible make use of machinery for irrigation, then not only will the incidence of bad harvests be reduced by fifty per cent, but it will be possible to turn all the level dry land into fields for the cultivation of rice of moderate and of high gluten content.[36]

Official manors were sometimes supplied with treadle pumps (see page 81).

The use of wind power in farming seems only to have come to China some time after the medieval economic revolution was over. The earliest known reference is in Sung Ying-hsing's *The Development of Commodities by Nature and Human Skill* of 1637, where wind driven drainage pumps are noted for Yang-chou in the Yangtze delta. These pumps were built very differently from those of Europe, as may be seen from a gazetteer for Sung-chiang prefecture published in 1817:

> The people use [square-pallet chain] pumps for the irrigation of their fields . . . Each pump needs from three to six men to irrigate twenty *mou* of farmland. In some cases, the pumps are turned not by men but by an ox. A [horizontal] wooden plate like a cartwheel, but with a larger circumference, is fitted with cogs that turn the drive-shaft of the pump. This economizes on the [human] energy needed to make the pump go round, and is twice as effective. In some cases, not even an ox is employed, but the wind is used to turn the pump. The method of construction resembles the ox-powered pump, but sails are set [on masts mounted vertically around the rim] on the [big] wheel, and advantage is taken of the wind to make it rotate. This is the most ingenious of all the machines used in farming. It is not suited for common use, however, for when great winds arise the pump is liable to be smashed.[37]

The sails used to drive these wind pumps were free to move within limits set by the length of a fixed sheet made fast to the boom of each sail. They would thus set approximately at right angles to the line of flow of the wind while moving with it; but, on the return journey, would swing into a position roughly parallel with the line of flow while moving against it, so offering the minimum degree of resistance.[38] It is my suspicion that the Chinese sailing-ship type of wind pump was more efficient in light breezes than the European airscrew variety.

Horizontal windmills with rigid vanes, and half casings to shield the vanes from the wind while they are moving in a direction contrary to it, go back to Persia in the seventh century. The date of the distinctive Chinese modification of this design, which did away with the half casing and was clearly inspired by the fore and aft rig of a ship, is not known. This may be one of the very rare instances of a useful invention being made in China *after* the medieval economic revolution had drawn to its close.

Trade and specialization

Lastly, expanding markets for all sorts of agricultural produce led farmers to move away from self-sufficiency as an objective and to concentrate instead on growing those crops which did best in their own particular area, with a corresponding rise in efficiency and output. This was perhaps most evident in Fukien, which produced lychees and oranges for foreign export, and a host of other products for sale in other provinces. Fang Ta-tsung described the prefecture of Hsing-hua in the thirteenth century:

> The four upper prefectures [namely Chien-ning, Nan-chien, Shao-wu and T'ing-chou] are the most productive of rice in Fukien, yet they are forbidden the cultivation of rice with a high gluten content, the manufacture of wine from it, the growing of oranges, and the excavation of ponds for the rearing of fish. The reason for this ban is the desire that no inch of land should go unfarmed, no grain of rice uneaten. If regions which produce a surplus of rice take such precautions, how much more should those whose harvests cannot supply half their needs! These days, the fields of Hsing-hua have been taken over by rice of a high gluten content [for wine-making], and there are I know not how many thousands of piculs of it carried each year into the prefectural capital. The fields of Hsien-yu county have been consumed by sugar cane, and there are I know not how many tens of thousands of jars of the stuff transported each year to Huai-nan and Liang-che. There can be no doubt but that sugar cane is an obstacle in the way of rice fields.[39]

Other major exports from one province to another were tea, timber, paper and lacquer. This specialization of production was of course sustained by the increase in the volume of trade and by counterbalancing flows of foodgrains from complementary regions. By the twelfth century, Fukien's coastal prefectures all relied regularly on rice imports from Kuang-nan and Che-hsi; and comparable areas, such as the Tung-t'ing hills in Lake T'ai where only oranges were grown, were in a similar state of dependence.

*

By the thirteenth century China thus had what was probably the most sophisticated agriculture in the world, India being the only conceivable rival. It was the base upon which a remarkable superstructure of commercial activity and urbanization was to be built. At the same time large differences remained between the various regions of China as regards technical skill in farming. Looked at in another way, these differences represented a potential capacity to expand total output by bringing the lagging areas, especially Hunan and Hupei, up to the level of the more advanced. The Chinese population under the Northern Sung was well over one hundred million. By 1580 it was at least half as big again, say somewhere between 160 and 250 million (see pages 310 et seq.). In a long term perspective, therefore, and ignoring the fairly drastic demographic decline of the thirteenth and fourteenth centuries and the subsequent recovery, it was the generalization, over the country as a whole, of the best Sung techniques without a correspondingly large expansion of the area of farmland that fed these increased numbers. It was thus that the foundations of China's enormous present population were laid.

10 · The revolution in water transport

Better transport and communications were almost as important as better agriculture in promoting the medieval economic revolution. They also contributed greatly to the integration and maintenance of the united empire of T'ang and Sung times. Progress was made mainly in the techniques and organization of water transportation, through which the economy began to pulse with a hitherto unknown vigour. But improvements in land transport and in government communications should not be overlooked; and we may usefully begin with a brief survey of road building and the official postal system before passing onto the main theme.

Both the T'ang and the Sung governments kept up and improved the main land routes of the empire. This was essential for economic development as the expansion of commercial traffic seems often to have had a destructive effect upon the existing road surfaces. Early in the eighth century Chang Chiu-ling was ordered to construct a new highway across the pass that links northern Kwangtung with southern Kiangsi, and observed of his work:

> The road up from Kwangtung was previously in a state of decay. People found the steep gradients difficult and travelled on roundabout paths . . . Thus, if they made use of carts, there were no ruts for them to roll in; and if they carried their goods, it had to be on their backs. Yet there was a continual flow of trade with countries overseas, and a profusion of teeth, hides, feathers, furs, fish, salt and shellfish sufficient to meet the needs of the imperial storehouses and the demands of the people of the lower Yangtze and Huai regions . . .[1]

A passage from the *Sung Digest* for the early thirteenth century is even more striking:

> Repairing roads and boundaries, and watching over defiles, plains and marshes, are the primary duties of local government and something

to which the authorities should pay attention in due season . . . From Lin-an [Hang-chou] to Chin-k'ou [Chen-chiang] is a distance of a thousand *li*. [Another variable Chinese measure. For general purposes, it may be taken as one-third of an English mile.] This road is used for the easy passage of boats [for which it presumably served as a towing-path] and of carts, for the relays of the official postal service, for the transport of the government's tax grain, and the despatch of contingents of soldiers. The prolonged and heavy rains of the past years, and the battering of flood waters, have caused the dyked banks to disintegrate and the roadway along them to subside, while the bridges have fallen in ruins . . . In consequence, carts and mounted riders coming and going, and those who are hauling boats, lose their footing and fall. Many types of person suffer from this . . .[2]

The state carried out the necessary repairs.

Sometimes upkeep was a very expensive business. This was particularly true of the perishable wooden bridges and galleries on the main road south into Szechwan from the north-west. In 1043 the county magistrate of Pao-ch'eng in Hsing-yuan prefecture memorialized:

The main road in Szechwan runs from Feng-chou through the passes of Li-chou and Chien-men straight to Ch'eng-tu. The way is long, and the bridges and galleries amount to over 90,000 *chien* [a unit of space corresponding to a room, or the distance between two pillars]. Every year, the soldiers assigned to the post stations gather wood in the nearby hills, and do repairs so that through passage is possible. Recently, . . . they have been going more than twenty or thirty *li* into the forests because of the difficulty of finding timber to cut. I would like to ask that the command be given that, along both sides of the official road into Szechwan, the soldiers at the post stations shall every year cultivate the timber which will be needed, so that it may be there in readiness.[3]

It was also common for trees to be grown along the roads to provide shade for travellers.

The quality of the main roads is hard to evaluate. T'ang records suggest that the Chinese had trouble building highways that did not become impassable in the summer rains. By Sung times, however, not only were a good number of city streets paved with stone slabs, but surfacing inter-city routes with bricks or stone seems to have been quite common. Thus Fan Ch'eng-ta noted in his *Travel Journal* late in the twelfth century:

We reached Ch'ü-chou. The road from Wu-chou [Chin-hua] to Ch'ü-chou is entirely bricked, and we no longer suffered from a muddy surface. In times past, there were two rich persons, one in each of these prefectural capitals, whose families were linked by marriage. They wished to visit each other in convenient fashion, and so they together bricked the road.[4]

While this was clearly something of an exceptional case, Fan's critical remarks on the roads of southern Hunan suggest that elsewhere he generally found paving of some sort in a fairly good condition:

> The route from Heng-chou to Yung-chou consisted entirely of small hills. The roadway was of a coarse inferior quality, not having been solidly laid down. That is to say, the stones were so ill-fitted that there were gaps between them. There was also mud. In spite of the fact that we had had clear weather for more than ten days, it was still not dry . . . On the whole, they do not maintain their roads in Hunan.[5]

Some other roads are known to have been bricked in Sung times, such as the ten miles of mountain highway across what is now the Kwangtung-Kiangsi border. In general, the later part of the T'ang dynasty and the Sung dynasty seem to have seen a steady extension of the main road network, most notably in southern China. Thus Wang Hsiang-chih's thirteenth-century *Geography of the Empire* observes of Hsin-chou, then in the province of Chiang-nan-tung, that: 'The roads to Fukien, Hunan and Hupei, and Kiangsi all lead off from here. In times past, it was an out-of-the-way place. Today, it is a centre of communications.'[6]

Something of the speeds attainable along the major land routes is revealed by the workings of the government postal system. It was 4210 *li* from Ch'ang-an to Canton by the shortest route; and in T'ang times the fastest horses could cover about five hundred *li* in twenty-four hours, while the swiftest runners could perhaps manage two hundred to three hundred *li*. In terms of communications, therefore, the capital of the middle Chinese Empire was only eight to fourteen days away from the most distant city of any importance. Ordinarily, of course, travellers went much more slowly. One T'ang official estimate gave seventy *li* a day as an average for a man mounted on horseback, fifty *li* for someone riding a donkey or going on foot, and thirty *li* for a cart. In Sung times the best foot-runners seem to have been rather faster than their T'ang predecessors, but the general levels of speed were still roughly comparable.

Better land communications after the T'ang made it possible for the government to move officials and documents more efficiently around the empire. Relay hostels, with horses and food for travelling bureau-crats, were set up along all main roads and some of the lesser roads as well. Boat travellers enjoyed the use of relay hostels set up along the rivers. In the middle of the T'ang dynasty, this system was developed into a regular government postal service; and the use of special mes-sengers for official communications was largely dropped. The post relied both on mounted couriers and, because of the shortage of horses, on foot-runners. Official goods were also carried in this way, sometimes making necessary the use of very large numbers of men. Thus delicate sea foods, which had to arrive at the court in fresh condition, were taken from Ning-po to Ch'ang-an by 9,600 runners working in relays.

Such luxuries apart, the new system made possible important political and economic developments. One such is described by the *Comprehen-sive Mirror for the Assistance of Government*:

> Liu Yen [the late eighth-century statesman] possessed both energy and insight. He knew in the minutest detail whether or not there were going to be shifts in the balance of circumstances. He regularly spent large sums of money to hire good runners; and set up relay stations in contact with one another, with the task of observing and reporting the prices of commodities everywhere. It took only a few days for all the news from distant places to reach the authorities. The power to con-trol the prices of goods lay entirely within his hands.[7]

Another improvement in the links between the central government and the country at large was the Sui and T'ang system by which a senior official from every one of the 350 or so prefectures had to visit the capital early in each year, to report on prefectural affairs and be questioned about them. After the disruption caused by the An Lu-shan rebellion in the middle of the eighth century it proved impossible to continue this system, too much power having shifted into the hands of the semi-independent military governors. Instead, these military men kept 'Courts for the Forwarding of Memorials' at the capital; and these served for the two-way transmission of information, orders and requests. The officials in charge of these courts privately copied out important government documents, relating both to the area concerned and to the empire as a whole, and circulated them to their masters. This practice in due course developed into an official gazette issued by the Sung government, the world's first national newspaper.

*

The political significance of a swifter administrative nervous system, based on land transport with its superior speed, was surpassed, great though it undoubtedly was, by the economic advances in water transportation which permitted cheap long-distance carriage of everyday goods in large quantities. South and central China were soon covered by an intricate web of itineraries along which travelled boats of an astonishing range of sizes and designs, beautifully adapted to the different natural circumstances with which they had to contend, and to a multitude of different cargoes. The coastal seas became highways for heavy junks sailing north and south with the seasonal alternation of the monsoon winds. On the oceans Chinese vessels, armed with the mariner's compass, star charts and navigator's manuals, crossed the Asian world from Japan to the Arabian littoral.

This was not a period when the Chinese were contentedly uninformed about what went on beyond their frontiers. On the contrary, it was the golden age of Chinese geography and cartography, which reached, through contacts with Arab sea captains and later with envoys and travellers across the Mongol Empire, as far west as the Maghreb and the shores of the Atlantic. Even the approximately triangular shape of Africa was known and recorded.

The origins of Chinese shipping went far back. In the sixth century BC the state of Ch'i in the north-east traded in bronze and iron with the south by river. A little later, there was also some seaborne trade between the Shantung peninsula and the Yangtze delta. This coastal commerce was mostly in the hands of the Yueh, the people in Fukien and Kwangtung before the coming of the Han Chinese; and as they merged with their conquerors they probably became the backbone of later 'Chinese' skill in seafaring. A new upturn next seems to have occurred in the third century AD. Wide commerce between north and south at this time is hinted at in the following report made by two officials from Wei about the contacts between Sun Ch'üan, ruler of the rival southern state of Wu, and the then dependent area which is now southern Manchuria:

> The 'rebel' Sun Ch'üan . . . has in recent years again been sending ships long distances across the high seas, relying upon a profusion of commodities to win over the coastal people in deceitful fashion. The coastal people are ignorant and have dealings with them. No one, from the officials downwards, is willing to put a stop to it. When he sent Chou Ho with a hundred vessels, they choked the coastal inlets; and

since no one entertained any antagonism towards them, they were presented with excellent horses.[8]

The appearance about now of the proverbial saying 'Go by boat in the south, in the north take a horse' suggests that river traffic was also on the increase.

It was however in T'ang times that Chinese shipping came into its own. In the later part of the seventh century Ts'ui Jung described how

Boats gather on every stream in the empire. To one side they reach into Szechwan and up the Han River valley. They point the way to Fukien and Kwangtung. Through the Seven Marshes and the Ten Swamps, the Three Rivers and the Five Lakes, they draw in the Yellow River and the Lo, embracing also Huai-an and Hai-chou. Great ships in thousands and tens of thousands carry goods back and forth. If they lay unused for a single moment, ten thousand merchants would be bankrupted. If these were ruined, then others would have no one on whom to depend for their livelihood.[9]

A hundred and fifty years later, Li Ch'ao was able to assert that: 'There is no commandery or county in the south-east in which water communications are lacking. Therefore most of the empire's profits from trade depend on the use of boats.'[10] T'ang poets customarily associated travelling merchants with water transport. Chang Chi speaks of them as 'living out their lives on shipboard, enjoying their existence amid wind and waves'. In Po Chü-i's famous lines on the salt-merchant's wife we read that 'wind and waves are her village, her ship her mansion'.[11]

So far as can be estimated, the volume of shipping was impressive. In the eighth century, for example, Liu Yen, then Commissioner for Salt and Iron, had 2,000 boats built for service on the Yangtze. Each had a capacity of about 50,000 kilograms, so together they carried almost a third of the total carried by the British trading fleet in the middle of the eighteenth century. The *Old T'ang History* mentions a storm in 721 in Yang-chou and Jun-chou during which houses and trees were torn from the ground, and over a thousand state and privately owned ships sent to the bottom. The *T'ang Digest* likewise refers to a fire in 751 among the transport ships at Shan-chou on the Yellow River which was responsible for burning 215 official grain vessels and a million piculs of rice, killing 600 sailors and destroying several hundred boats belonging to merchants.[12] In the same year, tides whipped up by a typhoon at

Yang-chou sunk several thousand boats. Liu's fleet can therefore have only represented a fraction of the total tonnage on the rivers.

The mastery of the open oceans came rather later. The Chinese in T'ang times were content to rely on South-east Asian, Persian and Arab ships for the trade with what are now Vietnam, Cambodia, Malaya, Java and India. Li Ch'ao observed: 'The ships that sail the southern seas are foreign ships.' Chinese ships did go, however, to Korea and Japan. The seagoing vessels of this period were probably rather like the Persian ships described by the late T'ang writer Liu Hsun in his *Record of Strange Things Beyond the Southern Ranges*:

> [Foreign] merchants' ships do not employ iron nails. They only use coir fibre to bind [the planks] together and olive oil glue to stick them. Once the glue has dried, it is extremely hard and goes through the water like lacquer.[13]

By Sung times, Chinese junks had become very much more sophisticated. They were built with iron nails, and waterproofed with the oil of the t'ung tree, a superb natural preservative. Their equipment included watertight bulkheads, buoyancy chambers, bamboo fenders at the waterline, floating anchors to hold them steady during storms, axial rudders in place of steering oars, outrigger and leeboard devices, oars for use in calm weather, scoops for taking samples off the sea floor, sounding lines for determining the depth, compasses for navigation, and small rockets propelled by gunpowder for self-defence. Understandably, from about the beginning of the second millennium AD, foreign merchants chose when possible to travel on Chinese ships.

For speed and cheapness sea transport was pre-eminent. The Chinese sail, being made of narrow sections of canvas or matting stretched between transverse batons of bamboo, rather in the manner of a Venetian blind or a fan, was less efficient than the curved Arabian or Western sail, but was easier to control when closehauled or damaged. Junks achieved quite impressive speeds by using the monsoon winds, as Liao Kang records in the twelfth century:

> [Seagoing ships] take advantage of the reliability of the seasonal winds. They go south in the winter and come north in the summer, never the other way around. For this reason, the ships travel steadily and evenly without the need for any great attention. Since the nature of the winds is favourable, they cover about a thousand *li* a day without difficulty.[14]

It was possible to go from Fukien to Korea in from five to twenty days; and the journey from Ning-po to Mi-chou in southern Shantung could take as little as three. The early fifteenth-century statesman Sung Li estimated that, for an equal cargo of grain, a seagoing ship needed twice as many men as an inland waterway vessel; but the superior speed of the seagoing ship (even conceding Sung's probably inflated figures) still made it cheaper. In 1487 Ch'iu Chün stated in a memorial: 'Transport by inland waterway is thirty per cent to forty per cent cheaper than transport by land. Sea transport is seventy per cent to eighty per cent cheaper than transport by land.'[15] The proportions probably did not greatly differ in Sung times.

The chief problem at sea was safety. The introduction of the compass, first mentioned in a nautical context in 1119, marked a great step forward. In Yuan and Ming times, charts with compass bearings marked on them began to be widely used. Investigations were made into the tides and the weather, and some of the results published by the government. The *Record of the Sea Transport of the Great Yuan Dynasty* lists mnemonic rhymes on such matters introduced with the following explanation:

> [The official grain transport] sails ten thousand *li* across the seas out of sight of land. Cloudy weather and storms arise in unpredictable fashion. They rely on the chart with compass bearings to set the vessel's course, and gaze up at the configuration of the skies to forecast the weather. Ships' captains therefore attach a high value to recruiting an experienced helmsman to have charge of these matters. The official grain, and the lives of those on board, all depend on him. If he makes the slightest error, extremely serious harm can result . . . We have therefore summarized and set out the fruits of our enquiries into tides, winds and weather. Although this is but vulgar talk, yet repeated experiences tally. We have not shunned the possibility that we shall be ridiculed, but have combined items into mnemonic rhymes in the hope that they will be easy to remember and recite.[16]

In spite of these and other aids Chinese medieval sailing ships remained extremely vulnerable. Thus the Ming *Classic of the Seaways* noted with regard to the mouth of the Yangtze:

> If an easterly wind is encountered, the situation may become critical. Unfavourable currents present an urgent problem. The vessels [of the grain transport] become crowded close together; and if one of them is driven back, it becomes entangled with the others, anchors intertwin-

ing, rigging snarling, prows and sterns striking one another. Winds and rains attack together, and the crews are helpless. If they are forced onto the sandbanks, then wrecks are inevitable. This is something about which it is necessary to be most careful.[17]

In the mid fifteenth century, Li Hsien wrote about the sea transport of grain from what is now Tientsin along the coast of the Gulf of Pohai to the frontier garrisons:

> There were numerous storms; and when the boats reached the seashore they would not dare to proceed hastily. They always delayed for up to ten days, or even an entire month, until the wind had become calm, before venturing to make the crossing. Sometimes the winds and the waves would rise up suddenly in mid-journey, and they would be blown off course or overturned. Every year, no less than several tens of vessels were lost, and tens of thousands of piculs of grain perished.[18]

These were small ships, of course, which also had to be able to navigate some of the inland waterways; yet the level of losses was high. The northern seas were not really mastered until the seventeenth and eighteenth centuries, one of the few clearly identifiable technical advances made in this later period although the reason for it still remains unclear.

*

The greatest economic impetus was given by the growth of river and canal shipping. It was at this time that ways were found to pass through or around previously unpassable difficult places in rivers. In consequence, a number of hitherto separate waterway systems were now linked into an integrated whole, and formed the foundation for the nationwide market which emerged at this time. An obvious example of one such barrier is provided by the Yangtze gorges, up which boats were hauled by teams of trackers moving on special paths cut into the cliffs above the river. Lu Yu's *Record of a Journey to Szechwan*, written in the later twelfth century, describes the passage up from Chiang-ling as follows:

> They took the yardarm off the mast and installed rowlocks, since for the ascent of the gorges only oars and 'thousand-foot hawsers' are employed. Sails are no longer set. The thousand-foot hawser is made

of strips of large bamboos split lengthwise into four, and is as thick as a man's arm. The boat on which I travelled had a capacity of 1,600 piculs, and used in all six oars and two thousand-foot hawsers.[19]

Already in the ninth century, Li Ch'ao had noted that 'at dangerous places such as the Three Gorges in Szechwan, the Three Gates rapids on the Yellow River, the O-ch'i River [in Kwangtung] and the Kan-shih shoals [on the Kan River in Kiangsi] there are locals who act as polemen'. When goods had to be trans-shipped into smaller craft, or portaged, there were often specialized workers for these purposes. The *Sung Digest* describes the ascent of the Han River thus:

> Going upstream from Han-k'ou to Ying-chou there are still but few rapids and submerged rocks; but from Ying-chou and Hsiang-yang upwards there are the dangers of the thirty-six rapids. When a convoy has brought its cargoes this far, it is necessary for them to be loaded into several hundred smaller craft, a practice which is called 'trans-shipping past the rapids'. The boats are all hauled upstream with thousand-foot hawsers made of bamboo.[20]

Fan Ch'eng-ta gives this account of the Pai-kou Gorges in what is now western Hupei:

> When one reaches the New Rapids, which have the worst repute of any in the Three Gorges, if one wishes to avoid either ascending or descending them, then one has to trans-ship and go by land, the rapids being negotiated by the unloaded boat. There are many inhabitants on both banks called 'Rapids Men' who make their living solely by transporting goods past the rapids.[21]

The invention of the double lock in the eleventh century may also be regarded as a means of easing passage past a difficult point. According to Shen Kua's *Dream Pool Essays*, when one of these was built at Chen-chou, where the northern arm of the Grand Canal met the Yangtze it 'effected an annual economy of five hundred workers and one-and-a-quarter million cash in expenses', presumably by removing the need for ships to be hauled over a ramp. It also enabled ships of up to 1,600 piculs capacity to use the canal, whereas previously the largest had not carried more than three hundred piculs.[22]

Many types of propulsion were used on inland shipping, suited to the nature of the waterways. On the biggest rivers, notably the lower reaches of the Yangtze and the Yellow River, sails were common. This may be seen from the following two poems, the first by Wang Yun and the second by Yuan Chüeh:

Sails

Yellow reeds are woven into foot-wide mats.
Section by section they constitute a sail.
It can be made long or short as required,
Tightened or slackened as desired.
Along one side the 'foot-rope' is attached,
Controlling the connected series like a net's main rope.
Northerners use linen sails;
Our custom on the Yangtze is to make them out of reeds.

Greedy for heavy cargoes, the captains of these ships
Hoist their sails high to catch the winds.
Both with the current and against the waves,
The great bird on the prow is given wings.
Seen from afar, coming from distant shores,
They seem a streak of dusky cloud.
Past misted isles they cut their headlong path,
Heavy with drenching in the Yangtze rains.

A hundred *li* have flown before the morning's past,
Through effortless use of favouring circumstance.
As in the failing sunlight the evening's anchorage gleams,
They fold in piles the many-pleated sails . . .[23]

The Boats of the Yellow River

The boats of the Yellow River are like slices of cut melon
Covered with iron nails for scraping the sandy shallows.
Their towering masts are not secured at the base
But guyed by ropes on every side.
They come like floating mountains of bundled firewood,
Scattering before them the boats of Huai and Wu.
Between the north and south they ply to make their living,
And know but little of the Yangtze River.
With the wind set fair, a thousand sails
Will move at different speeds . . .
Forward, they rear pigs and donkeys in one pen,
Using the donkey's strength for hauling.
Unsparingly they lay the lash on, much better
Than in Kiangnan, where men do the work of beasts.[24]

As these last few lines suggest, hauling and poling were also used where there were hauling-ways and shallow water. These techniques are also mentioned in an imitation boat-song written by Fang Hui in the thirteenth century:

> Southward bound to Hang-chou and northward bound to Ch'u-chou,
> By the Three Rivers and Eight Dykes the waters flow unbroken.
> Hauling-board and punting-pole – these are their ricebowls,
> Freed from the bitter toil of working with the hoe.
> Shifting heavy cargoes brings them their meagre wages,
> The father pulling forward, while the son punts behind.[25]

A variety of oars, sculls and sweeps were used in deeper waters. The most important was the long heavy single oar counterbalanced by its handle, and worked over the stern in a fishtailing motion – a uniquely efficient method of rowing. According to Wang Yun:

> The Yangtze River boat is an enormous fish,
> With fishtail oar for fins, and rudder for a tail.
> Where water's deep and sweeps inadequate,
> The fishtail oar is fastened at the stern,
> Joining its efforts with the sweeps in front,
> The most important of the five
> Things needed for navigation.[26]

Finally, paddle-wheel boats were sometimes used as tugs in harbours.

The family was the basis of the majority of shipping enterprises. A poem by Yuan Chüeh gives a picture of life aboard in the lower Yangtze region:

> Wu boats are oval-shaped, turtles with tucked-in heads.
> Families sail them all year round without returning.
> Their plot of land, their thatched cottage having long since
> vanished . . .
> Every morning, they endure the pain of travelling,
> But all year round are spared the pain of leaving home.
> The eldest son, just eight years old, skips with sure-footed
> assurance,
> While younger brother learns to treat the junk as terra firma.[27]

Sometimes these family units would be organized as the dependents of well-to-do merchants. In the later part of the twelfth century, Yeh Shih observed of northern Hunan:

> The rivers and lakes are linked together so that by means of them one can go everywhere. When a boat leaves its home port, there are no

obstacles to its planning a journey of ten thousand *li*. Every year the common people use for trading all the grain that is surplus to their requirements for seeds and food. Large merchants gather what the lesser households have. Little boats become the dependents of the greater vessels and engage in joint operations, going back and forth selling grain in order to clear a solid profit. It is a regular custom for sons to succeed their fathers, and to grow old in their turn facing the winds and the waves.[28]

Partnerships were also common. Ch'in Kan, writing in the later eleventh century, had this to say in an epitaph on a famous Buddhist monk who had been born in the great seaport of Ch'üan-chou:

He joined up with several persons from the same locality as he was, and they went off trading, sailing the seaways from Kwangtung and Fukien up to Shantung, coming and going across the seas for more than ten years. He became extremely rich. In the Huang-yu reign-period [1049–53], after having sacrificed before his parents' graves, he became a monk . . . His father and mother had vowed when he was a boy that he should be a monk, and his name had been registered with the K'ai-yuan Temple in Chang-chou. He now suddenly abandoned all his business pursuits, gave his wealth to his business partners so that they might take care of his family, and entered the monastery penniless. He shaved off his beard and his hair, and observed all the abstentions, much to the wonderment of the local people.[29]

Many partnerships were dissolved after each venture, and the profits shared out; some, like the above, were obviously more permanent. Large merchants also built up trading fleets under delegated managers, sometimes of as many as eighty ships. The separation of ownership and financing on the one hand and management on the other also took the form of investment by persons of quite modest means in ventures undertaken by others. Pao Hui, writing about the outflow of copper cash from Southern Sung China, reveals this in indirect fashion:

The households of the middle and lower grades who live along the seacoast are not able to cause any large outflow of cash, but harm is caused by 'leakage through entrusting', a phenomenon so far little remarked upon. Its cause is that all the people along the coast are on intimate terms with the merchants who engage in overseas trade, either because they are fellow-countrymen or personal acquaintances. Leakage through entrusting occurs when the former give the latter money to take with them on their ships for the purchase and return conveyance of foreign goods. They invest from ten to a hundred strings of cash, and regularly make profits of several hundred per cent.[30]

Finally, it is worth noting with respect to the scale of combination in the shipping business at this time that, when the Southern Sung government began to requisition commoners' boats in large numbers, in some ports up to sixty merchants would combine resources to build a number of vessels held in collective ownership, half of them going to the state on the understanding that the remainder would not be commandeered.

From the economic point of view, the shipping brokers were the linch-pin of the entire water transport system. Located in some numbers in every port, it was they who undertook to buy or arrange for the purchase of the cargoes from the ships calling there. It was they who had the warehouse facilities to store goods until a suitable moment came to put them onto the market. It was they who found cargoes for ships leaving port, and acted as middlemen for chartering or hiring vessels. Junk captains were not ordinarily familiar with local market conditions and customs formalities, and they needed as quick a turn-round as possible. Nor could merchants seeking transport be fully conversant with all the intricacies of the business, or be confident of captains and crews. Thus the specialized knowledge of the shipping brokers made them vital intermediaries through whose hands almost everything had to pass. Since ships without engines could not keep tight schedules, the flexible arrangements provided by the brokerage network probably worked better than any attempt to plan times and cargoes in advance. Under the Yuan dynasty, a three-sided contract had to be concluded between the hirer, the shipping broker and the shipmaster; and a standard form for such a contract was current by the fourteenth century. Even so, boatmen regularly pilfered cargoes and had an unenviable reputation for all sorts of sharp practice.

Thus medieval China was distinguished not only by the productivity of its farming but also by the cheapness and, on the whole, the good organization of its water transport system. We may fittingly end with the words of Marco Polo, a native of the greatest seaport in the Europe of his day, describing the Yangtze where it passes through the city of I-ching:

> I assure you that this river runs for such a distance and through so many regions and there are so many cities on its banks that truth to tell, in the amount of shipping it carries and the total volume and

value of its traffic, it exceeds all the rivers of the Christians put together and their seas into the bargain. I give you my word that I have
seen in this city fully five thousand ships at once, all afloat on this river.
Then you may reflect, since this city, which is not very big, has so
many ships, how many there must be in the others. For I assure you
that the river flows through more than sixteen provinces, and there
are on its banks more than two hundred cities, all having more ships
than this.[31]

11 · The revolution in money and credit

When more money in real terms circulates in an economic system per member of the total population, or circulates faster, we have a valuable if rough-and-ready indicator of economic progress. It suggests a shift from localized self-sufficiency towards the interdependence of regular exchange relationships. In a relatively well-monetized economy it also points, given constant prices, to a growth in real wealth per person. Advances in the means of creating money and credit, which are partly technical in the narrow sense and partly organizational and political, further an increasing volume of economic transactions, and hence growth generally. It is therefore significant that the period between the late T'ang and the early Sung should have seen a financial revolution.

Copper money was widely used in the early Chinese Empire, but during the confusion of the third century AD and the period of fragmentation that followed the fall of Lo-yang in 311, it tended to disappear and reappear according to the degree of political stability in the various regions. This phenomenon is clearly described in the biography of Chang Kuei, ruler of Liang-chou in the extreme north-west during the fourth century, contained in the *History of the Chin*:

> So Fu, General of the Treasury, observed to Chang Kuei: 'In antiquity metals, cowry shells, hides and silks were used as currency to overcome the disadvantages of using grain and silk [*sic*] for reckoning accounts. During the Former and the Later Han dynasties, the copper cash weighing five *shu* was exchanged everywhere without impediment. In the course of the T'ai-shih reign [265–74] the region west of the Yellow River was plunged into disorder; and consequently money was not used. People split up lengths of silk into sections; but after the cloth had been worn out, exchanges in the markets also became difficult . . . Although the central provinces are now in a state of rebellion, it is peaceful here and we ought to revive the five-*shu* cash in order to facilitate exchanges.' Chang Kuei agreed, and instituted

standardized cash which had a wide circulation and upon whose useful qualities the people depended.[1]

Two centuries later, even in the less-troubled south, the use of money was still sporadic and mainly confined to the large cities. According to the *Sui History*:

> At the beginning of the [southern] Liang dynasty [502–57], it was only in the capital of Nanking and in the provincial capitals of Wu, Ching, Hsiang, Liang and I that people used money. In the other provincial and commandery capitals, use was made without distinction of grains and fabrics for exchanges. In the territory of the provinces of Tonking and Kwangtung, gold and silver were exclusively used as units of currency.[2]

During the sixth century demand for money began to rise again. Shortage of copper led to the proliferation of iron coins, as the same source also records:

> Iron was cheap and easy to come by, so everybody secretly made money. After 535–45, iron coins therefore piled up everywhere. The prices of goods rose like an arrow. Those who carried out commercial transactions took cartloads of money with them. People no longer counted coins but only strings.[3]

Debasement forced the Liang state to control the currency by setting up scales at the entry to markets to detect underweight coins; and persons with underweight coins, or coins which contained lead or tin, were punished. By the time the empire was reunified under the Sui in 589, the Chinese economy may have been as monetized as in the heyday of the Han, but is unlikely to have been much more so.

A shortage of money persisted in the T'ang dynasty. There was widespread counterfeiting in spite of government efforts to establish a plentiful and uniform copper currency. By the early eighth century over 300,000 strings of cash were being minted annually; but by 834 this had fallen away to little over 100,000. There was not enough copper; and to mint and transport the new coins cost twice their face value, according to a report of 780. By the ninth century the various provinces were allowed to manufacture their own cash, and some twenty-three varieties resulted. Debasement increased, as did the use of less than the full number of cash in each string of a nominal 'one thousand'. The government banned hoarding and the use of copper for any purpose except coins and mirrors. To ease the pressure on the scarce coinage, it was also decreed that for medium and large transactions a mixture of cash, cloth and other commodities should be used rather than cash alone.

The pressure of the demand for money at this time came in other forms too. Taxes assessed in money affecting the majority of the male population were levied for the first time. These were the 'household levy' and, after 780, the land tax itself. Shortly after the fall of the T'ang, the first general tax to be levied in money, the poll tax or 'personal cash', made its appearance in the south, becoming nationwide after the Sung reunification.

There were regional variations in the degree to which money was actually used to pay taxes. In T'ang times Yang-chou paid both its land tax and other levies in cash; and the lower Yangtze area was generally ahead in this respect. Even here, however, the tenth century was still at most transitional. This emerges from a plea made by a statesman in the state of Southern T'ang, which covered what are today the provinces of Kiangsi, Anhwei and northern Kiangsu. He asked that the payment of taxes in cash should be stopped because of exceptional circumstances:

> [Around 920] officials were deputed to draw up registers and to determine the rates of taxation. Tax on the best land was assessed at two strings and 100 cash per *ch'ing*. On land of intermediate quality, it was one string and 800 cash; and on poor land 1,500 cash. This was all to be paid in ready cash in full hundreds. If ready cash was not available in sufficient quantities, the tax might be commuted at the going market rate to gold or silver. The poll tax and other imposts were likewise to be levied in cash. Sung Ch'i-ch'iu was a junior secretary in a ministry at this time, and he sent up a memorial asking that taxes should be commuted instead to silks valued at artificially high prices. 'Since the end of the T'ang,' he said, 'the Yangtze and Huai region has been the scene of warfare. Hostilities have only now ceased. The common people are at peace for the first time. If they are compelled to pay entirely in ready cash, or else commute it to gold or silver, it will be impossible for them to come by this money by means of farming. They will have to trade to get it. This is simply teaching the people to abandon what is fundamental for what is peripheral.'[4]

Hsu Chih-kao, the king of Southern T'ang, accepted this advice. Silks, overvalued at three to four times their market price, were temporarily accepted in lieu of money.

In the eleventh century, this situation of fluctuating monetization gave way to one where the volume of money in circulation vastly exceeded that of earlier times, and the monetary economy reached right down into the villages. Annual output of new copper cash under the Sung rose to 1·83 million strings early in the century, reaching a maximum of over six million strings after 1073. This was about twenty times the T'ang maximum and still only part of the picture. There was also an increase in the use of bills, tallies and tickets, of primitive sorts of fiduciary money, and above all of the newly invented paper money, which made its first appearance under government auspices in Szechwan in 1024. By the twelfth century China had already experienced the printing-press inflation; and proposals with a curiously modern ring were being made in the following century on the need to back paper currency with a suitable proportionate metallic reserve.

An immediate impression of the change may be had by contrasting late T'ang literature with that of Sung times. Thus Han Yü in a memorial on the salt monopoly, written in 822, said:

> Apart from the prefectural towns themselves, those who buy salt with ready cash will be less than two or three out of ten. Most of them will employ miscellaneous goods or grain, and barter them [to obtain salt] . . . In other cases, [the salt merchants] will sell on credit against amounts of grain, and agree to be repaid at harvest time.[5]

Fang Ta-tsung, writing four centuries later about his travels in Fukien, could note: 'Trade in the markets is customarily carried on by means of strings of a thousand copper cash. The people from the country villages exchange their produce there for these strings.'[6] And Shu Yueh-hsiang could write the following verses on T'ai-chou in Chekiang:

> In the remote hamlets the women sigh
> At the small return from the sale of vegetables –
> Turnips smoother than mother's milk,
> Globes plump as lambkins.
> With sacks across their shoulders, *and cash stowed in their belts*,
> They go to town to buy their meat.
> Vegetables are far more profitable than paddy;
> They can buy rice and have no fear of hunger.[7]

A flood of Sung copper coins spread overseas, especially to Japan and to south-east Asia. *The Record of the Customs of Cambodia* observed of that country: 'For small transactions they use rice and Chinese currency.'[8]

*

What were the causes of this monetary revolution?

One factor was the growing interdependence of the regional Chinese economies, based on the higher agricultural productivity and improved transport already described. This can be seen clearly during the brief period of political division known as the 'Five Dynasties and the Ten Kingdoms' which lasted approximately from 907 to 959, between the T'ang and the Sung. China at this time was a congeries of units about the size of the larger European states (see map 3). 'International' trade, in other words the inter-regional trade in times of unity and the related problem of the balance of payments, began to govern the financial stability and hence the currency policies of many of the governments of this time. This is worth examining in some detail as it has implications for the theme of Part One. Above all, it shows internal economic pressures, as the economy advanced, making political fragmentation rather than political unity the inherently unstable condition.

Thus the inland state of Ch'u in present-day Hunan had to buy most of its salt from the state of Southern T'ang, which controlled the Huai salt-fields in northern Kiangsu. The money to pay for these imports could only come from the deliberate state-sponsored promotion of the production and export of tea to north China. Conversely, Southern T'ang revenues depended to a great extent on its earnings from exporting salt. The loss of the Huai region between 955 and 958 to the state of Northern Chou in the north China plain, and the need thereafter to purchase salt from 'abroad', dealt it a blow from which it never fully recovered, succumbing to the Sung not long afterwards.

Actions taken in the field of monetary policy by one government were apt to have repercussions across the whole of China and provoke reprisals and countermeasures. An instance of this was the adoption of a lead currency by the state of Min in present-day Fukien. This threatened other states, through foreign trade, with the loss of their copper cash and silver in exchange for the inferior Min coins. To avert this danger the state of Southern Han, in Kwangtung and Kwangsi, followed suit a few years later with its own lead coins. In 924 or 925 the state of Ch'u, which had close commercial relations with Southern

Han, did likewise. The eleventh-century historian Ssu-ma Kuang explained Ch'u's action as follows:

> Merchants from all quarters converged upon Hunan. The land produced an abundance of lead and iron, so Ma Yin [its ruler] followed the proposal put forward by military judicial commissioner Kao Yü that they should cast lead and iron coins. Merchants were unable to use these coins outside the area, so they used them to buy other commodities before they left. In this way Ma Yin was able to have the surplus produce of his region exchanged for all the products of the world. His kingdom prospered because of it.[9]

The dynasties of the north China plain were also affected by the policies of the southern states. Thus in 924 the Later T'ang, perpetually unable to export enough goods to pay for its southern imports, and its currency adulterated with southern lead coins, banned absolutely the export of copper cash from its cities. This proved to be unworkable, and was modified two years later to prohibition on the export of amounts above five hundred copper coins. On the other hand, the richest state of all, that of Wu-Yüeh in present-day Chekiang and southern Kiangsu, resisted pressures to go over to a lead or iron currency. When a proposal was put forward in 946 to introduce iron coins, the younger brother of the ruler opposed it in these terms:

> There are eight harmful consequences attendant upon the minting of iron coins. The first of these is that once the new coins have entered into circulation, all the old coins will flow into neighbouring states. The second is that, since the new coins will be usable in our country but not in other countries, merchants will cease their activities and the circulation of commodities will come to a stop . . .[10]

Eleven years later, notwithstanding these opinions, iron coins were cast. The Southern T'ang also avoided using iron or lead currency until some time after 960, when its economic viability had been undermined by the loss of its salt-producing areas. It seems likely that it was the strong position of these last two states as exporters of salt, grains, silk and teas, for which payment in copper could often be demanded, that allowed them for a time to avoid debasing their currencies.

This world of nations at once trading and competing with each other produced policies in some ways like the mercantilism and bullionism of the West many centuries later. Rulers attempted to hoard large reserves of copper for strategic purposes, and to prevent any net outflow of the metal from their domains. One offshoot of such a policy was the famous pottery currency of north-east China in the early tenth century:

> Liu Jen-kung, the military governor of Lu-lung, was proud, extravagant, greedy, and possessed of a violent temper. He was continually anxious about the weakness of the city walls of Yu-chou and so he built a fort on the Ta-an mountain . . . He collected all the copper cash within his territories and stored them in the hills. He ordered his people to make their cash of clay, and he also forbade tea merchants from Kiangnan to enter his lands. He had grasses gathered from the hillsides and sold them as tea.[11]

Hung Tsun's *Treatise on Coinage*, published in 1149, says of Liu Yen who founded Southern Han:

> He did not have enough money to meet government expenses and so he had lead coins minted, ten of which were exchanged for one copper one. After the Ch'ien-ho reign-period [during the 940s], the government acquired a large reserve of copper cash. Inside the cities lead was used, and outside the cities copper. It was forbidden to take it either out or in. Those who disobeyed were punished with death. Official salaries were only paid in copper as a special favour.[12]

Liu Jen-kung banned tea merchants lest they cause a drain of copper. Liu Yen forbade copper in the cities presumably because it was here that all large-scale foreign commerce was conducted.

Underlying all these manoeuvres, then, was the shortage of copper; and the search for additional supplies was carried on with a single-minded intensity that had both its grim and its humorous aspects. States either prohibited altogether or limited the casting of copper utensils. Sometimes they also kept the prices of such utensils artificially low as a disincentive to the melting down of coins to make them. In 938, under the Later Chin dynasty then ruling the north China plain, another strategy was tried: it was decreed that anyone who wished to do so might cast his own coins:

> Currency is the most important thing on which a state depends. The abuse of melting it down is widespread. Additional minting is unheard of. We are therefore issuing these regulations in order to make our people wealthy and numerous. The order is to be given that . . . all those who have copper, whether they are private persons or in the public service, are to be permitted to mint copper cash . . . We are

deputing salt and iron commissioners to cast samples and issue them to the various provinces . . . If there is still anxiety in any place about an insufficiency of copper, then the order should be given to the various provinces that any of the common people who open up long abandoned copper-works may carry on refining as they please, and are to enjoy the right of permanent ownership. The officials are not to tax them. Their raw or refined copper may as before be everywhere sold to the state. They may also themselves cast cash for circulation; but any remaining copper may not at pleasure be cast into copper utensils.[13]

Since there was no profit in casting copper coins unless they were debased with lead or tin, this attempt to solve the problem by means of laissez-faire was unsuccessful.

Emperor T'ai-tsu of the Later Chou, the dynasty which followed the Later Chin as the masters of northern China, proclaimed death for anyone melting down coins. His successor, the emperor Shih-tsung, issued the famous 'Edict Sweeping Away the Buddhas' in 956:

Currency is the foremost matter of profit for a state. Under recent dynasties minting has long ceased. People have not even been prevented from melting down coins. Abuses have grown worse with the passing of time. We are now extracting copper, having it refined, and setting up an Inspectorate to mint cash, in the hope that this will benefit both public and private interests. Regulations must be promulgated. Henceforth, except for the Buddhist objects at court, for weapons of war, official objects, mirrors, bells, chimes, cymbals, drums (?), fire-pearls [that is, burning-mirrors], and hand-bells, all other copper objects are without exception to be forbidden. The copper used for religious statues, for utensils and for all kinds of ornaments and shears throughout the two capitals and the provinces must be broken up and handed in to the government within fifty days. Copper handed in by private persons shall be paid for in cash according to its weight.[14]

Although proof is lacking, it seems that only those Buddhist statues in temples not on the official lists, and those in private homes, were affected. Emperor Shih-tsung is however said personally to have smashed the Buddha of Great Compassion at Chen-chou, remarking with dry humour to his prime minister 'The Buddhist religion considers that one's head, one's eyes and one's brains should all be put ungrudgingly at the service of the multitude of living creatures. How much less should it begrudge a copper statue!' Pious legend has it that he was

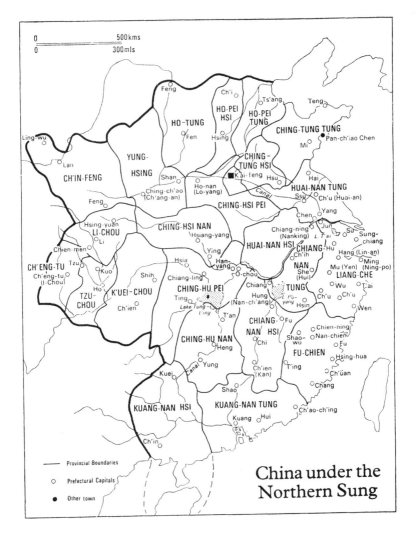

Map 5

later afflicted with an abscess on his chest in the very place where he had first struck the image.

From one point of view the iron, lead and pottery currencies of the tenth century may be regarded as primitive fiduciary currencies. In other words, they were paper money made of metal or clay. The convention of using strings of cash with less than a hundred or a thousand coins on them as equivalent to a hundred or a thousand may likewise be seen as a move in this direction, if one imagines the process continued to its logical conclusion when nothing is left but the piece of cord itself. With such practices widespread and copper in critically short supply, it is not surprising that in the early eleventh century true paper money was invented.

Bills for the transfer and exchange of cash and commodities had been known since T'ang times. The earliest of all were probably the 'food tickets' of the divisional militia mentioned in chapter 5. In the eighth century, the T'ang government developed the so-called 'flying cash' system on the basis of the complementary north–south flows of money arising from the tax system on the one hand and the tea trade on the other. Merchants could pay in money at the capital and receive in return a certificate from the government which, when presented at any provincial treasury, entitled the bearer to draw an equivalent sum. Both state and merchants were thereby spared the hazards of the transport of large sums of copper cash.* The Sung dynasty operated an essentially similar system under the name of 'money of convenience'. According to Ma Tuan-lin's *Comprehensive Study of Civilization*, a work compiled in the thirteenth century:

> In the time of emperor T'ai-tsu [960–75] the old T'ang system of 'flying money' was adopted. Commoners were permitted to pay in cash at the capital and draw it out in the provinces . . . Originally, merchants were allowed to pay in their cash to the Treasury of the Left and be repaid out of provincial funds; but when they presented their applications to the financial authorities and then paid in their money to the Treasury, the offices through whose hands the matter passed would illegally deduct twenty cash from every string of a thousand. In 970 the Bureau for Money of Convenience was established. It was ordered that merchants who paid in cash should present their applications to this Bureau, which would on the same day pass them on to the Treasury of the Left and issue certificates. As before, the provincial authorities were commanded that, whenever a merchant arrived bearing one of these certificates, payment should be made to him on the same day without procrastination, any offenders against this provision to be fined. After this, no one suffered from delays. By 997 merchants were drawing over 1·7 million strings

---

* There was an analogous system in Rome, the *publica permutatio*. See J. P. V. D. Balsdon, *Rome: Story of an Empire* (London: 1970), p. 53.

worth of money of convenience [annually]. By 1021 the sum had risen by a further 1·13 million strings.[15]

The chief weakness of this rudimentary nationwide remittance system was that it worked in one direction only, from the capital to the provinces. Like the postal service, however, it was both symbol and cause of a higher degree of imperial integration.

During the period of the later T'ang and the Five Dynasties the private sector also produced a number of paper credit instruments. Deposit shops stored cash, gold and silver for a fee, and would honour cheques drawn against these funds by a depositor. Both they and the gold- and silver-smiths issued promissory notes which in the course of time came to be used much like money. These notes, or something very similar, are mentioned in the *Treatise on Money*:

> Ma Yin [the ruler of the tenth-century state of Ch'u] began by casting lead coins. These circulated in the cities while outside the cities copper cash were used. Many merchants melted down these lead coins and carried them off north of the Yangtze. Kao Yü requested the minting of iron coins six inches in circumference . . . and exchanging at the rate of ten for one [copper cash]. Since these coins were so thick and heavy, exchanges in the markets were carried on by means of certificates on which the quantities were marked.[16]

These notes or bills were the immediate ancestors of paper money.

Paper money itself first appeared in Szechwan, as the result of a combination of circumstances. The state of Later Shu, which ruled this area during the mid tenth century, had introduced an iron coinage alongside the existing copper money as a means of financing its military preparations. Initially, therefore, Szechwan resembled the rest of China south of the Yangtze when the new Sung government began to undertake the task of restoring a unified copper currency throughout the empire; but the relative economic isolation of the great inland region with its four provinces made it possible to treat it differently. Ostensibly as a temporary measure, its copper coins were drained off to remedy the shortage elsewhere in the south. Then, in 979, this policy was reversed. The ban on bringing copper into Szechwan was lifted; and a phased ten-year plan was adopted for the conversion of all taxes and excise on government monopoly goods to payment in copper. The results were disastrous. The state made the error of setting the conversion ratio for the percentage of iron coins cumulatively phased out year by year at a cash-for-cash parity with copper, a much more valuable metal. Demand for copper rose steeply. Merchants who imported it into Szechwan could exchange one copper cash for fourteen of the local iron cash. As they then had to buy Szechwanese goods with their profits, iron not being legal tender elsewhere, the value of iron relative to copper in Szechwan was still further depressed. In 982, the year for which it was decreed that thirty per cent of taxes had to be paid in copper, the people of Szechwan in their desperation are said to have 'hacked pieces from Buddhist statues, melted down utensils, and pillaged old burial-grounds to get four or five copper cash'. The phased scheme had to be abandoned. Szechwan continued to have a different monetary system from the rest of China, and to suffer from cumbrously inconvenient coins.

In this situation paper promissory notes came into their own. Large quantities were issued by sixteen officially recognized merchant houses but around 1022 this system broke down from abuse. The government itself had to step in and take responsibility for the paper money, in order to prevent what would otherwise have been a disastrous economic recession. The full story is given by Li Yu in his *Factual Account of the Sung Dynasty* written about a century later:

> Originally, more than ten wealthy commoners in I-chou [Ch'eng-tu] mutually guaranteed each other for the issue of notes of exchange. Every year [in return for this privilege] they provided the officials with the personnel for measuring the tax-grain taken in summer and autumn at the granaries, and with men and materials for the repair of damaged dykes. These rich persons would meet at regular intervals and [agree] to print the notes on the same kind of paper. The printed design would feature buildings, trees, men and other objects, and bear the seal of the shop of issue. Each one would have a secret super-scription in interlocking red and black to serve as a private mark. The value in strings of cash would be written in, there being no maximum or minimum amount. These notes of exchange were issued in return for the ready cash which people deposited. They circulated in enor-mous quantities without regard for distance, and were exchanged in the streets and markets. If anyone wanted ready cash in place of a note of exchange, the merchants would deduct thirty cash per string of a thousand as their profit. Every year, just before the silk cocoons, the rice, or the wheat were about to come to maturity, they would print off more such notes of exchange, either on one of these occasions or two, with as much celerity as one would mint coins. They would then

buy up huge stocks. They owned a profusion of inns, shops, mansions, gardens, fields and precious goods. There were also some people who counterfeited these notes, which provoked not a few lawsuits. Sometimes many people would come to demand their cash, pressing their claims in a crowd. The shops would seal up their doors, and so provoke a riot. The authorities would then send out officers to bring the situation under control, and the poor people would be defrauded by receiving only seven or eight hundred cash for each string of a thousand. Kuan Chen, the Remonstrancer in charge of [Ch'eng-tu] Prefecture, memorialized:

> When I took up my post here, I urged Wang Ch'ang-i and the other issuers of notes to close their note-shops, seal up their printing tables, and issue no more. It took them until the spring of this year to settle their repayments. There are issuers of notes in the other outlying counties, and they have all submitted statements that they have destroyed their printing tables. I would beg that the order be given to I-chou that henceforth it shall be illegal for people to set up shops for the issue of notes of exchange after the manner of former times.

The imperial decree replying to this told transportation commissioner Chang Jo-ku and the magistrate of I-chou, Hsueh T'ien, to settle this matter together. They memorialized:

> Iron coins are used in Szechwan. Ten strings of small cash weigh sixty catties, and exchange for one string of large cash weighing twelve catties. It is difficult to carry more than three to five of these strings when buying and selling in the marketplace; and the system of notes of exchange has long been a convenience to the people. At the present time, there are no notes of exchange circulating in the markets. The system ought to be taken over by the government . . . and a separate bureau instituted for the purpose . . . The notes of exchange which it issues should have precisely the same dimensions as those previously put out by the common people, and be sealed with the copper prefectural seal . . .

An imperial decree then commanded Wang Chi-ming, the provincial judge of Tzu-chou, to come to a final decision with Hsueh T'ien and Chang Jo-ku and report back. They said:

> Since a stop was put to the notes of exchange, the merest handful of people have been coming to the markets to buy and sell. It would have a useful stabilizing effect if private notes were to be abolished and official ones produced in their place . . . As previously, we would request that a register be established and that notes be issued in denominations of from one to ten strings, imprinted with a seal, entered in the register, and sent to the office of the official in charge. When persons bring in iron cash of either the large or the small

variety, they shall pay them to the treasury at the regulation discount and be issued with notes matched by number with stubs so that they may enjoy the convenience of their use . . . When notes are returned, the stubs in the register are to be checked off.[17]

Thus was paper money born.

Like the merchants' notes which they replaced, early government notes were normally issued against the deposit of money by members of the public. Their period of issue was limited to three years, after which they were recalled to be exchanged for new notes or coins, perhaps because the paper tended to have worn out by this time. Apart from the discount charged for issue, they were fully convertible. For them to become exactly like present-day paper money a few further developments were necessary. The state had to issue notes directly up to a specified limit, without waiting for public demand. The fixed periods of circulation had to be done away with. A cash reserve had to be set up representing a proportion of the value of the total issue. The option of inconvertibility had to be opened. All of these, except for the last, seem to have come about fairly rapidly, though the changes are hard to document. The temptation to print notes without adequate backing first became great when the government began to suffer from financial troubles as a result of the war with Hsi-hsia, the Tangut Kingdom which from 1032 to 1227 controlled what is now the western part of Inner Mongolia and the province of Kansu. Some 1·2 million strings worth of unbacked notes were issued in what is now south-east Kansu province shortly before mid-century; and the ill effects flowed back into Szechwan. By the 1070s notes with face value 1,000 were only worth between 940 and 960 cash.

By the end of the eleventh century paper money had spread into much of north China; and under the Chin and the Southern Sung governments in the twelfth century it became established on a regular basis in both north and south. In 1161, the Southern Sung put into circulation about ten million notes, worth about double that number of strings of cash, keeping several more millions in the official treasuries and a small but apparently adequate cash reserve. These notes circulated alongside the copper currency, as the *Sung History* explains:

> With the exception of payment for government monopoly salt, which had to be in cash, those provinces without communications by inland waterway were permitted to make their tax payments entirely in paper money. Prefectures and military prefectures located by rivers paid

half in paper and half in cash. A similar practice was followed among the common people for the mortgaging or sale of fields, houses, horses, cattle, boats and carts, but complete payment in notes was [also] permitted.[18]

Under the Chin Tartars, notes almost ousted cash altogether; and the Mongol rulers issued notes for as little as five or even two cash. Under the latter dynasty, silver and gold rather than copper were used as a reserve, and in 1268 so-called 'Equitable Ratio Treasuries' were set up in each province at which paper notes might be exchanged for either metal. According to Liu Hsuan, who was president of the ministry of personnel late in the thirteenth century:

> If there was the slightest impediment in the flow of paper money, the authorities would unload silver and accept paper as payment for it. If any loss of popular confidence was feared, then not a cash's worth of the accumulated reserves of gold and silver in the province concerned would be moved elsewhere. At that time, still very little paper money was issued without a reserve to back it, and it was therefore easy to control . . . For seventeen or eighteen years the value of paper money did not fluctuate.[19]

The removal of the provincial reserves to the capital under the tyranny of Ahmed late in this century, together with the excessive issue of notes, led to the first dose of inflation. Liu pleaded in astonishingly modern fashion for deflationary policies and cuts in governmental expenditure:

> The only way to relieve the situation is to stop any further printing of paper money of denominations of a thousand cash or over, and to print merely the smaller denominations. The latter should be issued to the various treasuries so that they may give them in exchange for notes that are worn out or illegible. This will facilitate the making of small payments by the people. It is necessary to reassure the public by having due regard to our basic reserves of gold and silver when issuing these notes . . . National expenditure should be calculated with reference to government income. Thus, if the annual yield from taxation amounts to a value of one million ingots of silver then annual expenditure should be set somewhere between 500,000 and 700,000 ingots. The remaining surplus of old paper money should be destroyed by burning. If we act on these lines for the next ten years, then prices will be reduced to half their present level, even if they do not sink to their original level. There is no short cut. Producing a new kind of paper money in order to bolster up the old would only amount to a

change of names. It would in no wise be comparable to creating a gold and silver backing, and so preventing further damage to military and administrative finances.[20]

A penetrating analysis, but his advice was not taken. Fifty years later, as the dynasty began to collapse, there was a second and much more severe inflation. 'In order to pay the army, countless notes were printed every day. They were loaded onto an endless line of boats and carts . . . At the capital, paper money worth ten ingots would not buy one tenth of a picul of grain.'[21] In spite of strenuous efforts by the Ming dynasty, a satisfactory system of paper money was never again established in China by the government until modern times.

An analysis of the reasons for this must be deferred until the last part of the book (see pages 221–2, 293–4). Here we may simply note that, from having begun as a brilliant solution to a shortage of copper cash, paper money gradually turned into a bureaucratic monstrosity that hampered the productive forces whose growth it had originally done much to foster. In general terms this was a part of the obscure but profound transformation of Chinese society and economy which began in the fourteenth century, and which was to render late traditional China very different from the China of the period of economic revolution.

*

Paper money, important though it was, cannot be considered apart from the proliferation of public and private devices for providing credit or transferring funds in Sung and Yuan times. Hung Shih, prefect of Hui-chou in what is now southern Anhwei around the middle of the twelfth century, commented on the widespread use of private notes there, observing that if the order had been suddenly given that all government transactions were to be in ready cash, 'the cash would all be used up within a year or six months and there would be no means to restore it to circulation'. Commodity bills for quantities of tea, flour, bamboo and wine were often used as money under the Mongols; and within circumscribed areas so were the notes of hand and wooden or bamboo tallies put out by the proprietors of tea-houses, wine-houses, bath-houses and brothels in the large cities. The ordination licences of Buddhist priests were titles to exemption from taxes; and they were therefore issued as a means of raising funds, themselves becoming negotiable and an important form of quasi-money. In Shao-chou in

Kuang-nan-tung the government bought lead and tin from miners with 'lead and tin notes'. These were redeemed for cash in sequence by date of issue, and only some considerable time after this date. At least one speculator made a handsome profit (before he was impeached) by buying up these notes from the miners at a discount. In 1131 the state used 'cash certificates' to induce merchants to bring supplies to Wu-chou, a relatively inaccessible part of Liang-che province. Merchants were paid locally for their goods in these certificates which they could then cash at the capital or Shao-hsing with ten cash per thousand added as a bonus.

Credit mechanisms were also routinely inserted into the organization of production, storage and distribution. Hung Mai has a description of this in the twelfth-century hemp cloth industry:

> Ch'ien T'ai was a commoner from Fu-chou prefecture [in Kiangsi] who made his fortune by selling hemp cloth. Every year he advanced capital as a loan to spinners in the counties of Ch'ung-jen, Le-an and Chin-chi. In the counties of Chi-chou prefecture he had brokers to take charge of his affairs. In the sixth month he would go in person to collect the cloth from them, only returning late in the autumn. This went on for a long time.[22]

A glance at map 5 will show that Ch'ien's operations probably covered a span of over a hundred miles. He also advanced money to his brokers so that they could build storehouses holding several thousand lengths of cloth.

Among merchants credit had become commonplace, as may be seen from the following none too moral tale, again told by Hung Mai:

> Mr Chang was a wealthy inhabitant of Hsing-chou [in present-day Hopei]. He originally made his living by selling hemp goods in partnership with other small merchants. One evening, after having closed the door of his tea-house, he heard a man moaning outside. He went out to take a look and found there a criminal who had that morning been flogged to death by the market police. This man said to him:
> 'My vital breath was cut off but I have revived. If I have some water I can still live. If the patrolmen see me, I am afraid that I shall die a second death.'
> Chang at once dragged him into his house, gently loosened his bonds and after laying him on a bed covered him with a rush mat so that he fell into a sleep. He and his wife tended him carefully and fed him on dumplings and gruel. Not even their son and daughter-in-law

were aware of what was going on. After two months had passed, the scars on the man's ribs had healed and he was able to walk. Chang gave him travelling money and personally escorted him out of the city before dawn, never having asked him his name, or where he might come from.

Ten long years later, a great merchant came riding on horseback with a retinue of followers, bringing five thousand lengths of hemp cloth to market. The big brokers all outdid each other to welcome him but he said:

'Is broker Chang here? I want to consign my goods to him!'

Everybody tittered and went off to call Chang. Chang excused himself, saying:

'The capital of my firm does not come to more than a few tens of thousands of cash. For a big transaction like this you should select several persons of wealth and standing.'

'I must insist on putting you to this trouble,' answered the merchant. 'Simply find me a good shopkeeper to whom you can sell the cloth on credit, hand the contract to me, and wait for me to return. I shall be back before very long to collect my money.'

Chang hastened to do as he had been told. A few days later the merchant said to him:

'You must get ready some wine for us to drink, but don't invite any other guests.'

When he arrived, he summoned Chang's wife to drink with them. When they were merry he rose and said:

'Don't you recognize me? I am the man whom you cared for beneath your bed ten years ago. All my life long I had been a robber. I came and went through a dozen prefectures and never met with failure. Only in Hsing-chou was I caught the moment that I appeared. From your hands I received the favour of a second life. After leaving your doors I pointed to Heaven and swore an oath: 'I shall never murder anyone again but make a great sum of money with which to repay Mr Chang, and after that never thieve again!' Just then I was crossing the T'ai-hang hills and met a man travelling by himself. I robbed him of over a thousand strings of cash and set myself up as a merchant. Today I have lands and mansions in Chin and Feng [that is, in Shensi], and have specially brought you this cloth to repay you and your wife for the kindness which you did me. Here is the original contract. You may keep all the money and use it in your business. I shall not be coming back.'

So saying, he bowed in farewell and departed.[23]

12 · The revolution in market structure and urbanization

Even before the foundation of the Ch'in empire in the third century BC, commerce played an important part in the Chinese economy. But mercantile life did not put down such deep roots as it did in some other Old World cultures. In lower Mesopotamia the activities of traders and money-lenders figured prominently in written legal codes before archaic Chinese civilization had even begun to take on distinctive shape. We have records of partnerships, loans at interest, and deeds of sale and purchase from the Babylonia of the early second millennium BC. For China before the Han dynasty there is nothing comparable.

Around the third century BC there seems to have been an upsurge in trade, and a powerful merchant class came into being. According to Ch'ao Ts'o writing early in the following century:

> Well-to-do merchants accumulate goods and redouble their profits, while the less well-off sit in their shops and sell. They control the markets and daily enjoy their ease in the cities. They take advantage of the pressing needs of the government to sell at twice the normal price. Their sons do not plough or hoe. Their daughters do not raise silkworms or weave. They have fancy clothing and stuff themselves on millet and meat. They earn fortunes while suffering none of the hardships which the farmers suffer. Their wealth enables them to hobnob with princes and marquises, and to dispose of greater power than the officials. They wear themselves out in the search for profit . . . and grow plump by means of hard dealing.[1]

The Han historian Ssu-ma Ch'ien describes how in 'centres of communication and the great cities' it was possible to buy an astonishing assortment of alcoholic drinks, prepared foodstuffs, silks, hemp cloth, dyes, hides, furs, lacquerware, copper and iron goods. 'The large entrepreneurs,' he wrote, 'make their way to the commandery capitals, middling ones to the county capitals and minor ones to the country villages in numbers too great to be counted.'[2] Fortunes were made from such commonplace items as pickled food; and in a few areas manor organizations and well-to-do peasants made cheap textiles for sale.

Even those otherwise outside the market economy were often forcibly drawn into it by the government's requirement that certain taxes be paid in specified commodities. Not infrequently these had to be bought. Taxes and other levies, which touched the entire empire, were the precursors of the deeper commercialization of later times. Political pressure acted as a pumping mechanism to create a circulation of goods of which economic demand by itself was incapable. The expenditure of wealth derived from taxation created new industries and new trade in the service of the upper classes, but generating skills that were in course of time to be of wider use.

Most of the population remained little affected by commerce. Apart from iron tools and salt, production for the market during the Han dynasty was largely limited to supplying the needs of the upper classes. Legal trading was confined to specified areas in, or just outside, the main administrative centres, where shops and stalls in the same line of business were placed together under government control. Thus the *Han History* tells us, in its chapter on cruel officials, that Yin Shang had merchants and artisans in the capital, who had not been officially registered, buried alive in batches of a hundred with other malefactors in a subterranean dungeon. Succeeding dynasties down to and including the T'ang continued this restriction of commerce to specified areas and firms. Something of the nature of this system may be glimpsed from an account written by Liu Yü-hsi in 808 on the moving of the market at Lang-chou, a small prefecture in north-western Hunan:

> On the day when the order to move the market was first issued, those responsible for the market register all came and marked off the different sections on either side of the road. They set out the spaces for stalls in exactly the same order from left to right, and sequence from front to rear as was used in the walled market place within the city. Notices proclaimed the names of the various rows and sections, and made known the prices and named the commodities on sale.[3]

In the larger cities, and especially in the enormous markets of Ch'ang-an, which covered the area of all medieval London, there were correspondingly more elaborate arrangements for policing, and for the control of weights and measures, and prices.

Without government permission it was illegal to set up markets other than those officially sanctioned and supervised. Yet these markets were too few and usually too distant to serve the needs of the peasantry once better techniques of production and transport began to provide them with a marketable surplus. In consequence, a separate system of unofficial markets, usually held once every few days, gradually grew up in the countryside to cater for the needs of the farmers. An early mention of this is in Shen Huai-yuan's *Gazetteer for Southern Yueh*, which was compiled in the third or fourth century AD:

> The markets of Yueh [that is, of south-eastern China] are 'empty places' and mostly found on village commons. Merchants are either invited beforehand to come, or are attracted by displays of singing and dancing. Ching-nan [Hunan] and Ling-piao [Kwangtung] are similar.[4]

By the later part of the T'ang dynasty such markets were sufficiently numerous for Tu Mu to write: 'In the region of the lower Yangtze and the Huai the sites of village markets are all at the confluence of rivers. In them live many rich and powerful households.'[5] The official markets thus faced a growing challenge from the multiplying unofficial markets. At the same time bureaucratic controls on the city markets were slackening, and merchants were setting up shops and stalls wherever they pleased in the urban areas, rather than just in the quarter set aside for them. The old system gave way during the ninth century to an era of vastly increased commercial freedom.

A deeper transformation was also at work. The Chinese rural economy was becoming linked with the market mechanism. Trade was no longer just the supplier of luxuries, but also the provider of necessities. A large interregional traffic developed in staples such as rice; and a 'national market' appeared in the sense that many local products, such as particular types of paper, became both nationally known and nationally available.

One consequence of this was the creation of a national internal customs network, which replaced the system of market regulation as the means by which the state controlled and taxed commerce. Already in the later eighth century there had been 'officers in the major cities in the provinces to inspect the goods of merchants and to levy twenty cash per thousand'.[6] In the next century, the military men who held most of the local power turned the control stations which the government had set up along main roads (inspecting the travel permits of persons passing along them) into de facto customs-houses levying a tax on merchants' goods. Po Chü-i observed that 'Most of the control points on the land and water routes in every region demand a percentage levy.'[7] Sometimes the rates charged by this still only semi-legal system were so heavy that commerce was impeded, or the merchants took to the sideroads in an effort to bypass the customs houses. In the tenth century the Later Chin dynasty regularized the situation, distinguishing goods simply in transit from those to be sold within the locality concerned. By 1077, under the Sung, there were about two thousand customs houses for such transit and sales taxes, and the number increased with time. By 1205, for example, in the three prefectures of Kuang-chou, Ch'ao-ch'ing and Hui-chou alone there were eighty-three customs posts, all of them 'at the sites of village periodic markets'. If this was representative of the average national density, there would have been close to ten thousand customs houses in north and south China by this date. Clearly they must have accounted for much of the government's revenue.

★

Increased contact with the market made the Chinese peasantry into a class of adaptable, rational, profit-oriented, petty entrepreneurs. A wide range of new occupations opened up in the countryside. In the hills, timber was grown for the booming boatbuilding industry and for the construction of houses in the expanding cities. Vegetables and fruit were produced for urban consumption. All sorts of oils were pressed for cooking, lighting, waterproofing, and to go in haircreams and medicines. Sugar was refined, crystallized, and used as a preservative. Fish were raised in ponds and reservoirs to the point where the rearing of newly-hatched young fish for stock became a major business. Paper production soared as a result of the demand from the printing industry and a bureaucratic government. Besides being used for books, documents and correspondence, it was also employed for money, for articles of clothing, for lampshades, for wrapping and for toilet-paper. Hemp, ramie and silk textiles were produced in countless villages. Growing mulberry leaves became in itself a profitable undertaking, and there were special markets for mulberry saplings. Peasants also made lacquer goods and iron tools.

When villagers lacked raw materials they often imported them. In

Chu Mu's geographical compendium *The Triumphant Vision of the World*, published in 1240, it is noted of Wen-chou in Chekiang that:

> Wen-chou is situated on salty land impregnated with mud. The soil is meagre and hard to cultivate. The people work hard and prosper as a result of their efforts. Thus although the region is unsuitable for mulberry trees they weave silk, and although it is unsuitable for the lacquer-tree they make lacquer vessels.[8]

In the early fourteenth century, baby fish from the Chiang-chou hatcheries were regularly carried up to two hundred miles in special containers to be raised in the ponds of peasants in Fukien and Chekiang for eventual sale in the market. Conversely, in many areas specialization often meant that food had to be imported from outside. Shen Kua mentions the case of a Hunan county so wholly devoted to tea cultivation that even the countryfolk bought their vegetables in the markets. A gazetteer for Hui-chou in the later twelfth century describes that prefecture's economy:

> The hills produce fine timber which is every year bound up into rafts. Those who go down the Che River obtain great wealth . . . The Ch'i-men River flows into the P'o-yang Lake. The people take tea, lacquer, paper and wood along it to Kiangsi, *upon which they depend for their supply of rice.*[9]

Ch'en Fu's *Treatise on Agriculture* tells how completely silk had displaced rice as the basis of the peasant economy of An-chi county in Hu-chou:

> Some of the people there rely exclusively upon silkworms for their living. A family of ten persons will raise ten frames of silkworms. From each frame twelve catties of cocoons will be obtained; and from each catty comes 1·3 ounces of silk thread. From every five ounces of thread one length of small silk may be woven, and this exchanges for 1·4 piculs of rice. The price of silk usually follows that of rice. Thus supplying one's food and clothing by these means ensures a high degree of stability. One month's toil [at sericulture] is better than exertion all year round [at farming]; and they are afflicted neither by parching drought nor overflowing floods.[10]

A comparable situation was to be found in the Tung-t'ing hills of Lake T'ai, the slopes of which were given over entirely to growing oranges, and whose grain supply was entirely imported.

*

The growth of a system of local markets was both consequence and cause of this commercialized peasant economy. Most of these markets were small-scale affairs held once every few days for a few hours early in the morning. Some verses written by Chou Mi as a commentary on a painting give a good idea of their character:

> The small market –
> People with their bundles of tea or salt,
> Chickens cackling, dogs barking,
> Firewood being exchanged for rice
> Fishes being bartered for wine.
> Here and there –
> Green tavern flags
> Where elderly gentlemen sit propped,
> Drowsy with drink.[11]

At the larger markets a degree of internal organization and control was necessary. Some idea of this is given in the poem 'On the Way to Kuei-tsung Monastery' by the eleventh-century poet-monk Tao-ch'ien:

> The morning sun not yet risen from the lake,
> Bramble thickets seem for a moment like gates of pine.
> Aged trees steep the precipitous cliffs in gloom;
> The apes' desolate calls float down.
>
> The path turns, and a valley opens
> With a village in the distance barely visible.
> Along the track, shouting and laughing,
> Come farmhands overtaking and overtaken in turn
> Off to match wits a few hours at the market.
>
> The lodges and stores are countless as the clouds.
> They bring linen fabrics and paper-mulberry paper,
> Or drive pullets and sucking pigs ahead of them.
> Brushes and dustpans are piled this way and that –
> Too many domestic trifles to list them all.
> An elderly man controls the busy trafficking,
> And everyone respects his slightest indications.
> Meticulously careful he compares
> The yardsticks one by one,
> And turns them over slowly in his hands.[12]

The main power behind a market was usually the influential local persons or merchants who had contracted to collect the taxes on trade for the government. In the largest markets of all an official controller's office would be responsible for the levy of customs and for security. If two market towns were too close together, there would be intense rivalry between the leading citizens of each, who would try to obtain exclusive recognition for their own market and have the other suppressed. Four to eight miles seems to have been the closest that village markets could come at this time without such friction arising.

These local markets were the foundation of a national hierarchy of higher markets linking almost the entire Chinese economy. There were three main regions: north China, centred on K'ai-feng; south China, centred on the complex of cities north and south of the T'ai Lake; and Szechwan, centred on the cities of the Ch'eng-tu plain.

Within each of these regions there was, in Sung times, an increase in economic interdependence between localities, particularly in staples such as grain and cloth. This may be illustrated by the trade in rice in the southern region during the twelfth and thirteenth centuries. There were three areas which normally produced a surplus for export: the Yangtze delta, the Canton delta and the central Kan River valley. Rice flowed from these into the chronically deficient areas along the southeastern coast, into localities specializing in non-agricultural products, and into the major cities. Thus Chou Pi-ta wrote of Fukien that 'The land of Min is cramped and its fields few. Every year they rely on rice from Kuang-nan, and are constantly worried lest the merchant ships fail to arrive on time.'[13] On the prefecture of Yen-chou one preface to a local gazetteer observed 'The common people's daily purchases of rice come from the merchant boats of Ch'ü-chou, Wu-chou, Su-chou and K'ua-chou.' The twelfth-century statesman Lü Tsu-ch'ien also said of it that, 'If there is no rain for ten days, so that the streams run dry and the merchants' boats cannot come through, the price of rice rises abruptly, and great and small will make a clamour just as in a year of dearth.'[14] Yen-chou was a poor prefecture whose main source of revenue was from its position as an entrepôt in the timber trade. Ch'ih-chou was another chronically deficient area. According to Yuan Shuo-yu:

Land in this prefecture is limited, and the people are poor. Even when there has been a good harvest, the inhabitants must rely for rice to eat upon the merchant boats from the upper Yangtze which come down-river and sell it near the prefectural capital, if they are to have enough.[15]

The capital at Hang-chou was supplied by merchants with about 116,000 tons of rice a year, in addition to the massive amounts of tax grain and private manorial grain which it presumably consumed. Chien-k'ang, now Nanking, required about half this amount and O-chou, now Wu-ch'ang, depended on rice brought to it from as far away as Heng-chou, three hundred miles distant by river. Just as important as the regular rice trade were the temporary shipments made to almost any and every area following a bad harvest, when prices made it worthwhile for merchants to divert grain in its direction. There was also an extensive intraregional trade in other bulky commodities such as timber, sugar and iron. Thus a fourteenth-century gazetteer for Ning-po noted that: 'Pig iron comes from Fukien and Kwangtung. Ships regularly come here to sell it. It is cast into implements and utensils.'[16] Thus an industrial raw material was habitually brought over seven hundred miles by sea.

The trade between the regions was on the whole in more valuable items. In the *Continuation of the Comprehensive Mirror for Aiding Government* there is the following description of the town of Pan-ch'iao in southern Shantung in 1088:

> Merchants from Kuang-nan, Huai-nan and Liang-che come to this town in seagoing junks to sell such dutiable goods as spices and drugs. [Northern] merchants from the provinces of Ching-tung, Hopei and and Ho-tung come bringing copper cash, silk thread, silk floss, silk gauze and thin silk, and do an extremely thriving trade with them . . . The trade of Ming-chou [Ning-po] and Hang-chou is limited to one province, but Pan-ch'iao has the commerce of merchants from several provinces in the north-west. Its silk thread, floss, double-thread silk cloth and silk are also commodities which are desired by barbarian merchants. From this one can see that it is the place to which north and south hasten to meet for trade.[17]

Commerce between Szechwan and the other two regions seems to have been rather more limited, although the medicine fairs at Ch'eng-tu and elsewhere drew itinerant Taoists and other vendors of cures from all over the country.

There was also a flourishing international trade, especially with Japan and south-east Asia. To the latter China exported copper and iron goods, porcelain, silks, linens, chemicals, sugar, rice and books, receiving in exchange spices and other exotic items. Parts of the Chinese rural economy became directly linked to production for the overseas market, as may be seen from Ts'ai Hsiang's *Manual of the Lychee*:

> [In Fukien], when the trees are bearing blossoms, merchants make estimates of the crop grove by grove, and on this basis draw up contracts [with the cultivators]. They can tell if the coming harvest is going to be plentiful or meagre. All the fruit, regardless of its colour or complexion, is preserved in the brine of the pickled plum dyed red by the rose of China, and taken by land or water to the capital. Some of it goes abroad to the northern barbarians and to Hsi-hsia. Some of it goes in ships to the east and to the south – to Korea, to Japan, to the Liu-ch'iu Islands and to Persia. Everyone appreciates lychees and handsome profits may be made from them. For this reason, merchants are trading ever more extensively in them while fewer and fewer country folk are growing them. Although the annual output is an incalculable number of tens or hundreds of thousands, very few peasants are in a position to overeat as a result. This is because they sell on a grove-by-grove basis.[18]

No quantitative measures are available; but in a loose and qualitative sense it may be concluded that the Chinese economy had become commercialized.

★

One sign of this development was the increased complexity of the structure of business. A kind of managerial class emerged, albeit sometimes in a quasi-serflike relationship to the owners of the money and property which it handled. There was a wide variety of business associations, some linking larger and smaller merchants, some joining essentially equal partners. Functions, too, became more specialized. Storage, for example, became an independent trade in itself, sometimes very sophisticated, as in the warehouses of Hang-chou with their moats for protection against fire and their permanent staffs of watchmen. State-licensed brokers, previously restricted mostly to mediating, recording and taxing deals in real estate, livestock and (before the Southern Sung) in human beings, now became the key agents, resident in every market centre, who co-ordinated the activities of travelling merchants and retailers. In the largest cities there were specialized guild heads and go-betweens for the hiring of almost every kind of labour, for the provision of almost every kind of commodity including sites for burial, and for the sale of such refined services as those of a comprehensive travel agency.

Good business managers were keenly sought after. Hung Mai describes one such case as follows:

> Shen Shih-meng from Tsao-yang [in Hupei] had a reputation as a manager of commercial affairs throughout Kiangnan, Hunan and Hupei. The wealthy Mr P'ei sought and obtained his services, making him extremely welcome and entrusting him with a capital of 100,000 strings of cash with which he was allowed to do as he liked. Within three years Shen had doubled this sum, and gave the profit to his employer. He then further increased the total to 300,000 strings. When old Mr P'ei died a few years later, Shen went to Lin-an to mourn him, and as before to return the funds. P'ei's sons gave him thirty per cent of it, which amounted to 20,000 ounces of silver.[19]

Most managers were more closely controlled than Shen Shih-meng; but the centrifugal tendency of capital which the passage suggests – in other words, the inclination of wealthy people to disperse their funds when investing them rather than to form greater concentrations of resources – is not untypical of the times. Building up a large commercial empire was most efficiently done by decentralizing decisions as far as possible. This is well brought out in a cautionary tale recounted by Yang Wan-li in the twelfth century:

> In a certain place there was a rich man. He owned 10,000 *ch'ing* of agricultural land and his goods filled 1,000 ships. [These figures should not be taken literally. The story is presumably fictitious and simply meant to point a moral.] He grew rich not by his own activities but by making use of others to act for him. One day someone said to him:
>
> 'You, sir, have known how to amass wealth, but you don't understand how to put it to work. Your 10,000 *ch'ing* of land bring in a mere 5,000 [strings of cash] a year, your 1,000 ships of goods a mere 500 [strings of cash]. This means that you, as the owner, are not getting all the profits because you are sharing them with subordinates.'
>
> The rich man forthwith personally took over the farming of all his fields and the trading engaged in by his boats. Within three years he was poverty-stricken. Why was it that, formerly, he had shared and yet been wealthy; and that, latterly, he had kept everything to himself and yet become poor? His income had been extensive; now it was restricted. His outgoings had previously been slight; now they were ruinous. How can one take away from others all the profits in the empire and appropriate them to oneself?[20]

It is not entirely clear how far merchants who worked together on a basis of equality (usually in groups of about five to thirty) co-ordinated their individual operations. Profit-sharing according to the amount of capital contributed was normal, but associates seem to have traded with a fair degree of autonomy. Organizational integration was still limited.

It would be wrong to imply, however, that large-scale operations did not exist in the private commercial sector. One entrepreneur with a sizeable workforce was Wang Ko, who flourished in Southern Sung times:

> Having heard that it was possible to make a living by smelting and by farming, he crossed the Yangtze and settled in Ma-ti, which is thirty *li* from Su-sung [in present-day Anhwei]. There were hills here from which firewood could be obtained, and he gained possession of them, calling together vagrants to work at charcoal-burning [to provide his smelters with fuel]. He also erected an iron-smelter at the side of his house and another at Ching-ch'iao, in charge of which he put Ch'ien Ping-te . . .[21]

His arrogant behaviour led to charges of plotting rebellion; and the attempt then made by the government to suppress him caused him really to rebel:

> He ordered one of his sons to raise the charcoal-burners, and the other son to raise the men at the furnaces. The charcoal-burners were all peasants and unwilling to follow him. They scattered as fast as they could. The furnace-workers did follow him, however, most of them being absconded criminals. He mustered his army at night, dividing it into groups under the command of his cronies Kung Ssu-pa, Tung San and Tung Ssu, and his two sons. *They had altogether over five hundred men.*[21]

If this was the number of men working at the furnaces, then the total workforce, including those who mined the ore, cut wood, burned charcoal, and provided transport to the furnaces, probably numbered several thousand. Wang Ko was therefore an ironmaster on a scale not to be surpassed until the creation of the Urals iron industry in Russia in the eighteenth century. The Chinese state armaments factories operated on an even greater scale. Nor was such gigantism limited to the metal industry. Li Fang, writing in the early Sung, mentions a certain Ho Ming-yuan, a wealthy inhabitant of Ting-chou in T'ang times who had five hundred looms in his own home for the weaving of silk damask, as a result of which he became very rich.

★

The economic advances just described culminated in an urban revolution. Throughout eastern China, cities spilled out from within their walls and spawned suburbs until the original nucleus was all but lost in the surrounding conurbation. Thus, when the walls of T'ing-chou in western Fukien were built in the middle of the eleventh century, they surrounded a city about half a mile in diameter. By Southern Sung times, however, the original three inner wards were dwarfed by the twenty-three which lay outside the walls and which had even engulfed a former satellite town about a mile and a half away. The proportion of urban inhabitants in the prefecture also rose rapidly. In the later twelfth century they were still only six per cent of the total population (counting only males); but by the middle of the thirteenth they amounted to twenty-eight per cent. Nor was this percentage exceptional for administrative areas with major cities. At the beginning of the thirteenth century, twenty-four per cent of the inhabitants of Tan-t'u county, which contains the city of Chen-chiang, were city-dwellers; and by the end of the century this figure had risen to thirty-three per cent. The timing of this spurt is indirectly confirmed by medical evidence. Large cities are hazardous to health because the greater density of population, and the related problems of sanitation, make it easier for epidemics to spread. Better communications also convey diseases more rapidly between urban centres. The rate of epidemics, formerly low, rose to about one in every five years by the twelfth century, and it is about now that the typical 'crowd diseases' such as influenza and eruptive typhus first appear in Chinese medical writings. The worst epidemic of this period was that which struck K'ai-feng in 1232, shortly after the lifting of the first siege of that city by the Mongols. The precise nature of the disease is not known, but it is said to have carried off, in between fifty and ninety days, from 900,000 to 1,000,000 of the inhabitants. Other indirect evidence of the urban revolution is that urban landownership first became an important source of profit in Sung times, and urban real estate a specific and separate object of taxation.

The proportion of the total population living in cities is virtually impossible to determine with any certainty. There must have been major regional variations, as with most other aspects of the economy. In 1100 there were seven prefectures which contained over 200,000 households, two of them in the north and five in the south. There were fifty-one prefectures with over 100,000 households, of which fourteen were in the north, two in Szechwan, and thirty-five in the south. These contained all the cities of any great size. If we now assume that there were five persons per household, we can make an educated guess as to the percentage of the population that lived in cities of a substantial size. This involves the strictly speaking improper step of combining the population figures of 1100 with an average ratio for urbanization in prefectures containing large cities derived from the handful of thirteenth-century figures available, namely Tan-t'u – 33 per cent, T'ing-chou – 28 per cent, She – 26 per cent, Yin – 14 per cent, and Han-yang-chün – 13 per cent. The first, third and fourth of these are counties, and county rates are possibly too high for use in this way with prefectures. A ratio of 20 per cent seems about right, bearing in mind that none of the biggest known conurbations are included in the handful of ratios just cited. This yields a city population of six million or between 6 and 7·5 per cent of the registered population. This is probably a fairly close estimate for those residing in large cities (i.e. those with over 100,000 inhabitants), since we have ignored all prefectures with less than half a million total population. In absolute terms, six million undoubtedly understates big-city population. Yeh Meng-te observed in the twelfth century that: 'When Chien-k'ang [Nanking] enjoyed peace, there were more than 170,000 registered inhabitants in the urban areas, *not including* the migrants, merchants, peddlers and itinerant labourers who came and went.'[22] Whether non-registration in the cities affected a greater proportion of the population than it did in the countryside, with its landless tenants and serfs, cannot yet be said. On the other hand, no account has so far been taken of those who lived in market towns or in the cities of the 220-odd Sung prefectures with less than half a million inhabitants each. Although in the 1930s about as many persons lived in market towns as in cities of the county capital level and above, the great period of market town development came in the Ch'ing dynasty, and it cannot be assumed that this ratio held in Southern Sung times. Still, it seems reasonable to think in terms of a figure of at least ten per cent for the nation as a whole. In the more advanced areas the urban population was presumably considerably higher.

Qualitatively, the task is easier. Chinese cities in the thirteenth century were the wonder of observers. 'Su-chou,' said Marco Polo, 'is so large that it measures about forty miles in circumference. It has so many inhabitants that no one could reckon their number.' The former Southern Sung capital at Hang-chou he declared to be 'without doubt the finest and most splendid city in the world'; and it was his opinion that 'anyone seeing such a multitude would believe it a stark impossibility that food could be found to fill so many mouths'.[23] If the recent estimate by T. H. Hollingsworth, on the basis of an ingenious internal analysis of Polo's figures, that Hang-chou in the late thirteenth century had from five to seven million inhabitants, is correct, then the Chinese case is even more remarkable than had hitherto been suspected. The quantity of grain sold by merchants in the city, given on page 171, would however only have fed 6–700,000 people, assuming a daily ration of about sixteen ounces each, which fits with the passage quoted on page 82. In either case, though, we are compelled to conclude that China at this time was the most urbanized society in the world.

Yet Chinese cities did not play the same historic role as their much smaller counterparts in medieval Europe. They were not centres of political or personal freedom, nor did they possess distinctive legal institutions. Their inhabitants developed no civic consciousness (as opposed perhaps to a certain regional pride) nor served in any autonomous citizen armies. They were not communities of merchants at odds with an alien countryside and its rulers. Manor did not conflict with market. The countryside was commercialized; most manors produced for the market. It seems to have been precisely the expanding market for surplus agricultural produce that made the exploitation of serfs and tenants so attractive. The basic reason for the divergence between China and Europe was rather that the continuing existence of a unified imperial structure, examined in the first part of this book, made independent urban development in China as impossible as the development of a true feudal political and military structure. These can only happen under conditions of prolonged administrative fragmentation. It is true, of course, that the city-state tradition of Western antiquity had no Chinese parallel; but this tradition was largely extinguished by the later Roman Empire, and it is unlikely that it would have revived had Western imperial history followed a Chinese course.

It is still too soon for us to be able, with any confidence, to contrast the pattern of urbanization in Sung China with that of Ch'ing China. But one hypothesis does suggest itself. By 1900 only about four per cent of the Chinese population lived in cities of 100,000 inhabitants or more,[24] – that is *less*, in relative terms, than in the later thirteenth century. At the same time, as we shall see in chapter 16, the eighteenth and nineteenth centuries saw a rapid growth in the number of market towns. What would seem to have happened between about 1300 and 1900 is that the trend towards the growth of great cities stopped or reversed itself; and that there was a lessening of the contrast between these great cities and the countryside as the relative importance of small to middle sized urban centres increased. So far we have treated urban growth simply as the consequence of technical improvements in agriculture, transport and other parts of the economy. In theory, an equally plausible case could be made for the converse: that it was the markets created by the growth of cities, and the attractions of city life, which prompted these improvements.[25] So if the dynamics of Chinese urbanization during the medieval economic revolution (growth of large cities) were different from the dynamics of the late traditional period (growth of market towns), it is possible that this was in part the cause, as well as the effect, of the spate of inventions in the medieval age and the relative stagnation which followed. We shall have to postpone this argument, however, until we have looked further at technology and the late traditional economy in the chapters that follow.

13 · The revolution in science and technology

From the tenth to the fourteenth century China advanced to the threshold of a systematic experimental investigation of nature, and created the world's earliest mechanized industry. A few examples will illustrate the range of these achievements. In mathematics, a general technique was found for the solution of numerical equations containing any power of a single unknown. In astronomy, a new level of observational accuracy was achieved with the casting of much larger instruments and the perfection of hydraulic clockwork. In medicine, a start was made upon systematic anatomy with the dissection of cadavers; more precision was attained in the description of diseases; and a vast number of new remedies were added to the pharmacopoeia. In metallurgy, coal certainly (and coke possibly) was used for the extraction of iron from iron ore. In warfare, gunpowder changed from a material for fireworks into a true explosive; and flame-throwers, poison gas, fragmentation bombs and the gun were invented. At the same time there was an increasing tendency to try to relate existing theoretical systems more closely with the mass of empirical information collected in the preceding centuries, most notably in pharmacology and chemistry.

This period was the climax and also the end of many preceding centuries of scientific and technical progress. Its foundation, above all else, was the art of woodblock printing, invented in the ninth century and in general use by the tenth. The dissemination of ancient scientific texts inspired scholars to master and surpass the conquests of antiquity. It also created a nationwide community of scientific discourse, and helped to democratize knowledge by making personal instruction from a master less essential. We should not exaggerate. There remained significant differences in scientific culture between north and south. The theoretical mathematics and theoretical medicine of the former were transplanted with difficulty, if at all, to the more practically-minded world of the Yangtze valley. The famous fourteenth-century doctor Chu Chen-heng, who lived in Chekiang and was in many respects an autodidact, only learnt about northern ideas already two hundred years old when by good fortune he was instructed by a scholar whose own teacher was from the north and who owned the relevant books, most of them printed. The great mathematician Chu Shih-chieh, trained in the northern school, migrated south to Yang-chou, where his books were printed but he could find no disciples. In consequence, the more sophisticated of his achievements became incomprehensible to following generations. But the basic scientific texts at least were common property everywhere.

The main driving force behind this renaissance of learning was the government. The only area in which it may possibly have hindered enquiry was astronomy, which was 'classified' because of its connection with portents and the calendar. The T'ang Code had punished with two years' banishment any private person possessing astronomical books or studying astronomy, but under the Later Chou in the tenth century the penalty was merely the destruction of privately owned books. Under the Sung scholarly families connected with the bureaucracy could safely study the stars in private. The Sung government pursued a policy of editing and printing the standard texts on mathematics, medicine, agriculture and warfare, besides of course the Confucian scriptures, the dynastic histories, law codes and writings of the more important philosophers. It also sponsored new publications, such as the eleventh-century herbal of Su Sung, a work based on original drawings of plants presented by different localities to the Northern Sung court. Such books were either distributed to provincial government offices or sold. Editions of these works were not large by modern standards. The two printings of 1,500 copies each made in 1273 of the *Essentials of Agriculture and Sericulture* constituted one of the largest. But they raised the national level of knowledge to new heights, as chapter 9 has shown in the case of books on farming.

Official publications were supplemented by a system of state-sponsored education in the prefectural and the more important county capitals. Though literary and philosophical subjects had pride of place in the curriculum, dry but practical matters as administration, hydraulics, military studies and mathematics were studied too. A separate system of state medical education also prepared a quota of three hundred students for posts in the state medical service. The examinations were practical as well as theoretical: no one passed who did not cure the prescribed percentage of patients. Sung and Yuan officials were thus not simply literary mandarins but had a considerable fund of immediately useful knowledge.

Private printing also flourished, although from time to time efforts were made to control or even stop it. Apart from Buddhist books, the most popular privately printed items in the early period of the art were calendars; and this provoked an immediate clash with the government, which felt that the emperor's right, as the Son of Heaven, to regulate the relationships between the movements of the heavenly bodies and earthly affairs, was being impaired. In 835, Feng Su observed:

> In all the provinces of Szechwan and Huai-nan [that is, present-day Anhwei and Kiangsu] printed calendars are on sale in the markets. Every year, before the Imperial Observatory has submitted the new calendar for approval and had it officially promulgated, these printed calendars have flooded the empire. This violates the principle that [the calendar] is a gift of His Majesty.[1]

In 881, when emperor Hsi-tsung took refuge in Szechwan from Huang Ch'ao's rebellion, he found disputes among merchants because of differences between the official calendar and privately printed ones. By 953 the Later Chou government was forced to print its calendar, so severe was the private competition. In Sung times it also became profitable to print books. In 1108 one statesman complained that scholars did it simply for the money; but there were also publishers who were famous men of letters, such as Yao Shu, one of whose disciples used movable types to print the works of the philosopher Chu Hsi.

These private publishers produced works on agriculture, elementary arithmetic and the technique of the abacus. Typical of such books was Yang Hui's *Mathematics for Daily Use*, printed in 1262. According to the author it was designed to be 'a slight help in the contingencies of everyday life, and to assist in the education of the young'. More sophisticated was Chu Shih-chieh's *Introduction to Mathematics*, published in 1299 and notable for its examples drawn from contemporary city life. The availability of these and similar works made medieval China the most numerate as well as the most literate nation in the world.

Woodblock printing was a somewhat primitive process. A block had to be cut specially for each page, and the impressions were taken not with a press but by placing a sheet of paper over the inked block and rubbing the reverse side with a dry brush. The result was often far from satisfactory, as may be seen from Liao P'i's comment on the printed primers of calligraphy and composition on sale in Ch'eng-tu in 883 that 'the ink had spread and it was impossible to read every word clearly'. Efforts were also made to speed up the process of composition by using movable types. The first account of this is in Shen Kua's *Dream Pool Essays* of 1086:

> Under the T'ang dynasty, the printing of books from wooden blocks was still not fully developed. After Feng Ying-wang had first printed the Five Classics [in 932], all the canonical works were printed by means of blocks. In the Ch'ing-li reign-period [1041–9], a commoner named Pi Sheng also devised movable types. His method was to cut the ideographs in sticky clay to the depth of the edge of a copper cash each one constituting a separate piece of type. These were then baked to make them hard.
>
> He would previously have prepared an iron plate covered with a mixture of pine resin, wax, and paper ash. When he came to print, he would place an iron frame on this plate and in it set up the pieces of ideographic type in a closely-packed fashion, so that when the iron frame was full it amounted to a block. He would warm it near a fire so that the composition would melt slightly; and then press a level board on the surface of the type until they became as flat as a whetstone. This method was too cumbersome for merely printing a few copies, but marvellously quick for printing tens, hundreds, or thousands of copies.
>
> He would usually have two iron frames in operation, so that while one of them was printing, the type could be set up in the other. Thus, as soon as the first was finished with, the second would be ready. By means of this alternation the job could be done in the twinkling of an eye. There were several pieces of type for each ideograph. For those like 'of', 'it', 'him', and 'is' he had more than twenty pieces of type so as to be ready for their repeated use on one page. When pieces of type were not in use, they were stored in wooden cases differentiated according to rhymes, each of them being marked with a paper label. Rare ideographs, for which type was not normally kept, could be instantly cut and baked in a straw fire, the whole process only taking a moment. He did not use wood, because the closeness of its grain varied and if it became moist it expanded in an irregular fashion, so making a level surface impossible. Wood would also have adhered to the resin

composition, and have been impossible to remove. The baked clay type, however, came out quite unsoiled at the merest touch of a hand, when the composition had been melted again after use.[2]

Pi Sheng's technique was not continued after his death, although it seems that sometimes clay type was set into a clay base and then baked solid, a procedure which would have ruled out distribution and re-use of the type after printing. Presumably unequal shrinkage in the course of baking made it difficult to align the type accurately. The earthenware may also have absorbed too much of the ink, which was based on water, not on oil as in later European printing.

Movable types were only used in any quantity after the later thirteenth century, at which time Wang Chen also invented the rotating circular type-case for easy access to the pieces of type during the process of composition. These later types were mostly made of wood. Tin type was also tried, but it did not hold the ink well and wore out too fast to survive long runs. Both wooden and metal types had to be held in place either with rods running through them, or pads placed between them. Neither cutting nor casting were precise enough to permit solid setting. Certain improvements were later made in metal type, first in Korea and later in China, but on the whole the wooden block and wooden type dominated Chinese printing until the end of the nineteenth century. Presumably an ideographic script, with four thousand to five thousand characters in frequent use, as against an alphabetic script with less than a hundred letters and signs, made the perfection of movable metal type a less attractive goal.

Printing apart, a diversity of causes lay behind the scientific and technological revolution. Medicine was faced with new diseases, both the epidemics which hit the new dense urban populations, and the unfamiliar sicknesses of southern China where more and more of the Chinese people now lived. Need for quick commercial calculations led to the introduction and spread of the rod-and-bead abacus. The deforestation of north China and the resulting shortage of firewood prompted the use of coal for cooking, heating and iron-smelting. Coal fumes spoilt the taste of food, and this led to the invention of coke, and probably its later use in metallurgy. Demand for weapons, armour and money meant a greater output of iron and copper, and prompted the invention of the wet-extraction of copper from deposits left on thin iron sheets immersed in the copper sulphate solution obtained from mine-waters. An increasing demand for cloth, and perhaps a labour shortage in north China in the twelfth century, produced a water-powered machine for spinning hemp thread. The introduction of cotton brought with it, perhaps from India, the cotton gin, while a spinning-wheel with multiple spindles and driven by a foot treadle was soon invented. New aesthetic and gastronomic sophistication led to the breeding of new kinds of fancy goldfish, the more expert manufacture of wine, and a passion for horticulture expressed in special books on plums, chrysanthemums, peonies and bamboos.

Religion also played its part. The desire of Buddhist missionaries to propagate their faith was the immediate cause of the development of wood-block printing. (A necessary precondition was of course the existence of paper, made at this time only in China, Korea and Japan.) The first surviving printed book is a *Diamond Sutra* of 868. From geomancy (the art of siting graves and buildings in harmony with supposed occult terrestrial forces) came the magnetic compass. Out of Taoist numerical nature mysticism grew an advanced algebra. The search for the secret of changelessness and of constancy through change, the presumed keys to an elixir of immortality, led to investigation of the chemical properties of gold and mercury/cinnabar. The government's concern with a well regulated calendar, not just as a matter of practical convenience but as a link between Heaven and the Son of Heaven, and so the symbol of political authority, favoured the development of hydraulic astronomical clockwork.

Rather than try to do justice to all these aspects of our theme, we will look in detail at medicine, mathematics, and textiles as a representative sample.

Medicine

Medicine in Sung and Yuan times may be considered both as a body of knowledge and pseudo-knowledge, and as a system of human organization for the combating of disease. As regards the first, an outstanding characteristic of the period was a dissatisfaction with past ideas, and an awareness that the nature of many diseases had changed since antiquity. Chang Yuan-su, a physician of the thirteenth century, said quite bluntly:

> In the ordinary course of events, when one is treating diseases, one does not use the old remedies ... The movements of the internal

ethers are not the same. The past and the present follow different tracks, and to use the old remedies for the new illnesses is ineffective.[3]

As regards the second aspect, the most striking feature was the determination of the government to make medical information as widely available to the public as possible. Indeed, no other medieval nation seems to have been so conscious, both publicly and privately, of the problem of health. Huge drainage systems were built in the major cities. Spittoons, powdered soap, toothpaste and, at the very end of the period, the toothbrush came into general use.

Chinese clinical observations of the new diseases were detailed, matter-of-fact and often remarkably accurate. The first account of eruptive typhus is in the *Service of Parents among Scholars*, an exposition of the theories of the eminent doctor Chang Ts'ung-cheng written by Ma Chih-chi in the thirteenth century. After detailing the onset of the fever, the sense of chill and the headaches, he adds:

> On the fourth or fifth day reddish pustules begin to appear, initially below both armpits or sometimes on the ribs, and subsequently over the surface of the entire torso then gradually spreading to all four limbs.[4]

Influenza first appears in the official pharmacopoeia of the Southern Sung, *The Prescriptions of the Board of Great Peace for Showing Favour to the Masses and of the Board of Harmonious Pharmaceutics*:

> There is a high fever and a severe cold. The head hurts and the body aches. The nose is chill and the throat dry. The chest is congested. [Sensations of] cold and warmth come and go. The patient coughs up phlegm. Mucus and saliva are thick and gummy.[5]

Similar diagnoses of the diseases typical of the south – filariasis, schistosomiasis, malaria and others – were also given for the first time during the Southern Sung. As an illustration, we may cite Yang Tzu-ying's description of schistosomiasis in 1264:

> Diagnosis: The face becomes a greenish yellow. The strength fails and the body aches. Lips and mouth become parched. The sufferer is depressed as if by excessive heat. The chest is congested. The stomach distends and the skin covering it grows hard. The belly feels queasy and there is a cutting pain in it, like worms biting, and also like worms moving about. The urine dribbles, and the faeces come out mixed with a bloody pus. Everything that the sick man eats is transformed

into these worms, which invade and consume his vital organs. When they have all been eaten, he dies.[6]

It is quite plausible that the development of irrigated rice agriculture, which meant long hours barefoot in the water where these worms bred (some of them no doubt deposited there in the human excrement used as manure) led to an increase in this disease. By the twentieth century, about one Chinese in ten living south of the Yangtze was afflicted by it. If this did in fact happen, then it offers a new, and hitherto unsuspected, explanation for some at least of the declining economic vigour of south China in later traditional times.

Knowledge of anatomy also advanced. Although dissection was first practised in China under Wang Mang in the early years of the first century AD, it was only under the Northern Sung that reasonably accurate charts showing the main internal organs were compiled. A primary motive for doing this was to systematize the technique of acupuncture, a peculiarly Chinese mode of therapy which consists of inserting needles into the patient, often to a considerable depth, with the obvious risk of serious damage if the wrong place is chosen. In 1027, two bronze models of the human figure were cast by imperial order, at the same time that the T'ang acupuncture charts were being revised. These models were probably coated with wax and filled with mercury, being so constructed that if a student pierced the right spot the fluid would flow out.

The first recorded dissection in Sung times was that performed in 1045 on fifty-six captured rebels, whose stomachs were slit open so that drawings might be made of their viscera. These were later revised; and in 1113 Yang Chieh, professor of medicine at Ssu-chou, compiled the *Diagrams of the Internal Organs and Blood Vessels*. These showed the lungs, heart, stomach, kidneys and other organs, and were transmitted to the West through the work of the Persian scholar Rashid al-Din al-Hamdani.

Progress was also made in the analysis of the causes of diseases. Occupational illness was recognized as such, as may be seen from the following passage in the *Anthology of Conversations*, a work probably written by K'ung P'ing-chung in the eleventh century:

In the silversmiths' workshops in the rear [imperial] park where gold-plating is done, there are exhalations from the mercury employed. Both the heads and the hands of the workmen tremble. Those who watch the ovens in the pastrycooks' shops all suffer early from impaired eyesight. Rockdust injures the lungs of those who gather rocks in the Chia-ku hills; and when their lungs have become dried out, they die. The workers employed by the Inspectorates to cast copper cash are never old men with white hair. The hardships of the work see to that.[7]

Environment was regarded as one of the basic factors in causing sickness; and phenomena such as the connection of malaria with stagnant water (though not with mosquitoes) were well understood. The regular ban on cattle markets at times of cattle-pest also indicates a rudimentary knowledge of how diseases were transmitted. Sometimes, during severe epidemics such as those at the Southern Sung capital in 1181 and 1187, the inhabitants would be forbidden by the government to travel. The main theoretical controversy was between those who believed that illness was simply the result of the invasion of the body by noxious external influences, and those who argued that prior weaknesses in the body itself made such an invasion possible. The first school stressed direct action with drugs to combat the harmful influences and drive them out. They used preparations to reduce fevers, and to induce sweating, excretion and vomiting. The others thought that illness often arose from such causes as immoderate eating and drinking, excessive effort, sexual indulgence and emotional disturbance. They therefore adopted a strengthening approach which aimed primarily at restoring the body's own defences.

Practical therapeutics was helped by the printing of a series of herbals, continually revised and emended. The nucleus of Chinese drug-lore dated from Han times, and was contained in the *Herbal of the Divine Husbandman* and other works now lost. This herbal listed 365 drugs, one for each day of the year; and its material was organized by criteria which cannot really be regarded as scientific, although they show a certain systematizing spirit. Among these criteria were correspondences with the male and female cosmic principles, with the 'botanical' aspects of root, stalk, flower and fruit, with the 'seven humours', the 'five flavours' and the 'four ethers'. There were also careful descriptions of the drugs' curative powers. Around 500, a thorough revision was undertaken by T'ao Hung-ching, a hermit-scholar who was the descendant of a long line of doctors. He took out much of the theorizing, supplemented the initial list of drugs with a second list of the same length again, and added many practical details such as where drugs could be found, what they looked like, how to distinguish genuine from fake, and how best to store them. T'ao's illustrated *Classic of the Herbal of the Divine Husbandman* in turn served as the foundation of the *Newly Revised Herbal*, with coloured illustrations, completed in 659 at imperial order by Su Ching and a committee of scholars. It was also around this time that simple formulas for compounding medicines were first introduced into this and other herbals.

The first printed Chinese pharmacopoeia appeared in 973, and was a revised version of Su's text. New editions came out in 974 and 1061. In 1062 over nine hundred new illustrations of over six hundred plants were made and printed at the imperial command. These were later joined to the 1061 herbal, with the addition of much extra commentary selected from a wide variety of sources, by the Szechwanese doctor T'ang Shen-wei. A version of T'ang's work was printed in 1108 under the title *Herbal in Readiness for Emergencies, Drawn from the Classics and Histories, and Verified According to Category*, a further edition coming out eight years later. This book treated of some 1,748 basic drugs and summarized almost everything discovered up to this date. It was a thesaurus of medical information and natural history, presented in an essentially practical form.

The older pharmacological writings were given a critical scrutiny rather than reverence for the halo of antiquity which surrounded them. Typical of Sung unwillingness to accept on authority what had been found to conflict with experience was the remark of the eleventh-century polymath Shen Kua that 'very old books like the *Herbal of the Divine Husbandman* contain numerous errors'. The Drugs Office set up in 1076 under the Board of the Grand Physician was specifically charged with testing new remedies submitted by the provinces. Only if they proved satisfactory were they included in government-sponsored compilations. Some of the remedies first produced around this time attest a real degree of chemical sophistication. In 1061, for example, Shen Kua manufactured steroid sex hormones with the help of a Taoist adept. Datura was used by surgeons to induce total anaesthesia.

In the twelfth and the thirteenth centuries, doctors in north China tried to find a theoretical system that would integrate what was known empirically about the nature of drugs and of diseases. They hoped to find a method of healing that would transcend art to become science. One can see this aspiration in the preface written by the southern physician Chu Chen-heng to his own *A Further Discussion of the Investigation of Things* in 1347:

> When Chu Chen-heng was thirty years of age his mother suffered from pains in her spleen, and every remedy was tried, but to no avail. In consequence, he conceived the desire to master medicine, and obtained and read the *Classic of the Yellow Emperor on Corporeal Medicine* [the standard Han work on theory]. After three years it seemed to him that he had gained some profit from it . . . When he was forty, he re-read it and thought it over in a straightforward way, thereafter studying morning and evening, treating as defective those points that were doubtful and understanding those that were comprehensible. Four years later, he obtained Lo T'ai-wu as his teacher, and consequently saw the books of [the northern masters] Liu Wan-su, Chang Ts'ung-cheng, Li Kao and Wang Hao-ku. For the first time he understood that the majority of sicknesses were caused by dampness, heat and fire [three of Liu Wan-su's 'six ethers']. He also learned that doctors could not write books without the *Classic of the Yellow Emperor* as their theoretical basis; and that without the herbals there was no means of establishing what remedies should be. To have had the remedies but no theory would have meant that there was no way of knowing what illnesses were. If one had had the theory but no remedies, in what way could the former have found its exemplification? Now the *Discussion of Illnesses Contracted through Cold* [or *On Fevers*] by Chang Chung-ching [of the Later Han dynasty], with its hypothetical questions and answers, had given the details of external influences; and Liu Wan-su's [recent] works, which gave a clear exposition of natures and flavours [the underlying physiological elements], offered a detailed account of internal injuries. With this, writings on medicine had for the first time become complete, and the way of the physician had for the first time become clear. In consequence, he was bound to feel doubts about the preparations of the government pharmaceutical board.[8]

What this new synthesis meant in practice was that the old Han medical theory, previously not systematically related to what was known empirically about drugs and diseases, was now so related – or at least the attempt was made. It is impossible without a special study to evaluate this theory. Was the desire to link theory and observation for a practical end a step forward? Or was the whole process a forced imposition of inadequate concepts upon a rich body of data, worse than useless?

Two elements of Han medical theory were particularly important in the new synthesis. These were 'pulse' theory, and 'ether' and 'flavour' theory. There was thought to be a circulatory system of twelve pulses covering the body and linking the viscera with the hands, the feet and the head. Along these pulses passed two kinds of ether, the 'blood ether' and the 'vital spirits ether', making a complete circuit fifty times a day. The twelfth- and thirteenth-century theorists classified all drugs as affecting one or other of these pulses. A combined theory of physiology and pharmacology was built up out of the Han concepts of the four ethers and the five flavours. The ethers were cold, warm, moist and cool, or, in Liu Tsung-su's formulation, wind, damp, dryness, cold, heat and fieriness. The flavours were acrid (that is, the taste of onions and leeks), sweet, sour, bitter, salty and sometimes also bland. Each flavour was believed to have a different effect on the metabolism. Salty weakened strong; sour livened up sluggish; sweet calmed down over-urgent, and so on. Flavours were assigned to specific drugs, and to specific parts of the body. The *Potions and Materia Medica* of 1246 asserted that an excess of the salty flavour stopped blood flowing properly and caused its colour to change, while too much of the sweet flavour made bones hurt and hair fall out. Drugs were also divided into ten categories, some of which like 'decongestants' seem reasonable enough, but some a little puzzling, such as 'light drugs' and 'heavy drugs'.

These theories were not substantially improved upon in traditional China. What was it that kept the Chinese from the secret of micro-organisms as the carriers of disease? Why did they not pursue the relationships between ethers, flavours and pulses until problems of internal consistency and correspondence with observed phenomena made them re-think their concepts? Possibly because medicine was too complex, as compared for example with ballistics or planetary motions – typically European areas of interest which seem to have held little attraction for the Chinese. Progress would have been easier first in a simpler field. In those rare cases in which a real advance was made in later times, it was usually done by ignoring the earlier theories and observing again with a fresh eye. This is evident in the case of Wu Yu-hsing, the seventeenth-century epidemiologist, whose conception of disease entities as members of a class of 'miscellaneous ethers', only detectable by their effects but causing specific diseases in specific species (such as men, cows, or chickens) and passed from one member of the species to another, comes quite close to modern ideas. His work, *On Epidemics* (*Wen-i lun*), written in response to the great epidemic of

1641, explicitly attacks Liu Wan-su's view that the origins of diseases could be explained in terms of a mere six 'ethers'. It is curious that, to my knowledge, no successor built on Wu's potentially fruitful ideas.

The social and organizational aspects of Chinese medicine in the middle ages are likewise worthy of attention. 978 saw the compilation of the *Prescriptions of the T'ai-p'ing Reign, Provided by Imperial Favour*, listing over 16,000 prescriptions and remedies, most of them derived from the *General Discussion of the Origins and Symptoms of Diseases* of 610. When printed in 992 it filled a hundred volumes, copies of which were distributed to the prefectural governments. A five-volume selection, called *Simple Remedies for the Masses*, was printed in 1051 as a handbook for country doctors. Tropical illnesses also caused the government concern. In 1018 Ch'en Yao-sou's *A Collection of Tested Remedies* was printed and issued to officials in Kuang-nan and in 1048 the *Good Prescriptions of the Ch'ing-li Reign* was produced specially because of the lack of suitable remedies in the south. Around the end of the eleventh century famous doctors throughout the empire were ordered to submit their secret formulas to the government for evaluation; and early in the twelfth century this resulted in the publication of two new works: the *Remedies from the Office of the Grand Physician*, which listed 297 selected medicines, and the five-volume *Remedies from the Board of Harmonious Pharmaceutics* which, enlarged, became the standard reference work under the Southern Sung. The preparations it listed were made at the capital by state drug factories, the first of which was set up in 1076, and put on sale to the public at prices which were, in principle, two-thirds of the usual market price.

The government also printed the major medical classics. 1026-7 brought the *Classic of the Yellow Emperor on Corporeal Medicine* and two other important early works. In 1057, the Board for the Editing of Medical Books was established; and from 1061 to 1069 ten basic texts were either published or re-published, including the *Discussion of Illnesses Contracted through Cold*, which was to be the principal inspiration of the northern school. Five medical classics were issued in a small type version in 1088, and five more in 1094, all of them enjoying a substantial sale. By about 1100, therefore, the best medical knowledge of the past and present was generally available to the Chinese public.

The state also ran a nationwide medical hierarchy which at its peak, in 1114, contained over a thousand medical officials, though this number was not maintained for long. The Board of the Grand Physician gave instruction to a quota of three hundred students at the capital, and in 1113 provincial medical schools were also established. There were three levels of examination; and at all but the lowest a demonstration of practical competence was required as well as written tests. Ten specialized sections, each with its own professors, handled such matters as childbirth, acupuncture, the mouth and throat, the eyes and ears, war wounds, and the pulses. Some government specialists wrote monographs on their subjects. An example is Ch'en Tzu-ming's *Essentials of Surgery* of 1263. Forensic medicine was also important. In 1000 AD autopsies on persons thought to have been murdered were made compulsory. Sung Tz'u's *Sung Dynasty Compendium Concerning the Righting of Wrongs by the Provincial Judicial Authorities* was probably the world's first book on medical jurisprudence; and it was followed by others, notably Wang Yü's *No Grievances* in the Yuan period.

The Sung ideal of free medical treatment for travellers was another pre-echo of modern practice. According to Li Yuan-pi's *Guide to Country Magistrates*:

> If a merchant falls ill and is unable to proceed on his way, the innkeeper shall, at his convenience, report the matter to the heads of the administrative village and their constables. A nearby doctor shall be summoned to examine the sick man and to write out a diagnosis on the same day for submission to the county magistrate. If the heads and the constables pick up an ill person on the road and lodge him at an inn, he must also be examined according to this procedure, so that nothing needful is overlooked. Once his condition is relatively better, he shall visit the county magistrate's office, together with the heads and the constables, to provide witness on the basis of which money or goods may be given to the proprietor of the inn and the doctor.[9]

Officials often tried hard to raise the level of medical practice in the areas which they administered. When Liu I (1015–86) became the prefect of Ch'ien-chou in Kiangsi, he called together the 3,700 local doctors and gave them each a copy of the *Remedies which Correct Customs*, written by himself, in the hope that they might be persuaded to adopt sound medical techniques. Medicine was one field of science at least in medieval China where a gentleman might without fear of social stigma aspire to be an expert.

Mathematics

The development of Chinese algebra in north China during Chin Tartar and Yuan times demonstrates another aspect of the medieval Chinese science: its dependence upon regional centres, and consequent vulnerability if these centres suffered disruption. The underlying motivation for new mathematical techniques that had no immediate practical application was a numerical mysticism rooted in Taoist ideas. It was thus that a new algebra originated in southern Shansi, an area characterized by a vigorous Taoism, and the scene of a Taoist revival led by Wang Chung-yang and his Complete Truth Sect in the later twelfth century. The distinctive basic idea was that of a positional array in which the powers of x were indicated by location in the array, and their coefficients by the numbers of counting-rods placed there. It was probably originated by Ch'en Fu, a Taoist mathematician and expert in the *Book of Changes* who had retired to southern Shansi during the early part of the Northern Sung. The earliest surviving accounts come rather later, being found in two works by Li Yeh, the *Sea Mirror of Circle Measurements* (1248) and the *Amplification of the I-ku-chi of Chiang Chou* (1259). Li Yeh spent the early part of his life in Luan-ch'eng, a centre of politics and learning in present-day Hopei province; but after the Mongol conquest he became a wandering scholar in Shansi. He derived at least some of the ideas in his books from P'eng Tse and other Shansi scholars; and the Chiang Chou whose work he built upon came from P'ing-yang in this same province. Li's positional algebra handled one unknown; but in the course of the later thirteenth century this was extended, under certain restrictions, to four. Our present knowledge of this comes from Chu Shih-chieh's *Precious Mirror of the Four Unknowns* (1303). Chu was born near Peking, and later settled in Yang-chou. It is clear, however, from the comments of Tsu I-chi in the preface that both Li's and Chu's precursors were mostly mathematicians from southern Shansi:

> Later Chiang Chou from P'ing-yang [Shansi] wrote the *I-ku-chi*; Li Wen-i of Po-lu [Hopei] wrote the *Chao-tan*; Shih Hsin-tao of Lu-ch'üan [Shansi] wrote the *Ch'ien-ching*; Liu Ju-hsieh of P'ing-shui [Shansi] wrote the *Ju-chi shih-hsiao*; and Yuan Yü from Feng [Shansi] wrote the *Hsi-ts'ao*. Through these works later generations first knew of positional algebra. Li Te-tsai of P'ing-yang [Shansi] subsequently wrote the *Liang-i ch'ün-ying chi* in which he succeeded in handling a second unknown at the same time. Liu Ta-chien, styled

Jun-fu, who was a distinguished disciple of Huo Shan-hsing, wrote the *Ch'ien-k'un kua-nang*, at the end of which are two problems containing three unknowns. My friend Chu Shih-chieh has long practised mathematics, searched out the depths of heaven, earth and man, and investigated the secrets of the [Han classic] *Nine Chapters on the Mathematical Art*. By using 'heaven', 'earth', 'man' and 'things' [technical algebraic terms], he has achieved the treatment of four unknowns.[10]

This catalogue of lost works by forgotten authors is not exciting reading, but it proves the geographical concentration of this type of mathematical activity. Even the greatest of the southern mathematicians, such as Ch'in Chiu-shao (from a Shantung family that had migrated to Szechwan, it is true, but for most of his life a resident of Nanking), contented themselves with relatively practical problems, like perfecting indeterminate analysis for calendar work, and extending techniques already well known.

By Ming times, there was no one left who could understand the more advanced positional algebra of the Chin Tartar and early Yuan periods; and this continued until the later seventeenth century. It seems plausible to explain it by the disruption of north China, both during the Mongol conquest, and during the wars when the Mongols were driven out in the middle of the fourteenth century. Above all, the motivation for the pursuit of advanced mathematics must have disappeared. The techniques and ideas involved in Chinese positional algebra were capable of bearing rich fruit, as is shown by the invention largely on this basis of determinants by Seki Kowa and the calculus by Ajima Chokuyen in seventeenth- and eighteenth-century Japan, though Seki made important use of a written notation, either invented by himself or learned from Westerners. It is therefore important to remember the fragility, in a period before the process of discovery had become as routinized as it has today, of traditions such as the Shansi Taoism which sustained the creative impulse.

Textiles

The pattern of advance followed by decline appears most clearly in the textile industry. Some time in the Northern Sung dynasty a machine was perfected for reeling silk. Worked by a treadle, this device drew a number of filaments simultaneously from a tub of boiling water in which silkworm cocoons were immersed. The filaments passed through eyelets, and hooks on a ramping arm, to be laid down in broad bands on a rotating open-work reeling-frame. In the thirteenth century, the reeling machine was adapted for the spinning of hemp thread. A spindle carrying hemp roving was substituted for the cocoon wound with silk fibres. Hollow bobbin-rollers, twirling to impart a twist, were put in the place of the eyelets; and the entire device could be powered by men, animals or water. The first surviving account of this breakthrough into mechanical spinning is in Wang Chen's *Treatise on Agriculture* of 1313.[11] Its thirty-two spindles, he said, could spin a hundred catties (or approximately 130 pounds) of thread in twenty-four hours. This effected a notable saving in labour costs, for the device was 'several times cheaper than the women workers it replaces'. The best model was driven by water power, which was 'far more convenient than the land-based machine'. As he wrote in a poem in its praise:

> It takes a spinner many days to spin a hundred catties,
> But with water power it may be done with supernatural speed.

These machines were widespread, unlike some famous early inventions which failed to find acceptance because of an underdeveloped economic environment. 'This device,' said Wang of the land-based kind, 'is used in all parts of north China which manufacture hemp.' Of the water-driven variety he added that 'Many of these machines have been installed in those places in the north China plain which are near to running water.'

The technology employed emerges clearly from Wang's account of the mechanism:

The Large Spinning Machine

It is so constructed as to be more than twenty feet long and about five feet wide. A wooden framework is first built as a base and uprights about five feet in height are erected at each of the four corners. Through the centre runs a horizontal cylinder. Light struts complete the structure at the top. The iron axles of the long reeling-frame onto which the hemp thread is wound rests in two ridged grooves in these struts. Next, a long wooden base-board is fixed to the main frame. Sockets set into it receive the iron bearings at the bottom of the bobbin-rollers. (These are tubes made on a lathe and one [Chinese] foot two inches long and one foot two inches around. There are thirty-two of them, and the thread is wound [or twisted] inside them.) Iron rings

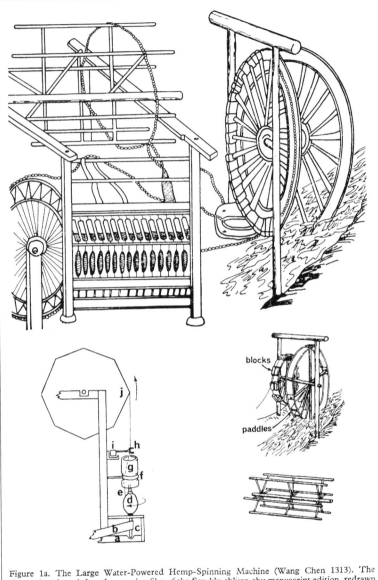

blocks

paddles

Figure 1a. The Large Water-Powered Hemp-Spinning Machine (Wang Chen 1313). The illustration above is based on a microfilm of the Ssu-k'u ch'uan-shu manuscript edition, redrawn in order to make the main features more readily apparent. The reader should note that the original artist's treatment was highly impressionistic. The sketches on the lower right, showing the presumed alignment of the wheels and the possible structure of the reeling frame, are based on other illustrations in Wang Chen's book. The figure on the lower left illustrates a possible reconstruction of the spinning mechanism. A spindleshaft (c) rests on a baseboard (a), and is rapidly rotated by a driving-belt (b). A bobbin (d) carrying the roving is set loosely on the spindleshaft, and a bobbin-roller (g) is firmly attached to the top of the spindleshaft and rotates with it, held steady by an iron ring (f). The roving (e) is drawn off the bobbin into a duct in the bobbin-roller, from which it passes through a small iron fork (h) to the reeling-frame (j). The horizontal beam (i) on which the fork is set moves slowly back and forth so that the yarn is laid down in broad bands on the reeling-frame.

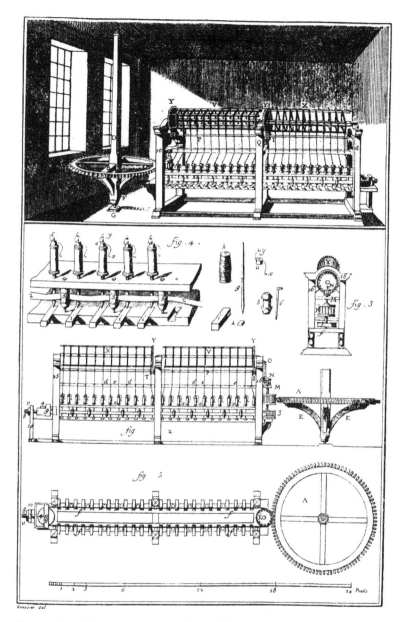

Figure 1b. A European machine of the eighteenth century, from Diderot's *Encyclopédie*.

at the end of rods are used to hold the tops of the bobbin-rollers steady. Furthermore, on the front of the top strut is set a line of small iron forks which separately seize the rovings and transmit them upwards onto the long reeling-frame. What is more, to the left and the right of the framework are two wheels set on separate stands. They are joined by a leather driving-belt. On its lower traverse it passes through the line of bobbin-rollers, and on its upper traverse shuttles past the revolving drum of the reeling-frame. Motion is imparted to the large wheel on the left-hand side either by a man or by an animal. The driving-belt is moved by the rotation of the wheel, and every part of the mechanism is set in motion. The upper and lower portions respond to each other at the appropriate relative speeds. In consequence they cause the rovings to be stretched and wound upon the reeling-frame.

Wang's keen delight in the automatic nature of the process is evident from the poem which he appended to his description:

> There is one driving-belt for wheels both great and small;
> When one wheel turns, the others all turn with it.
> The rovings are transmitted evenly from the bobbin-rollers.
> The threads wind by themselves onto the reeling-frame.

A provisional reconstruction of the mechanism is given in figure 1.

This machine was clearly not very efficient, but if the line of advance which it represented had been followed a little further then medieval China would have had a true industrial revolution in the production of textiles over four hundred years before the West. What is puzzling is that the rather modest and simple changes needed to make it much more efficient were not made. This point can be illustrated by a comparison with the late seventeenth-century and early eighteenth-century flax- and silk-spinning machinery described in Diderot's *Encyclopédie*. One of these machines, for retwisting flax thread, is also shown here in the figure (and the resemblance to Wang Chen's machine is so striking that suspicions of an ultimate Chinese origin for it, possibly via the Italian *filatorium* for spinning silk, are almost irresistible). A continuous belt turns a line of bobbins, surmounted by freely-turning fliers, from which the spun thread rises through guides to be wound upon an open-work reeling-frame. But the burgeoning mechanical genius of Europe had already laid its hand on this machine. The inefficient tangential transfer of power from the belt had been improved by the use of counterset rollers (5 in figure 4 of 1b). A screw device had been inserted to allow the operator to tighten or slacken the belt as he desired (left-hand of figure 5). The relative speeds of bobbins and reeling-frame had been regulated by gearing rather than by a second belt. Little lead weights had been fixed under the bobbins to ensure, fly-wheel fashion, the regularity of their rotation. Sockets of glass had been sunk into the pieces of wood marked i in figure 4. Earlier versions probably resembled the Chinese model more closely, whether or not they were actually derived from it, but further improvements were to come. The irregularities in the speeds at which the bobbins rotated, which were the result of irregularities in the transfer of power from the belt, led to the invention of a machine with the bobbins in a circular array so as to increase the angle of lap. Later still, when difficulties arose from the varying distances of the bobbins from the reeling-frame on account of the circular layout, the bobbins were arranged in an oval.[12] None of these simple and useful advances, including the use of gearing (which was used in hydraulic clockwork and water mills) was out of the reach of Chinese skill in the fourteenth century. None of them was ever made, and perhaps in consequence the machine gradually fell out of use and finally disappeared altogether. We are compelled to conclude that, at least in the case of textiles, the basic obstacle in the way of further technological progress in China after this time was *not* a lack of better scientific knowledge. Rather, it must have lain in a weakening of those economic and intellectual forces which make for invention and innovation.

The last part of this book is devoted to the explanation of this obscure, but profoundly important change.

Part Three · Economic development without technological change

14 · The turning-point in the fourteenth century

The medieval economic revolution did not continue. Between about 1300 and 1500, for reasons which are still largely inexplicable, the Chinese economy fell into a decline from which it only recovered slowly. More importantly, some time in the fourteenth century, the internal logic of Chinese historical development began to change. In saying this, I do not simply mean that Chinese society in 1700 was different from Chinese society in 1300. There were of course great differences, though of a subtler kind than those characterizing western Europe at these two dates. What is important, however, is the alteration in the causal patterns at work over the long run. Technology provides the most obvious and perhaps most basic example of this. During the period of the medieval economic revolution, economic growth had been accompanied by the invention of new techniques of production; but between 1500 and 1800, when there was a renewal of vigorous economic growth, invention was almost entirely absent. Some of the other changes of this sort have already been mentioned in preceding chapters, such as that in the pattern of urbanization (see pages 177–8).

The chapters that follow describe the distinctive characteristics of this late traditional period. Chapter 15 tells of the dissolution of serfdom and the manorial order. Chapter 16 shows how the multiplication of market towns was both cause and effect of an industrialization of large parts of the countryside. Chapter 17 shows the inadequacy of the conventional explanations of China's failure to create industrial capitalism on her own account. It also develops a new theory: that technological invention was inhibited by the establishment in the economy of a high-level equilibrium trap.

The present chapter is concerned with how the dynamic quality of the medieval Chinese economy disappeared. This seems to have happened some time around the middle of the fourteenth century. The most important change was probably that an economy in which an expanding frontier had played an important part had begun, in terms of people and resources, to 'fill up'. Next in importance was the reduction in overseas trade and in contacts with foreigners. The Chinese economy was temporarily denied much-needed supplies of foreign silver, and Chinese society became inward-looking. Lastly, there was a change in the attitudes of philosophers towards nature. Interest in systematic investigation was short-circuited by a reliance on introspection and intuition. There were therefore no advances in science to stimulate advances in productive technology. These three aspects are treated in turn below.

Migration, resources and productivity

The basic demographic evidence for the correlation of a rise in the rate of migration from north to south with the medieval economic revolution, and its reversal with the period of relative stagnation, is set out in graphic form in figure 2. The depth of the fall in the percentage of the population living in the north was the result of the disorders arising from the Chin Tartar and Mongol conquests; but the overall pattern is too pronounced for it to be simply the consequence of such accidental

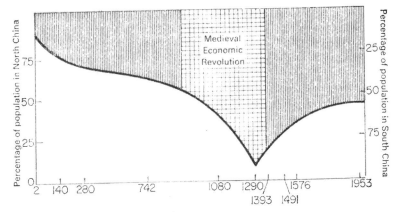

Figure 2. Distribution of population, AD 2–1953.

factors. A more detailed picture, derived from prefectural population data, is given in maps 6 and 7. The first of these shows the increases and decreases in registered households between 606 and 742, two years in which particularly good censuses were held. There is a fall in almost every northern prefecture, and marked rises in Szechwan and in the south-east. The second map shows the changes between 742 and 1078. There has been a slight recovery in parts of the north; the rate of increase in Szechwan and the lower Yangtze valley has somewhat slowed down, and the extreme south has begun to grow a little faster. The main picture of southerly movement and expansion continues.

As qualitative evidence of this demographic and economic transformation we may cite a passage from Chang Ju-yu's *Further Bibliographical Inquiries from the Mountain Hall*, of the early thirteenth century:

Our dynasty [the Southern Sung] possesses southern China, and so south of the Great River [the Yangtze] and Chien-ko [in northern Szechwan] all is calm and controlled. Furthermore Pa, Shu and the northern bank of the Yangtze join to form an outer screen. Compared with the twenty-three provinces of the Yuan-feng reign [1078–85], as regards registered population and amount of cultivated land, [southern China] constitutes two-thirds of the empire. With respect to geographical extent and wealth, it constitutes three-quarters. The north-west corner was formerly three-quarters of the empire. Now it is but one-quarter. In ancient times, Confucian scholarship flourished in Tsou and Lu [Shantung]. Today, it does so in Min and Yueh [Fukien and Kwangtung]. Once skill in the textile industry lay in Ch'ing and Ch'i [Shantung and Hopei]. Now Pa and Shu [Szechwan] are reputed for it. The north in the past profited from dates and millet, neither of which southern China has had at any time. Nowadays, the south enjoys abundant profits from perfumes and teas, neither of which has ever existed in the north. The north benefits from its hares, the south from its fish. None of these things has been possessed by both north and south; but the northern specialities yield only a slender profit, while the southern specialities give rich returns. Thus, although the population which lives to the south of the Great River and of Chien-ko only occupies a part of all China, yet it has two-thirds of its total wealth . . . At the present time, the profits of both land and sea are to be found first and foremost in Chiang-Che [the Yangtze delta]. There is no question of the north-west. The use of irrigation is today more developed around Lake T'ai than anywhere else in the empire . . .[1]

This was a dramatic reversal of the situation in earlier times, when three-quarters of the population had been in the north.

There were limits to the amount of easily farmed land available even in the relatively empty south; and with time the frontier largely filled up. The older regions of settlement begin in their turn to send out migrants to more distant areas. This two-phase process can be followed particularly well in Fukien. The table below gives the number of registered households in the province at successive dates, and the percentage which they represented of the national total.[2] The Southern Sung Empire was smaller than that of the Northern Sung, and this of course affects the figures in the last column:

	approximate date	households in Fukien	per cent of national total
	713	115,311	1·4
T'ang and	742	95,586	1·1
Northern	806	74,467	3·1
Sung	976	467,808	7·2
	1068	992,087	6·7
	1078	1,044,235	6·3
Southern	1131	1,330,000	11·5
Sung	1208	1,599,214	12·6

The number of administrative units grew in similar fashion. In Sui times there was one prefecture and four counties. By early Sung there were eight prefectures and forty-five counties. Inevitably, a shortage of land developed. In 686, Ch'en Yuan-kuang had written in a memorial: 'Half the people here [in Chang-chou] are barbarians, who button their coats on the left and have unkempt hair. There is a surplus of dry fields for cultivation.'[3] But, early in the twelfth century, Fang Cho observed that:

> The land in the 'seven prefectures' of Fukien is limited in extent and not very fertile. Rivers and springs are shallow and remote. The people work extremely hard, but the means by which they make their living are inferior to those anywhere else. Rich persons open up terraces on the hills for cultivation, and these rise level upon level like the steps of a staircase.[4]

As the passage from Fang Ta-tsung quoted on page 129 indicates, there

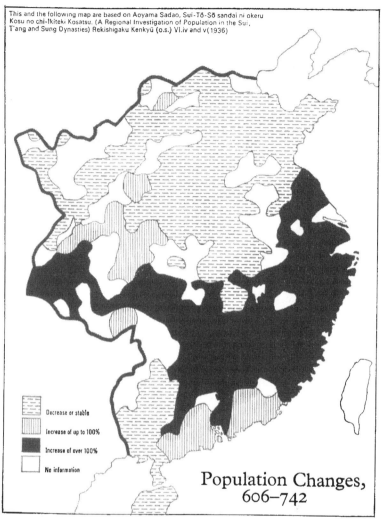

This and the following map are based on Aoyama Sadao, Sui-Tō-Sō sandai ni okeru Kosu no chi-Ikiteki Kosatsu. (A Regional Investigation of Population in the Sui, T'ang and Sung Dynasties) Rekishigaku Kenkyū (o.s.) VI.iv and v(1936)

Decrease or stable

Increase of up to 100%

Increase of over 100%

No information

Population Changes,
606–742

Map 6

were four prefectures in thirteenth-century Fukien in which fish-pools, orange-growing, and the cultivation of rice for the manufacture of wine were forbidden in order to increase the supply of foodgrains. By the end of the eleventh century, the province was fourteenth among the provinces for land area under crops, but sixth for population. Not surprisingly, regular imports of rice became a necessity.

The other resources of Fukien contributed to the Chinese economy in a variety of ways. Fukien teas acquired a national reputation and output expanded. Sugar became a major provincial export. By the later part of the Northern Sung dynasty, mining had grown to the point where Fukien accounted for more silver than any other province, provided a substantial amount of copper, and was China's chief source of lead. Overseas trade and the building of ships became mainstays of the provincial economy. Lu I-hao declared in the twelfth century that: 'Fukien holds the first place for seagoing junks, being followed by Kwangtung and Kwangsi, and then by Wen-chou and Ming-chou.'[5] Ch'üan-chou was the leading seaport; and in 1120 its governor wrote:

> Ch'üan-chou is fifty-four postal relay stations distant from the capital. It links together thirty-six overseas countries. Within the city walls eighty wards are marked out. The population is about 500,000.[6]

In Southern Sung times the prefecture passed the million mark.

The cultural transformation of the province was equally rapid. Early in the ninth century Liu Yü-hsi could observe:

> Although Fukien has riches resulting from its position on the seacoast, its people are fierce and customs demonic. Those who live in caves and stockades, or who make their homes on rafts, are not conversant with the Chinese language.[7]

Yet in Sung times Lin Shang-jen could say:

> In the 'seven prefectures' of Fukien the people excel others in talent in the same way as the landscape is outstanding . . . and therefore half of those in the empire who put their satchels on their shoulders and come to take the examinations at the capital are customarily Fukienese.[8]

And Fang Ta-tsung, of his own county of Yung-fu:

> Every peasant, artisan and merchant teaches his sons how to read books. Even herdsmen, and wives who bring their husbands food at their work in the fields, can recite the poems of the men of ancient times.[9]

The growing pressure of population on the land, and the high educational level of the province, led many Fukienese to give up farming or to emigrate elsewhere. In the twelfth century, according to Tseng Feng:

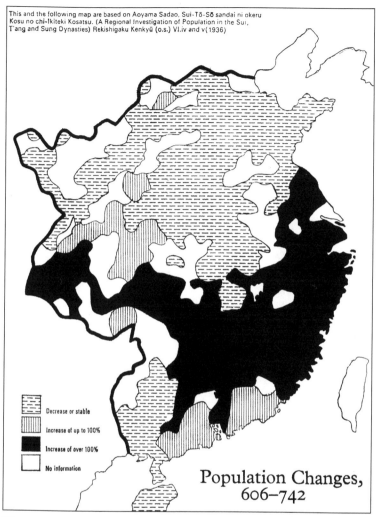

This and the following map are based on Aoyama Sadao, Sui-Tō-Sō sandai ni okeru Kosu no chi-Ikiteki Kosatsu. (A Regional Investigation of Population in the Sui, T'ang and Sung Dynasties) Rekishigaku Kenkyū (o.s.) VI.iv and v(1936)

Decrease or stable

Increase of up to 100%

Increase of over 100%

No information

Population Changes, 606–742

Map 7

Everywhere these days there are persons leaving agriculture to become scholars, Taoists, Buddhists or professional entertainers; but those from Fukien are the most numerous. The land of Fukien is cramped, and inadequate to feed and clothe them, so they scatter to all the four quarters.[10]

Wang Hsiang-chih, in his *Geography of the Empire*, quotes a source as saying that in Mei-chou in present-day Kwangtung:

> There is plenty of land in the prefecture, but the people are idle and few of them work at agriculture. They rely entirely on migrants from T'ing-chou [in Fukien] and Kan-chou to do the farming.[11]

Elsewhere he notes that:

> Nine out of ten pawnbrokers in Hua-chou [in Kwangtung] are Fukienese. The Fukienese resolutely put their empty hands to work; and those who come south over the mountains often become rich.[12]

Thus a province which had absorbed great numbers of in-migrants from north China at the beginning of the medieval economic revolution was now, towards its end, sending out-migrants to the less crowded lands further south. This pattern may be taken as a paradigm for what happened in most of south China.

Another way in which the long-term filling up of the south may be traced is through the changing pattern of interprovincial flows of rice. According to Wang Yen's *Literary Works from Shuang-ch'i*, written in the twelfth century:

> In the Liang-che, the prefectures of Hu-chou, Su-chou and Hsiuchou have the reputation of being rice-producing areas. In a year when the harvest has been good, boats and carts will usually set out in all directions.[13]

Kuang-nan-tung also exported rice to other provinces at this time and even overseas. In 1288, for example, it was officially reported that:

> The officials and commoners of Kuang-chou who purchase rice in the country villages in hundreds, thousands, or even tens of thousands of measures, frequently transport it overseas to Champa [central Vietnam] and other foreign lands, where they sell it in the hope of realizing substantial profits.[14]

These passages have to be compared with later ones showing that these former areas of surplus had now to import supplies. Thus a decree of 1785 stated that: 'The people of Kiangsu and Chekiang regularly rely for rice on Szechwan and Hukwang.'[15] Likewise a memorial written in the early eighteenth century observed:

> The population of Kwangtung is dense. The rice produced in this province is not sufficient for the people to eat. They always rely upon Kwangsi and Hunan to sell and transport rice for their relief.[16]

By this later time there was no longer anywhere promising for peasants to migrate. They had a choice between the poor farmlands of regions like the Hupei–Shensi–Szechwan border, or the medical hazards of valley floors in the jungles of the extreme south-west. Manchuria was the only exception; and under the Ch'ing dynasty Chinese emigrants were legally barred there until 1860, although a certain trickle of illegal settlers did make its way through.

Exploitation of the major resource frontier which the south constituted probably gave a dynamic impulse to the medieval Chinese economy; and when it was gone this dynamism likewise ebbed and vanished. It is worth analysing why this should have been.

Consider the following simple model, which roughly approximates to the situation in China at this time. Let us suppose that a county has two regions at different levels of economic development. Assume that some small change (possibly a technological advance) now allows the technology of the more advanced region to be transferred fairly quickly into the less advanced one. The chief means of diffusion is migration, and effects deriving from migration, the movement of North Europeans into the North American continent being a suggestive if imperfect analogue. Further assume that the advanced region has already reached a density of population at which, failing any new technological progress, extra labour added to the labour force will produce less than the average output of labour – in other words, that there is marked population pressure on natural resources. The less advanced region is, by comparison so lightly populated initially that extra labour using the best techniques from the advanced region will produce more than the average outputs in the advanced region. An historical example is the migration-led agricultural boom in Manchuria in the first third of the present century, in which traditional techniques were almost exclusively used. In other words, there is an abundance of untapped and potentially tappable resources. The result should be brisk growth in both regions. Higher productivity in the new region will create a larger marketable surplus, and stimulate internal trade by causing a greater demand. It may also increase the rate of saving and capital formation. This state of affairs will last until the growth of the population in the less developed region has raised the ratio of people to land, water, and other resources to somewhere near the level of the older region.

The demographic evidence presented in figure 2 and maps 6 and 7 suggests why, by about 1300, agriculture was losing its capacity to act as a leading sector. Much new land remained to be cultivated, and there were areas whose techniques had still to be brought up to the level of the best; but after this time the expansion of acreage and improved practice only kept pace with population growth. They no longer ran ahead of it. Invention and innovation in farming almost stopped. A few new fertilizers were used in the late traditional period, notably soybean cakes. The New World food complex of maize, peanuts, sweet and Irish potatoes was introduced, though as late as the early 1930s it only accounted for about seven per cent of total crop acreage. There were probably many small refinements connected with the increasing inputs of labour per acre in later times. But there was nothing comparable to the earlier agricultural revolution. Unlike the medieval migration into the south, the reverse demographic swing towards the dry-farming lands of the north after 1300 was not associated with marked increases in the productivity of labour.

The filling up of China must also be considered from the point of view of resources. A sudden increase in the supply of a raw material can prompt technical advances, the cotton gin of the thirteenth century being a case in point. About ten times as much cotton fibre can be produced from a given area as hemp fibre; so when hemp cultivation gave way to cotton cultivation there was something of a glut of raw cotton. 'In times past,' wrote Wang Chen in his *Treatise of Agriculture* of 1313, 'rollers were employed [to remove the seeds from raw cotton]. Nowadays, the gin is used . . . It is several times more advantageous than the use of rollers . . . Even if there is a large quantity of cotton, the use of this method permits one to get rid of the seeds immediately, and to avoid a backlog piling up.'[17] Similar considerations probably apply to the treadle spinning wheel with multiple spindles for cotton, also introduced around this time in the Yangtze delta.

But why did progress in cotton manufacture stop here? The thirteenth-century hemp spinning machine described at the end of chapter 13 was not suitable, without substantial modifications, for spinning the short fibres of the cotton plant. Yet why, since the feasibility of machine spinning had already been established, was there not a determined, and ultimately successful, search for a way to do the same with cotton as with hemp? The answer may be in part that the relative glut of raw cotton, and both the challenge and the opportunity which it gave, did not last long and could not, under the economic circumstances of late traditional China, be re-created.

By the sixteenth century there was an acute shortage of cotton in the lower Yangtze valley, then the main centre of the cotton industry. It intensified with the passing of time, as the case of Chia-ting county shows. According to its gazetteer for the Wan-li reign (1573–1619):

Our ancestors considered that water control [for rice agriculture] was a major concern. During the Cheng-te and Chia-ching reigns [1506–1566] the effects of their efforts were still in evidence. At the present time eighty or ninety per cent of the channels have silted up and disappeared. Those that remain are like the belts on clothing. People's lives therefore depend upon cotton. The nature of cotton is such that it is best if its cultivation can be alternated with that of wet-field paddy; but in Chia-ting it is grown for several decades on end with no possibility of a change.[18]

As in areas like Hu-chou, Hang-chou and Chia-hsing, where peasants specialized in silk production, rice had to be imported:

Our county does not produce rice, but relies for its food upon other areas. When the summer wheat is reaching ripeness, and the autumn crops are already rising, the boats of the merchants which come loaded with rice form an unbroken line . . . If by any chance there were to be an outbreak of hostilities . . . such that the city gates did not open for ten days, and the hungry people raised their voices in clamour, how could there fail to be riot and disorder?[19]

By the beginning of the Ch'ing dynasty, around ninety per cent of the land was under cotton; and in the neighbouring county of Shang-hai the figure was seventy per cent. Yet interregional imports were essential, in spite of this concentration upon cotton cultivation. An early seventeenth-century gazetteer for Sung-chiang prefecture, in which Shanghai was situated, and next door to Chia-ting, observed that: 'Sung-chiang cotton cloth clothes the empire . . ., but *most* of the raw cotton used in it is grown in the north.'[20] Of Chia-ting county, its gazetteer noted that: 'Every part of Honan and Hukwang knows how to grow [cotton]. They load their bales of it into an unending line of boats, and come down to Kiangnan to sell it.'[21] According to a roughly contemporary gazetteer for Yen-chou in Shantung:

The land here is suited to cotton. Merchants sell it in Kiangnan, where they have set up shops. It is more than twice as profitable as growing grain.[22]

The south-east coast and Kiangsi relied even more upon imported cotton. A Ch'ing dynasty work on Kwangtung province records that cotton cloths from Sung-chiang and Hsien-ning in Hupei were 'the chief articles of trade, together with raw cotton'. For 'Kwangtung does not produce sufficient raw cotton to meet the requirements of its ten prefectures'.[23] Chu Hua, the eighteenth-century Shang-hai cotton expert, wrote that merchants from Fukien did not buy cotton cloth, 'but only our ginned cotton, with which they return home, their thousands of boats with multiple decks loaded to capacity with sacks', the reason for this being that 'the people of their province are capable of spinning and weaving for themselves'.[24] An early Ch'ing gazetteer for Hsin-ch'eng county in Kiangsi noted: 'Our raw cotton is provided by Honan and Kwangtung. The local people grow a certain amount but not much.'[25] Ch'en Hung-mou's notes on Ku Yen-wu's *Record of Knowledge Day by Day* also mention of Shensi province that 'Raw cotton and cotton cloth come from Hukwang and Honan.'[26]

When, in the later part of the seventeenth century, a cotton manufacture began to develop in north China, overcoming the problem of the dry atmosphere causing the threads to snap by spinning in moist underground cellars, it could take advantage of local supplies of cotton free of transport costs; and the Yangtze delta had to turn to Manchuria. In 1746, the ministry of Works reported that bannermen* and commoners there were 'selling their entire crop to merchants, losing the use of the cotton which they have grown and having besides to meet the expense of buying cloth every year'.[27] Slightly later, Kwangtung turned to India, importing on average 27.4 million pounds of raw cotton annually between 1785 and 1833. Beancake fertilizer made from soybeans was also extensively used in the Yangtze delta area to increase cotton yields. Imports of beancake for this purpose from Honan and Shantung were already significant in the sixteenth century. With the opening up of the Manchurian trade in the late seventeenth century, a fleet of about 3,500 ships, each carrying between 65,000 and 400,000 pounds of cargo, made several trips a year between Shanghai and south Manchuria exchanging cotton cloth and tea for beans, beancake and wheat.

In one sense, these interregional flows of raw cotton and fertilizer are impressive evidence of local specialization and the development of commerce. In another, they point to a shortage of supplies relative to the size of the Chinese population. Land that was used to grow cotton was

* The 'banner' was a unit of the Manchu military and social organization.

land that could be used to grow grain; and by the sixteenth and seven-teenth centuries there was very little land available in China for any crop except foodgrains. Any expansion in the supply of raw cotton be-yond bare parity with population growth depended on raising higher a per-acre agricultural productivity that was already the highest in the world, or on increased imports of food or cotton. There was no Chinese counterpart to the West Indian and South American cotton which, added to the imports from the Levant, made possible a *tripling* of British cotton consumption between 1741 and 1771–5. The size of China's population made an increase of this order impossible; and the excellent commercial network prevented any long-lasting atypical local economic effects which might have paralleled the British experience. A mechanized cotton industry would have had to take away supplies from the existing handicraft industries, and its total output would have been no greater than before. As will be shown in chapter 16, other factors inhibiting invention were also at work; but clearly the persistent difficulty of obtaining raw materials cannot have made the creation of *labour-saving* machinery seem an urgent necessity.

Increasing isolation from the non-Chinese world

During the period of the medieval economic revolution, China's con-tacts with southern Asia, the Islamic world, and even the east coast of Africa, were expanded through foreign trade. Geographical and anthro-pological knowledge of the outside world surged forward. Numerous foreign merchants settled in China's coastal cities, some of them even attaining government office. The period of decline coincided with a government policy of reducing contacts between Chinese and foreigners, and of stopping private ventures overseas by Chinese merchants. This caused demonstrable harm to the economies of the coastal provinces, especially Fukien. It probably also deprived China of stimuli which could have triggered new scientific and technological departures. An example is the fate of Ptolemy's *Almagest* and Euclid's *Elements* in China. Persian copies of these works, the keys to traditional Western astronomy and geometry, were in Peking by the end of the thirteenth century. They served as the basis of the work of the Moslem observatory set up in 1271. But on Chinese thought they made no lasting impact, al-though translations were made in Ming times and the Moslem tradition of astronomy was given imperial support until the early Ch'ing.[28]

The cause of this neglect is uncertain; but it is natural to ascribe it to the growing xenophobia and intellectual isolation of the late traditional empire.

The degree of isolation imposed by Chinese governments after the later fourteenth century varied greatly from time to time. It is also hard to give a precise date for the change from an open to a closed policy because one trend, that of overseas expeditions sponsored by the government, came to its climax early in the fifteenth century, long after restrictions had been clamped down on private ventures. The main events in a complex story were as follows:

The regular taxing of imports began in the middle of the eighth century when a superintendent of foreign trade was appointed at Kuang-chou (Canton). At this time, the court and its officials had priority in purchasing foreign goods; but ordinary people were not forbidden to deal with foreign traders. In 979 the Sung dynasty instituted a state monopoly in a number of specified goods, and private trade with foreigners in these was forbidden; but three years later Chinese with official licences were allowed to do so once all the official buying had been concluded. In 1104, rules for the trading activities of foreign merchants in China by means of a system of permits and route-checks were promulgated, the object being to prevent the loss of customs revenue. Nonetheless the Sung, and especially the Southern Sung, encouraged foreign trade, as may be seen from an ordinance of 1146 which declared: 'The profits of maritime trade contribute much to the national income. We ought to continue the old system by which people of faraway countries are encouraged to come and abundantly circulate goods and wealth.'[29] Laws were passed to protect foreign merchants who were shipwrecked on the China coast.

The Sung government equally insisted that Chinese ships going overseas to trade had to obtain official licences. According to Chu Yü's *Talks from P'ing-chou*, written in 1119:

> Large seagoing junks carry several hundred men, and small ones rather more than a hundred. Important merchants are made group leader, assistant group leader(s) and purser. The superintendency of foreign trade gives them vermilion seals, permits them to inflict the bamboo upon their followers, and, if there are any who die, to confiscate their property.[30]

If merchants did not obtain a permit their goods were liable to be seized.

The early Mongol government conceded freedom of foreign trade, but in 1284 the state was made the sole agent legally entitled to trade overseas. Officials financed ventures, and took seventy per cent of the profits. This does not seem to have been a permanent system however; and it appears that the Sung licensing system was the type mainly used. Every licence had to be guaranteed by a shipping broker, the purpose of the voyage had to be stated, and any weapons kept on board had to be deposited with the government authorities during the ship's time in harbour.

The first moves towards a policy of restriction came in the early fourteenth century, when the Mongol government stopped Chinese merchants trading overseas in certain goods; and then, in 1309, going overseas at all. In 1303 the seven superintendencies of foreign trade were closed down, though three of them were reopened in 1314 along with new rules resembling those of 1284. In 1320 there was a further ban on merchants (presumably those not within the officially controlled system) dealing with foreigners.

The emperor T'ai-tsu, founder of the Ming dynasty, converted this Mongol system of controlled trade into purely tributary trade from foreign nations acknowledging Chinese suzerainty. In 1371 coastal people were forbidden to go overseas, and in 1390 an edict stated:

> At present the ignorant people of the Liang-kuang, Chekiang and Fukien are frequently in communication with the outer barbarians, with whom they carry on a smuggling trade [in metals, textiles and weapons]. This is therefore strictly prohibited.[31]

Private overseas trade continued in spite of these prohibitions, and in 1394 ordinary Chinese were forbidden to use foreign perfumes and foreign goods. Another severe edict was issued in 1397. The only ships from abroad that were allowed to trade were those on an official tributary mission from another state. In 1375 the periodicity of this tribute was subjected to controls, and in 1383 a licensing system was begun to distinguish lawful from unlawful trading junks. In 1401, after negotiations with the Ashikaga shoguns, trade through licensed ships was started with Japan; and this lasted until 1549, when confusion caused by rivalries among Japanese merchants led to its abolition. The general philosophy was that granting trade to barbarians was a favour, to be manipulated in order to control them. According to Wang Ch'i, writing in the sixteenth century:

Tribute ships and foreign merchant ships amounted to the same thing. For the outer barbarians who brought tribute there were established superintendencies of foreign trade to control them. They were allowed to carry other goods with them, and the officials established brokers for their trading with the common people. This was called an 'exchange market'. If there were tribute ships there was an exchange market, but if no tribute was presented then the exchange market was not allowed.[32]

The emperor Ch'eng-tsu (1403–24) continued T'ai-tsu's isolationist policy in the main. Thus, in 1407, after the annexation of Annam, he issued the following edict:

> Annam is adjacent to Champa and the hundred barbarians, with all of whom frontiers should be maintained, so that there are no encroachments or transgressions. Likewise, neither civilians nor soldiers should be permitted to cross the frontier, or privately go on the seas and trade with barbarian countries.[33]

New maritime edicts, with increasingly savage penalties for disobedience, were issued in 1433, 1449, and 1452. At some point – when is not clear – the ban was extended to coastal shipping, so that, in the famous phrase, 'there was not an inch of planking on the seas'.

In the course of the sixteenth century the pressure of illegal trade grew so great, and the damage caused to provinces such as Fukien so manifest that, after one vigorous attempt had been made to put down smuggling, the bans were partially lifted in 1567. Chang-chou was opened as a port from which Chinese could sail to south-east Asia, Taiwan and the Philippines to trade in certain commodities. The interdict on both coastal and overseas trade was reimposed in the last few years of the Ming, and then again by the Ch'ing dynasty until 1684 as part of their campaign against Coxinga, a pirate leader based on Taiwan. In the course of the eighteenth century, after a brief period of freedom, the prohibitions were once again gradually brought back. In 1717 Chinese were forbidden to go privately overseas, a ban that obviously excepted the officially-sponsored copper trade with Japan. In 1727 Chinese were forbidden to live abroad, a measure which separated overseas Chinese from their compatriots at home. In 1757 Canton was made the sole legal port for foreign trade, and all dealings there had to pass through a member of a small group of officially approved merchants. This system remained in force until 1842 when China was compelled by Great

Britain to sign the Treaty of Nanking and open other ports to unrestricted international commerce.

Some measure of control over foreign trade thus characterized Chinese policy during most of the medieval economic revolution; but the deliberate restriction of foreign trade and contacts coincided on the whole with the subsequent period of decline, recovery and renewed but technologically sterile growth. It now remains to explain the change of policy and its effects.

One motive for controlling overseas trade was always the Chinese government's desire to extract revenue from it. This should not be confused with the desire to restrict or suppress it; the lure of revenue was in fact used in the fifteenth and sixteenth centuries by Ming statesmen who were trying to persuade the government to lift the maritime interdict. The initial cause of the Mongol's restrictive policy seems to have been the desire to starve out the Japanese and other pirates, whose depredations first began to become a problem in the last part of the thirteenth century. (Since pirates are a predatory species who need a certain supply of prey to support them, their appearance may be indirect evidence of the swelling volume of maritime trade at this time.) This is a speculation; but the importance of the pirates is suggested by the fact that two of them who had been won over were entrusted with the task of transporting the government's grain supplies from the Yangtze valley to Peking in the years prior to 1303. T'ai-tsu, the first Ming emperor, believed that 'people who lived along the sea-coast went privately to foreign countries to trade in perfumes and goods, and that this induced barbarians to become pirates'.[34] Since some of the followers of his former enemies had taken to piracy, he had to be particularly wary of them; and Hu Wei-yung's attempt in 1380 to stage a revolt with the help of Japanese pirates under the cover of a tributary mission can only have confirmed him in his views. But, early in the fifteenth century, the threat from pirates was largely eliminated. This was partly the result of negotiations with the Ashikaga shoguns, and partly of the destruction of the pirate lair at Wang-hai-t'o on the Fukien coast in 1419. They were still something of a menace, though a declining one, until 1446 but thereafter only made four more recorded appearances in the rest of the century.[35] To see the maintenance of the maritime interdict simply as an anti-pirate measure does not make very good sense, except on the assumption of remarkable administrative inertia.

The analysis of the development and decline of the Chinese navy offers an alternative approach to the problem. In 1281, the Mongol dynasty had put together an armada of 4,400 ships to attack Japan. Twelve years later they sent 1,000 ships against Java. Both expeditions were unsuccessful, but they testify to an impressive naval capacity. The early Ming navy contained 6,450 ships, the largest of them able to carry 500 men, and was probably the most powerful seaborne force at this time anywhere. Its most spectacular triumph was the series of voyages undertaken between 1405 and 1433 to Ceylon, India, Persia, Arabia and the east African coast under the leadership of the eunuch-admiral Cheng Ho. Thenceforth, however, it was allowed to decline, and by the middle of the next century had virtually vanished. It was revived for the wars in Korea against Toyotomi Hideyoshi in the 1590s; and Ming naval cannon were a decisive factor in his defeat. The immediate reasons for this decline are well known. The voyages, though profitable, were mainly prestige ventures; and the lustre which they shed on the eunuchs irritated many of the regular bureaucrats. The funds used for the navy were also needed for land defence against the Oirats. These, however, were temporary phenomena. The reason for the thoroughness and the permanence of the government's withdrawal from the sea lies elsewhere. No Chinese government which depended on sea transport of grain to the north could afford to run down its naval capability beyond a certain point. While the sea transport lasted, the early Ming government therefore had a fundamental interest in preserving its navy. With the successful reconstruction of the Grand Canal to Peking in 1411, and the abolition of the main sea transport in 1415, the navy became for the first time a luxury rather than a necessity. Moreover, travel by sea was dangerous, especially perhaps in government-built ships, which were flimsy because of the excessive economies in their construction. Wang Tsai-chin recalled:

> My family grew up along the seashore, and I have heard the old men say that when the people were compelled to transport grain across the seas, the father was parted from the son and the wife separated from her husband. They received sacrifices while alive; and after they were dead, empty coffins were prepared and their souls summoned home. They appeared and disappeared like duckweed. Their life and death were like a dream. If they were lucky enough to miss the maws of the whales they would consider that they had been born again into another life.[36]

There was thus every reason to avoid having a navy.

The maritime interdict was probably preserved because, once the government had withdrawn from the sea, it had no wish to return to it. The underlying assumption of the policy makers was presumably that a large overseas or even a coastal trade would lead to centrifugal coastal centres of power, and the need once again for naval forces if they were to be controlled, which was bound to be difficult, dangerous and expensive. Economically, the policy was disastrous. Above all, in so far as it was effective, it made it difficult to relieve the shortage of acceptable money; and this may have been a major cause of the recession in the fourteenth century.

The Mongol dynasty had limited legal tender among merchants to copper cash and official paper money. A memorial submitted in 1282 by the government of Chi-ning (in present-day Shantung), while indicating that this ban was not widely respected, testifies in passing to the currency problems besetting trade:

> Apart from copper cash, only paper money should be used to determine prices in all the contracts used in commerce, for all that dealings are in fact carried out in all sorts of commodities. It is absolutely forbidden for them to be drawn up in terms of gold, silver, silk thread, silk cloth, brocade or hemp cloth, or other miscellaneous goods. It has come to the attention of the Chi-ning government that the majority of transactions of all kinds are in terms of silk thread, whose value rises and falls with market conditions, and for this reason continually gives rise to lawsuits.[37]

Reckless issue of inconvertible notes by the later Mongol rulers led to a flight of silver from China into Western Asia. The early Ming economy was therefore faced with a liquidity crisis, an emperor who was set on a policy of economic self-sufficiency, and inadequate domestic sources of copper, silver or gold for the money supply it needed.

The Ming inconvertible paper currency was a concomitant of the isolation policy. Both policies ultimately proved impossible to enforce; but the attempt to enforce them must have caused great damage not only economically but politically, by increasing the alienation of people and government. In 1428 a fine amounting to ten thousand strings of cash (or about ten ounces of silver at this time) was prescribed for making a purchase with one ounce of silver; but the next year a censor reported that:

> There are many rich and crafty persons, both of military and commoner status, who store up goods in their houses, which come to

resemble warehouses. Sometimes they trade with each other on board ship. All of them insist on using gold or silver.[38]

To counter this tendency, special 'paper money customs stations' were set up along the Grand Canal to tax all boats carrying goods other than their owners'. Between 1465 and 1488, however, the currency regulations affecting commerce were largely abandoned as unworkable. After 1529, merchants could pay their taxes in silver even at the paper money customs stations.

Around 1400, ordinary people were also forbidden to use anything except paper money for the purposes of trading. As a result they were badly hurt by the inflation brought about by the excessive issue of notes to finance military expeditions. A picul of rice cost two-and-a-half 'strings of cash' (paper) in 1385; by 1426 it cost fifty 'strings', and by 1457 from 200 to 250. Partly as a consequence of popular pressure and partly because specie was cheaper to transport and store than grain, permission was given in 1436 for part of the land tax to be paid in silver; and by 1500 the practice had become widespread.

The currency situation was saved by illegal and semi-legal foreign trade. A certain flow of silver from south Asia was maintained; Japan became a major supplier of silver to China early in the Ming period, though this was offset by her importing of Chinese copper cash in exchange; and in the sixteenth century Spain and Portugal poured in New World silver through Manila and Macao. Relief from smuggling obtained this way was bought at a price. Given the demographic filling-up of southern China, already well under way by this time, probably the only way to sustain the momentum of medieval economic development would have been by a vigorous overseas expansion in the later manner of Europe. The means and the men were to hand. Instead, the energies of the tough seafaring folk, which might have been turned outwards, were spent in running contraband and fighting with government troops. In the early modern West, government power and piracy often ended by being more or less linked. This was not the case in China.

The only class with the power to defy the government ban on coastal and overseas trade was the local gentry. From their role as the protectors and organizers of the massive smuggling that arose in the later fifteenth and early sixteenth century they derived so much wealth that they came to have something of a vested interest in the maritime interdict – so long as it was not too rigorously enforced. A few of them, such as Lin

Hsi-yuan, author of *The Opening of the Seas*, did plead for a relaxation; but most undoubtedly felt that the legalization of seaborne commerce would have removed the need of the merchants for their well-rewarded protective services. As Wang Shih-chen observed of the situation in the middle of the sixteenth century:

> The criminal merchants and sly people of Fukien and Chekiang, seeing the fat profits to be made, secretly trade with foreigners in prohibited goods. They all of them entrust themselves to the protection of the gentry and the authorities do not dare to enquire into what is going on.[39]

Chu Huan, the governor of Chekiang from 1547 to 1549, was even more specific:

> When retired officials live at home, they feel no concern about their moral reputation. They call together rogues and become involved in subversive activities. They spread wide their claws and teeth, tyrannizing their localities and holding the local officials in their grasp. Persons who go down to the seas to have dealings with foreigners borrow the capital of these retired officials, and also make use of their boats and crews. They often go about their business quite shamelessly, asserting that they are on official duties. When they return with their ships and cargoes, they first pay back the original loan, calculate the interest due on the capital, and then divide the remaining loot in equal fashion. This practice is not limited to one year only, nor to just one family![40]

Chu caused economic havoc in the south-east by his clamp-down on smuggling; and infuriated the local gentry and officials by revealing how far they were involved in the illicit trade. He was successfully impeached; and not long after his downfall there was a prodigious increase in the frequency of 'pirate' attacks along the coasts, rising to over a hundred a year in some of the years between 1552 and 1563. The underlying causes of this are still obscure, but they may have been related to the efforts of groups of middle and small merchants to break free from the control of their gentry masters. When seagoing merchants had not been paid what was owing to them by the powerful land-based merchants and gentry, they were often driven to piracy out of economic desperation or a desire for revenge. The gentry, for their part, sometimes tried to avoid paying their debts by denouncing the seagoing merchants to the authorities as 'pirates'. All in all, the futility of the maritime interdict as a security measure, particularly given the run-down state of the Ming military forces at this time, was amply demonstrated; and the policy was largely abandoned in 1567 as the result of a plea by the governor of Fukien province.

Chinese overseas trading ventures, already important again during the last decades of the interdict, now expanded even further. The gazetteer for Chang-chou prefecture in the Ch'ung-chen reign (1628–44) noted:

> The men of Chang-chou often build great vessels and trade with foreign countries far away. Those of moderate means pool their capital; and it also happens that those of means lend money for the purpose.[41]

A contemporary gazetteer for Hai-ch'eng county in this same prefecture confirms this:

> Rich families supply capital, and poor persons their labour, to transport Chinese products swiftly to distant lands. They exchange these for local products as a return cargo. Profits can be a thousand per cent, and the people therefore take pleasure in it.[42]

Chinese sailing manuals survive from this time which give instructions for voyages such as Canton to Nagasaki, Atjeh to Calicut, and Calicut to Aden, with directions on the sequence of courses to be set by the compass and the stars, and also information on the reefs, landmarks and the nature of the sea floor.[43]

It is thus apparent that government policy caused Chinese overseas and coastal trade to go through a prolonged depression, beginning in the fourteenth century and ending in the sixteenth. During the same period Chinese naval power fell from its position of world pre-eminence to a shadow of its former self. The currency problem was also exacerbated by the policy of isolation, in so far as the latter was effective. These developments, among many other causes, halted the period of medieval economic growth.

It should be noted in conclusion that it was the great size of the Chinese Empire which made the adoption of the policies of the Ming emperors possible. In a Chinese subcontinent made up of smaller independent states, like those of the Five Dynasties and the Ten Kingdoms, no government could have afforded so to close itself off. International economic interdependence (as that between regions would

have become) would have removed this option; and the need for diplomatic and military alliances, and revenue from foreign trade, would have
made isolationism undesirable. With smaller states, there might also have
been, as there was in north-western Europe in early modern times, a
closer conscious identification of the governed with their countries and
rulers. Prior to modern communications, the immensity of the empire
precluded nationalism.

The changing conception of natural phenomena

Finally (though this is a topic that really lies outside our present scope) a
word about what appears to have been a turning-point in thought. The
fourteenth century marks a divide in the way in which the Chinese looked
at the world; and this seems to have had indirect but powerful links
with a slow reorientation in philosophic outlook. The consequences
for scientific and technical creativity may have been of importance.

Professor Max Loehr believes that whereas Sung painting was
'the last word . . . in objective and highly differentiated images of the
visible world', and possessed of 'an almost scientific character', there
was a profound change around 1300. The art that followed was 'a sub-
jective, introspective, expressionistic, or intellectualized art . . . no longer
concerned with the image of nature or external reality'. In his view,
Ming painting was 'entirely preoccupied with rational (rather than
sensible) matter'.[44]

Sung Neo-Confucian philosophy was initially a powerful attack on the
Buddhists' denial of the permanent existence of any forms, and on their
vision of forms, things and people as mere momentary phenomena in a
great flux of cause and effect that, lacking any enduring characteristics,
was ultimately meaningless. Against this the Neo-Confucians asserted
the reality, the meaningfulness, and the goodness of human life and the
nature in which it was embedded. In doing this their object was to
establish social order and social morality on a firm philosophical basis.
Their strategy was to maintain that Nature embodied principles, or
patterns of construction and operation, showing the morally correct
principles for human society. An understanding of Nature was therefore
part of the process by which human beings came to grasp these principles,
and progress to the sagehood that was the ultimate goal of human
existence. Thus, at this time, scientific pursuits had a philosophical

significance of which some scientists, such as the physician Chu Chen-heng, were consciously aware.*

But this approach raised a number of philosophical difficulties. If society and man were a part of this Nature, how could the existence of evil in them be explained? If Nature produced evil, then Nature could no longer be taken as the source of morality. Man's own nature, as part of all Nature, had to be good, given the initial premises of a natural morality; but to deny that evil existed would have been socially disastrous, and at variance with the moral norms which the philosophy was designed to support. An element of dualism was therefore introduced. It was argued that while the basic nature of man was good and identical in all men, they possessed different kinds of 'substance' or disposition. In so far as a man's substance was 'turbid' he was a fool, unenlightened, and so by implication wicked; in so far as his substance was 'clear', he was a sage. The logic of this argument, however, tended to drive principle out of a nature thus contaminated by a morally ambiguous 'substance' and make it into something transcendental existing above and beyond Nature, rather than something just immanent in it. In consequence, Nature could no longer serve as a basis for social and moral norms.

The only option remaining was to make man's own judgment the source of moral authority; and this was the core of the theory of moral intuitionism developed in the sixteenth century by Wang Yang-ming. Against the proponents of the older view, he argued that Nature was in any case simply a derivative of man's consciousness. Things existed solely in the mind. 'Outside the mind,' he said, 'there are no principles. Outside the mind there are no phenomena.' So, whereas the great synthesizer of Sung dynasty Neo-Confucianism Chu Hsi had urged 'seeking for principle in everything', Wang now insisted that 'one must look for the principle of filial obedience in oneself'. There was thus a shift in philosophy analogous to the shift in painting: away from the conceptual mastery of external nature and towards introspection, intuition and subjectivity. The new emphasis on Mind devalued the

---

* Others, notably Shen Kua, seem to have had no philosophical motivation for their investigations. Sakade Yoshinobu has even said that Shen looked at nature 'not with the eyes of a scientist, but of a great technologist'. This is too harsh a judgment on a thinker with Shen's appreciation of the importance of experiment, quantification, and the building of models; but it may help to explain the disconcertingly unstructured nature of his thought. See Sakade Yoshinobu, 'Shen Kua no shizenkan ni tsuite' (Shen Kua's View of Nature), *Tōhōgaku* XXIX (Mar. 1970).

philosophical significance of scientific research by draining the reality from the world of sensory experience, though in a less absolute fashion than did Buddhism. Furthermore, 'Mind' had a variety of meanings and tended to become identified with 'Spirit' as the ultimate causal principle. This hindered the growth of a mechanistic and quantitative approach to phenomena; and also suggested that the individual mind of the philosopher-scientist, as part of the totality of Mind, could get into direct contact with the latter, rather than having to master it analytically from the outside.

These effects may be seen with particular clarity in Fang I-chih (1611–71), who was probably the ablest scientific thinker in seventeenth-century China. On the surface, he was firmly within the well established Chinese encyclopedic tradition. His best-known work, the *Brief Record of the Principles of Things* (1664), consists mostly of short articles quoted from previous writers on such topics as 'ether', light, astronomy, anatomy, mineralogy, botany, zoology and uncanny phenomena. What distinguished him was a concern with methodology, a scepticism towards received opinion, and a desire to explain where in general his predecessors had been content merely to record. There is also evidence that he performed some simple experiments. He was interested in the scientific knowledge being brought to China at this time by the Jesuits from Europe; and his book contains accurate accounts of the nature of solar and lunar eclipses, and of the circulation of the blood, derived from their writings. Yet during the years from 1631 to 1650, when he was most preoccupied with science, he made no real new contribution to it; and it is important to see why.

His articles on optics show the quality of his thought. For example:

Inversion of the Image in a Concave Solar Burning Mirror Shen Kua [the Sung dynasty polymath] says: 'Objects reflected in a concave solar burning mirror are inverted. Diviners refer to this as a "technique of interchange". The phenomenon resembles the resistance offered by the pivot of an oar. When a kite flies through the air, the bird's shadow moves with it. But if [the transmission process] is constricted at its midpoint by a small aperture in a window, then the kite and its shadow will move in opposite directions. If the bird goes east, its shadow will go west; and the converse is likewise true. Furthermore, if the image of a high building is constricted at the midpoint [of its transmission] by a small opening, it too will be inverted. This is the same phenomenon as that exemplified by the concave solar burning mirror. Such a mirror has a concave surface; and if one brings one's finger close to it then the reflection will be the right way up. If one then gradually draws the finger away the image will first disappear and then reappear inverted. The point at which the image is not visible is precisely the same as the small aperture and the pivot of the oar. It resists [the transmission of the image] so as to produce the [hourglass-shaped] pattern of a waist-drum. Opposite ends change place and/or direction, as in the case of the two ends of an oar. So, if one moves one's hand upwards then the shadow or image will go downwards, and vice versa. We can now see that if the concave solar burning mirror is turned to reflect the sun, it will gather all the light at a point one or two inches distant from the reflecting surface, and about the size of a hempseed. Objects brought into contact with it will catch fire. This is the smallest point in the waist-drum configuration' . . . As a general rule, if a precious stone has a convex surface, the light from it will form a single ray. If it has several edges there will always be a thin and slightly curved spectrum of five colours. 'Light-emitting stones' have six faces and rock-crystal paperweights have three. Such coloured glass and three-faced rock-crystal will also produce a spectrum. If the sun shines into a ravine and strikes a leaping spring, a spectrum will result. So will it if a jet of water is directed towards the sun from behind the shelter of a wall. We know therefore that the colours of the rainbow, the haloes of the stars and the moon, and five-coloured clouds all have this principle in common.[45]

Thus while Shen Kua had simply described the phenomenon of the focal point, Fang I-chih, by comparing the effect produced by the burning mirror with those produced by prisms and lenses, was trying to establish a more general principle: that of the refraction of light. He was also much concerned with the means by which light and images were transmitted. In the article *On Light* he wrote:

In my view, it is the principle of light that it should pervade both brightness and darkness, just as the male cosmic principle runs through both the male and female cosmic principles [in some degree]. Fire has no extension but inheres in objects. It manifests the light by which one may determine extension. In the same way Mind has no extension but inheres in phenomena. It makes manifest the principles from which one may determine the germinal elements of causation. On a moonless night, when earth has blotted out the sun, space has light of itself. If a man sleeping in a dark room suddenly opens his eyes, his eyes have light of themselves. It is not surprising then, is it, that tigers, owls, cats and rats can see in the dark? When ether congeals it becomes form. When it is emitted it becomes light or sound. It is as if the formless ether which has not yet congealed into any shape were interacting with itself, exhaling and inhaling. Thus the function of what has form lies in its being delimited; but the function of light and sound lie in their constantly overflowing into everything else.[46]

Fang's disciple Chieh Hsuan added the point that 'All things contain light, whose nature it is to make use of ether to acquire extension.' On the basis of these physical concepts, Fang I-chih's son Fang Chung-t'ung attempted a more detailed analysis of image-inversion:

Water can assimilate [the images of] objects so that they enter into it. When the objects are close to the water their images lie on its surface, and when they are far away they lie upon its bottom. Now trees and people reflected in a pool all have inverted images. When formless ether adjoins the earth it belongs to the category of water. Therefore it can assimilate [the images of] objects, and these images will likewise be inverted. There will be an image in space of every object on the ground, the reason for this being that space is all ether. If one cuts a small round hole in a dark room in the direction of the light, all the [images of the] objects outside can come in and be assimilated onto the wall. These images will all be inverted. This is the assimilation of the inverted images in the ether that fills space.[47]

If Fang Chung-t'ung had realized that his theory implied that an image in the ether was *already* inverted before it passed through the aperture, and so conflicted with the observation that it was the passage through the aperture that effected the inversion, he might have been driven to reconsider his whole conception of light. But it was precisely at this kind of analysis that the Chinese seem to have been weakest; and it is necessary, given their generally sophisticated level of argument at this time, to ask why.

*

The answer almost certainly is that such a problem would have been given only cursory attention. It was not in the main line of intellectual advance for a seventeenth-century Chinese scientist, who, if not concerned with strictly practical matters, would probably have thought of knowledge, as did Fang I-chih, as an ordered progression from the empirical/analytical study of phenomena to an intuitive grasp of the workings of Mind or Spirit as the ultimate reality. In Fang's own words:

> Everything in heaven and earth is an object of existence. Man is born in their midst; his life is lodged in his body; and his body is lodged in the world. All that he sees or makes use of are things; and things are objects of existence. The sages established implements and beneficial practices to make men's livelihoods secure; they made manifest general principles so as to govern their minds. Implements are of course objects of existence. The mind is an object of existence. If one speaks at a deep level of discourse, then life is an object of existence. If one takes an overall view of heaven and earth, they too are an object of existence.
>
> When one infers the unknowable, it is by means of an extension of the known that one assimilates it, learning of what is hidden by the expenditure of one's efforts. The single reality of manifold mystery – this is the profound germinal cause which makes both things and spirit(s) what they are. To seek the origins of the obscure silent responses is called 'reaching to the germinal elements'. Objects of existence have their causes. To investigate them, whether they are as great as the cosmos or as small as the grasses, trees or insects, classifying them according to their character, seeking out what is good and bad in them, inferring what is constant and what changeable, is called 'substantive research'. It is substantive research which contains concealed within it [the possibility of] reaching to the germinal elements. If one sweeps aside substantive research and in impetuous fashion takes up reaching to the germinal elements, with the aim of making clear the spirit of what is mysterious, then this is to neglect the objects of existence. What is it that conjoins the internal and the external, linking together the one and the many, but spiritual intelligence?[48]

Fang Chung-t'ung used even stronger terms to stress the nature of scientific investigation as a process which led to, but was different from, a kind of enlightenment:

> When one is genuinely free from delusion, then it is through the objects of existence that one touches upon the fundamental emptiness of these objects of existence.[49]

This point is all the more important because the Fangs, father and son, were pursuing intellectual rather than moral illumination. Fang I-chih drew a careful distinction between normative and natural laws. The Sung dynasty Confucians, he said, had 'only concerned themselves with normative principles. As regards the general principles of objects of existence and the order of temporal periods they did not reach the truth.' And he added, 'When one is speaking exclusively of government and indoctrination, then normative principle is involved. But when one is speaking exclusively of reaching the germinal elements of causation then what is at issue are the ultimate general principles which make the objects of existence what they are.'[50]

The first step in the process envisaged by Fang, that of 'substantive research', was the one which we might view as the most genuinely scientific. Several of his contemporaries, such as the philosopher Wang Fu-chih, also thought it his most important contribution. But Fang himself thought it inadequate on its own and criticized the Jesuits in China as being 'well-versed in substantive research, but inept at reaching the germinal causes'. Some of his criticisms of Western astronomy were indeed not without substance, though others were unfortunately vitiated by incomprehension of optical principles and consequent distrust of the telescope. His ability to make these criticisms seems, however, to have satisfied him that where method was concerned he had nothing to learn from the West. In his own words:

> [The various Western schools of thought] use a variety of techniques for their swift computations, but they are still out of touch with general principles. How can one rely on what they say?[51]

It was the second step that mattered. After 'substantive research' had established specific natural laws, these had in turn to be used to infer general principles:

> All objects of existence are compounded of ether. Space is entirely filled with ether. Objects of existence have their laws. Space likewise has its laws . . . These laws are the means by which general principles may be verified.[52]

But – and this is the point – the transition from laws to general principles could not be accomplished by the analytical understanding alone. We have noted his view that 'spiritual intelligence' alone could bring the otherwise unco-ordinated and unrelated objects of existence into harmony, 'conjoining the internal and the external, linking together the one and the many'. General principles were 'spiritual' in nature. He observes at one point that for the sage, 'spiritual general principles are interfused in the objects of existence'. This spiritual quality made general principles inaccessible to solely rational knowledge: 'Spirit resides in [general principles]. It is by Spirit that they are comprehended, being known and yet not known [in a rational sense].'[53] To a disciple he wrote:

> It is not from the interplay of the male and female cosmic principles that the essential comes. That which makes the male and female cosmic principles what they are is unknowable Spirit. Spirit is known by the mind. To know with the unknowable is called 'magical apperception'. What is there that is not Spirit, not Mind? If one minutely examines their character then one becomes aware of the general principle that is hidden but omnipresent.[54]

★

What then was this 'mind' that alone could grasp general principles?

As to cognition, Fang was insistent that things in themselves, if there were such, were unknowable. 'Since it is only the mind which knows and perceives, everything is shadows and echoes.'[55] Therefore, inexorably, 'The laws of the objects of existence, or the laws of nature, are simply another way of referring to the laws of the mind.'[56] But the mind of the individual had no arbitrary control over what it perceived or over the laws governing the 'shadows and echoes'. Rather, in the words of I-chih's father, Fang K'ung-shao, whom he quotes with approval, 'The germinal elements in the ether and the germinal elements in the mind are two and yet one.' At this point we meet a problem. As we have seen, according to Fang, 'the mind is an object of existence', and in saying this he is presumably referring to the 'mind which knows and perceives' as it belongs to individuals. At the same time, however, he clearly also thinks of mind as the mental aspect of the totality of all that is.* He insists that he is not a dualist:

> The ultimate general principle that there is no dualism in the objects of existence is hidden and invisible. Substance is all ether. To verify the initial germinal elements one cannot depart from the configurations [of the Book of Changes]. Those who would sweep away matter to speak of function, hoping to find out without effort about all that is hidden, have lost their sense of balance. As they are, heaven has hung aloft the configurations of the sun, moon, stars and planets. As they are, heaven has shown forth the senses, limbs and pulses of the human body. As they are, the sages have made the [mystic, numeralogical]

---

* Where this sense is clearly uppermost, I suggest it by the capitalized form 'Mind'.

Diagram and Chart, the trigrams and the divining-slips to be their hidden standards in which the germinal elements are contained in summary form. There is nothing that is not an object of existence. There is nothing that is not Mind. Can one still make any dualistic division?[57]

By merging these two different senses of 'mind', the mind of the individual and the mental aspect of the universe, Fang is able to conclude that 'Only mind can reach through heaven and earth and the ten thousand things, know their origins and find out all their nature'.[58] This could not be achieved in one sudden intuitive jump that 'neglected the objects of existence'. It had to follow the gradual process described above. But what was gained was, ultimately, not a conscious and analytical knowledge. It was a state of mind intuitively responsive to the fine causal stirrings in the World-Mind. It was here that the techniques of divination came in, above all the *Book of Changes*, because they enabled one to bring one's subconscious into a suitably responsive state. The sage was one who used his capacity to do this in the best interests of his fellow men.

The consequences of this philosophy for Chinese science were disastrous. As the result of a highly sophisticated metaphysics there was *always* an explanation – which of course was no explanation at all – for anything puzzling which turned up. Thus Fang I-chih wrote in his article on thunder:

Shen Kua of the Sung dynasty found 'thunder wedges' under a tree that had been struck by lightning. They had the shape of axe-heads but without the hole. It was his view that the mysterious doings of the spirits cannot be fathomed.* In my view this occurrence too was pervaded by general principle. So I assert that *all is Mind, all is Spirit(s)*. Here, too, it is merely a case of the nature of its pervading being covered over.[59]

Given this attitude, it was unlikely that any anomaly would irritate enough for an old framework of reference to be discarded in favour of a

---

* Shen was characteristically cautious about the probable limitations of human understanding. He did *not* believe that a mind in contact with some universal mind could 'reach through heaven and earth'. This appears clearly from his discussion of 'dragon fire': 'Men can only know of phenomena which take place within their own world. Yet is there any end to the phenomena which take place outside the human sphere? Is it not difficult for us if we wish, with our petty knowledge of everyday events, to plumb the depths of ultimate principle?' See Shen's *Meng-ch'i pi-t'an* (Dream Pool Essays) (1086–91), ch. 20, sect. 10.

better one. Here then was the reason why China failed to create a modern science of her own accord, and the deepest source of resistance to the assimilation of the spirit of Western science both in the seventeenth century and later.

15 · The disappearance of serfdom

During the Ming dynasty (1368–1644) and the earlier part of the Ch'ing (or Manchu) dynasty, the manorial order with serfdom and a serf-like tenancy continued to dominate the countryside, though with diminishing vigour as time passed by. In the course of the eighteenth century they finally disappeared, and a new and distinctive rural order took shape. The landlord and the pawnbroker took the place of the manorial lord; financial relationships displaced those of status. The members of the gentry who ran rural projects now did so as professional managers, and not as owners of land directly interested in the outcome of their labours. Class consciousness and social mobility among the peasantry increased; and society became restless, fragmented and fiercely competitive.

The expulsion of the Mongols by the founder of the Ming dynasty meant new owners for large estates, but it did not greatly affect the tenure system. The new emperor distributed large quantities of manor lands exempt from all taxes to the nobility he had created, and to deserving officials. Later in his reign, he tried hard to reduce the size of these holdings, being well aware of the damage they did to the exchequer and the long term political threat which they posed. But neither he nor his successors achieved this. Manor lands grew larger through imperial gifts, purchases, forcible encroachment on neighbouring holdings, and the practice of commendation (*t'ou-hsien*), by which a peasant entrusted his land to a lord in the hope of thereby escaping his taxes.

Some of the resulting estates were enormous. In the early fifteenth century, the manor lands of the eunuch Liu Yung-ch'eng, augmented by illegal appropriations, brought him an annual income of 150,000 piculs of rice and over 4,000 ounces of silver. In the sixteenth century, according to Hai Jui, 'South of the Yangtze, the poor and the rich rely on each other, the weak all commending their land'. This seems an extreme statement, but a survey in 1567 showed the four prefectures of Su-chou, Sung-chiang, Ch'ang-chou and Chen-chiang alone to have 1·9 million *mou* of commended land and 3·3 million *mou* of land falsely registered to make large holdings appear smaller. The *Ming Veritable Records* for 1387 had observed: 'The rich people of Liang-che . . . deceitfully entrust their lands to relatives, neighbours, tenants and serfs'; and presumably the practice continued. Later, if Prince Fu, favourite son of the Wan-li emperor (1573–1619), had been given all of the 40,000 *ch'ing* of manor lands in Honan promised him as a consolation for not being made heir to the throne, it was estimated that the manor lands simply of princes would have taken up half the total acreage of that province. Just before the fall of the dynasty, between seventy and eighty per cent of the farmland in the counties of Ch'ang-sha and Shan-hua in Hunan was in the hands of the descendants of Prince Chien, the seventh son of emperor Ying-tsung (1457–65).[1] The exact extent of manor lands both legally and actually exempt from taxes is hard to tell; it was clearly a significant percentage.

Being a tenant on the manor of a member of the Ming nobility, or a high official, probably meant personal subordination. The *Ming History* records of Li Shan-ch'ang that, when he retired in 1371 on account of illness, the emperor gave him not only some land but also 1,500 families of tenants, a statement which only makes sense on this assumption. The government certainly took it for granted that commendation led to a serf-like dependence. A decree in the *Collected Statutes of the Wan-li Reign* stated:

> It is forbidden for any soldier or civilian to commend himself to a powerful family so that he becomes their servant, and to conspire with the manor managers recklessly to commend land that pertains to the common people.[2]

As the *Commentary on the Ming Code* said: 'It is to be feared that many meritorious officials will use their power to obtain fields and mansions on a wide scale, and take possession of the population.'[3] For a more detailed picture of life on the lands both of such officials and well-to-do commoners, however, we have to turn to unofficial sources.

A not untypical estate of mid-Ming times was that belonging to Madame Kung, the aunt of Wang Shih-chen, a well-known official:

> Madame would make her toilette at dawn, seated in her bedroom. Her hundred serfs, young and old, male and female, would all come

to report upon what they had been doing. Madame would pick out the laziest and have them given a flogging. For those who had toiled diligently she would prepare a goblet of wine with her own hand and mix in marrow to make it ready for drinking. Those who tasted this wine would leave flushed with happiness, and compete with each other to work hard, unmindful of their burdens. Those who had been beaten would blame themselves and say, 'What point is there in not making every effort for her ladyship, and being rewarded with a beaker of wine?' In this way everyone whom Madame employed proved himself capable; her lands supported cattle by the hundred, her streams bred fish and turtles by the picul, and her gardeners tended fruit, melons, mustard and vegetables by the tens of acres.[4]

Numerous estate owners of these times are described as having 'led their serfs in person', going into the fields themselves. The famous statesman Ho Liang-chün wrote of his father, who probably farmed around 1500, as follows:

He bought a large number of serfs for his rich and splendid agricultural properties. Depending upon the season of the year, he would supervise ploughing, sowing, cutting down undergrowth, dyke-building and the repair of the irrigation ditches. From one year's end to the next he would disregard the wind, the rain, the cold and the heat to go regularly in person to see to matters. He never missed a day out of idleness. A programme of work was laid out for each of the serfs whom he organized. He would give them encouragement if the going was hard and, since he had a shrewd idea of the inner feelings of other people, they all had confidence in him and worked diligently. For this reason his income gradually increased until it was ten times as much as he had had to start with.[5]

Some large properties in Ming times were probably also run by hired labour. This is illustrated by a contemporary description of the brothers T'an Hsiao and T'an Chao, who farmed in T'ung-lu in Chekiang:

Much of the land along the lakeshores in the countryside was swampy and overgrown. The country people had all left it to become fishermen. The fields that had been deserted could be counted in tens of thousands. Hsiao and Chao found the price negligible, so they hired [literally, 'purchased and employed', which suggests the peasants were those described as 'hired serfs'] more than a hundred of the country people, fed them, and had them make pools of the lowest-lying places, and open up the rest for cultivation by surrounding them with high dykes. Their yearly income was three times that from ordinary land. Their ponds could be reckoned in hundreds, and in all of them they reared fish. Above the ponds they built grass huts on beams in which they reared geese and pigs. The fish fed on the manure and grew still fatter. On the dykes they cultivated all kinds of plum and peach trees. In the marshes they grew mushrooms, dye-plants, water chestnuts and water lilies. There were thousands of walled areas where they cultivated vegetables at all seasons of the year. They netted and sold all sorts of birds and insects.

In their house they set up several tens of caskets; and every day they divided their earnings, putting so much into such and such a casket for fish, so much into such and such a one for fruit, and so forth. When one was full of money, something which happened several times a month, they would take it out. Their income was three times more again than that which they obtained from their fields.

Both Hsiao and Chao were frugal. Being careful of their expenditure, they did not wear silk clothes; and they only slaughtered an animal if there was an important reason. Their wealth therefore increased daily.[6]

These hired workers should not be seen as necessarily entirely 'free'. Thus an amendment made in 1588 to the Ming code in the section 'When a male or female serf fights with the head of the family' said:

Henceforth, in the families of officials and commoners, all persons hired by contract to work for a period of a year shall be treated as 'hired workers'. Only those who have been hired for a short period of months or days, and have not received any great quantity of wages, shall be treated as 'ordinary persons'.[7]

Legally, the long-term hired hand was assimilated in some measure to the status of the serf. His low economic status is also suggested by Wang Tao-lung's remark about 'those without agricultural property of their own' in early sixteenth-century Hu-chou that 'they repress their feelings and use up all their strength'.

The survival of serfdom in the lower Yangtze valley into Ch'ing times is indicated by the gazetteer for Chia-ting county in the K'ang-hsi reign (1662–1722):

In Chia-ting county the distinction between master and serf is very strictly observed, for a serf depends wholly upon his master for the provision of food and clothing, and for the contracting of his marriage.[8]

A similar observation is made by the Ch'ien-lung reign (1736–95) gazetteer for nearby Pao-shan county.

*

There are two main obstacles to estimating the extent of serfdom in China at this time. The first is that sometimes 'tenants' were treated as if they were serfs. The K'ang-hsi reign gazetteer for Kiangnan tells us that: 'The great families call their tenants "serfs of the manor" and do not allow them to go elsewhere.'9 In other words, they were bound to the soil. The second obstacle is that owning serfs was technically illegal in Ming times for anyone not a member of the official classes. Wang Meng-ch'i, who wrote a work on the conduct of family affairs, made this perfectly clear:

> The laws have provisions for making people enter official households to be serfs [as punishment for a crime], but how can the families of scholars and ordinary persons [legally] own serfs? For this reason serfs are called 'adopted sons' and female serfs are called 'adopted daughters-in-law'. Young ones are called 'adopted daughters'. They are given the same designation as our own daughters-in-law, sons and daughters. Although there is a distinction between persons of titled and unfree status, these latter are not dogs and horses who are of a different species from ourselves . . .10

There was, however, a slight but persistent difference between serfs and 'adopted sons'. Thus one official wrote early in the fifteenth century:

> As to the practice known as 'great households giving protection', powerful families with wealth and titles either exploit the fact that debts are owing to them to take the debtor's person in settlement, or use their power to take forcible possession of their children. Either the entire family is employed to cultivate, or the household is split so the serf can live under the master's care (?). In some cases they give him their surname, regarding him as an adopted son; in others, they change his personal name and order him about as a serf. Once these people have become their dependents they are no longer liable for land tax or forced labour. They submit with pleasure and no one dares to question it.11

When Hai Jui was the magistrate of Shun-an county in Chekiang from 1558 to 1562, he tried to make the inhabitants treat their 'adopted sons' better:

> As regards serfs: everyone everywhere is a commoner of the empire The law limits the bestowal of serfs to the families of meritorious officials. The other ordinary families have only hired labourers or 'adopted sons' who have begged to be provided for. Hired labourers

only work for a term of months or days. Those called 'adopted sons' are like a person's own sons. They are therefore assigned seniority among the elder and younger brothers according to their age, and rank as uncles with respect to his grandsons. They perform labour and are provided for, which is a natural principle. Although it is impossible for them to be loved equally with the others, yet their clothing, food, marriages and mourning should not be very different from those of one's own sons and grandsons. I have heard that in Chien-te county [in Chekiang] the people treat their 'adopted sons' more or less in conformity with the laws. Customs are not thus in Shun-an. Here they treat them simply as serfs, and this needs to be reformed.[12]

The kinship implied by adoption thus had some real substance. In so far as it was simply a legal cover for serfdom, however, it obscures the extent of the institution.

Another complication is the fluctuating number of serfs. Thus the section on 'Auspicious and Unnatural Events' in the gazetteer for Shang-hai county in the Chia-ch'ing reign (1796–1820) observes:

At the end of the Ming period the gentry had acquired numerous serfs, whom they held in hereditary subjection. *There were almost no free commoners in the county.* However, if a master's power ever grew weak they would kick over the traces and leave. Sometimes they would even rebelliously take possession of their masters' fields, seize their masters' possessions, and transfer their allegiance to some other person who had newly acquired high rank. The original powerful family would enter a lawsuit over this, but the authorities would treat it solely on the basis of who was the strongest. When a state of affairs has reached an extreme, a reaction is bound to set in. For this reason, as soon as [the rebel] Ku Liu had issued his call [see page 246], a swarm of persons arose to follow him. Later an imperial decree was issued telling the gentry to have some self-respect [in other words, not to acquire serfs], and the accumulated abuses of the past were thus cleared away; yet the sons and grandsons who were in hereditary subjection enjoyed no change in status.[13]

It is interesting that a serf uprising was categorized by the writers of the gazetteer as a violation of the natural order – like a swarm of locusts or a monstrous birth. More to the present purpose, however, is the way the passage implies that there had been fewer serfs here in the middle of the Ming. This is to some extent confirmed by a document on famine relief written in 1568 and cited in the 1630 gazetteer for Sung-chiang prefecture (in which Shang-hai county was situated). This states that: 'In this region all of the poor people farm as tenants [or "tenant-serfs"] of the rich. We should order the rich not to be stingy, and to lend to those who pay them rent.' Just possibly, the second sentence implies that the duty of a manorial lord in an earlier era to succour his tenant-serfs, exemplified in Chu Hsi's blueprint for famine relief quoted on page 70, no longer held. Perhaps, then, a cash rather than a status nexus prevailed and these persons should be regarded as tenants rather than tenant-serfs. If so, their position probably deteriorated in the last part of the sixteenth century, but the evidence is too thin to permit any definite conclusion.

The status of a serf was usually established by a written bond, which his master kept. According to an anonymous Ming work:

> The customs of our county of Lou [in Sung-chiang prefecture] lay the greatest emphasis upon master and serf. If a man enters a wealthy household as a serf, he draws up a personal bond; and to the end of his life he will not dare stand on a level of equality with them. If there is a job to be done, they summon him and he will not dare to do anything amiss. What is more, his sons and grandsons from generation to generation will not be able to divest themselves of this status. There are some who are wealthy and redeem themselves for a great sum of money, but this is a nominal redemption for they can never rub shoulders with their masters on a basis of equality. This is the law by which serfs are governed.[14]

In later times, at least, it seems that in the absence of such a bond the serf relationship could not be legally maintained.

In the sixteenth century a change gradually came over the attitudes of manor owners towards their serfs. It derived from a greater sense of the precariousness of the master–serf relationship, and of the need for the master to balance strictness with kindness. The following passage written by Hu Hung in the twelfth century is a useful yardstick for the later Ming material:

> Masters should see to it that their tenants have a secure livelihood. They should encourage them in their farming, and give them a fair share of the harvests. They should show sorrow at their misfortunes and congratulate them upon happy events, so that while they are alive they may have sufficient to be content and may die without a feeling of resentment. If a master acts in this way, they will serve him for generation after generation. Even if he drove them away, they still would not go.

If a master does not know how to give loving protection to his tenants, bawls orders at them as if they were slavish dogs, makes use of them as if they were cows or sheep, causing their parents, their wives and their children to exchange angry glances, to lose their feeling of contentment, to forget their natural sentiment of cherishing the soil, and to be anxious only to leave as fast as they can, then it is the master who is at fault. Under such circumstances an official should rebuke the master and reject his plaint.[15]

The Ming work *A Compilation Concerning Everyday Affairs* quotes an almost similar view:

In dealing with inferiors one cannot just rely on one's authority. When officials direct their subordinates and masters direct their serfs there is a right way to go about it . . . As to the master directing his serfs, . . . although there should be a strict distinction as to status, yet kindness and moral influence should also be extended towards them. Although one makes use of coercion, yet sympathy should also be shown for the happy and the sad occasions in their lives. If one approaches them solely on the basis of authority, and follows after them with angry abuse, or harasses them with one's orders, then one's moral influence will decline day by day and the hearts of one's inferiors will become increasingly estranged.[16]

What is new here is the note of apprehension, sounding still more clearly in the *Notes on Family Instruction*:

In controlling the family serfs one has to be strict. Otherwise they will immediately be able to do ill against us. But one should normally also treat them kindly. Merely using authority is not appropriate.[17]

That the old status order was no longer as secure and permanent as it once had been appears from another Ming set of family rules:

When a family has long been rich, it declines and collapses. This is due to eating food produced by others without having any achievements to justify so doing, . . . and is a course which brings retribution from heaven. Therefore, after riches and ease have long been enjoyed, decline will ensue. Worse yet, you will become serfs or oxen, and your sons and nephews will have no choice but to toil at farming.[18]

Serf management grew more sophisticated. Thus in a work on agriculture composed in the first half of the seventeenth century, the author points out:

According to the old standards . . . the common people were docile and the masters authoritative. The men of the present have a proud and lazy air. It is not possible to urge them on without food and wine. They are very dissimilar to those of a hundred years ago . . . My way of providing for them is generous. In hot weather, when the days are long, they will be hungry and weary after midday. In the harsh cold of winter, it is hard for them to go out early with empty stomachs. So in the summer they should be given extra snacks, and in the winter given early rice-gruel. If, in the winter months, the weather is rainy and they have to handle mud, I give them hot wine, and stuff them with food and drink, after which I allocate their duties. They thank me silently, and I can control them by the expression on my face. As to the women and serf-girls, although they do not have any bitter work to do, they too should be given something pleasant to taste. If they pass a whole month without tasting meat, how will it be possible not to have some of them pilfering? . . . According to the old system, in spring and autumn they had one day with strong-tasting food [i.e. meat] to every two with only vegetables. Now it has to be every other day, and when life is especially difficult meat should be given every day. In the spring and the winter, it used to be one day with meat and three days with only vegetables. Now it is meat on every third day, and when life is burdensome more meat is added. According to the old system, every three men would get one ladleful of wine. Nowadays, one has to pay attention to the conditions of their life. When the going is hard, each man ought to have one ladleful; when moderately hard, each man ought to have half a ladleful. When circumstances are easy, and they stay at home, or in rainy weather, one gives them no wine at all . . .[19]

And he goes on to detail other ways in which times have changed. Another work comments on punishments, recommending that:

Sons and younger brothers should not be allowed to flog the male serfs in person; nor should their wives be permitted to beat the female serfs in person. If a crime has been committed then it should be reported to the head of the family, who will take steps to correct or to dismiss the culprit. The head of the family likewise should not himself administer the lash, lest he be provoked by a passing fit of rage. The number of strokes inflicted should be specified, and ought to correspond to the lightness or the gravity of the offence. The questioning should be done slowly, which will not only nourish an air of authority, but also the fear of the serfs themselves.[20]

Of their female serfs masters were told that they 'should deduce everything which they desire or do not desire in the recesses of their heart, but about which they do not dare to speak'. An authority in the *Essential Handbook of Human Life* added to this the following advice:

> Although girl serfs are of a very low status, yet they too should be induced to have a sense of shame . . . If they are frequently scolded and repeatedly abused, they may be disgraced but they will not feel shame; and without modesty and shame they will be unemployable.[21]

Underlying this sophistication was an awareness in the masters of how much they needed their serfs, and the uncertain nature of their hold over them. Thus in the *Family Admonitions of Wang Meng-ch'i* we read:

> Once a family attains relatively comfortable circumstances it is necessary to keep male and female serfs. They rely on us for their upkeep, and we rely on them for their labour. In other words, all are mutually interdependent for their living. Since they have their labour power, how should it be that they could not rely on others? To say that but for us they would have no means to survive is quite erroneous.[22]

It would seem that dissatisfied serfs were not necessarily unable to change their employers.

They were also becoming increasingly disobedient and rebellious. The section on 'The Imperial Cartographer' in the enormous eighteenth-century *Collection of Works Ancient and Modern* quotes a certain Li Ta-pi as saying of Ching-shan county in Hupei that:

> Before the Ch'eng-hua reign-period [1465–87] the ways of the county were simple and characterized by but little contriving . . . When the elders had something that needed to be done, their juniors would do it for them. Sons, younger brothers *and serfs* were loyal, reliable, and but little cultured. Later, it developed a reputation; cultured pursuits flourished; the population grew, and scheming minds were as many as the quills of a hedgehog. Strong and weak were divided from each other; people began to plot to appropriate each other's possessions, so much so that literary skill perverted official decisions and the stupid people were helpless . . . In general, the first real change in the ways of the county was during the years 1522 to 1523. Later still, it became closely linked with the prefectural city. A multitude of horses and carriages met together. One after the other the most ingenious men from the five quarters of the empire sought supremacy. Merchants and peddlers became rich with little effort, and all types of crafts gathered together. In general, there was another change in the customs of the county around 1546 and 1547.[23]

Another source which hints that tenant and serf disobedience were connected with the growth of commerce and a market network is the Wan-li reign (1573–1619) gazetteer for Ch'üan-chou prefecture in Fukien:

> As to what the tenant farmers obtain [for their living], in the mornings they go up into the dykes and fields, and in the evenings they trade in the markets. They even go so far as to make agreements with each other that they will not pay their rent to the great households. Up to the present this custom has not changed. The slyest of them sometimes act in collusion with the government clerks and runners, whom they make their protectors. Those who live off their rents have a hard time.[24]

The following chapter suggests that the network of local markets began to grow denser during the sixteenth and seventeenth centuries. If this is correct, then it seems plausible that the regular meetings of tenants and serfs in these markets would have given them a sense of common interest as a class, and allowed the discontented to see that their grievances were not just against a particular master or family, but against a system.

Tenant and serf rebellions prior to the seventeenth century, such as that of the 'Levelling King' Teng Mao-ch'i in Fukien in 1448, seem to have left little permanent impact. However, Teng's uprising did mark a definite advance in the level of class-consciousness among the peasantry. He was a tithing-general in the canton and tithing system; and in this capacity devoted himself to securing the reduction of the burdens borne by tenants. He rose in revolt when a warrant was issued for his arrest. The origins of double landownership in Fukien, discussed on pages 253–4, may perhaps be traced to this rebellion. But when we reach the outbreaks between the 1630s and 1640s, many of them explicitly aimed at overthrowing the existing status order, these do seem to have been significant in bringing serfdom to an end. The following account of a small uprising in Kiangsi is a good illustration of their general character:

> There had earlier been a major disturbance in Chi-chou in 1644 and 1645. The serfs had risen in swarms, and had been followed by the tenant-tithings and a crowd of mean and worthless fellows. They formed societies with the [ritual] slaughter of a bull and a pig, and engaged in shameless pillaging. In every village there were hundreds

or thousands of them under rebel leaders. They ripped up pairs of trousers to serve as flags. They sharpened their hoes into swords, and took to themselves the title of 'Levelling Kings', declaring that they were levelling the distinction between masters and serfs, titled and mean, rich and poor. The tenants seized hold of their masters' best clothes. They broke into the homes of important families and shared their mansions with them. They opened the granaries and distributed the contents. They tied the masters to pillars and flogged them with whips and with lashes of bamboo. Whenever they held a drinking bout they would order the masters to kneel and pour out the wine for them. They would slap them across the cheeks and say: 'We are all of us equally men. What right had you to call us serfs? From now on it is going to be the other way around!'[25]

The demand for the return or the destruction of the bonds of servitude was a common feature of these uprisings. According to the Pao-shan county gazetteer for the Ch'ien-lung reign:

During 1644 and 1645 in Ming times, [the serfs] took advantage of the [disorders of the] occasion to plot revolt. It began with the serfs of the Ch'ü family in Chiang-tung [the lower Yangtze valley], and spread to Chu-chia-k'u in Kiangsi. The poison was widespread. Thousands joined together, burning houses and seizing bonds. The sky was covered with smoke. The serfs occupied [the houses of the rich] as squatters and their masters offered them food. If the latter showed the least sign of reluctance, they flogged them on the spot. It was an uprising such as has not been seen for a millennium.[26]

In Chia-ting county 'crafty serfs formed bands and demanded the return of their bonds of servitude from the heads of their families. If there was the slightest delay they would plunder and burn.'[27] In Shang-hai county:

The serfs of Chu Sheng-yao seized knives and butchered their master and his son, after which they burnt them to ashes. The trouble spread to the great households in the other rural communities, all of which were burnt and pillaged. Moreover Ku Liu and others led a band of serfs from various families into the county capital. They went first to the houses of the gentry to seek out the bonds recording the sale of their persons. Once the gentry's houses had been reduced to rubble, and the masters flogged and insulted, the owners hastily wrote out deeds of manumission. The great houses which had been burnt and looted all stood empty on this account.[28]

According to a source quoted in a later gazetteer for Hupei province:

In the central Yangtze valley the serfs of the upper classes are the most numerous in the empire, and foremost in the central Yangtze valley is Ma-ch'eng. The serfs of the powerful and titled families of the Mei, the Liu, the T'ien and the Li were not less than three thousand to four thousand [each?]. They lorded it over the village communities. At the end of the Ming dynasty roving bandits arose in great numbers, and these families made their own preparations to meet them. They allowed their serfs to form into bands, cemented with a pact based upon libations and sacrifices, and called 'Societies for Local Altruism'. They competed in decking them out with clothes and armour so as to dazzle them. After this, all the serfs roasted meat and wore fine apparel to the same extent as did their masters.[29]

Nonetheless there were several serf risings in Ma-ch'eng.

Similar events occurred in Kwangtung province. In K'ai-p'ing county, for example, 'serfs . . . rose in rebellion merely because they wished to free themselves from their servile status'. In Shun-te county in 1646 'serfs murdered their masters; then attacked the county capital and looted the treasury'.[30] There is also evidence, though slender, of scattered serf uprisings Szechwan, Honan and Shantung. It was a widespread movement which engulfed the greater part of south and central China.

There were several reasons why the rebellions were successful in undermining serfdom. In the first place, they coincided with the uprisings in the north-west of mobile groups of bandits led by a variety of leaders of whom Li Tzu-ch'eng and Chang Chung-hsien are the most famous. These marauders did not represent the cause of social justice as did some of the southern leaders; they were rather a symptom of the growing weakness of Ming governmental structure. There therefore seems no justification for characterizing these north-western movements as 'peasant rebellions', though it is perhaps worth noting that Li Tzu-ch'eng's father was a peasant forced by extreme poverty to transfer his family to an 'official manor' held by rural gentry. It was these bandits' depredations, together with the military pressure exerted by the Manchus on the north-east frontier, which brought the dynasty down and in part created the conditions for the widespread serf revolts. Murdering of serfowners further made it plain to the upper classes that keeping serfs was a dangerous business, and to the new Manchu government that it constituted a source of social and political weakness. In 1681 the K'ang-hsi emperor approved a memorial from the governor of Anhwei to the effect that: 'Henceforth, when landlords are buying and selling land they must allow their tenants to do as they please. They may not sell them along with their fields or compel them to perform services.'[31] Early in the next century, the Yung-cheng emperor (1723–35) finished off the task of liberation by freeing all remaining hereditary occupational groups, including certain types of serf.[32]

A second reason was that far-reaching economic and social developments had weakened the manorial system. One of the most important was the changing pattern of investment. People with money were no longer putting it into land to the extent that they had done previously. Trade, pawnbroking, and urban real estate offered much higher returns on capital. Thus a miscellany composed in Ming times by Hsieh Ch'ao-che noted: 'Most of the great merchants of Kiangnan do not own land, for the profits are small and the taxes heavy.'[33] The prevailing conventional wisdom is summed up in a comment on the customs of Su-chou attributed to Keng Chü:

> There are one-fold profits in agriculture and it needs very great labour. Fools do it. There are two-fold profits in manufacture and it needs great labour. Those who have skilful fingers do it. There are three-fold profits in trading, and little labour is needed. Those who are prudent and thoughtful do it. There are five-fold profits in the [illegal] sale of salt, and labour is not necessary. Bad and powerful people do it.[34]

By the eighteenth century agricultural land ranked low in the few great fortunes of whose composition we have detailed knowledge, ranging between two per cent and twenty per cent.[35] Land was valued for its security. This is the tenor of Chang Ying's *Remarks on a Regular Livelihood*, written early in the Ch'ing period:

> If any commodity in this world is at some time new, it will inevitably be old at another. In the course of time, houses will crumble in ruin. In the course of time, clothes will become worn to shreds. With the passing of time horses, cows and personal followers grow old and die . . . Only land is a commodity that is continually new, even after a hundred or a thousand years . . . From of old until the present there has never been any anxiety that it will rot, decay, crumble, or be destroyed, nor any worry that it will run away or get less . . . Always when goods are gathered together in this world there is fear of floods, fires and robbers. The rarest of precious objects easily attract the swiftest misfortunes . . . Only with land do we not worry about floods, or fires, or robbers and

do not exert ourselves to protect it. If there is fighting or drought or floods, we can leave our place of residence, coming back when the trouble has passed. There will be nothing in the empty houses, but a plot of land that belonged to the Chang family will belong to them still; and the same will be true of a plot belonging to the Li family. Those families who have opened up new land will still be rich . . .

My friend Master Lu, . . . who comes from Chekiang, prides himself upon his economics. I used to meet with him frequently at the capital. One day our talk naturally turned to the planning of a livelihood. What, in the last analysis, did we consider best? Master Lu thought for a long time and then he said: 'I have seen much of this world. Pawn-broking, trade, and lending at compound interest are such that one inevitably comes to ruin before long. Even if at first you quickly make rich profits, it is certain to come to nothing in the end. Only land and houses can be for long relied upon; and if these two are compared with each other, houses are not as good as land.'[36]

Even such an advocate of investment in land as Chang did not claim that it was very profitable. The sensible strategy, and the one that was probably most commonly followed in later traditional China, was to invest a modest proportion of one's capital in land, which would then serve as a safe reserve fund, but to look for profits elsewhere. In the words of a Nanking merchant, Hsu Huai-ch'üan, 'we use trade to raise our family up and agriculture to preserve it'.

Another reason why land was often a poor source of income was that tenants, as we saw on page 245, were increasingly disposed to resist paying their rents. By the middle of the eighteenth century, it was a 'fixed habit' in Kiangsu province for tenants to resist payment; and cases are known in which landlords had to borrow money in order to meet the taxes due on their land. It was often said that 'collecting rents was a path to be feared'. On the other hand, the collapse of the manorial order opened up a new means of exploiting the peasants, and one with the added charm of being more lightly taxed than land. This was pawn-broking. The advancing of money or grain at interest to cultivators suffering from seasonal difficulties because of the long turnover period in farming had previously been handled by the manorial organization. Now there were new openings; and this explains the phenomenal growth in the number of pawnshops during the eighteenth century. One seventeenth-century writer made the interesting observation that ten-ants 'would rather default on their landlord's rent than dare not to pay back their debt to the grain-lender, for fear that in the latter case they might be unable to borrow again the following year'. Another, in the eighteenth century, thought that 'these days the activities of rich persons in agriculture consist in the exercise of skill in lending money at interest'.[37] Financial resources were thus in many ways becoming a more important source of social and economic power in the countryside than ownership of land.

★

The consequences of this were major. Declining enthusiasm for investment in land meant that large estates were now fragmented by the Chinese system of equal inheritance among male heirs, without any longer being rebuilt in each generation by the rich and successful. Thus, by the beginning of the nineteenth century, the Chinese countryside was becoming predominantly a world of smallholders, that is to say of peasant owners and of petty landlords who owned on average only a little more land than a well-off peasant.

At the same time, the growth of commercial activities and perhaps also the amenities of urban living drew every landowner of any importance into a town or city. According to an eighteenth-century work on the town of Fu-li in Su-chou prefecture: 'Half of the fields of the highest quality belong to rich families in the prefectural capital.'[38] The prefectural gazetteer for the Tao-kuang reign (1821–50) has a passage to much the same effect:

> There are many landowners in Kiangnan, but forty to fifty per cent of them live in the county cities or their suburbs, and some thirty to forty per cent in the market towns. Ten to twenty per cent live dispersed in the country villages.[39]

Numerous sources show how tenants and serfs of this time thought of the cities as centres of landlord power. Here is one of the most dramatic, describing events in Ning-hua county in 1645:

> The great households in the county capital and the tenant labourers in the rural areas hated each other like enemies. It so happened that at this time Huang Tsu-fu had broken up the bones of Huang T'ung's father, Liu-ming, razing the latter's grave. T'ung repeatedly spoke of making his way into the county capital and exacting his revenge. The tenantry also had hopes of going to the county capital for the pleasure of working off their customary petty grievances; and they joined together to incite T'ung to carry out this plan.

Whenever any of the inhabitants of the county capital who were engaged in trade with other parts met T'ung's forces, they would be obstructed. In this way T'ung placed an embargo on all the fuel and rice which had previously been carried into the city from all sides. The people inside the city were unable to contain their grief and rage. Rascally market spies secretly brought news to T'ung of the state of the affairs within the walls, and he decided to take advantage of it. He came by stealth from An-lo and broke in through the north gate. The people in the county capital were taken by surprise, and were without any idea as to what to do. T'ung and his comrades thereupon proceeded to murder their enemies and to loot the rich. Each tenant had the satisfaction of vengeance. They burned down almost all the fortified posts outside the city and demolished more than a hundred feet of wall, having destroyed an incalculable amount of property within the city.[40]

Physical removal of the landowners from the countryside also weakened the control which they could exercise over their workpeople. An early nineteenth-century gazetteer from Fukien province remarks revealingly that 'The peasants near the suburbs still fear the laws, and do not dare to farm as if *they* were the landlords'![41] The nature of tenancy changed; it became less a status relationship than an economic relationship unsoftened and unstrengthened by personal contacts. If a large landowner now came to the countryside at all, it was probably only at harvest time. Otherwise his sharecroppers would only see him when they carried his rents into the city. If, as sometimes happened, he had set up granaries in the countryside to spare them the journey, they would only see his agents. A document in an anthology on the collection of rents in Shan-yang county in northern Kiangsu vividly reveals this separation of landlords from the land:

When a tenant defaults on his rent and usurps the cultivation of his land, he relies entirely upon the district-general [a post that seems to have approximated to that of village headman] and other officers of the sub-bureaucracy to conceal the fact. The tenants of their district will be long familiar with them, and it is the custom of the rural communities that the tenants all give them wheat, rice and fuel in summer and autumn. Because the land-generals [i.e. the district-generals] and the tenant farmers become more intimately acquainted day by day, they become firmly linked together. They even conspire with the tenants to deceive the landlords and make them accept their losses gladly . . . Hitherto each district has had a prompter whose special responsibility it has been to see that the rents on widely scattered fields are paid in full. The rental rice is the landlord's, and the task of prompting payment falls to the local warden. Since there is the custom in the local communities [referred to above], many of the prompters also act in collusion. For the 'porterage rice' with which the landlords recompense them has a fixed yearly quota whereas the tenants, in return for the help which they have received, always give double this. Thus those who serve as the rent-collectors have turned into the corrupt agents of resistance and misappropriation.[42]

Some points in this passage are not entirely clear, but it suggests that individual absentee landlords normally used the lowest-level officers of the local government to collect their rents against a consideration, otherwise having nothing to do with their tenants. The practice is known to have been employed a little later by landlord bursaries or rent-collecting agencies in Kiangsu, and so this interpretation is probably correct.

Other factors reinforced the independence of sixteenth- and seventeenth-century serfs and tenants. It seems certain, for example, on the basis of Japanese experience with rice agriculture a century or so later,[43] that free tenants working family-size units were more productive than larger groups of unfree labourers working larger units as a managed work force. In many cases landowners must have found it profitable to turn their serfs into tenants of this sort, though I have so far found no direct evidence to support this. The most suggestive hint is in a passage on the lower Yangtze region in a seventeenth-century treatise on agriculture:

I would reckon that managing four *mou* of land involves a cost of four ounces of silver [a year]. Planting eight *mou* of land, after the deduction of taxes, yields a profit of eight piculs of rice, which in ordinary times are worth ten ounces of silver. Apart from this, there are the expenses of banking up the fields and hiring short-term labour [in the busy season]. These are met with the spring crops and rice straw, or in vulgar parlance 'meeting item with item'. No profit is left at all. It necessitates much early rising and late going to bed, and much expenditure of thought and strength. In the rural communities to the west all the land is rented out, and the owners peacefully enjoy the profits of idleness. Isn't that excellent? Here [probably Lien-ch'uan in Chekiang province], however, there is no custom of letting land. If one owns land, one must have it cultivated; and if one is to have it cultivated, one must engage long-term labourers and toil diligently all year round – this is simply unavoidable.[44]

Such a state of affairs was probably typical of a transitional period during which the manor and the managed estate were disappearing. Landholdings also became more fragmented. According to the Su-chou prefectural gazetteer for the Tao-kuang reign (1821–50):

> Boats can row anywhere in the watery land of Kiangnan. Therefore many of those who live in one district also have land in another district. Many of those who live in the county capitals, or their suburbs, also have property in various districts. Even if their fields do not exceed several tens of *mou* they will still be scattered all over the place.[45]

Cases are also known where tenants rented land from more than one landlord at the same time. Under such conditions, co-ordinated management and strict discipline were impossible.

Greater income from part-time or full-time handicrafts, which will be described in the next chapter, also made the peasant without land of his own much less dependent on the goodwill of a landlord in order to earn his living. This is illustrated by an eighteenth-century account of the counties of Wu-hsi and Chin-kuei:

> There are five counties in Ch'ang-chou prefecture, and only in ours is cotton not cultivated. Yet we make a greater profit from cotton cloth than the other counties. The country folk only live off their fields for the three winter months. When they have paid their rent, they pound the husks off the rice that remains and deposit it in the bins of the pawnshops . . . During the spring months they close their doors and spin or weave, eating by exchanging their cloth for rice. There is not a grain to spare in their houses. In the fifth month, when the demands of farming become pressing, they once again pawn their winter clothes . . . The autumn is somewhat rainy, and the noise of the looms' shuttles is once again to be heard everywhere in the villages. They trade the cloth in order to have rice to eat. Thus, even if there is a bad harvest in our counties, our country people are not in distress so long as the other counties have a crop of cotton.[46]

Finally, absentee landlordism brought its familiar concomitants: rights of permanent tenure and multiple ownership. In much of southern China the original proprietor had the so-called rights to the subsoil, while the permanent tenant had the rights to the surface, both of which could be sold separately. How this arose is not entirely clear. Sometimes landlords granted permanent tenure as an incentive to more efficient farming and to improvements; but perhaps the simplest explanation is the Chinese proverb: 'Long tenancy becomes property.' The forces at work may be sensed from the following obscure but suggestive passage from an early nineteenth-century gazetteer for a department in Fukien:

> Lung-yen is a mountainous land. Not much of it is fit for agriculture. There are numerous peasant farmers and often, when they see that there is some surplus land available for renting, they will offer a large sum of money [to the incumbent tenant] so that they may privily take over the tenancy. This causes a steady drain on their resources. If there is a bad harvest, they will beg for their rent to be reduced; and even in good years they will be dilatory without paying. When their unpaid debts to the landlord have piled up over a number of years, these tenants are in effect farming as if *they themselves* were the landlords . . .
>
> In recent years the landowners have started numerous law-suits [against tenants] on account of the latters' resistance to paying rents, and their cultivating lands without having been given permission to do so. The authorities punished Ying-shih rural area, and its obstinate tenants were somewhat subdued. The other areas have, however, imitated these evil practices; and they have by no means been completely rooted out. Even lands which have been bequeathed by the ancestors of a clan to provide for sacrifices will, if given to tenants for cultivation for many years in succession, simply be occupied by the latter as their hereditary property. In cases of this sort there have been changes of tenancy, with several changes of surname, without any attention being paid to the landowner; and the rent for the surface has been double the original [subsoil] rent.[47]

The like was probably also true of Kiangsu. The collection of materials on Shan-yang county mentioned above indicates that new tenants were meant to sign a three-sided contract between themselves, the landowner and the district-general, the last being supposed to evict them if they failed to pay the rent, though in fact he usually protected them. Moreover, 'It is not allowed for a private succession [to the tenancy] to be received from the former tenant.'[48] Whatever the causes, by the early twentieth century between one-third and two-fifths of the land farmed by tenants in the lower Yangtze valley was held in permanent tenure.

Figures collected by organizations with widely different political views in the early 1930s[49] indicate the end result of this steady process of transformation. According to John Buck, then of the University of

Nanking, in the north China plain at this time over four-fifths of the cultivated area was farmed by those who owned it. In the Yangtze valley the corresponding proportion was about three-fifths, and in Kwangtung and Szechwan slightly over half. The median size of farm was 3·31 acres. The amount of land held by landowners who did not themselves farm was clearly too small to serve in and of itself as an adequate basis for a distinct and socially dominant class. This picture is confirmed by the Communist land-reform documents from Kiangsi province during the same period. The differences between those categorized as 'landlords', 'rich peasants', 'middle peasants' and 'poor peasants' were so fine that there was constant difficulty in assigning persons correctly. In Sheng-li county, for instance, the initial investigation turned up 1,576 'landlord' and 'rich peasant' households. When Mao Tse-tung did a follow-up survey, he uncovered 536 more such households. Subsequently however 941 of the new total of 2,112 managed to clear themselves of 'landlord' or 'rich peasants' status. Mao also complained that: 'The majority or the great majority of landlords and rich peasants in many places . . . have not yet been found out.' Such a statement only makes sense given a social continuum with a restricted overall range.

The social and political consequences of the end of the manorial order

The disappearance of the manorial order, and of serfdom and serflike tenancy, had profound effects on the development of Chinese society. It was in part responsible for the tremendous demographic upsurge which took the Chinese population from over 200 millions in 1580 to about 410 millions in 1850. It led to greatly increased social mobility and to greater geographical mobility. It probably contributed to the higher agricultural productivity which enabled the greatly expanded population to be fed. And obviously it meant the formation of an essentially new type of power structure at the grassroots, one in which rural power was not linked to landholding so much as to institutional position or financial strength, and located in the market towns and cities. None of these causal connections can at present be documented as one would wish, yet the logic of the case is compelling.

Let us turn first to the question of population. As we have seen on page 238, serfs depended on their owners' good offices if they were to get married. In the words of the Ch'ien-lung reign gazetteer for Pao-shan county: 'Serfs are all provided with wives, food and clothing by their masters.'[50] In conditions of a relative shortage of land it was not necessarily in the interests of the masters to have their serfs breeding at a great rate, especially as there was no well-established market for the sale of children. The sales that are mentioned as taking place seem to have been solely by parents under economic duress. The Ch'ien-lung reign gazetteer for Hsiang-shan county in Chekiang says of the peasants there:

> Even if they suffer from extreme poverty, they are not willing to sell their sons and daughters to be serfs or maid-servants. Sometimes there are years of bad harvests and they do sell their sons. The rich families may also bring them up as adopted sons.[51]

It would also have been thought deeply shocking for a well-to-do family deliberately to separate serf children from their parents. That there was no or little gain to be had from serf-breeding appears from the *Family Rules of the Chiang Clan*:

> Girl serfs should be married off before they are nineteen years of age. Sometimes they are given to male serfs; sometimes one selects a [free] husband for them to marry. *One should not be greedy for profit* [and hold onto them].[52]

In fact owners often chose not to relinquish the labour power of their female serfs. Light is thrown on this by the biography of Yao Yung-chi, a native of Shang-hai in the latter part of the Ming dynasty:

> When he first became magistrate of Tung-yang county [in Chekiang] . . . it was the custom for the hair of the female serfs of the powerful households to grow white without their being able to marry. Yao Yung-chi gave instructions that if any serf-girl over nineteen years of age was without a husband, her master should be punished. If any hid such girls and did not report them, their neighbours would be punished. Thus this evil custom was abruptly reformed.[53]

We also know of a Mr Chang whose female serfs 'were never married off all their lives long, but were always treated with courtesy'. According to a gazetteer for Chi-an prefecture in southern Kiangsi:

> [In An-fu] it is the custom in the rural communities for those tenants of the manor who rear girls to present silver to their landlord before

giving the child its name . . . For this reason many tenants drown their daughters.[54]

The passing of serfdom thus increased the proportion of the female and probably also of the male population available for reproduction. There may also have been some long-term weakening of other demographic controls. In the twelfth century an official had observed of Fukien province:

> People give birth without limit; and since the number of persons has multiplied in this fashion, when there are three adult males in a family, generally one or even two of them will abandon secular life and enter a Buddhist or Taoist monastery.[55]

As monks they were of course subject to vows of chastity and celibacy, but did this make any great difference to the state of the population? It is hard to be certain. Fukien was, of all the provinces of the empire, the most devoted to Buddhism, and therefore presumably something of a special case. The 1817 gazetteer for Sung-chiang prefecture (in Kiangsu) quotes figures for 1341–67 which show that at that time there were in this prefecture 6,566 Buddhists and Taoists in 667 religious establishments, out of a total population of 177,348 households. At the contemporary local ratio of persons to households of about 5·4, this meant about 0.7 per cent of the total population or something over one per cent of the adult population. Such a percentage is not very persuasive evidence that the religious life was a significant form of birth-control. But if this was so, why should the founder of the Ming dynasty have thought it important to ban the private establishment of new Taoist or Buddhist monasteries, to limit the number of religious who might be licensed in each administrative area, and to reduce religious establishments by forced amalgamations? In the later fifteenth century an edict prescribed punishment for anyone from a household of less than three grown males who became a monk, presumably because this would have made it hard for the household to pay its taxes. About the same time a decree limited the holding of religious foundations in Fukien to a mere one hundred *mou* each. These measures all suggest administrative concern. Yet by 1486 the number of monks and nuns reported in the empire had only risen to somewhere between a quarter and a half million (from an unbelievable low of 57,200 religious officially registered in 1372); and this too can hardly have exceeded one per cent of the adult population. The *economic* position of the monasteries may, however, have been out of all proportion with the numbers of monks and nuns. In 1525, for example, the tax rice in Fukien amounted to 849,000 piculs, and the rice taken from their land by the monasteries as rent to 128,000. Given what is known about the proportions of official and commoner land, this may indicate a monastic holding of up to fifteen per cent of cultivated land. Perhaps this explains the degree of government concern, and the decrees like that limiting monastic landholdings (which was patently ineffective). From a demographic point of view, it must be remembered that it was quite common for people to become monks or nuns in old age, when they no longer wanted or were capable of bearing children. Some monks, who got tonsured to avoid the state labour services rather than out of any sense of pious devotion, are known to have kept wives and concubines. It is therefore hard to develop even an impressionistic feeling for the part played by monasticism in holding back population growth. What does seem certain is that the concern of the government with the institution had waned almost to nil by the seventeenth and eighteenth centuries; and that monastic landholding and the relative numbers of monks and nuns seem all to have declined during roughly the same period that serfdom was passing away.[56]

How the decline of serfdom and serflike tenancy increased social mobility needs little elaboration, except for one caveat. There were times when the institution itself was a means of upward mobility. Several Ming works advised a master against giving a serf his own surname on the grounds that, as one of them put it, 'as the years passed by and numerous sons were born, the false would inevitably become confused with the genuine and throw our system of succession into disorder'. If a serf were able he might also be made a manager of his master's affairs and come to be much richer and more powerful than many free persons.[57] The general assumption of most writers on the subject, however, was that serfs were labourers; and cases of this kind must therefore be regarded as exceptional.

Chinese rural society in the nineteenth century and the early twentieth century was thus one of the most fluid in the world, lacking any of the status or caste restraints which typified late pre-modern Japan or India. The Communist land-reform documents of the 1930s again give proof of this. According to a Communist party ruling, it took only three years to establish 'landlord' or 'rich peasant' status; and there are a number of references to the problems of dealing with those who had been landlords for only a short time, and of categorizing characters like a certain Chou

Tsung-jen who had risen in the space of twenty years from a hired labourer to a landlord and moneylender. A document on the 'rich peasant problem' observed of 'rich peasants of an initial stage character' that, 'though they do not collect land rent or exploit hired labour, yet they make loans at usury and in addition, sell their surplus foodstuffs whenever an opportunity offers . . . This category of rich peasants, by virtue of the above-mentioned two forms of exploitation, gradually accumulates its capital and moves in the direction of joining the ranks of the rich peasants of a capitalistic and a semi-landlord character.' Other documents refer to the intermittent hiring of labour, i.e. 'exploitation', and to peasants who had had 'good luck' a year or two before the Communist takeover and had become 'landlords'. Everywhere there was a constant competition, without benefit to society as a whole, in which the fortunes of individual peasant families continually rose and fell. It was a society that was both egalitarian and riven with mutual jealousies. The economic closeness of exploiter and exploited, and the lack of any ideologically sanctioned inevitability in the social differences between them, made for hostility rather than harmony.

The ownership of land, though useful, was in no way necessary for upward mobility in the countryside. For example, the management of collective lands belonging to clans, temples and associations could bring substantial wealth. According to a decree issued by Mao Tse-tung and others early in the 1930s: 'There is no doubt that the management of landholdings of public bodies is a sort of exploitation when the landlord class and rich peasants have concentrated large amounts of land and other properties through the medium of this system. As the management of landholdings of public bodies has been monopolized by a handful of people, the act of such management constitutes, of course, one of the factors for the determination of class status . . . However . . . some of the smaller public bodies are managed by turns by the masses of workers, peasants and poor people and accordingly make for very little exploitation.' Loans and commerce were also important. According to one Communist document: 'All kinds of rich peasants have in common two ways of exploiting the poor and miserable masses, namely, loans at usurious rates of interest (interest on loans of money, grains, pigs, oxen and vegetable oils), and the sale of foodstuffs and like commodities . . . Besides, many of the rich peasants are concurrently engaged in commerce – running small stores and peddling farm produce – thus exploiting the poor and miserable masses.' 'Buying when prices are low and selling when prices are high, and running small stores' were the 'principal forms' of rich peasant exploitation. (Perhaps significantly, 'small landlords' and 'rich peasants' were said to exploit more ruthlessly than large landlords.) This commercialization of the countryside is the main theme of the next chapter.

*

Finally, the nature of power in the countryside changed when manorialism had gone. In broad terms this change may be characterized as a shift from landlord power localized in the country to managerial gentry and sub-bureaucrat power based mostly in the towns and cities. The tasks of maintaining order, collecting taxes, and directing such projects as hydraulic works not large enough for state intervention, were until the seventeenth century the responsibility of the powerful landowners. After this time, there were no longer enough big landowners living in the country for the old system; and the fragmentation and geographical dispersion of holdings made it hard to assign a landlord specifically to any one administrative area (see the quotation from the Su-chou prefectural gazetteer on page 253). The local government clerks and various wardens and headmen appointed by the county magistrates therefore took over. Then during the eighteenth century the local 'gentry' (that is to say those with official rank but living at home, and those with official academic degrees) moved in as co-ordinators of tax collection, managers of local projects, and a little later as the directors of local institutions like the charities which sprang up in great numbers around and after 1800. 'Gentry' in this sense had of course been active previously in local affairs as landowners, though exempt from the chores of formal administrative service. Now they operated under official supervision as professional directors, often owning little or no land. This change may seem a subtle one. In fact it was fundamental to the evolution of late traditional Chinese social structure.

The basic Ming system of local administration is described in the *Veritable Records of the Ming Dynasty* for 1381:

> One hundred and ten households will form a canton. In each canton the ten men [i.e. heads of households] with the highest tax assessment will be chosen as leaders. The remaining hundred households will be divided into ten tithings, each of ten men. The canton administrator and the tithing-heads shall be responsible for managing the affairs of the canton.[58]

In other words, formal administrative power was put into the hands of the biggest landowners (see page 80, where the Sung system is outlined). For the collection of the tribute grain needed to feed the capital, the founder of the Ming dynasty chose grain administrators from 'rich families who possessed much grain and many labourers'. Initially at least they were given extensive privileges. Thus in 1375 it was decreed:

> If a grain administrator commits robbery or a crime which merits the death penalty or banishment, he shall merely be flogged.[59]

A gazetteer for Chia-ting county observed:

> Bearing in mind that the collection of taxes is connected with the great policies of state, and that 'if people are wealthy they are virtuous', His Majesty used rich families to provide grain administrators, and direct the taxes of their areas. Each was responsible for from ten thousand to several thousands of piculs . . . At that time fathers and mothers and elder brothers gave instructions to their sons and younger brothers with the object of fitting them to hold the post of grain administrator and enjoy high esteem. They had no desire for the glory of the state examinations, for this was not so easy to transmit through numerous generations.[60]

In 1435 the county magistrate of Ch'ang-shu, after deploring the abuses committed by the grain administrators, asked for 'rich persons with many taxable males in their families, and spoken well of by the multitude' as replacements.

These conscripted administrators were not normally of the official gentry class, but wealthy landowning commoners. In his seventeenth-century *Survey of the Age* Yeh Meng-chu makes this clear, at least of his own county of Shang-hai:

> [In Ming times] these services were all performed by persons who possessed land, but the gentry had by law a privileged exemption and did not participate in them. Senior licentiates, imperial academy students and licentiates only had a privileged exemption for a hundred *mou* of land. It was the rich families, with numerous fields but no privileged exemption, who had together to fulfil these obligations. By and large, the rural gentry who held the metropolitan doctorate were not liable for any administrative labour service at all, regardless of what official rank they held and how extensive their lands might be. For those with the provincial doctorate, official rank was taken into account. Those with a high rank could be exempt of obligation for

two or three thousand *mou*. If a senior licentiate had had an official career his rank might also be taken into consideration. If he had a high one, he might be exempted of liability for a thousand *mou*; if a low one, for not more than three to five hundred *mou*. Imperial academy students who had had no official career were on a par with the licentiates, which meant that they benefited but little from their promotion.[61]

The organization of tax-collection and water conservancy works is described by a late Ming gazetteer for Sung-chiang prefecture as follows:

There are 14,350 canton administrators enrolled in the Yellow Registers [in which the Ming government recorded tax obligations]. Each year some 1,435 of them perform the duties in rotation. The remainder are off-duty administrators. There are 1,435 elders, old men of good conduct being picked to fill this post. There are 209 grain administrators, men of good conduct and liable for both labour service and grain tax being chosen for this post. There are also 209 dyke administrators. Each county has jurisdiction over a certain number of wards. Each ward controls a certain number of divisions. Each division controls a certain number of districts [which seem to have been the same as the cantons]. The numbers differ from case to case. Each district shares out a ten-year period among its ten tithings, and for each of these a tax prompter is enrolled, though the post may either be filled by a single household, or by two or three together . . . Each year it is the turn of one of the tithings to have special responsibility for managing the tax payments of the households in their district. Suppose, by way of example, that the first tithing, assigned to the first year of the ten-year cycle, is filling the post of tax prompter. Then the tenth tithing, assigned to the tenth year, which is to say the year before, will fill the post of annual overseer, and the ninth tithing, assigned to the year before that, will fill the post of tithing-general [with responsibilities for law and order]. The annual overseer has to undertake such chores as gathering together labourers, having the waterways dredged, and mud and undergrowth removed . . . Out of the annual overseers in a given division it is the one who has served as general divisional tax prompter [i.e. the richest] who becomes dyke administrator. His special duty is to direct the labourers from the various districts in undertaking the water conservancy works of the division . . .[62]

Sung-chiang was exceptional in some details, but the spirit of the system was entirely typical.

In the later sixteenth and seventeenth century the Ming local administrative structure was dismantled, though at different times in different parts of the country. Reform came to Shang-hai county in 1667. 'Everyone paid in their own taxes, and there was no need for others to act as prompters.' Dyke administrators were abolished on the assumption that, 'If sometimes there are [large-scale] tasks which must be undertaken, these too will be suitably assigned according to the acreage [held by each landowner].' This apparently applied with equal force to the members of the official gentry, for they are said to have been 'aggrieved at the lack of distinction made between the honourable and the mean, . . . and to have wanted to restore the canton labour services'.[63] Immediate cause of the reform was the mounting corruption among the clerks in the county sub-bureaucracies. This had led rich people to do all they could to avoid such once esteemed positions as that of grain administrator, which were now subject to all sorts of unjust and unreasonable demands. The clerks' depredations may have been inadvertently encouraged in the Chia-ching reign (1522-66) by this latter post going not only to powerful persons, but also to the less well off as a way of 'repressing the strong and supporting the weak'. The weak of course could not stand up to the clerks. The underlying cause of the breakdown, however, and the reason why the new and vigorous Manchu dynasty could not restore the old system, was that suitably qualified rural landlords to man it grew ever fewer.

*

What was the system that replaced it?

Some of the clearest changes can be seen in the management of local hydraulic projects, which may therefore serve as a model for the pattern of change as a whole. The county of Shang-hai is once again an illustrative case.[64] In 1678 an official who was a native of the county proposed that an assistant county magistrate should 'be deputed *in conjunction with the rural gentry*' to manage the county's dredging. The first record of the actual participation of the 'gentry and scholars' in a hydraulic project appears in a gazetteer entry dated 1684, but referring to some years earlier. These were isolated incidents, however, and the management of conservancy works during most of the next hundred years stayed mainly in the hands of official deputies* and canton clerks. They were at best a portent of what was to come.

* Deputies were expectant officials assigned to a particular province. They gained their administrative experience chiefly through this sort of work.

In 1720 it was proposed that the official in charge of a conservancy project 'should select several upright and capable members of the gentry or scholars from the cantons, who will help him to spread his influence downwards'. In 1753 we again find such assistance being provided by the local gentry, and in 1763 the new system began to take definitive shape with the proposals of Chang Shih-yu, an official deputy, for a scheme which he described as 'seasonable, sweeping and bold':

> The method is three-fold: . . . When it is necessary to request government funds, the local officials shall be ordered to undertake the repairs . . . In those cases [of somewhat smaller undertakings] where the acreage has to be estimated district by district [in order to determine the landlords' obligations for the provision of labour], the order shall be given for the gentry and scholars of the county involved to gather for discussions and publicly select leaders. The local officials will be used to supervise them. In this fashion the network of personal obligations will work in its accustomed way, and neither public nor private interests will be thrown into confusion. When there are repairs which need to be done in rotation year by year, the landlords . . . shall be ordered to carry out this maintenance dredging by themselves.

In 1775, according to the county gazetteer for the T'ungc-hih reign (1862–74) for a clearance of the major and minor waterways of the county capital, 'this year *for the first time* the levying of funds and the [direction of the] dredging were done by the gentry and scholars; and hereafter all the work done on the market rivers of the county capital followed the proposals first made [on this occasion]'. In this and the following year members of the gentry took charge of two projects in the countryside. Lest this development should be thought peculiar to Shang-hai county, it is worth stressing its occurrence in other parts of China at about the same time. For example a gazetteer for the huge polder of Sang-yuan-wei in Kwangtung province noted that:

> For dealing with the repairs each year: initially the Sang-yuan-wei area was divided into [fourteen wards] which were assigned to fourteen sectors under the management of the *landlords*. Nowadays each ward entrusts its *gentry and scholars* with deciding upon two knowledgeable persons to help supervise these matters. Everything that is done has to be in accordance with the decisions of the Dyke Board [which they constitute].

By the early nineteenth century, members of the gentry who administered hydraulic projects, either on their own or along with official deputies, were being referred to as 'gentry directors' – a new term – in recognition of their services as professional organizers rather than as interested or responsible landowners.

The gentry directors, unlike their conscript predecessors, were not forced to administer hydraulic projects. Their power to do so, although it enjoyed the formal backing of the state, depended in fact upon that 'network of personal obligations' of which Chang Shih-yu had spoken. For this reason, whenever there was any difficulty over conservancy policy or a departure from commonly accepted routine, they worked through consultations either with the magistrate, or with each other, or with the landowners, merchants and common people. A representative example of the kind of collective advice which the gentry directors and others might be called upon to give to the authorities is the case of Ch'ao-chia Creek in 1870:

> Chu Feng-t'i, the acting county magistrate, called together the directors and wardens of the county capital and the countryside. It was concluded after a discussion that: in 1836 the whole county had provided labourers on the basis of acreage, no wages being given for the quantity dredged and administrative expenses being provided by the officials. In 1858 a payment had been made for the amount dredged, and administrative charges had all been met from unallocated levies and fines, no money being taken from the landowners and tenants of the county. In recent years the officials had become poor and the commoners rich . . . They requested that . . . a levy on acreage should be imposed . . . The gentry directors [also] suggested that the best thing to do would be to make an additional payment for the difficult parts.

There are other instances of a magistrate using an assembly of gentry for advice on a hydraulic project; and the proposals made seem invariably to have been accepted.

The voice of the gentry in local policy-making was not unique to Shang-hai county. In 1902, for example, K'ang Yu-wei wrote:

> There are at present as a matter of course in our various provinces, prefectures, departments and counties, public boards where the gentry and scholars meet for discussions. If there are important matters, the Hall of Human Relationships in the Confucian Temple is opened for a public debate, and the authorities usually send a deputy to attend it . . . In my native Kwangtung . . . the gentry of these boards are selected by the gentry and authorized by the officials. When

there are important matters, all the gentry and scholars are able to give their opinions and in this closely resemble the members of assemblies in other countries . . . However, the state has not laid down a system, the assemblymen and the heads of the boards are not selected by the people; and for this reason there has often arisen the abuse of powerful gentry from families of long standing keeping an arbitrary hold upon them.[65]

Consultative procedure might also involve the low-status headmen and wardens, who were appointed by the county magistrates to handle the dirty work of day-to-day control. An example of this is the so-called Rural Compact boards of Wu-hsi and Chin-kuei counties. These boards had originally been concerned with giving edifying public lectures, but had grown to be auxiliary organs of government. Their regulations, published in 1869 as part of a collection of documents relating to charitable foundations, indirectly reveal this. When the county magistrate and the gentry directors, they say, come on one of their regular visits to an area, the scholars and commoners 'ought to wait until the lecture is finished before they discuss at the board all public matters of benefit to the locality regarding which something may usefully be done'. The link between the gentry and the lower-level professionals, who were known locally as 'Rural Compact leaders', emerges later:

> The rural area directors must come in rotation to the boards in order to facilitate discussions. In each sub-district they shall visit the board twice a year . . . At these times, one day before they come to the board, the directors of the sub-district shall call together the various canton directors in their sub-district, and also the rural compact leaders of the various urban and rural areas, to a meeting in their own sub-district office, at which they will proceed to discuss all local matters which may with advantage be acted upon. Then, when the appointed time comes, each sub-district director shall go with four or five canton directors *and* the rural compact leaders from the urban and rural areas to the general board, where they will report upon the matters discussed in the various cantons, with the intent that further deliberations and then action will be taken.[66]

It is unlikely, simply on the basis of the numbers involved, that all those called 'directors' here had imperial academic degrees; but they must either have had them or have been notables for some other reason. The Rural Compact leaders, if the analogous 'wardens' of Shang-hai may be taken as a guide, were probably persons of low social status who had bought their posts, and lived off the 'squeeze' they extracted from the populace.

The gentry also played an important part in the collection of taxes. This is clear from a passage in the Ch'ing dynasty's *Veritable Records* for 1806:

> It has been reported that, when the tribute grain is collected, the local officials in the provinces collect more than the amount sanctioned by law. They make arrangements to have gentry of bad character act as their agents in coercing payment. They first make enquiries as to who among the gentry are habitually fond of meddling. Then they bribe them in advance, granting them the right to contract for a certain portion of the tribute grain. The rustics and the poor have a redoubled burden because these persons can levy an excess amount from them just as they please.

T'ao Chu (or Shu), an official chiefly famous for reforming the salt monopoly, commented on this practice in 1827:

> Some of them do not own a single *mou* of land, yet contract for the payment of up to several hundred piculs' worth of tax. There are cases, too, when not a pint of rice is taken but only 'tribute rice silver', in amounts ranging from several tens to several hundreds of ounces. In the most densely populated areas there may be as many as three hundred holders of the first degree, and the tribute rice money may amount to from 20,000 to 30,000 taels.[67]

It is likely that prosperous grain merchants also contracted for the collection of taxes. Certainly they could be important local figures. Thus in 1814 a censor reported that:

> In the region of the two market towns of Shuang-ho and San-ho, in the neighbourhood of Liu-an in Lu-chou in this province [i.e. Anhwei], there is a rice merchant called Lu. He has built granaries along the river for over twenty-three miles, and has dominated this area for many a year. At harvest time he gathers in a million piculs, buying cheap and selling dear.[68]

Power in the countryside no longer resided solely or even primarily in the ownership of land, though obviously it might sometimes be *reflected* in such ownership.

In what, then, did it primarily reside? The short answer is: trade, finance, education, and institutional position, in ascending order of importance; but for this answer in full it is necessary first to turn to the two following chapters.

16 · Rural markets and rural industries

We have just seen that the social matrix in which the second period of sustained economic growth took place in pre-modern China was significantly different from that of the first. This chapter will show the organizational matrix also to have been different, and that this had far-reaching implications for the *type* of growth that took place.

Some time in the course of the seventeenth century the number of market towns, at least in the more economically advanced part of China, began to multiply at a rate exceeding that of the population increase. This phenomenon is illustrated for the case of Shang-hai county by the maps grouped under map 8. The recent researches of Professor Shiba indicate a broadly comparable pattern for Ning-po prefecture in northern Chekiang; one suspects that a good part of China was affected in much the same way. The late Ming work *A Record of the Customs of Wu* observed that:

> The large villages and famous towns all developed shops which sold every kind of commodity, so as to monopolize the profits; and those who carried goods on their backs between the towns and villages were all in distress.[1]

Interestingly, the increase in market towns in Shang-hai county seems to correlate with the rise of guilds concerned with interregional trade located in the county capital; figure 3 shows this. Professor Ho Ping-ti has shown that the accelerated growth of such guilds through the eighteenth and nineteenth centuries, so striking a feature of the Shang-hai case, was almost nation-wide.[2] Shang-hai in this respect was not exceptional.

The origins of these market towns were many and varied. They grew up around temples, around the manors of great landlords and the country residences of important merchants, and even around industrial undertakings such as pottery works. They appeared at nodes in the transport system, at bridges, at the intersections of waterways, at resting-spots along main water-routes, and at customs houses in 'places through which merchants have to pass'. They were the by-products of the location of official salt stores, military stations and arsenals. Sometimes they were set up by influential persons as a deliberate act of will. In other instances they were the outcome of accident, as when bad harvests in a region forced the inhabitants into commerce, or rebels overlooked a village in their otherwise thorough plunder of a countryside. Some of them straddled county borders. All of them helped the flow of persons, goods, money and ideas locally, regionally, and nationally. Anyone who is tempted to think of the late traditional Chinese rural economy as 'cellular', 'self-sufficient', or 'uncommercialized' has only to look at this network and its density to realize how inapplicable these terms are.

As further qualitative evidence for this here are two passages showing the extent of trade in everyday necessities. The first, from a censor early in the seventeenth century, relates to the customs-houses in the southern part of the country:

> Throughout the prefectures, the departments and the counties of Kiangnan there are waterways everywhere. Everywhere there are local specialities. Everywhere there is trading. At the present time there are controls on all this. At the river ports of every county and pre-fecture even such commonplace articles as rice, salt, chickens and pigs, and even such coarse ones as firewood, coals, vegetables and fruits are all affected. Every commodity is subject to a tax. Every person is subject to a tax. In no county is there one village at peace, and in no village one family at peace. People are being interfered with everywhere. Rich and poor alike are being molested.[3]

The second, from the Chia-ching reign (1522–66) gazetteer for Ho-chien prefecture in what is now northern Hopei province reads:

> The merchants who bring goods to Ho-chien sell silk, grain, salt, iron and timber. Those who sell silk come from Nanking, Su-chou and Lin-ch'ing. Those who sell grain come from Wei-hui, Tz'u-chou and the region around Tientsin along the Grand Canal. They come to buy grain, or go to sell it, depending on whether our harvest has been good or bad, transporting it in carts. Those who sell iron mostly deal in agricultural implements. They come from Lin-ch'ing and Po-t'ou in small carts. Vendors of salt come from Ts'ang-chou and Tientsin. Sellers of timber come from Chen-ting. Those of porcelain and lacquer objects from Jao-chou and Hui-chou. The resident traders are mostly

from the prefectures and counties of Hopei. They are all called 'shop-keepers'. Since goods have begun to circulate there have also been people in the prefectural capital here, and in the departments and counties, who have travelled with them . . . Their principle in going to market is to exchange what they have for what they do not. Markets are held at midday, and everyone gathers at the appointed time. Those in the departmental and county capitals meet five or six times a month. Those in the rural market towns meet two or three times a month. In the prefectural capital there is a market every day.[4]

The markets in the department and county capitals presumably stocked travelling merchants and peddlers with goods to sell at a number of smaller markets held on a cycle of days arranged, where possible, to avoid two nearby markets coinciding.

This second passage, and some other evidence as well, suggests that markets were still a comparatively new phenomenon in many areas. Thus a gazetteer for Shao-hsing prefecture from the Wan-li reign (1573–1619), after noting that 'the large markets are those in the administrative capitals; they meet daily', observes that the capital of Hsin-ch'ang county only had a market after the Ch'eng-hua reign (1465–87). Country markets, it adds, were only held 'once or twice in each ten-day cycle'. At the same time, the most advanced regions were already moving on from such periodic rural markets to permanent markets.

This last development had profound implications for the structure of subsidiary peasant handicrafts. We can see this in the cotton industry. It was probably the largest single industry in China in late traditional times; and also showed in unusually clear form many features which pervaded other industries but less obviously. Cotton moreover is of particular interest in the context of the problem of industrialization, because in most developed countries it has been one of the first sectors to be mechanized.

By the seventeenth and eighteenth centuries it was normal for those who spun or wove cotton in the countryside to make *daily* trips to the market to buy their raw materials. According to a late Ming gazetteer for Hu-chou:

Merchants from other prefectures buy raw cotton and set up shops on our land. The poor people take what they have spun or woven, namely thread or cotton cloth, and go to the market early in the morning. They exchange it there for raw cotton [or yarn] with which they return to spin or weave as before. On the morrow they again take it to be exchanged.[5]

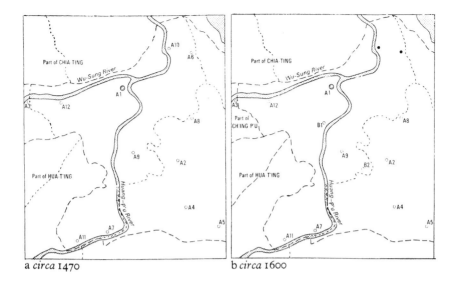

a *circa* 1470   b *circa* 1600

The growth of market towns in
Shang-hai county, 1470–1910

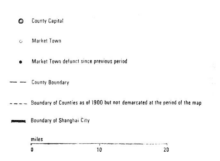

○ County Capital

○ Market Town

● Market Town defunct since previous period

— — County Boundary

– – – – Boundary of Counties as of 1900 but not demarcated at the period of the map

▬▬ Boundary of Shanghai City

miles
0   10   20

Map 8

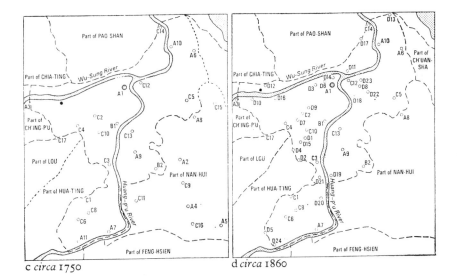

c *circa* 1750

d *circa* 1860

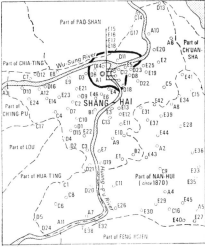

e *circa* 1910

This could just possibly refer to isolated rural supply depots rather than to markets; but not so the Ch'ien-lung reign (1735–95) gazetteer for Shang-hai:

> It is not only in the country villages that spinning is to be found, but also in the county capital and the market towns. In the morning the village women take the thread which they have spun and go to the market, where they exchange it for raw cotton, with which they return. The following morning they again leave home with their thread, never pausing for an instant.[6]

Tung Hsien-liang's *Weaving Song*, written in the Ming dynasty, describes the role of the market as a source of supplementary raw material:

> He tends his cotton in the garden in the morning,
> In the evening makes his cloth upon the loom.
> His wife weaves with ever-moving fingers;
> His girls spin with never-ceasing wheels.
> It is the humid and unhealthy season
> When they finish the last of the cotton from their garden.
> Prices go up and up, if outside merchants come to buy;
> So if warp's plentiful a lack of weft brings grief.
> They therefore buy raw cotton and spin it night after night.[7]

Hsu Hsien-chung's *Prose poem on Cotton Cloth*, which is an account of Shang-hai county in the middle of the sixteenth century, gives a vivid picture of peasant dependence on the market:

> Why do you ignore their toil? Why are you touched
> Only by the loveliness that is born from toil?
> . . .
> Shall I tell you how their work exhausts them?
> By hand and treadle they turn the rollers of wood and iron,
> Feeding the fibre in between their fingers;
> The cotton comes out fluffy and the seeds fall away.
> The string of the cotton bow is stretched so taut
> It twangs with a sob from its pillar.
> They draw out slivers, spin them on their wheels
> To the accompaniment of a medley of creakings.
> Working through darkness by candlelight,
> Forgetful of bed. When energy ebbs, they sing.
> The quilts are cold. Unheard, the waterclock flows over.
> . . .

> Then in the freezing cold they send the shuttle flying.
> One up, one down, the warp-threads through the heddles run.
> And as the footbar moves they rise and fall in turn.
> A thread snaps; and is painfully joined again.
> . . .
> The chill night stretches out
> As one foot, then another foot, is done.
> The hens are cackling in the morning cold
> When the piece is wound off its roller
> And they hurry to market.
> . . .
> When a woman leaves for market
> She does not look at her hungry husband.
> Afraid her cloth's not good enough,
> She adorns her face with cream and powder,
> Touches men's shoulders to arouse their lust,
> And sells herself with pleasant words.
> Money she thinks of as a beast its prey;
> Merchants she coaxes as she would her father.
> Nor is her burden lifted till one buys.[8]

Reliance of the rural subsidiary industries on the market network thus characterizes this period.

This dependence takes on an added significance when we remember that in Sung times what amounted to quite large-scale putting out had existed in the rural hemp textile industry (see page 162). This seems to have disappeared in the second period of pre-modern economic growth, presumably because the market mechanism was so good as to make it unnecessary. If a peasant with virtually no working capital could have daily access to a market for his or her materials, there was no place for a putting out system. Proof of the absence of such a system is not easy, since the argument is basically ex silentio. Thus in Tung Hung-tu's *Complaint of the Weaving Wife* we hear of the pressure exerted by the landlord and the tax-collector, but not of the putter out coming to collect his goods:

> Hungry, she still weaves.
> Numbed with cold, she still weaves.
> Shuttle after shuttle after shuttle.
> The days are short,
> The weather chill,
> Each length hard to finish.

> The rich take their rent;
> The clerk the land tax,
> Knocking repeatedly with urgent insistence.
> Her husband wants to urge her on,
> But has no heart to do so.
> He says nothing,
> But stands beside the loom.
>   . . .
> The more she tries to get it done
> The more her strength fails her.
> She turns away, choking down tears,
> And consoles herself that their neighbours are
>   poorer – and lonelier –
> For they sold their loom
> And next had to sell their son.[9]

The only possible evidence we have for putting out in the cotton industry is unfortunately unclear on the nature of the organization involved. The best passage is a tombstone inscription for Hsi She-jen, a member of a family of cotton merchants, written by Wang Yuan late in the seventeenth century. This says:

> I made several trips to Tung-t'ing Tung-shan . . . At that time the women in the hills had no subsidiary occupation and ate in empty-handed idleness. Much later, weaving became known and was to be met with in every highway and byway. When I enquired as to who had brought this about, they told me: 'She-jen taught it to girls whom he recruited in the neighbouring prefectures.' I asked them from where they obtained their raw cotton, and also their spinning wheels and looms. They answered: 'She-jen gave them.'[10]

Was this a single act of charity or a continuing commercial operation? The phrasing is tantalizingly vague. So too is that of an early eighteenth-century gazetteer for T'ai-shun county in Chekiang prefecture: 'The women workers rarely work at embroidery. They only practise spinning or weaving. Some of them are poor and unable to buy cotton or ramie fibre. Therefore they spin or weave on a sharing basis for others, so as to sustain themselves.' There is also an account of the Sung-chiang stocking industry by one Fan Lien, though this may refer to the sewing, rather than the spinning or weaving, as being put out:

> Formerly there were no shops for summer socks in Sung-chiang. Most people wore felt socks in the hot months. After the Wan-li

reign [1573–1619] Yu-t'un cotton cloth was used to make thin summer socks which were extremely light and attractive. People from distant places competed to purchase them. As a result, more than a hundred shops for summer socks were opened in the hinterland to the west of the prefectural capital; and men and women throughout the prefecture made their living from the manufacture of these socks. They were supplied and paid from the shops. It was a new occupation of benefit to the people.[11]

The first incontrovertible evidence of putting out in the spinning and weaving of cotton comes from the end of the nineteenth century and does not properly belong to China's pre-modern economic history.

If this analysis of the seventeenth- and eighteenth-century Chinese rural cotton industry is correct, certain conclusions follow regarding the absence of technological progress. The industry was based mainly on subsidiary labour, often with a marked seasonal aspect to it (see the passage on page 253 on Wu-hsi and Chin-kuei counties). Therefore income from spinning and weaving constituted only a portion of the total income of a peasant household, and their simple equipment lay unused for many months in the year. Taking all such households together, there was an enormous reserve of unused productive capacity. Moreover this industry was co-ordinated through a market mechanism by merchants with no direct involvement whatever in the process of production itself. Therefore both a rising and a falling demand for cotton textiles exerted a much weaker pressure on the technology of the industry than it would have done had the workers been full-time, and co-ordinated through putters out or the owners of factories.* For consider – when demand was rising the enormous reserve capacity in hundreds of thousands of peasant households was brought into play as needed by diverting labour from agriculture as price levels determined its marginal return. And, when demand was falling, the damage only affected a portion of the total composite income of each peasant household; and even this could be alleviated by directing labour back into farming. Thus in times of boom there were no great prospective rewards for inventors; and in times of slump there were few penalties severe enough to drive the inefficient permanently out of business.

Secondly, the excellence of the market mechanism made it unnecessary for cotton cloth merchants to become directly involved in

---

* There were some factories in China at this time, most notably in the tea-processing industry outside Canton. See p. 282.

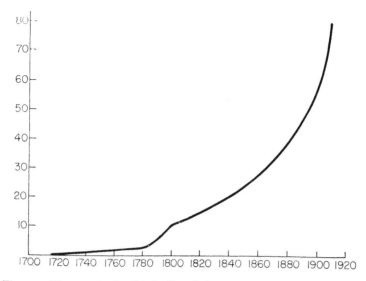

Figure 3. The growth of guilds in Shanghai.

production. They could hold almost all their capital in relatively liquid form as working capital and avoid tying it up as fixed capital. This gave them much greater potential freedom of action, and spared them embezzlement of materials by spinners and weavers. With no benefits to be had from acting otherwise, this arrangement was in any case congenial to the merchant temperament.

Thus those with the keenest awareness of market forces, and the capital and skills for new initiatives, were so placed that they were very unlikely to have any deep personal appreciation of how their product was manufactured and any ideas as to how it might be improved. In so far as the rural cotton industry had a structure of this kind, one can argue the paradoxical proposition that the Chinese countryside was both overindustrialized and overcommercialized.

Was the organization of the urban cotton industry different?

There is reason to suspect that it may have been. At least in the hemp and silk industries there were weaving shops with hired labour. Consider, for example, the following remarks of Chang Han, who came from Hang-chow:

My ancestor I-an was of modest social status, being a dealer in wines. In 1471 there were floods . . . and he abandoned this business and bought a loom. He wove all kinds of hemp [or ramie] cloth, exceedingly finely worked. Whenever he had finished a piece, people would compete to buy it, and he made a profit of twenty per cent. After twenty years he bought a second loom; and finally he had more than twenty of them. Outside his doors there was a constant crowd of merchants, and he still could not supply them with all they needed. As a result the family became extremely rich. Four of my forebears later continued in this business and each amassed several tens of thousands of ounces of silver.[12]

It is of course only likely, not certain, that this passage refers to urban production. There was a somewhat comparable situation in the silk industry, if the report made by Ts'ao Shih-p'in on the disturbances among the silk weavers of Su-chou in 1601 may be trusted:

Very few [of the Su-chou people] have a regular agricultural livelihood, but in every family one will find looms and woven silk. The 'loom households' provide the capital, and the weavers provide the labour, each relying upon the other to prolong their days . . . [Besides setting up customs stations which interfered with trade, the followers of Sun Lung, the eunuch director of taxes] also recklessly proposed taxing every loom 0·3 of an ounce of silver. All the loom households closed their doors, and the weaving workers, who were faced with the prospect of death by starvation, responded at once [with a riot] . . . The people without families who wander around in search of a living cannot make plans in the morning for the evening of the same day. If they find employment, they live. If they lose employment, they perish. When the dyeing shops closed, I saw several thousand dyers scattered. When the loom houses closed I saw a further several thousand weavers scattered. These were all worthy people who supported themselves by their own efforts.[13]

The daily labour markets in Su-chou and Ch'ang-chou at this time also show the extensive use of hired workers in the silk industry.[14]

We do not yet have incontrovertible proof of a comparable system in the Kiangnan urban cotton industry. The most suggestive text is the following passage from a writer of the early nineteenth century:

Mr Wang from Hsin-an set up the Beneficial and Beautiful wholesaling firm by the Ch'ang Gate of Su-chou city. He was a cunning business man. He gave secret orders that tailors who used his firm's cloth should be rewarded with 0·02 of an ounce of silver. The tailors, greedy for this small profit, all extolled the beauties of Wang's cloth, and users competed to buy it. He calculated that [normally] he sold about a million full lengths each year, making a profit of a hundred cash per length [i.e. a total profit of 100,000 strings of cash], and that if he laid out 20,000 ounces of silver [in rebates to tailors] in addition to the cloth, he increased his [gross] profits to 200,000 strings of cash [or, in other words, he doubled them]. For ten years he was the richest of all merchants, and his cotton cloth was sold ever more widely throughout the empire. He subsequently went on a tour of duty as an official, and, having to relinquish the business, consigned it to a relative called Ch'eng. Ch'eng later returned it to Wang, and for some two hundred years now there has been no place, either north or south, that has failed to consider Beneficial and Beautiful [cloth] to be lovely.[15]

The figures in this passage are almost certainly notional rather than real. In the first half of the seventeenth century, when Mr Wang flourished, the price of a full length of good quality Kiangnan cotton cloth was between 0·15 and 0·18 of an ounce of silver. The rapid rise in the copper/silver exchange ratio during the last years of the Ming dynasty only allows one to determine the percentage profit represented by a hundred cash for specific years. As of about 1628 the ratio used in the provinces would have made a hundred cash equal to 0·09 of an ounce of silver. At 0·18 of an ounce per length this means a profit of one hundred per cent over cost, which is surprising though not necessarily impossible.

What is clear is that something like four thousand weavers, and several times that number of spinners, would have been needed to produce the million lengths of cloth which Mr Wang sold in a normal year, for it took a weaver between one and two days to weave a standard forty-foot length. Unless the reputation of Beneficial and Beautiful rested solely on Wang's skill in public relations, he must have exercised some control over its production. Did this extend to weaving? Or did he simply rely on the superior talents of his purchasing agents, and his own care in arranging for the dyeing and finishing of the cloth? Almost certainly the latter. Wang was one of a number of cotton wholesalers outside the Ch'ang Gate of Su-chou, and organizing dyeing and finishing seems to have been their main concern.

What is more, the structure of this dyeing and finishing industry seems to have been deliberately designed to prevent direct merchant participation in production. Its essentials were described by Li Wei, governor-general of Chekiang, in a memorial of 1730:

In the prefectural capital of Su-chou . . . the green and blue cotton cloth from the various provinces is bought and sold. After it has been dyed it has to be given lustre by being calendered with large stone foot-rollers. There is a class of persons called 'contractors' who make ready large stones shaped like water chestnuts, wooden rollers, tools and rooms. They gather together calenderers to live there, and advance them firewood, rice, silver and copper cash. They receive cloth from the merchant houses to be calendered. The charge per length is 0·0113 of an ounce of silver, all of which goes to the aforesaid workers. Each of them, however, gives to the contractors each month 0·36 of an ounce of silver as representing the rent for the workspace and the tools . . . Formerly there were only seven or eight thousand men in the various workshops . . . Now a careful investigation of the area outside the Ch'ang Gate of Su-chou has shown that there are altogether over 340 persons acting as contractors, and that they have set up more than 450 calendering establishments, in each of which several tens of men are employed. There are over 10,900 calendering stones, and the number of workers must equal this.[16]

There were therefore three main groups involved in the process of production: cloth merchants, contractors and artisans. There may also have been a fourth, peripheral, group consisting of landlords who owned and leased the premises where the work was done. The relationships between these three (or four) groups was an odd blend of organizational fragmentation and structural rigidity.

At the head of the pyramid stood the Su-chou cotton cloth wholesalers (like Mr Wang), of whom there were about seventy at the beginning of the eighteenth century. They drew their supplies either from their own branch shops or from cotton dealers in major towns such as Wei-t'ing. According to a gazetteer of the early nineteenth century, 'The cotton cloth shops are in the eastern market of Wei-t'ing. Outside merchants from various areas and the wholesalers from the Ch'ang Gate of Su-chou all have shops here for buying.'[17] These latter, in their turn, were supplied by merchants operating in the smaller market towns. Thus an early nineteenth-century inscription observes:

Sung-chiang prefecture is an area which produces cotton cloth. The people of the towns and villages of Shang-hai depend on the weaving and sale of cloth for their living. It is therefore decreed that the cotton cloth shops, and those who buy and sell cotton cloth in the villages and in the market towns, shall not henceforth prettify their cloth with flour, and that the cotton cloth brokers and the cotton cloth wholesale firms shall not purchase cloth so powdered.[18]

Two levels in the market structure thus normally intervened between the Su-chou wholesaler and the weavers of his cloth.

The wholesaler was also separated from those who did the finishing work by the contractors. These intermediaries had a legal monopoly of the right to allocate work to artisans. No one might enter the business unless he had been guaranteed by those already engaged in it. In return for this privilege the contractors had to assume full liability for cloth entrusted to their care. According to an inscription of 1644, 'If any of the calenderers steals or absconds with stolen materials, or acts in an evil manner, then the responsibility shall fall upon the contractor. It shall be no concern of the wholesalers or of the proprietors of the dye-shops.'[19] An inscription about fifty years later stressed that 'when the contractor receives the cloth and passes it on, the personal record of the calenderers, and any loss or damage to the goods, shall be the concern not of the cloth merchant but of the contractor'.[20]

These arrangements seem to have been devised by the wholesalers themselves, wealthy businessmen with much influence over the local officials. Rates of pay, both to the contractors and to the artisans, were fixed at a level favourable to the merchants until some time in the 1860s. The latter counted on playing off one contractor against another in order to obtain the best service. Early in the nineteenth century, the wholesalers strenuously resisted the efforts of the contractors to get greater predictability in their operations by having the wholesalers advance them money for work to be done later (their pretext being the difficulties created by rising prices). In 1834 the wholesalers decreed:

> The workshop proprietors [contractors] undertake to calender cloth for the wholesale firms. This resembles the way in which a *tenant* undertakes to cultivate a field for its owner. If the tenant is in arrears with his rent, the owner may dismiss him and engage someone else in his place. If the artisans in some workshop do not give a high enough lustre to the cloth, how can it be that the merchants should not be able to go elsewhere?[21]

This is a striking example of commerce substituting for management. It shows the gap, so characteristic of the cotton industry in late traditional China, between the merchant's concern with the market and the artisan's concern with production. Chang Han's prosperous ancestor I-an, with his twenty looms for hemp cloth, must have had some counterparts among the urban cotton weavers; but on the whole it would seem that an industry enormous in the aggregate was created not by expanding the size of the units of production but by linking a growing multitude of small producers through a market mechanism, with a minimum of direct functional integration between the various parts of the structure.

How typical, then, of Chinese industry as a whole was cotton? Generally speaking, it would seem that it was. Merchants became financially involved in production only when special conditions, such as the need to make sure of supplies in advance in a highly competitive market, or expensive raw materials, meant that they had to. The tea and silk industries show this happening.

Most of China's tea for export, the sector about which most is known,[22] was grown in the back-country hills of Fukien, Kiangsi, Chekiang and Anhwei. These areas had nothing approaching the dense market network of Kiangnan, and yet there was commercial production on an impressive scale. There were three main groups concerned with production and processing. These were the so-called 'hill households', family-sized units for whom tea was sometimes only a subsidiary occupation, the 'tea-firms' and the merchants of the Co-hong (a small group of favoured businessmen at Canton enjoying the official monopoly of foreign trade). In the eighteenth century, cultivation of the shrubs was mostly in the hands of the hill households; but in the nineteenth, with the stimulus of overseas demand, large tracts of hill land were leased and operated by the tea-firms, though under what system of management is unfortunately not clear. To make sure of their supplies of leaves the tea-firms also frequently advanced money or rice to the hill households against the coming harvest. The financing of this often went back a step further to the Co-hong merchants, who equally wanted to be sure that they could obtain supplies of tea.

The processing of the coarsest and the primary processing of most better-quality teas was usually done by itinerant professionals hired by the hill households, or else by the hill households themselves. The more delicate processing was undertaken by the tea-firms, whose largest sheds gave employment to well over a hundred men. Further processing took place in or near the major tea centres, Canton being the most important. This was done in real factories, the biggest containing several hundred workers, for re-roasting, sorting, blending and packing. In this last stage the Co-hong merchants also played a part, perhaps because they were interested in quality control. In the tea business commerce was clearly not separated from production to anything like the degree that it was in cotton. It would be dangerous, however, to assume that management by the tea-firms was necessarily of a direct or integrated kind. We see why in the silk textile industry, where we know much more.

Low grade silk was produced in the countryside in much the same fashion as cotton cloth. Higher grade silks were mostly made in the cities, and by more complex organization. This was due both to the expense of the raw materials and to the more sophisticated looms for weaving patterns, which required two or three persons to operate. The supply of raw silk was relatively inelastic, because any increase in output made it necessary to bring new mulberry trees to maturity. It seems that the rapidly rising demand for the fabric in the eighteenth century, as the result both of internal population increase and the growing overseas market, made it harder for the independent urban silk-weaving establishments with from three to twenty looms to survive. They had too little working capital to cover the greater costs of their materials. The consequence was a shift to a system of putting out financed by so-called 'account houses', some of which handled up to five hundred or six hundred looms. It was, however, putting out with a difference, Chinese style.

In the seventeenth century, small workshops or 'loom households' using hired labour were the norm. This may be seen from the official report on disturbances among the Su-chou silk weavers in 1601 quoted on page 278. At some later date the majority of the loom households became subordinate to putters out. There is, however, no clear statement of this until the latter part of the nineteenth century. One of the most striking of such statements, which shows how much had changed in the intervening period, is in a memorial by Liu K'un-i in 1896:

> As a rule, merchants themselves buy the silk for the warp and the weft, and issue this to the loom households to weave. They are called 'account houses'. The loom households stand in the same relationship to the account houses as tenants do to their landlord.[23]

But – and this is the crucial point – the account houses were divorced from actual production by one and sometimes two levels of so-called 'management contractors'. These independent intermediaries were, by guild law, obligatory in all dealings between the account houses and the loom houses, and most particularly in guaranteeing the contract made between these two parties at the guild hall to inaugurate their relationship. According to an inscription of 1891: 'The [putting out] firms may not, no matter whether business is good or bad, . . . themselves undertake to seek out wage households [i.e. weavers].' Moreover: 'The management contractor must make honest enquiries into the behaviour of his men and their technical capacity, so that he knows what kinds of silk they can weave. He should be careful with other people's capital, and if he bungles matters he should bear the responsibility.'[24] The underlying nature of this system, with its barriers between market and technology, was evidently all but identical with that of the calendering industry already described. One suspects, too, that similar arrangements may have existed on the plantations and in the processing sheds of the tea-firms, although no record of this has survived.

The putting out system in the urban silk industry probably first became of importance during the eighteenth century. A twentieth-century gazetteer for Wu county, in which Su-chou is situated, asserts that: 'Among the account houses there are some which have been established for more than two hundred years.'[25] Early nineteenth-century inscriptions refer to putting out and the use of 'management contractors' to handle loans of equipment and materials. Finally, the rescinding during the K'ang-hsi reign (1662–1722) of a previous ban on any firm controlling more than a hundred looms suggest that the scale of management was increasing.

We may thus conclude that the last three centuries of pre-modern Chinese history saw the creation of much larger units of private economic organization than ever before, and that the change here was qualitative as well as quantitative. In particular, rural industries were co-ordinated through a market network of rapidly increasing density, and urban industry, supplied with materials and customers through this network, developed new structures to handle larger numbers of employees. In one sense this was 'progress'; but, as we have seen, the methods of organization tended to separate those in commerce from those in production. It is therefore quite unwarranted to assume, on the basis of the evidence so far, that China was heading towards an industrial revolution. There was less technological progress during this time than at almost any other previous moment in two thousand years of Chinese history. But the paradox, at least to those schooled in European history, is deeper than this. There is so much evidence, beyond that already presented, of the heightened tempo of economic activity from the later sixteenth century that we are forced to ask 'Why did China not break through to modern economic growth at about the same time as Europe?'

17 · Quantitative growth, qualitative standstill

Reading in the literature of the China two or three centuries before the modern age, there are moments when it is hard to believe that an industrial revolution had not begun. The phrases of Wang Shih-mao's description of Ching-te-chen, the great porcelain-making centre in Kiangsi province, instantly summon up such a vision:

> Tens of thousands of pestles shake the ground with their noise. The heavens are alight with the glare from the fires, so that one cannot sleep at night. The place has been called in jest 'The Town of Year-Round Thunder and Lightning'.[1]

So too does Yen Ju-yü's account of the ironworkers of the Hupei/Shensi/Szechwan borders:

> Their iron furnaces are seventeen or eighteen feet in height and fenced about on all sides with *yuan* trees. They are square in shape and solidly constructed of clay, with an opening at the top to allow the smoke to escape. Charcoal is put in at the bottom and ore in the middle. For every so many hundred catties of ore a certain number of catties of charcoal have to be used, a precise quantity which may not be increased or decreased. At the side more than ten persons will take it in turns to work the bellows. The fire is not put out either by day or by night. The liquid metal and the slag flow out from separate ducts at the bottom of the furnace, the liquid metal turning into iron which is cast in slabs. Every furnace has an artisan who determines the timing of the fire and who can distinguish the appearance of iron in different stages of completeness. More than ten artisans are hired to serve each furnace. The largest numbers of men are needed for transporting timber and building the [charcoal] kilns in the Black Hills, and for opening up the seams and extracting ore from the Red Hills. The distances which the ore and charcoal have to be taken vary, but over a hundred men are required for each furnace. Thus six or seven furnaces will give employment to not less than a thousand men. Once the iron has been cast into slabs it is sometimes manufactured locally into pots and farm

tools. A thousand and several hundreds of men are also required for this work and for the transport [of the goods]. Thus the larger iron-works in Szechwan and the other provinces regularly have two thousand to three thousand persons, and the smaller ones with but three or four furnaces well over a thousand.[2]

In Kwangtung we read of water-driven hammers for pounding incense 'without any expenditure of [human] muscular effort'. In Kiangsi, according to a provincial gazetteer, similar hammers were used for husking rice:

> They are mostly found at present at important fords and places where merchants gather. Over a hundred of the machines may be installed in a line of buildings to supply the grain boats which come and go selling rice. Since prosperous farmers make use of much rice, it is particularly suitable that they should instal them.[3]

In Fukien, paddle wheels were fixed to the sides of boats anchored in fast-flowing streams and used to turn hammers for the manufacture of paper, so that 'the sound of pounding was like the whirr of wings'. Out of so widespread a mastery of the pre-modern mechanical arts it seems strange that no further technological progress should have come.

A number of explanations for this have been put forward by various writers in the past. Here, though avoiding personal polemics, I shall show that they are all unsatisfactory.

Inadequate capital and restricted markets?

Was there, for example, a shortage of capital, leading to the kind of low-level equilibrium postulated by Ragnar Nurkse? Nurkse, it will be recalled, argued for two interlinked vicious circles. Lack of capital leads to low productivity, hence to low income, hence to a small capacity to save and so to a lack of capital. Further, low productivity and hence low mass buying power leads to a low inducement to invest, which is thus a second cause of the lack of capital which leads to low productivity. Moreover, 'inducement to invest is limited by the size of the market'.[4] It is difficult to know how to relate this to the facts of the Chinese case. There were large markets for goods of mass consumption and also large concentrations of capital in merchants' hands, as is shown by Yeh Meng-chu's account of Shang-hai in the seventeenth century:

> *Cotton Cloth* Our county used to produce three grades ... The broadest and finest of them was called 'standard cloth'. The best

was made in the town of San-lin-t'ang, the next best in the town of Chou-p'u; that made in the county capital was the poorest. All three qualities went to Shensi, Shansi and the border areas . . . Rather narrower and longer than standard cloth was the kind called 'midloom'. It went to Hupei, Hunan, Kiangsi, Kwangtung and Kwangsi. The price was the same as that of standard cloth.

Under the preceding [Ming] dynasty a thriving business was carried on in standard cloth. The wealthy merchants who came to purchase it each possessed a capital of many tens of thousands of ounces of silver. The richest may have had several hundreds of thousands, the poorest perhaps ten thousand. For this reason the brokers treated the cotton cloth merchants as if they were princes or marquises, but at the same time struggled against them as if they had been a hostile army. No broker who did not enjoy the backing of a powerful family could stand up to them. Few merchants bought midloom, and those that did had a limited supply of capital. Thus not much of this latter cloth was produced.

Under the present [Ch'ing] dynasty few of the great merchants who dealt in standard cloth have continued to come. Recently none of them has brought more than ten thousand ounces, and some have brought as little as two or three thousand. Their profits have also been limited. The trade in midloom has, on the contrary, prospered. Those who used to deal in standard cloth have now turned to midloom . . . There also used to be a very narrow and short variety called 'smallcloth'. It was little more than a foot wide and did not exceed sixteen feet in length. It was only sold to places like Jao-chou in Kiangsi . . . After 1669, the Jao-chou merchants stopped coming and smallcloth consequently disappeared.[5]

The responsiveness of traditional industry to the ebb and flow of market forces is clearly apparent. So is its size, for Shang-hai was only one of many important Kiangnan cotton centres. The geographical range must also be grasped. Shang-hai cloth was sold in places up to eight hundred miles apart in a north/south direction, and on a western European scale would have been a flourishing international export industry.

The drying up of mechanical invention in the Chinese cotton industry cannot therefore be attributed to the smallness of markets or the weakness of commercial influences. The same conclusion holds for many other branches of manufacturing: iron pots from Fo-shan (Fatshan), silk cloth from Su-chou, Ching-te-chen porcelain. Nor was shortage of capital the critical weakness. There were even larger concentrations than those in the hands of the cotton merchants. The salt merchants of late Ming times commonly had some hundreds of thousands of ounces of silver, and sometimes more than a million. According to Hsieh Ch'ao-chih, writing in later Ming times:

> The great traders of Hsin-an [Hui-chou] make fish and salt their business. Some of them have stored away up to a million strings of cash. Others who have but two or three hundred thousand are only middle-grade merchants. Those from Shan-yu [in Shansi] deal in salt, silk thread or grain storage. Their wealth is greater than that of the Hsin-an [merchants].[6]

The great salt merchants of the eighteenth century and the members of the Co-Hong foreign trade monopoly had capitals of several million ounces of silver.[7] Nor, despite what we have just seen of the textile industries, were merchants always unwilling to invest in the means of production. Thus Yen Ju-yü on the backers of the Ta-yuan Wood Factory:

> The merchants who opened the factory and provided the capital live in Hsi-an, Chou-wu and Han-chung-ch'eng. Their general managers are called 'comptrollers' or 'managers'. Those who look after contracting, hiring and lodging are called 'secretaries'. The foremen who undertake transport at the water's edge are called 'shore receivers'. Those who lead the coolies by land and water are 'contractors'. The number of artisans in the Ta-yuan Wood Factory and those who haul by land and water is not less than three to five thousand men. The profits accumulated by these merchants are indeed a rich harvest from the mountains. When local millet is cheap they expand their operations; and their workforce increases. If there is a shortage of local millet and its price rises, they will close down the factory and lay off workers.[8]

A work on the clans of Hsin-an printed in the Wan-li reign (1573–1619) speaks as follows of a certain Chu Yun-chan:

> When he was young, he followed his elder brother to trade in Chekiang . . . He also followed him to trade in Fukien. For the most part they set iron smelters to work in the hills. He directed most of the hired workers and they strove to work so as to bring him credit. The business was very profitable.[9]

With such evidence it is hard to believe that there was not enough capital to finance the simple technological advances that would then have been appropriate, or that there were not big enough markets to make investment in such improved technology attractive.

Political obstacles to economic growth?
A second explanation with some initial plausibility is that political hazards for merchants were the inhibiting factor. It can be argued that the rapacity of the government, plus its inability to provide security from recurrent riots and uprisings, made it unsafe for merchants to concentrate their wealth in highly visible fashion. It was wiser to disperse it covertly in a variety of investments. Moreover, this argument continues, the insecurity of the merchants' life made the abler of them pursue a long-term strategy of entering the bureaucracy themselves, with the result if they were successful that they became subject to the legal ban on trading imposed on officials. Ingenuity was thus more profitably expended on cultivating liaisons with the powerful than on improving the techniques of production. We have therefore to ask how far government policy and government shortcomings are likely to have blocked a modern type of economic growth.

There can be no doubt that from time to time the officials and their underlings, in a time-honoured Chinese phrase, 'hunted and fished' the people, including merchants who had no official protectors. One example of this was given on page 269 in a censor's report on local customs stations. Ts'ao Shih-p'in's official report on the riots among the Su-chou silk weavers in 1601 provides another:

> When the tax [on cloth] was first imposed, [the eunuch director of taxes] Sun Lung spent a long time in Su-chou. He had a knowledge of the people's feelings that was the fruit of his own experience. He elaborated nine regulations and set up nine customs barriers at which only the travelling merchants, not the resident merchants, were taxed. The people soon accepted it, yet the fiscal net was as fine and close as autumn tea. I have already stated in a memorial how the local bullies had obtained a monopoly of the customs levies, and how this had reduced the circulation of goods in the city and the number of looms owned by the weaving households . . . In the early part of the fifth moon, Sun Lung went to Su-chou . . . The quota had not been fulfilled, and so he temporarily borrowed funds from the official treasury to forward to the capital. His personal follower Huang Chien-chieh was in league with some twelve families of local blackguards; and they took advantage of being deputed to inspect the customs levies to add a further charge without having had any authorization to do so.

They also recklessly proposed taxing every loom 0.3 of an ounce of silver, and this caused popular indignation and a spate of rumours. All the loom households closed their doors, and the weaving workers, who were faced with the prospect of death by starvation, responded at once. They killed Huang Chien-chieh with volleys of stones, and set fire to the houses of T'ang Hsin and the other [blackguards].[10]

There were other obstacles to the free circulation of goods besides customs duties. By the eighteenth century, the long distance trade between the north and the Yangtze Valley along the Grand Canal had almost become a de facto monopoly of the official grain transport boats. These vessels carried weapons and sometimes plundered ordinary merchant shipping under such pretexts as looking for stolen goods. According to the *Ch'ing Veritable Records* for 1833:

> The Canal runs for more than 233 miles through the provinces of Kiangsu and Chekiang. Every year as the grain transport boats return to the waterside granaries from which they departed, boats belonging to merchants and commoners are passing along it. The official boats extort cash from the smaller ones, and loot the larger without any restraint. They have two methods: either they block the Canal with the grain transport ships, allowing no boat to go by unless it pays them what is known as 'passage purchase money', or they select a narrow shallow spot in the waterway and anchor two boats in parallel there so that vessels going north and south are unable to get past, piling up in great numbers for three or four days while local bullies who live along the banks and are known as 'river speeders' demand money from them and deliver it to the grain transport boats.[11]

Not surprisingly, merchants who could contrive to have their goods carried on the grain transport boats regarded them as 'magic amulets' that warded off misfortune.

Originally the Ming government had conceded to the soldiers who ran the grain transport boats the right to carry a limited quantity of duty-free goods in addition to the main cargo of grain, the object of this being to save the state paying them adequate wages. Under the Ch'ing dynasty this concession went much further, both legally and illegally. In 1731 Hsieh Ning, the governor of Kiangsi, described the legal position as follows:

> Each grain ship is entitled to carry a hundred piculs of local products and the head steersman is allowed a further twenty-six piculs. There are seven thousand grain ships in all, and they carry a total of about one million piculs of local products.[12]

This was an underestimate. In 1799 one writer asserted that the load per boat was between one and two thousand piculs, or nearly their total capacity. Such was the ascendancy established by the official grain transport over non-official shipping that by 1824 it could be reported from Lin-ch'ing, a great city on the northern reach of the Canal: 'Recently goods have mostly been brought on the grain transport boats. Goods sold by merchants have been few.'[13] Prior to 1772 private cargo in excess of the permitted quota had simply been liable to customs duties, though it was rare for customs officers to search the grain ships properly, lest they be denounced for holding up the government transport. After 1772, surplus goods on the grain ships were regarded as tantamount to smuggled goods; but this seems to have had only the most limited effect on the practice of carrying them. The grain ships under their official overseers could even go so far, as in a celebrated case in 1834, as to smash through the customs barriers in order to avoid examination. It is thus obvious that the effects on Chinese economic life of official policies and official depredations cannot be lightly overlooked. Because big rewards went to those who could successfully bend or break the rules, there was a misdirection of energy and talent.

Yet it would be wrong to assume that trade and the holding of official rank or position were in fact mutually exclusive. While it did happen that a merchant entering official life might divest himself of his commercial interests, the case of Mr Wang of Hsin-an on page 278 being a good example, it is equally true that many officials made use of their position to engage in business. This is borne out by a censor's memorial of 1789:

> The [official grain] boats of the Hupei group were late. Investigation revealed that the cause of this was that the entire group was engaged in dragging through the water 1,800 mast timbers belonging to provincial judge Li T'ien-p'ei . . . If this official has timber for his own use, he ought to have it transported himself. How can he allocate its transport to the tribute grain ships in the hope of economizing on carriage costs and avoiding the customs duties – so holding up the grain transport?[14]

The commonest tactic was probably to work through agents, like one well-known Hsin-an businessman in late Ming times of whom it was recorded that: 'when he had become an official he ceased going in person to Chen-chiang and Hang-chou, and employed others like oxen and sheep'. Officials with accumulated funds to invest, but having no mercantile background, would often entrust them to important merchants to manage. This practice became very prevalent in Ch'ing times. As one example we may quote the *Ch'ing Veritable Records* for 1746:

> When Po Chung-shan was governor-general of waterways he managed river-conservancy work. Because of his many kinds of improper expenditure, the necessary treasury funds had to be greatly increased. We would observe that he owns houses in Peking worth not less than several thousand ounces of silver, and we have heard that his official capital has all been entrusted to a family of Huai-yang salt merchants to be managed on his behalf. We ordered Chi Ch'ing to investigate and report and he has now memorialized that:
>
>> Ch'eng Chih-chung, a Huai-pei merchant, has received 20,000 ounces of silver from Po Chung-shan for keeping, and Ch'eng's son-in-law Wang Shao-i has received 40,000 ounces from Po Chung-shan, with which he has opened a pawn-shop in Ch'ing-chiang. Furthermore, the merchant Ch'eng Jung-te has received 20,000 ounces from Po and the merchant Ch'eng Ch'ien-i has received 20,000 ounces from Po to employ on his behalf . . .[15]

There was thus a symbiosis between bureaucrats and businessmen.

By the beginning of the nineteenth century, if not somewhat earlier, many important merchants had acquired official degrees and titles, both by examination and by purchase. When, in 1826, the temporary blocking of the Grand Canal forced the Ch'ing government to transport more than a million-and-a-half piculs of its annual supply of rice by sea, it entrusted the task to forty-six merchants based upon Shanghai; and the records show that twenty-six of them were provincial graduates, Imperial Academy students, senior licentiates or holders of purchased rank, in other words 'gentry'.[16] Studying for the imperial examinations was expensive; and with the decline of large landholding in and after the seventeenth century, mercantile wealth must have been behind an increasing number of candidates. Any sharp dichotomy between 'officials' and 'merchants' is therefore misleading.

This was also a time when the political power of the merchants was increasing. Its most obvious form was the confederations of guilds which became the municipal governments of a number of cities in the course of the nineteenth century. Historically, this institution emerged in one of two ways. Sometimes a 'Great Guild' formed by in-migrants would become differentiated, as numbers grew, into constituent guilds for various trades and localities. This was the case at Kuei-sui (Huhehot),

the northern trade centre which linked Mongolia and Sinkiang.[17] Or
independent guilds of fellow-regional merchants would combine into
an overarching association. This was the origin of the Ten Guilds
of Hung-chiang, a market town in western Hunan, and the Eight Guilds
of Ch'ung-ch'ing (Chungking) in eastern Szechwan.[18] Both of these
bodies assumed governmental functions in the 1850s during the crisis
brought on by the Taiping rebellion. Their duties included welfare
work, education, the management of police and militia, the collection
of certain taxes, famine relief, standardizing weights and measures,
resolving disputes between members, and advising the authorities.
Other cities known to have had somewhat comparable bodies are
Sha-shih, Shan-t'ou (Swatow) and Chia-ting. There were probably
more.

But the confederations were not simply merchant institutions. A text
of 1888 refers to the 'gentry and merchants of the Ten Guilds' in
Hung-chiang; and almost all the leading Ch'ung-ch'ing merchants had
official titles or degrees. Furthermore, with time the differences between
the in-migrants of different regional origins tended to disappear (except
in the matter of which gods they worshipped); and the functions of
the guilds expanded from the service of their members to the service of
society at large. Although their origins, and those of their constituent
guilds, seem often to have been connected with interregional trade
and interregional migration, the guild confederations of the nineteenth
century were not organizations of powerful outsiders. Nor were they
organizations defending purely merchant against 'gentry' interests.
They symbolized the consolidation of the power of a new urban élite
based at least as much on commerce as on landholding. Businessmen
in late traditional China were not members of a disadvantaged caste,
but were respected and influential citizens.

Finally, in the sphere of monetary policy, government power was on
the whole used sensibly and constructively, once the ill-judged attempt
of the early Ming rulers to force an inconvertible and rapidly depreci-
ating currency onto their people had been abandoned. New mines for
silver and copper were opened up; and in the seventeenth and early
eighteenth century copper was even imported from Japan. When the
continuing expansion of Chinese trade and Chinese population made
paper money necessary again, this was brought in entirely through
private channels. The most important notes were the 'cash bills' issued
by money-shops. Such bills seem first to have appeared in the

seventeenth century. By the early nineteenth, they were an integral part of the economy of many provinces. When there was a proposal in 1838 that they should be forbidden, the governor of Shansi success-fully protested:

> For the trade in goods among the common people [silver] specie is only rarely used, and [copper] coins are frequently used. In the pro-vinces of Kiangsu, Chekiang, Fukien and Kwangtung foreign dollars are employed, while in Chihli, Honan, Shantung and Shansi cash bills are made use of. If cash bills were all of a sudden to be abolished, the people would be forced to make general use of foreign dollars; and the foreigners would exact a further increase in their exchange value. There is, moreover, only a little regular copper cash in the reserves of the provincial treasuries. The cash that have been hoarded by the common people are likewise insufficient. If cash bills were now to be abolished there would necessarily be ever less ready money available. I fear that both merchants and ordinary persons would be in difficulties . . .[19]

There were also silver bills; but they were basically a type of short-term credit, and often carried interest. Their importance in the commerce of advanced areas may be seen from this petition submitted to the county magistrate of Shang-hai by six gentry merchants in 1841:

> We are engaged in the money-shop business, and in the buying and selling of beans, wheat, raw cotton and cloth. We all depend upon the circulation of silver bills, which we either exchange for others when they fall due or redeem with silver coin.[20]

Money-shops normally issued bills well in excess of their silver reserves, and thus made more currency available.

The one drawback from which the late traditional Chinese monetary system did suffer was a multiplicity of types of specie, coin and paper in circulation. This required the good offices of an army of assayers and exchangers; but the problem was quite minor in comparison with the shortage of liquidity which might otherwise have arisen. Although a well managed unified paper currency would no doubt have been pre-ferable, there is no very compelling reason to criticize the Chinese government for failure to act in this direction. The difficulties of main-taining such a currency almost certainly made monetary laissez-faire a wiser choice.

Political obstacles to economic growth in late traditional times, it may be concluded, were minimal.

Enterprises small-scale and short-lived?

A third explanation sometimes given of why late traditional China missed an industrial revolution turns on the alleged incapability of the Chinese to create large private economic organizations. This, it is said, was partly because there was no commercial law worthy of the name, except perhaps that sometimes imposed by powerful guilds. Moreover, the Chinese found it hard to trust anyone to whom they were not related, or with whom they had no long-standing relationship. Therefore businesses tended to stay small and restricted in geographical scope; and their dealings with customers, employees and other businesses had usually to be mediated through brokers, guarantors, contractors or middlemen of some other kind. There is a measure of truth in these contentions, but they need to be qualified in a number of ways. Commercial contracts *could* be enforced in the lawcourts, at least up to a point. Thus we learn of a Hui-chou merchant named Hung Shih that:

> He traded in Pa-ling [in Hunan]. His landlord was a fellow-regional named Hu Yao; and because he was young, Hung recommended him, and Hu prospered. On three occasions Hu borrowed a thousand ounces of silver from him but he never enquired after it. When he returned to She county [in southern Anhwei] his family retainer sued Hu Yao before the authorities. Hung complained about this, saying, 'I would rather Hu Yao ruined me than that I was the ruin of him.' He went to the authorities and had Hu Yao released, after which they were on good terms as before.[21]

Likewise, kinship bonds and partnerships could be the basis of quite large businesses. We know of Ch'eng Sou, a Hui-chou merchant who flourished in the sixteenth century:

> He gathered together the worthy persons in his clan, thus obtaining some ten persons, and each of them contributed three hundred strings of cash for their common use. They traded in Hsin-shih in Wu-hsing. At that time the Ch'eng clan was prosperous, and the young bloods vied with each other in wasteful expenditure. Ch'eng Sou made a pact with his ten associates that they should reject such behaviour and face up to hardship . . . In the course of time their undertakings prospered and the ten became wealthy beyond measure.[22]

The device of commercial discipleship was used to extend the range of a business still further. Thus Wang T'ung-pao, a sixteenth-century moneylender who lived in Shang-hai, 'made an agreement with his disciples that they would reside in other counties, refrain from forcing loans on people, not mix up good and bad quality [coins], not charge interest for small sums of money or be concerned with the odd extra coppers, and not calculate charges on a daily basis. Everyone thereupon came in a stream to do business with them, including all the neighbouring prefectures. Before long they were very rich.'[23] What is of particular interest here is the network of branches extending over several counties. This device, under the name of 'association', was also much used by the merchants of Shansi. According to Shen Ssu-hsiao's *Account of Chin,* written in the later part of the sixteenth century:

> The great merchants of Tse-lu in P'ing-yang are the foremost in the empire. If they do not possess 100,000 ounces of silver they are not regarded as rich. Their economic practices are excellent, and they vie with each other in [good] conduct. When associates combine to trade this is called 'an association'. *One person puts up the capital and the associates jointly use it for commerce.* Although they do not swear an oath there is never any misappropriation. Yet if a father has contracted such a loan from someone and then died, the loan already being twenty or thirty years old, when his sons and grandsons learn of it they will make every effort to repay it. Other people with accumulated capital will compete to have these men as their associates, saying: 'If they do not forget the dead, are they likely to turn their backs on the living?' Thus these persons will lose a little of their profit to begin with, but will end by reaping a rich reward. In this way both those with capital and those without it are able to make a living. What is more, the rich do not store their wealth in their houses but entirely disperse it in these associations. If one is estimating a man's fortune, one merely counts how many large and how many small associations he has underwritten; and several hundreds of thousands or millions worth of wealth can be counted on one's fingers. This is the means whereby the rich cannot be suddenly reduced to penury, and the poor can make their fortunes.[24]

This method of business organization culminated in the famous Shansi banks, which were founded some time in the eighteenth century. They had a network of branches enabling them to remit funds from one end of the country to the other. The eight largest banks each ran more than thirty such branches within China itself; and in the later nineteenth century they also set up in Japan, Russia and Singapore. Their clients were merchants, financiers and officials. Capital was provided by the traditional partnership, with unlimited liability for all partners and profits distributed every three or four years. Decision-making rested mainly with the chief accountant, who represented the owners, and with the managers of the branches. When a man was appointed branch manager, his family was kept at head office as hostages for his good behaviour; and his letters to them were read by the firm. He was paid no salary but his expenses were met. After three or four years he would go back to Shansi to present his accounts and be cross-examined by his superiors. If all had gone well, he would be rewarded and reunited with his family. If anything had gone wrong, he would have to make good the loss from his own property and his family would be detained until the firm was satisfied. Assistants in the banks were dismissed for the smallest errors and the other banks would not hire them. In consequence few ever misbehaved. The standard of honesty achieved was legendary, and there were no known frauds until well into the twentieth century.

It is thus clear that while the organization of private business across the full breadth of the subcontinent needed extreme measures, it was in no way beyond the capacity of the Chinese in late traditional times. Economic and technical retardation cannot therefore in any great measure be put down to the small scale of pre-modern enterprise. There were too many enterprises anything but small.

Nor should it be assumed that Chinese businesses were always short-lived. Mr Wang from Hsin-an, whose skilful methods were described on page 278, founded an enterprise that lasted two hundred years. A certain Sun Ch'un-yang ran a large store in Su-chou selling all sorts ot dry goods and medicines around the end of the sixteenth century. Two hundred and thirty-four years later, it is recorded, 'His descendants still enjoyed its profits and no other family had replaced them.'[25] Some of the account houses dealing in silk cloth, and described in the previous chapter, were almost as old.

It would seem that none of the conventional explanations tells us in convincing fashion why technical progress was absent in the Chinese economy during a period that was, on the whole, one of prosperity and expansion. Almost every element usually regarded by historians as a major contributory cause to the industrial revolution in north-western Europe was also present in China. There had even been a revolution in the relations between social classes, at least in the countryside; but this had had no important effect on the techniques of production. Only Galilean-Newtonian science was missing; but in the short run this was not important. Had the Chinese possessed, or developed, the seventeenth-century European mania for tinkering and improving, they could easily have made an efficient spinning machine out of the primitive model described by Wang Chen. (See the discussion at the end of chapter 13 of the many minor improvements made to machines for re-spinning flax in Europe before the middle of the eighteenth century.) A steam engine would have been more difficult; but it should not have posed insuperable difficulties to a people who had been building double-acting piston flame-throwers in the Sung dynasty. The critical point is that nobody tried. In most fields, agriculture being the chief exception, Chinese technology stopped progressing well before the point at which a lack of basic scientific knowledge had become a serious obstacle.

We are therefore justified for the moment in concentrating on the economic aspects of invention. We need a theory which will explain the differences between late traditional China and early modern Europe as regards technical creativity while fitting the factual record satisfactorily. Can this be done? The rest of this chapter attempts to show that it can.

The high-level equilibrium trap

The problem is a difficult one. Throughout the Ming and the Ch'ing the Chinese showed resourcefulness in all the activities normally associated with invention. The adoption and diffusion of Western technology was in many respects considerable. New World crops were grown: maize, peanuts, sweet and white potatoes, and tobacco. The simpler kinds of Western cannon, handguns, clocks, telescopes and microscopes were successfully imitated, a fact which speaks for the high quality of the best Chinese craftsmanship. Small but significant improvements were made in a range of familiar indigenous techniques. Multi-colour woodblock printing was perfected; the smelting of zinc mastered. The ships sailing in northern waters learned to sail closer into the wind, which made them much safer. There was a continual refinement of the adaptation of agriculture to local ecological peculiarities. The introduction in the north of underground cellars to create the moist atmosphere needed for cotton-spinning is an example of a parallel ecological adaptation of industry. The best Chinese techniques spread steadily over the country. Cotton, for instance, replaced hemp and ramie as the main clothing fibre. There was a greater use of wells (first encouraged by the Mongol dynasty) for providing water for fields in the north. And of course there *were* a handful of Chinese inventions: the merry-go-round windpump with its gybing sails, the bulletproof vest used by the troops of Li Tzu-ch'eng, soybean cake and other new fertilizers. Wang Cheng (1571–1644), working under the influence of the Jesuits, devised improved tools for use on his own farm and wrote a book about them. Clearly, the term 'technological stagnation' is a misleadingly oversimple description of this period.

There were also organizational changes. Most of these we have already touched upon: the growth of money-shops and remittance banks, the guilds of merchants engaged in inter-regional trade, the decline in serf-like conditions of tenure for much of the peasantry, the growing density of the local market network. There were others, such as the attempt to use organizational means to combat insect pests. These developments further contributed to economic productivity.

Nor was entrepreneurship absent. Here is an account of how the price of fuel in Ching-yang county in Shensi was reduced:

County magistrate Lu Chen-fei submitted this memorial in 1629: I would observe that south of Ching-yang lies the Ching River, providing direct access to the Wei, on which there is a continuous flow of merchant shipping. Ching-yang, however, relies on the damming of waterways and loads are not carried by boat, the people being unaware of the advantages conferred on them by nature. Leaving aside the question of whether grain might be transported or timber floated in the form of rafts, this is even true of coal. Ching-yang is densely populated and has nothing to burn as firewood. The people depend on carriers and carts to supply them with fuel for cooking; and the effort used up in transport is a source of distress. A picul of coal never costs less than 0·4 of an ounce of silver, and may rise above 0·5 or 0·7 of an ounce. It is not always a lack of food-grains which prevents people from lighting a fire in wet or snowy weather. After having become aware of this, every time I went to the banks of the Ching River I would stand overlooking the current and gauge the depth. When I asked the boatmen about it they said: 'The Ching River is quick-rushing, with numerous rocks, and is of varying depth. Merchant ships do not dare to travel on it.' I sent my officials to inspect it, on foot along the riverside together with some boatmen. They reported that even in the shallowest places, if the water were only a foot or so deeper, it would take even a war-junk. I was delighted and declared it suitable for shipping. Even so, the people were apprehensive that accidental difficulties might arise. They grudged a small outlay, and so barred the way to subsequent profit. I therefore had a long, narrow boat constructed, and told sailors to pilot it to Ming-chiao-k'ou in Lin-t'ung county and fetch coal from there. They made the round trip [of perhaps 50 miles] and had the coal unloaded in a mere three days. The transport cost was only seventy per cent of that needed for carriers and carts. I further ordered Ma Shou-ts'ang and other boatmen from the foodboats at the various ferry-crossings to join with the above-mentioned boat and make several trips, giving them their wages in advance. Every picul of coal used to cost 0·4 of an ounce of silver. Now it is only 0·25 of an ounce. When the snow falls, the roads are muddy, and wheels and hooves unable to proceed, the benefit will be twice that in ordinary times.[26]

Economic enterprise would thus seem to have been alive in late traditional China. There was certainly a keen awareness of comparative costs, and this could demonstrably have its effects upon the kind of technology used – as the cost of fuel changed the pattern of salt-making in Ch'üan-chou in Ming times:

Salt may be produced either by boiling or by evaporation. From before the Sung and Yuan dynasties both of these methods were used. *Nowadays only the evaporation technique is employed.* The boiling technique used the salt left by the two highest monthly tides. When the tide went out, the salt soaked into the ground; and if there was a strong sun it would form white crystals. These were gathered and used to form salt-mounds, which were further sprinkled with brine. The 'salt-mound' was a hole in the ground under which there was a dripping pool, to which it was connected by a number of apertures fitted with reed tubes to draw off the brine. The water soaked through the salt-mound, ran down the tubes and dripped into the pool. The readiness of the brine for use was gauged by throwing in a hen's egg or a peach-kernel to see if it would float. The brine was then drained into an earthenware container by the side of the stove; and a tube was used to draw it into a pan for boiling. The pan was made of bamboos plaited into the shape of a pan and smeared with a cement made from clamshells. Large pans could boil two hundred catties of salt in a day and a night; the small ones half of that. The evaporation technique in like fashion involves gathering the saltiest parts of the ground and drying them in the sun until they are extremely dry. They are then put into a dripping-mound and [brine] is soaked through them into a dripping-pool. The water is taken from the pool and poured over the mound twice before it is fit for use. The evaporating pans are made of stone slabs very tightly fitted. It is the wind which reduces the water content, and so the salt is only a few feet thick. One man can also get two hundred catties a day by this method. In the Sung a catty of salt cost ten cash, and when dear, twice this. These days the price is never more than two cash. *This is because the evaporation technique needs no expenditure for firewood.*[27]

It is therefore reasonable to assume that perfectly rational short-run considerations lay behind many or most choices of technique. This being so, we have to ask how the availability of resources, capital and labour may have affected the decisions of Chinese entrepreneurs in the late traditional period.

Clearly the shortage of many resources grew more severe. In many areas there was a lack of wood for building houses and ships, and indeed machinery. There was a shortage of fuels, most obviously in the coastal regions where the reed-swamps which had once provided plenty of combustible material were now being turned into paddy-fields. There was a shortage of clothing fibres (though this was mitigated by the introduction of cotton, which yielded much more fibre per acre than hemp or ramie). Land which could be used for growing cotton was often needed for growing food. There was a shortage of draught-animals, and possibly therefore of animal manures, as northern grazing-lands were turned into fields. Metals were in short supply, particularly copper before the opening of the Yunnan mines in the eighteenth century, but also iron and silver. Above all, there was a shortage of good farmland: the quality of the new land brought under the plough in this period fell sharply. A major cause of these shortages was of course the continuing growth of the population under conditions of relative technological standstill.

One consequence of this lack of resources was that the cost of building even simple wooden machines might often be beyond the reach of many peasants. This is suggested by a passage in a gazetteer for Yung-p'ing prefecture (an area in present-day Hopei) describing a project for agricultural improvement undertaken by the Mongol government in the late thirteenth century:

> Where the land is so high that the water cannot be brought up to it, the officials should order the peasants to build water-pumps. *To those who are too poor to be able to afford to do so they shall make a gift of the materials,* and after the autumn harvest inspect those families using the water so that they may pay off the price in equitable fashion.[28]

The high cost of metal may have been the reason why the Western cylinder and piston pump, known in China since the seventeenth century, was not used in spite of its potential value to farming areas dependent on wells for water. According to the *Comprehensive Examination of Seasonal Practices*, compiled in 1742:

> In upland areas which I have seen where wells are used to irrigate the fields, the people either use the windlass and bucket or the well-sweep. Although these appear to be convenient, one may look up and down all day long without managing to water all of a *mou* of land. I have heard that in Shansi and Honan the people work extremely hard to irrigate fields with water drawn from wells. In a year of drought, eight people toiling day and night can only manage several *mou*. In other areas it is the custom to be lazier. Having seen the difficulties involved, people no longer enquire into the method of watering fields from wells. If the machine shown here is made, there is no need for a well-rope, bucket, windlass or well-sweep, and one man using it can do the work of several men. Used for irrigating fields, it can save about four-fifths of the labour needed.[29]

Unfortunately the pump had to be made in copper – solid money in a Chinese peasant's eyes – and was presumably too expensive, copper being in very short supply, for returns to justify investment. Merchant capital was of course available, and merchants did sometimes invest in the means of agricultural production. The irrigation system built outside Pao-t'ou early in the nineteenth century, in which 'water shares' were bought and sold independently of land, is an example. We can only guess that investing in a pump would not have paid as well as other possible investments.

Another example of knowledge not used is the Archimedean screw or 'dragon's tail pump', to give it its Chinese name. The screw was brought to China by the Jesuits; and the *Comprehensive Examination* is emphatic that it was more efficient than the traditional square-pallet chain-pump. The screw consisted of a helical pathway formed by a partition wall that rose in a spiral in the space between a central axle and an outer cylindrical casing. The whole cylinder was inclined at an angle of about twenty-five degrees, with the lower end just under the water. When it was rotated, the water entered at the bottom and then rose up the pathway until it poured out the top. Considerable inventiveness was shown by the Chinese in devising ways of building up the partition wall without using metal. One method, reminiscent of modern plastics technology, was to weave hemp or ramie fibres, or else splints, between vertical struts like a screen and then to waterproof them with a mixture of pitch/wax/ t'ung oil/lacquer and stone lime/pottery dust, according to what was available. Another method, which fancy might compare to the modern use of hydrocarbons, was to build up superimposed layers of mulberry or hibiscus bark held together with pitch or wax. Why this pumping device was little used is a mystery. Perhaps power transfer was a problem. When the screw was cranked by hand, it is unlikely to have surpassed the treadle-driven pallet pump, and the use of foot-power required wooden gear wheels, which was not the case with the simpler pallet pump. Practical experiment might yield interesting evidence on the balance of comparative advantage. Without this evidence, we can only conclude that there is no definite indication that the use of the screw would have significantly raised Chinese agricultural productivity.

One area where there was obvious room for improvement was land transport. The observations of an anonymous traveller who passed, disguised as a Chinese, through the south-eastern silk and tea districts in 1845, are to the point here:

The roads of central China are better than a stranger would expect to find them; *considering that they are not made for the passage of two-wheeled carriages, and only for foot-passengers, with occasionally a wheelbarrow, and a few animals,* the pathways are on the whole exceedingly good. In some places they were found fifteen feet wide paved with flagstones in the middle, and with well-laid pebbles on each side. For hundreds of miles, the traveller may be assured of meeting with good stone roads, at least three feet wide, formed of slabs of granite, mica, slate, sandstone or lime, according to the nature of the adjacent rocks, and the supply of stone in the neighbourhood. Over mountain passes, one or two thousand feet in height, roads are to be seen, cut into steps, six or eight feet wide, and laid with great care and exactness, for the convenience of passengers . . . At the distance of a mile from each other sheds are to be seen, built over the road, and provided with seats, where the weary traveller may refresh himself by a little rest, and prepare for further exertions. These roads and sheds, together with the bridges and canals, are, as far as can be ascertained, all the product of voluntary and benevolent effort . . . Another benevolent provision is the lighting of lamps along frequented roads, and near to dangerous bridges; these are made of thin layers of oyster-shells, fitted into a wooden framework, and either suspended from a lamp-post or fixed in a recess in a stone pillar; the light they afford is of course dim, but it serves to show where the bridge or road is.[30]

Why, then, was vehicular traffic so little developed? One plausible explanation is that, given the scarcity of grazing-lands and fodder for animals, and human overpopulation, men were often the cheapest form of transport. There is also another possibility which deserves consideration: that it was inhibited by the efficiency of traditional water transport.

The carriage provided by China's extensive system of waterways was so much cheaper than by land routes that the level of development in areas without water transport was usually far below that of those areas which had water transport. The difference was so pronounced that we can regard it as a case of pre-modern economic dualism. Illustrative evidence for this is provided by materials on Hunan province in the eighteenth century. In 1709 Chao Shen-ch'iao observed:

> The three counties of Ch'ang-sha, Shan-hua and Hsiang-yin in Ch'ang-sha prefecture, the county of Heng-shan in Heng-chou prefecture, the two counties of Pa-ling and Li-chou in Yo-chou prefecture, and the two counties of Wu-ling and T'ao-yuan in Ch'ang-te prefecture *are all on the banks of large rivers or have access to water routes. They likewise have places where rice is bought and sold* [on a large scale].

But,

> On account of shoals and the dangers of its waters, the prefecture of Yung-chou is entirely without [large-scale] merchants. That is to say, it does have the petty commerce which commoners carry on between themselves. Everyone takes goods by cart to Heng-yang to sell.[31]

Regulations issued in 1752 concerning the purchase of grain for the government made these observations on Ch'ang-sha prefecture:

> The six counties of Ch'ang-sha, Shan-hua, Hsiang-yin, Hsiang-t'an, I-yang and Hsiang-hsiang are all close to the water's edge. The government's instructions should be followed, and purchases of rice for the [government] granaries should be made in the markets of the county capitals and in the market towns, and at the various riverine ports. Although the counties of Yu, Liu-yang and Ch'a-ling are on navigable water routes, *these are either hill streams or else full of dangerous mudbanks, which makes transportation difficult. None of them have markets where [government] purchases can be made.* It is necessary at harvest time to order the local officials to send silver to families who have a surplus of grain, and to buy it from them at current prices . . . Furthermore, An-hua county is in a remote location among numerous hills. Boats cannot get to it . . . Although Li-ling county contains the

market town of Lu-k'ou, which is beside a large river, the latter is ninety *li* from the county capital. There is only this one navigable river, and it has shoals and treacherous places. It is very hard to haul the grain. Apart from the above-mentioned places, there are no riverine ports or places near rivers which produce grain.[32]

The dualism, depending on the availability or absence of water transport, is clear, at least as regards the degree of commercialization.

To the extent that this is a fair picture of the facts – and obviously it is not adequate to meet the full range of regional diversity – certain consequences follow. Even substantial improvements in land transportation techniques, along the lines of those made in eighteenth-century Britain, would not have brought costs down to the level of water transport. Adam Smith recognized this clearly when he wrote in *The Wealth of Nations*: 'Through the greater part of Europe . . . the expense of land-carriage increases very much both the real and nominal price of most manufactures . . . In China and Indostan the extent and variety of inland navigation save the greater part of this labour, . . . and thereby reduce still lower both the real and the nominal price of the greater part of their manufactures.'[33] In China, even in the early decades of the present century, railways and steamships made possible only modest cost reductions as compared to the traditional junk, and sometimes only a gain in speed and reliability.[34] It was therefore difficult, by improving traditional land transport techniques, to make goods produced in the backward areas competitive far away from home with comparable goods produced in advanced areas with access to water transport. The general economic incentive to search for improvements in land transport was therefore reduced, although it is possible to imagine exceptional cases in which they would have been attractive. Presumably, too, the water-based system with its lower costs, greater concentration of capital and customers, and its denser labour-force, to some extent attracted entrepreneurial interest away from the land-transport areas.

There must have been ways in which the water transport system could have been improved on the basis of existing Chinese technical knowledge. But big advances by simple means, such as that accomplished by the Erie Canal in the United States in 1825, were no longer possible in China. They had, as it were, already been used up. Chinese water transport was faced with something of a technological discontinuity: probably only a large jump forward into the world of steampower would have meant a significant gain. This discontinuity made any new dynamic shift in the economy through reduced transport costs exceedingly difficult.

There was another technological discontinuity, that in agriculture. Yields per acre were very nearly as high as was possible without the use of advanced industrial-scientific inputs such as selected seeds, chemical fertilizers and pesticides, machinery and pumps powered by the internal combustion engine or electricity, concrete and so on. Furthermore, there was not enough suitable land to raise the yields per worker for the Chinese farm labour force as a whole by using either eighteenth-century British techniques, which depended critically on the interdependence of crop-raising and animal husbandry, or nineteenth-century American techniques of extensive, low per-acre yield, mechanized cultivation.

Traditional inputs, whether in the form of irrigation works, fertilizer or labour, were also nearly as high as they could be without running into sharply diminishing, or even negative, returns. That the last is not merely theoretical fancy is shown by the numerous cases where new irrigation works seriously reduced the supply of water to existing systems or, in some instances, imperilled them by crowding low-lying lands, subject to periodic floods, with too many polders. Often, where there was in principle the possibility of improving per-acre yields, this was ruled out in practice by resource shortages. An example is the dry-farming of Hopei and Shantung. Investigations in the 1930s suggest that it could with profit have used more animal manure; but the supply of manure was inadequate because of the shortage of grazing land, which in turn reflected the need of a dense population to turn pasture into arable.

It is not easy to give substantive proof that (i) improvements in late traditional agricultural technology, (ii) increases in both investment and the provision of recurring inputs in farm production on the basis of this technology, and also (iii) the use of new resources (notably land) still available at this technological level, had all reached a point of sharply diminishing returns by the later eighteenth century. The diversity of the Chinese agricultural scene across both space and time makes aggregate measures of output poor indicators of the level of technology. The farm economy in Ming and Ch'ing times consisted of two widely different sectors: a high-yielding rice sector and a lower-yielding wheat and millet sector. The relative share of the latter rose significantly with the passing of time. Likewise, as demographic pressure forced the Chinese to bring poorer and poorer land into cultivation, the relative share of marginal soils in both sectors increased. This may have been of considerable significance. Surveys in the 1920s showed that in the north the yields of wheat grown on irrigated land were over two-thirds again higher than those of wheat grown on non-irrigated land. Under these conditions, a level of average per-acre output unchanged over time may conceal a marked increase in skill in working more favoured lands, or less favoured lands, or both. If, therefore, we compare per-acre yields in 1400 with those in 1850 we are not necessarily talking about otherwise comparable agricultural systems. Differences in crops, soil fertility, rainfall and temperatures make comparisons of per-acre yields between China and other countries even more potentially misleading as regards the level of the technology used.

After these cautionary remarks, we can consider a few statistics. The data presented in Professor D. H. Perkins' quantitative survey of Chinese agriculture since 1368 suggest that productivity per *mou* rose steeply from under 140 catties of grain to about 224 catties in 1600. It then fell to a little above 200 catties in the 1770s, after which it rose again, modestly surpassing its previous best at a little over 240 catties by the middle of the nineteenth century.[35] Much of the early rise must be attributed to recovery from the devastation of the Mongol period, though we have no means at present of saying how much. The pattern, which suggests only a small overall rise in output per *mou* between 1600 and 1850, depends largely upon the high figure for 1600; and this could be lowered on the quite plausible assumption that more land was in fact being farmed at this time than Perkins allows for. The late Ming period was notorious for the concealment of arable, and later increases look suspiciously fast. Quite properly, Perkins tends not to use the 1600 data as a base for his conclusions. For the moment, we can simply say that *if* we accept them they lend support to our view that increasing the productivity of land was harder during the last few centuries of traditional China than it had been for some time previously.

Second, the per-acre yields of unmodernized Chinese agriculture in the 1920s, the first date when we have reasonably reliable figures, were substantially above those in most of Europe on the eve of the industrial revolution. Thus Chinese wheat yields at this time were in the region of fourteen bushels per acre, whereas in France, under somewhat comparable conditions of peasant smallholder agriculture, wheat yields at the end of the eighteenth century were only about 9·5 bushels, rising to around thirteen by 1850.* Chinese rice yields in the 1920s were about fifty-six bushels per acre.

Third, the attempt made by the Chinese Communists between 1956 and 1959 to increase agricultural output largely by the use of an intensified traditional technology and organizational changes does not seem to have raised either yield per acre or yield per farm worker.[36] A policy of increasing industrial-scientific inputs, notably chemical fertilizers, was adopted shortly afterwards, and almost certainly for this reason.

Qualitative assessments by late traditional Chinese observers give further support to the view that agricultural output was near its premodern limits. Some time around 1740, Chu Lun-han wrote that: 'To use the limited acreage of farmland to feed an ever-expanding population is a means which leaves us little further leeway.'[37] The government became officially concerned over what it saw as a new problem: the continuing rise in grain prices even in years of good harvest. By the 1750s it was understood that this was due to population pressure. As Chu Yun-chin remarked a little later: 'There are no further benefits to be had from the land, yet population grows more numerous. This is why millet and rice cost more, and the prices of everything have gone up.'[38] The state encouraged the opening of new land by allowing the cultivator to become its legal owner once he had paid taxes on it. Land in the north-west and north was opened to migrants from China Proper, though their number was not large. Merchants were encouraged to import rice from abroad; and official degrees were offered to those who did outstandingly well. Maize and sweet potatoes, previously found mainly in Kwangtung and Fukien, were officially promoted.

Pessimism was, however, the order of the day. Hung Liang-chi, whose gloomy views have earned him the title of the 'Chinese Malthus', believed that population growth was bound in the nature of things to outstrip production, that natural checks could not contain it, and that government remedial measures could never hope to be adequate. The only important dissenting voice seems to have been that of Pao Shih-ch'en early in the nineteenth century. 'The land of the empire,' he

---

* English wheat yields were higher, though there were pronounced regional variations. In the later eighteenth century average output was over twenty bushels per acre, and by the first third of the nineteenth century in the neighbourhood of thirty bushels.

wrote, 'is the chief source of provision for the empire's people. If there are more people there will be more producers. A large population is the basis of wealth. How could it on the contrary cause poverty? There is not much unused land in the empire, but *productivity* does not conform to any such restraints.' He saw the failure to raise productivity as the fault of the scholars: 'They despise anything to do with farming, and do not research into it.'[39]

The views of Western agronomists who observed late traditional Chinese farming at close quarters also suggest a system working near the limit of what was possible by pre-modern means. This is most evident in F. H. King's *Farmers of Forty Centuries* (1927). J. L. Buck's classic *Land Utilization in China* (1937) is not so unreservedly enthusiastic about the Chinese rural economy, but characterizes it as 'one of efficient use of the land' in international terms. More importantly, Buck shows the output per farm worker increasing steadily with the size of the farm, fewer workers per acre the larger the farm, and yields per acre approximately constant whatever the farm size. This suggests that the optimum ratio of population to farmland for pre-modern technology had long since been exceeded. Furthermore, apart from organizational reforms, the few proposals he makes for raising per-acre yields without recourse at some point to modern technology are not without practical difficulties. For example, his advice that the straw, stalks and grasses often used for fuel (with the ash then serving as a fertilizer) be fed direct to animals for manure bypasses the problem of finding cheap alternative fuels.

The hypothesis that only inputs created by a fairly advanced stage of an industrial-scientific revolution (one that had not of course taken place in late traditional China) could have saved her agriculture from sharply diminishing returns to new methods, new investment, extra inputs and new use of resources, thus seems more plausible than the view that there was ample potential for progress within the terms of the old system. Accepting this, then, we are left with the question of why the population kept growing, and the pattern of its growth. For it was the expansion of the population which produced that combination of *high-level* farming and transportation technology with a *low* per capita income which perceptive economists since Adam Smith have recognized as the distinctive characteristic of China in the seventeenth and eighteenth centuries.

The general demographic pattern is well known. The Chinese

Map 9

 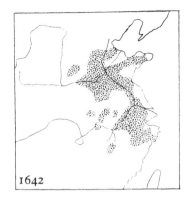

1588   1642

The extent of major epidemics

population reached a high point in the twelfth century, fell until the later fourteenth century, recovered to a new high point in the later sixteenth century, collapsed abruptly from then to about 1650, then grew until the end of the pre-modern period in 1850. The magnitudes of these changes are still sufficiently unclear to make analysis problematical. We do not know how high each peak advanced above the previous peak, nor what proportion of each phase of growth can be regarded as re-covery. A cautious guess would put the long-term increase from the middle of the twelfth to the middle of the nineteenth century as about three-fold, the population in 1850 being over 400 millions.

The major constraint on demographic growth in the late traditional period seems to have been epidemic disease. In 1586–9 and 1639–44 China suffered from the two most widespread and lethal epidemics in her recorded history, although their medical nature remains a complete mystery. In 1588, the worst year of the first of these outbreaks, ninety-two localities (that is, prefectures or counties) in thirteen provinces suffered severe mortality from epidemic disease. In 1641, the worst year of the second outbreak, seventy-nine localities in ten provinces were struck. Maps 9a and b show the geographical distribution for 1588 and 1642 respectively. Of the densely populated areas only Szechwan and Kwangtung escaped; and this immunity may only be apparent, because of inadequate evidence from these areas. By contrast, in the worst outbreak of the fifteenth century in 1455, only nine localities were affected. Sixteenth-century epidemics were worse, but before 1586 the most serious, in 1582, only saw twenty-five localities affected.

During the two great epidemics the death rate was very high. The local gazetteers often speak of twenty per cent, thirty per cent and forty per cent of the population dead. In some cases they record 'more than half the population dead', 'sixty to ninety per cent of the population dead' and 'ninety per cent of the population dead'. Dr T. H. Hollingsworth has pointed out that in a pre-modern population, with deaths normally close to fifty per thousand, it is probable that plague deaths have to reach at least ten per cent before chroniclers notice anything unusual. But most of the gazetteer entries for the two great epidemics do not refer to an 'epidemic' but to a 'great epidemic'. They stress the number of deaths with phrases like 'countless' and 'beyond reckoning'. If the average mortality was about twenty per cent on each occasion, the population may have fallen from thirty-five to forty per cent between 1585 and 1645.[40]

This temporary reduction in population eased the pressure on land for at least a century and a half, while the cultivated acreage continued to expand. By 1850 it was well over double its 1600 level. As a result, the amount of farmland per head of population was not very different in 1850 from what it had been around 1580. If Perkins' lower estimate for cultivated land is used together with his higher population estimate for these two periods, it actually appears as slightly greater.[41] But the average quality of the land had certainly fallen, though to what extent it is impossible to say. Speaking broadly, however, we can conclude that the statistical picture, shadowy though it is, suggests that impressive quantitative change in the form of population growth took place in Ch'ing times without much qualitative change in the farm economy. If there were technical improvements, they must have taken place mainly in the art of growing crops on poorer soils or under less favourable climatic conditions.

After 1644 there were no widespread epidemics for more than a century. In 1756 thirty-two localities were affected in the lower Yangtze region, and in 1786 forty-one localities, mostly in Kiangsu, Shantung and Honan. In 1820–22 came the first great cholera outbreak, which originated in Bengal in 1817 and spread to China by the sea-routes. In 1821, the worst year, it was recorded in over eighty localities in nine provinces. Mortality in Fukien, Chekiang, Kiangsu, Shantung and Hopei was probably substantial and must have temporarily eased the pressure of population there. The approximate coincidence of serious epidemic disease once again with a period when other evidence suggests that such pressure on land was becoming severe is perhaps noteworthy.

A final, more or less negative, confirmation of the trap in which China was caught is provided by Manchuria between 1905 and 1940. Before 1860, Manchuria was legally closed to Han Chinese in-migrants. It was opened at this time to provide some sort of demographic stiffening against evident Russian designs of annexation. The flow of migrants only became rapid, though, with the coming of railways early in the present century. In the later 1920s, gross in-migration for a brief moment rose above a million people a year. In consequence, the Manchurian population roughly doubled between 1905 and 1940. Cultivated area between 1919 and 1932 more than doubled however. Between 1914 and 1940 output of cereal crops rose over three-and-a-half times. Soybean production went up from 0·6 million metric tons in 1900 to 4·4 million metric tons in 1940.[42] This agricultural transformation was accomplished almost entirely by late traditional techniques, though one institution – the large land-development company – was new; and it proves that in the absence of severe resource restraints they were good enough to underpin an industrial revolution. Manchuria was industrialized under Japanese rule in the 1930s. The contrast with China Proper is impressive.

The foregoing discussion, though in some ways inconclusive, suggests a general solution to the question of China's retarded technological advance. It is that, through a number of interlocking causes, the input-output relationships of the late traditional economy had assumed a pattern that was almost incapable of change through internally-generated forces. Both in technological and investment terms, agricultural productivity per acre had nearly reached the limits of what was possible without industrial-scientific inputs, and the increase of the population had therefore steadily reduced the surplus product above what was needed for subsistence. This process is shown in figure 4. A falling surplus per head of population meant of course a reduction in effective demand per person for goods other than those needed for bare survival. Pre-modern water transport was close to a similar ceiling of efficiency; and few possibilities existed for increasing demand for goods by reducing transport costs.

For these technological reasons, the rising price of food in periods when population pressure on land was becoming severe could not induce a higher output of grain, except by means of migration and the opening

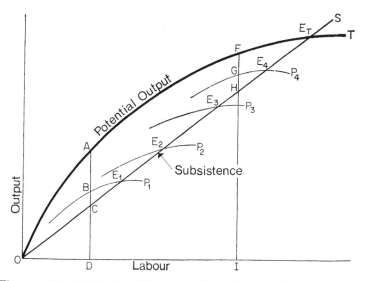

Figure 4. The high-level equilibrium trap in agriculture (after R. P. Sinha).
This illustrates the effects of a discontinuity or quasi-ceiling in late traditional
Chinese farm technology. OT shows potential output for a given input of labour
with best pre-modern methods. OS shows the proportion of output needed for
the subsistence of a given labour-force. With land constant, potential surplus
(e.g., AC and FH) shrinks, first relatively, then absolutely, as labour-force grows.
Actual surplus (e.g. BC and GH) depends on the level of 'practice', defined
here as investment and organization (especially commercialization and land
tenure). P_1, P_2, P_3, etc. show how at a given level falling returns per man as
labour input grows create intermediate equilibria E_1, E_2, E_3, etc. At E_T further
improvements in 'practice' are nil, and the ceiling on high-level pre-modern
technology leads to a trap that can be broken out of only by using modern
methods.

up of new land. Such migration took place on an impressive scale, and
was the chief means whereby the Chinese economy grew in quantitative
terms but with almost no qualitative change.

If the great size of the late traditional economy had any implications
for technological advance they were probably negative. Any significant
change in input–output relationships would have involved huge
absolute magnitudes of materials and goods. Britain's consumption of
raw cotton tripled between 1741 and the early 1770s, when effective
machine-spinning of the fibre first appeared. To accomplish this
tripling for China in a similar space of thirty-odd years would have been
beyond the cotton-production resources of the entire eighteenth-
century world. Between 1785 and 1833, the single province of Kwangtung imported on average from India each year six times as much raw

cotton as all Britain used annually at the time of Arkwright's first water-frame. Again, an expansion of Chinese exports of cotton cloth comparable to eighteenth-century Britain's both in its speed and in its relative size to the domestic market would have been too great for the available purchasing power of the world at that time. Perhaps smaller, localized, effects could have come about, more comparable to the British scale; but the high level of commercial integration in China, based on cheap water transport, made this rather unlikely except perhaps in the backward land-transport sector of the dualistic system relatively isolated from the influence of trade. The absolute size of a market is not without some importance, in that a given technology often demands a minimum scale of output if it is to be profitable. But it is of less importance so far as the creation of opportunities for investors and inventors is concerned than the *relative* magnitude of the change in its size over time. Beyond the minimum level required by production technology, moreover, the greater the absolute size of an economy or sector the harder it is to produce a large relative change in its structure or size.

Invention, as a social phenomenon, cannot be linked to immediate economic causes alone, though this is more nearly the case with the related acts of innovation and diffusion. Technology and science have long had a powerful interrelationship, and machines may be conceived of, like Leonardo's famous power-loom, long before there is any pressing economic need for them. All that we have shown here is that in late traditional China economic forces developed in such a way as to make profitable invention more and more difficult. With falling surplus in agriculture, and so falling per capita income and per capita demand, with cheapening labour but increasingly expensive resources and capital, with farming and transport technologies so good that no simple improvements could be made, rational strategy for peasant and merchant alike tended in the direction not so much of labour-saving machinery as of economizing on resources and fixed capital. Huge but nearly static markets created no bottlenecks in the production system that might have prompted creativity. When temporary shortages arose, mercantile versatility, based on cheap transport, was a faster and surer remedy than the contrivance of machines. This situation may be described as a 'high-level equilibrium trap'. In the context of a civilization with a strong sense of economic rationality, with an appreciation of invention such that shrines were erected to historic inventors (though, it is true, no patent law), and with notable mechanical gifts, it is probably a sufficient explanation of the retardation of technological advance.

*

What can we see of this in our own century?

It was the historic contribution of the modern West to ease and then break the high-level equilibrium trap in China. Opening the country to the world market in the middle of the nineteenth century led before long to rapid commercial and industrial growth at the main points of contact, especially Shanghai. Work done with and on foreign machinery trained the Chinese in modern technical skills, and laid the foundations of modern Chinese enterprise. A business representative of this trend was the Ta-lung Machinery Company in Shanghai. It was founded in 1902 by the son of a Chinese agent for a foreign firm; began by repairing foreign steamships; progressed to making units under contract for a British engineering firm which supplied blueprints and advice; and graduated in the 1930s to manufacturing a complete range of cotton textile machinery of its own design and suitable for export.[43]

Chinese creativity also reappeared in the interior. One of the earliest instances is Ch'en Ch'i-yuan's pioneering work in the Kwangtung silk industry in the 1870s. After visiting French Annam and seeing modern steam-driven filatures there he came home and built some in imitation, only worked by human power. He later advanced to steam-power, and put up a factory employing over six hundred men. This sparked off a protest from other silk-workers who were afraid of losing their livelihood, one of the few known instances of Ludditism in Chinese history. Ch'en survived, thanks to the help of the authorities, but was moved by his experience to invent a smaller silk-reeling machine suitable for those with only a little capital. It was widely copied.[44]

The introduction of modern methods at certain strategic points made possible new combinations of traditional elements. These linkages took a variety of forms. Steamships on major river and coastal routes, though they took away some traffic from traditional junks, stimulated the growth of the junk shipping serving subsidiary waterways. Tugs hauling strings of traditional vessels or specially built barges also became a common sight. The electric telegraph revolutionized the collection of business information, and business structure. It became possible, for example, for traditional-style banks in a number of cities to form networks.

Imported cotton yarn broke a raw materials shortage in Fukien and allowed a new handweaving industry to spring up. Rudolf Hommel in his *China at Work* (1937) noted of the Chinese blacksmith that 'for raw materials he relies nowadays very much upon the import of foreign iron'. Foreign demand allowed the expansion of such peasant industries as the production of tung oil in Hunan and Szechwan. The Japanese foot-treadle gin and the flying shuttle boosted the output of the traditional cotton industry. Small but useful items such as iron wire, kerosene and soap were introduced. Pumps worked by internal combustion engines appeared in the fields in a few places, such as Chia-hsing. Modern roads and railways increased the level of commercialization in their neighbourhoods.

An example of traditional/modern linkages is the rural textile industries of Kao-yang in Hopei.[45] This dry-farming area of about four hundred villages had links with the port of Tientsin by motor-road, telephone and waterway, and with Peking and Hankow by railway. These provided information, technology, new products, credit and markets. The influx of machine-spun yarn after 1909 brought an end to the local spinning industry, and a transformation of the weaving industry. The traditional wooden loom was replaced by a semi-automatic treadle loom (known as the 'iron wheel loom' from its heavy flywheel). This had been brought in by some Kao-yang men who had been to Japan, and the main suppliers were three Japanese firms in Tientsin. It was several times faster and wove broader cloth. The rising cost of outlays necessitated a rudimentary putting-out system. After a boom during the First World War there was a recession, but also further technical progress, especially roller calendering and Jacquard looms. In 1926 a method was discovered of sizing rayon so that it became strong enough to be used as warp as well as weft. This triggered a new boom, characterized by factories for weaving, sizing and preparing Jacquard cards. Collapse came in 1930 due to the world slump and the competition of the rival centre at Wei-hsien, which had lower transport costs.

This last example shows both the technological adaptability of the Chinese peasant, and the continuing problem of insufficient demand from the home market. If there had existed easy ways to improve agricultural output (and so raise home demand), this technological adaptability would surely have found them as it demonstrably found them in textiles. But to pursue these problems in detail would take us beyond the concerns of this book.

18 · Conclusion

A technology is the expression of man's working relationship with the natural world, the point at which environment and society meet and shape each other. His tools, his medicines and his weapons are the physical form of his conceptions, their effectiveness a matter of life and death. The means he uses to produce, preserve, organize and destroy give varying returns for effort; and these differences in efficiency account for many of the differences between the social institutions with which they are associated. In trying to discover why Chinese history has had its distinctive shape it has therefore seemed reasonable to make the changing pattern of the economics of technology our central point of reference. This procedure to some extent cuts across the usual subdivisions of history – politics, warfare, economics, institutions and ideas – emphasizing instead aspects of their interrelationship. Such an approach is a practical convenience, and implies nothing about the nature of historical causation. Its advantage is that it makes certain problems amenable to solution – the size and survival of the Chinese Empire, the Chinese medieval economic revolution, China's failure to create an industrial/mechanical revolution on her own initiative in late traditional times – that are otherwise nearly intractable. It would be rash perhaps to claim that this method is original, but I know of no other attempt to apply it systematically to the longer sweep of history.

Seen from this point of view, many familiar processes take on an appearance subtly but significantly changed. A difference in the relationship between the arts of production and destruction largely accounts for the differences between the fragmented political feudalism of the European middle ages and the consolidated state control of Sung China. The booming medieval Chinese economy, and especially its advanced metallurgical sector, could provide all its soldiery with armour and the best-known weapons, a luxury limited in the West by higher costs to a select minority. It was not the size of the eighteenth-century British market (tiny compared to that of China) but the speed of its growth that put pressure on the means of production there to improve. In eighteenth-century China, the high level of agricultural and water transport techniques, together with near to complete resource use and vast scale, made a comparably rapid growth in surplus and per-capita demand impossible. There is a sense in which, compared with China, western Europe in the early modern age enjoyed many of what Professor Gerschenkron has called 'the advantages of backwardness'. Again, nowhere in the world of 1800 was the hierarchy of urban central places so maturely developed as in the more advanced parts of China. Perhaps, then, it is an error to equate such maturation with a movement towards modernization? It is a plausible if disconcerting hypothesis that the perfection of a network of local and regional markets, efficiently connected and functionally differentiated, diffused and weakened the stimuli for new undertakings that might have arisen in a system with a more unbalanced urban concentration. The disproportionate development of the great Sung cities, like that of London and Paris at a later date, may well have been more closely linked with qualitative economic progress.

Many of the specific arguments put forward here are also new, at least in a work in a Western language. Typical examples are the analyses of the origins of the equitable field system and of Chinese paper money, the role of the late Ming epidemics and the structure of the late traditional cotton industry. There are two new points, however, which are of central importance and which depart considerably from the received consensus. The first of these is the insistence that serfdom and serflike tenancy from the Sung to early Ch'ing cannot be relegated to a minor historical role, and that its disappearance meant the rise of an essentially new type of rural society. The second is that technological innovation and invention during the period 800 to 1300 produced changes so great that the result can only reasonably be described as a 'revolution', and that Chinese growth thereafter slowed down not only relative to an accelerating Europe but also to its own earlier performance. These contentions will not be immediately accepted by everyone working in the field, and it is possible that they will at some future date have to be modified, perhaps along the line of regional differentiation; but the volume of evidence presented here is so massive that the burden of disproof is for the moment clearly on the other side.

What lessons may be drawn, however modestly, from what I have written? Two, I think: one for the historian of China and one for the historian of Europe. First, studies on particular aspects of Chinese history have been crippled by the lack of a suitable general view of the evolution of Chinese society into which they can be fitted, and from the partial modification of which their findings should gain their deepest significance. It is still too little understood that width is as crucial a part of historical understanding as depth, and that many patterns only show themselves at a distance. However inadequately, this book has begun to supply that perspective. Second, for European history whose long-term movements are relatively much better understood, comparison with the Chinese experience offers an unequalled source of fresh insight. The two histories are sufficiently alike for a study of the differences to be instructive. There are closely similar situations that later diverge, and widely different situations that later converge. Their investigation is the best way of determining which causes are crucial and which of little account.

Finally, does this book have any direct usefulness for our understanding of China today?

I think it may, provided that the expectations for this are not too great. A lesson which history has to teach is, after all, that the future is always different. Yet certain thoughts may be worth airing. The technological creativity of the Chinese people has deep historical roots, and slumbered for a while mostly for practical considerations. As it slowly reawakens, we may expect it to astonish us. Chinese agriculture, however, can only grow fast by using a vast and ever increasing quantity of industrial inputs, and can therefore never be a leading sector. If industry is to advance rapidly enough to let agriculture, and the economy as a whole, break out once and for all from the old high-level trap, it almost certainly needs to enter the international market to a far greater extent than hitherto. It is capable of doing this with an effectiveness that will come as a shock, if the decision to do so is taken. The consequence, however, will be a disruption of the control over information and thought which is essential to the survival of the Chinese Communist regime. Whether this latent contradiction is potentially lethal or merely troublesome is perhaps *the* riddle of the longer-term future of the country.

Felix qui potuit rerum cognoscere causas . . .

LIBRARY, UNIVERSITY OF CHESTER

References

A complete documentation of all the statements made in the text would be too cumbersome for a book such as this. References are therefore confined, with a few exceptions, to the sources of Chinese passages quoted. Roman upper case numerals (I, II, III, etc.) refer to volumes of Western books and journals and *chüan* of Chinese books. Roman lower case numerals (i, ii, iii, etc.) refer to issues of journals. The letters 'a' and 'b' refer to the *recto* and *verso* of the pages of Chinese books.

Chapter 1

1 CARLO CIPOLLA, ed., *The Economic Decline of Empires* (London: 1970), pp. 5–15, contains some remarks on this theme. Among the books on specific countries, A. Eck, *Le moyen âge russe* (Paris: 1933) deserves mention for its argument that the financial problems created by 'the imbalance between the density of the population and the territorial expansion of the Muscovite state' were at the root of the Russian system of land tenure and serfdom after the fifteenth century (pp. 320–1).

2 C. OMAN, *A History of the Art of War in the Middle Ages*, rev. ed. (London: 1924), I, 12.

Chapter 2

1 M. ROSTOVTZEFF, *The Social and Economic History of the Roman Empire*, rev. ed. (Oxford: 1957), p. 11.

2 R. L. WALKER, *The Multi-State System of Ancient China* (Hamden, Connecticut: 1953), pp. 27–8, 52.

3 HO CH'ANG-CH'ÜN, *Han-T'ang chien feng-chien t'u-ti so-yu-chih hsing-shih yen-chiu* (The Forms Taken by Feudal Land Tenure Systems from Han to T'ang Times) (Shanghai: 1964), p. 68.

4 HO CH'ANG-CH'ÜN (1964), p. 83.

5 *Han-shu* (Han History), Shih-huo chih, 24 *shang*. See also N. L.

Swann, *Food and Money in Ancient China* (Princeton: 1950), pp. 162 et seq.

6 *Han-shu*, Shih-huo chih, 24 *hsia*; Swann (1950), pp. 295–6.

7 HO CH'ANG-CH'ÜN (1964), p. 85.

8 HO CH'ANG-CH'ÜN (1964), p. 39. There is a somewhat different translation in E. M. Gale, trans., *Discourses on Salt and Iron* (Leiden: 1931), p. 96.

9 *Han-shu*, Wang Mang chuan, *chung*. See also C. M. Wilbur, *Slavery in China during the Former Han Dynasty* (Chicago: 1943), pp. 452–3 and Swann (1950), pp. 208–11.

10 A. H. M. JONES, 'Slavery in the Ancient World', in M. I. Finley, ed., *Slavery in Classical Antiquity* (Cambridge: 1960).

11 UTSUNOMIYA KIYOYOSHI, *Kandai shakai keizai shi kenkyū* (Studies in Han Social and Economic History) (Tokyo: 1955), p. 73; Ho Ch'ang-ch'ün (1964), p. 102.

12 *Han-shu*, Chang An-shih chuan; Wilbur (1943), pp. 170, 218, 365; Satō Takehashi, *Chūgoku kodai kōgyō shi no kenkyū* (A History of Industry in Ancient China) (Tokyo: 1962), p. 103.

13 HO CH'ANG-CH'ÜN (1964), p. 195. See also E. Balazs, *Chinese Civilization and Bureaucracy* (New Haven: 1964), p. 219.

14 HO CH'ANG-CH'ÜN (1964), pp. 248–9.

15 Ibid., p. 189.

16 Ibid., p. 233.

Chapter 3

1 HO CH'ANG-CH'ÜN (1964), p. 188.

2 Ibid., p. 291.

3 CHIN FA-KEN, *Yung-chia luan hou pei-fang ti hao-tsu* (The Great Northern Families After the Rebellion of the Yung-chia Reign-period) (Taipei: 1964), p. 27.

4 OCHI SHIGEAKI, *Gi-Shin Nan-chō no seiji to shakai* (Politics and Society in Wei, Chin and the Southern Dynasties) (Tokyo: 1963), p. 4.

5 Ibid., p. 28.

6 Ibid., p. 50.

7 Ibid., p. 12.

8 Ibid., p. 168.

9 Ibid., p. 191.

10 A. H. M. JONES, *The Later Roman Empire, 214–602: A Social Economic and Administrative Survey* (Oxford: 1964), II 781.

11 CHIN FA-KEN (1964), p. 147.

Chapter 4

1 CHIN FA-KEN (1964), p. 88.
2 Ibid., p. 95.
3 Ibid., p. 137.
4 HORI TOSHIKAZU, 'Kindensei no seiritsu' (The Formation of the Equitable Field System), *Tōyōshi kenkyū* XXIV.i and ii (1965): i, 48.
5 TANIGAWA MICHIO, 'Kindensei no rinen to daitochi-shoyū' (The Concept of the Equitable Field System and Large Landownership), *Tōyōshi kenkyū* XXV.iv (1967), p. 444.
6 TANIGAWA MICHIO, 'Hokuchō makki no kyōhei ni tsuite' (Local Soldiers towards the End of the Northern Dynasties), *Tōyōshi kenkyū* XX.iv (1962), pp. 415–6.
7 KANEKO HIDETOSHI, 'Hoku-Gi zenki no seiji' (The Government of the Early Northern Wei), *Tōyōshi kenkyū* XIX.i (1960), p. 32.
8 HORI (1965), i, 51–2.
9 TANIGAWA (1967), p. 440.
10 Ibid., p. 440. See also Wan Kuo-ting, 'The System of Equal Land Allotments in Medieval Times', in E. T. Zen Sun and J. De Francis, ed., *Chinese Social History* (Washington: 1956), p. 159.
11 HORI (1965), ii, 186, 192, n. 13.
12 TANIGAWA (1967), p. 455.
13 HORI (1965), ii, 186.
14 HO CH'ANG-CH'ÜN (1964), p. 321.
15 KU CHI-KUANG, *Fu-ping chih-tu k'ao-shih* (An Enquiry into the Divisional Militia) (Shanghai: 1962), p. 43.
16 Ibid., p. 30.
17 Ibid., pp. 37–8, 45–6.

Chapter 5

1 KU CHI-KUANG (1962), p. 102.
2 Ibid., p. 355.
3 Ibid., p. 187.
4 G. OSTROGORSKY, *History of the Byzantine State* (New Brunswick, 1957), p. 119.
5 L. BRÉHIER, *Les Institutions de l'Empire Byzantin* (Paris: 1949) p. 334.
6 HO CH'ANG-CHÜN (1964), p. 306. See also D. C. Twitchett, *Financial Administration under the T'ang Dynasty* (Cambridge: 1963), p. 216.
7 HO CH'ANG-CH'ÜN (1964), p. 309.
8 Ibid., p. 309.
9 KU CHI-KUANG (1962), p. 187.

10 Ibid., p. 203.

11 T'ANG CH'ANG-JU, 'Chün-t'ien chih-tu ti ch'an-sheng chi ch'i p'o-huai' (The Rise and Fall of the Equitable Field System), in *Chung-kuo li-tai t'u-ti chih-tu wen-t'i t'ao-lun chi* (Collected Discussions on Chinese Land Tenure Systems) (Peking: 1957), pp. 365–6. See also Sudō Yoshiyuki, *Chūgoku tochi seido shi kenkyū* (Studies in the History of Chinese Land Tenure Systems) (Tokyo: 1954), pp. 12–13.

12 HAMAGUCHI SHIGEKUNI, *Tō ōchō no senjin seido* (Unfree Persons during the T'ang Dynasty) (Kyoto: 1966), p. 38.

13 KU CHI-KUANG (1962), p. 148.

14 G. OSTROGORSKIJ, *Quelques problèmes d'histoire de la paysannerie Byzantine* (Brussels: 1956), p. 11.

15 SUDŌ (1954), p. 58 n. 8.

16 Ibid., pp. 58–9 n. 9.

17 Ibid., p. 17.

Chapter 6

1 KUSANO YASASUSHI, 'Sōdai no kokō-tōkei-jō ni iwayuru kakko ni tsuite' (The So-called 'In-migrant Households' in the Population Statistics of the Sung Dynasty), *Shien* LXXIX (1959), p. 122; Kusano Yasasushi, 'Sōdai no shuko, kakko, tenko' (Local/Landowning Households, In-migrant/Tenant Households and Tenant-serf Households in the Sung Dynasty), *Tōyō gakuhō* XL.i and ii (1963): ii, 74. There is a discussion of this passage by Tan Kyōji in his 'Ko ni kansuru ikkōsatsu – shuko kakko sei kenkyū no zentei' (An Inquiry into the 'Household' – A Preliminary Step in the Study of the System of Local/Landowning Households and In-migrant/Tenant Households), *Tōyōshi kenkyū* XXVII.i (Jun. 1968), pp. 49–51. He specifically attacks the idea that a distinction between tenant-serfs and 'families cultivating land belonging to others' may be inferred from it, on the grounds that the tenant-serfs of the 'families owning a moderate amount of property . . . but not [able] to provide in full for their tenant-serfs' are to be equated with those entered in the last category in the list. This is implausible for three reasons: (1) the quite different terminology used for 'tenant-serfs' and 'families cultivating land for others'; (2) the double counting of families which would result; and (3) the separation of the two categories in the list, which would be senseless if they were identical.

2 SUDŌ (1954), pp. 116–17.

3 Ibid., p. 121.

4 Ibid., p. 117.

5 Ibid., p. 120.
6 Ibid., pp. 118–19.
7 Ibid., p. 114.
8 NIIDA NOBORU, *Chūgoku hōsei shi kenkyū – dorei nōdo hō/kazoku sonraku hō* (A History of Chinese Law – Laws Concerning Slaves and Serfs/Laws Concerning the Family and the Village) (Tokyo: 1962), pp. 30–1.
9 SUDŌ (1954), p. 115.
10 WATANABE KŌRYŌ, 'Sōdai Fukken Sekkō shakai shōron – jikōnō o meguru shomondai' (Society in Fukien and Chekiang in Sung Times – Some Questions concerning Independent Farmers), *Shichō* XCV (1966), p. 31.
11 SUDŌ (1954), p. 131.
12 Ibid., p. 160.
13 SUDŌ YOSHIYUKI, *Sōdai keizai shi kenkyū* (Studies on the Economic History of the Sung Dynasty) (Tokyo: 1962), pp. 542–3.
14 KUSANO (1959), *passim*; Kusano (1963), i, 86.
15 KUSANO (1959), p. 110.
16 SUDŌ (1954), p. 223.
17 Ibid., pp. 264–5.
18 TAN KYŌJI, 'Sōsho no shōen ni tsuite' (The Early Sung Manor), *Shichō* LXXXVII (1964), p. 11.
19 SUDŌ (1954), p. 110.
20 FU I-LING, *Ming-Ch'ing nung-ts'un she-hui ching-chi* (Rural Society and Economy in the Late Ming and Early Ch'ing) (Peking: 1961), p. 81.
21 SUDŌ (1954), p. 252.
22 SUDŌ (1962), pp. 103–4.
23 TAN (1968), p. 53.
24 SUDŌ (1954), p. 155.

Chapter 7

1 YOSHIDA MITSUKUNI, 'Sōdai no tetsu ni tsuite' (Iron in Sung Times), *Tōyōshi kenkyū* XXIV.iv (1966), pp. 152–5; R. Hartwell, 'A Revolution in the Chinese Iron and Coal Industries during the Northern Sung, 960–1126 AD', *Journal of Asian Studies* XII (1962), pp. 154–5; R. Hartwell, 'Markets, Technology, and the Structure of Enterprise in the Development of the Eleventh-Century Chinese Iron and Steel Industry', *Journal of Economic History* XXVI (1966), pp. 32–3; R. Hartwell, 'A Cycle of Economic Change in Imperial China: Coal and Iron in North-east China, 750–1350', *Journal of the Economic and Social History of the Orient*, X (1967), pp. 104–5.

2 MIYAZAKI ICHISADA, 'Sōdai ni okeru sekitan to tetsu' (Coal and Iron in the Sung Dynasty), *Tōhōgaku* XIII (1957), p. 17.

3 YOSHIDA MITSUKUNI, 'Sō-Gen no gunji gijutsu' (Sung and Yuan Military Technology), in Yabuuchi Kiyoshi, ed., *Sō-Gen jidai no kagaku gijutsu shi* (A History of Science and Technology in the Sung and Yuan Periods) (Kyoto: 1967), p. 213.

4 Ibid., p. 212.

5 Ibid., p. 224.

Chapter 8

1 HAGIWARA JUNPEI, 'Doboku no hen zengo – keizai mondai o chūshin to shite mita Min-Mō kōshō' (Before and After the T'u-mu Incident – The Negotiations between the Ming and Mongols Seen from an Economic Point of View), *Tōyōshi kenkyū* XI.iii (1951), esp. pp. 9, 10, 11, 17.

2 See chapter 14, p. 216 et seq.

3 D. H. PERKINS, *Agricultural Development in China*, 1368–1968 (Chicago: 1969), p. 176.

4 HOSHI AYAO, *The Ming Tribute Grain System*, translated by M. Elvin (Ann Arbor: 1969), p. 33.

5 Quoted in Perkins (1969), p. 176.

6 P. DU HALDE, *The General History of China*, trans. R. Brookes (London: 1736), II 124.

7 OKUMURA SHŌJI, *Hinawajū kara kurofune made* (From the Matchlock to the Black Ships) (Tokyo: 1970), pp. 31–4, 53–4.

8 R. TAYLOR, 'Yuan Origins of the Wei-so System', in C. Hucker, ed., *Chinese Government in Ming Times* (New York, 1969), pp. 28–30, 36.

9 SHIMIZU TAIJI, *Mindai tochi seido shi kenkyū* (Studies on the Ming Land Tenure System) (Tokyo: 1968), pp. 235–354.

10 Ibid., pp. 367–83.

11 Ibid., p. 342.

12 FENG YING-CHING, *Huang-Ming ching-shih shih-yung pien* (Imperial Ming Handbook of Practical Statesmanship) (1603: Taipei reprint of 1972), pp. 482–8, and p. 1233.

13 HOSHI/ELVIN (1969), pp. 6–9, 83–5.

14 HOSHI AYAO, *Mindai sōun no kenkyu* (The Ming Tribute Grain System) (Tokyo: 1963), p. 27.

15 LI CHIEN-NUNG, *Sung-Yuan-Ming ching-chi shih-kao* (Draft Economic History of the Sung, Yuan and Ming Dynasties) (Peking: 1957), p. 116.

16 HOSHI/ELVIN (1969), p. 75.

17 SUZUKI CHŪSEI, *Shincho chūki shi kenkyū* (Researches into the History of the Mid-Ch'ing Period) (Toyohashi: 1951), p. 56.

18 SUGIMURA YŪZŌ, *Kenryū kōte i* (The Ch'ien-lung emperor) (Tokyo: 1961), plates 20–2. See also Ishida Mikinosuke, 'Pari kaichō Kenryū nenkan "Chun-hui liang-pu p'ing-ting te-sheng t'u" ni tsuite, (On the 'Pictures of the Pacification of Sungaria and Turkestan engraved in Paris during the Ch'ien-lung period), *Tōyō gakuhō* IX.iii (Sept. 1919), pp. 120, 137. T. Esper, 'The Replacement of the Longbow by Firearms in the English Army', *Technology and Culture* VI.iii (1965) makes illuminating reading in the context of this picture.

19 OWEN LATTIMORE, *Inner Asian Frontiers of China* (New York: 1940. Beacon edition 1962), pp. 138–9, n. 58.

20 HOSHI AYAO, *Min-Shin jidai kōtsū-shi no kenkyū* (Studies in the History of Communications in Ming and Ch'ing Times) (Tokyo: 1971), p. 351.

21 Ibid., p. 352.

22 SAEKI TOMI, *Shindai ensei no kenkyū* (The Ch'ing Salt Administration) (Kyoto: 1956), p. 174.

23 Ibid., p. 166.

24 CH'I SSU-HO, ed., *Huang Chüeh-tzu tsou-shu, Hsu Nai-chi tsou-i* (Memorials of Huang Chüeh-tzu and Hsu Nai-chi) (Peking: 1959), pp. 65, 75, 117, 121.

25 Historical Research Office of the Shanghai Academy of the Social Sciences, ed., *Ya-p'ien chan-cheng mo-ch'i Ying-chün tsai Ch'ang-chiang hsia-yu ti ch'in-lüeh tsui-hsing* (The Criminal Invasion of the Lower Yangtze by British Forces during the Last Phase of the Opium War) (Shanghai: 1964), p. 280.

Chapter 9

1 R. H. MYERS, *The Chinese Peasant Economy* (Cambridge, Mass.: 1970), p. 179.

2 SUDŌ (1962), p. 81.

3 Ibid., p. 91.

4 Ibid., p. 92.

5 Ibid., p. 45.

6 Ibid., p. 20.

7 Ibid., p. 38.

8 Ibid., p. 58.

9 SUDŌ (1954), p. 69.

10 Ibid., p. 86.

11 *Sung-chiang fu-chih* (Gazetteer for Sung-chiang Prefecture) (Sung-chiang: 1817), V 5a.
12 SUDŌ (1962), p. 92.
13 Ibid., p. 93.
14 Ibid., p. 94.
15 Ibid., p. 95.
16 Ibid., p. 82.
17 Ibid., p. 97.
18 Ibid., p. 144.
19 Ibid., pp. 146–7.
20 Ibid., p. 150.
21 Ibid., p. 275.
22 Ibid., p. 153.
23 Ibid., p. 230.
24 Ibid., p. 271.
25 Ibid., p. 156.
26 Ibid., p. 154.
27 Ibid., p. 154.
28 Ibid., pp. 161, 269.
29 SHIBA YOSHINOBU, *Sōdai shōgyō shi kenkyū* (Commerce and Society in Sung China) (Tokyo: 1968), p. 146. See also the translation of this work by M. Elvin, *Commerce and Society in Sung China* (Ann Arbor: 1970), pp. 52–3.
30 SUDŌ (1962), p. 366.
31 Ibid., p. 106.
32 Ibid., p. 169.
33 Ibid., p. 114.
34 Ibid., pp. 107, 110.
35 Ibid., p. 108.
36 Ibid., p. 114.
37 *Sung-chiang fu-chih* (1817), V 6a.
38 Diagram in J. Needham, *Science and Civilisation in China*, IV. 2 Mechanical Engineering (Cambridge: Cambridge University Press, 1965), p. 559.
39 SHIBA (1968), p. 148; Shiba/Elvin (1970), p. 54.

Chapter 10

1 AOYAMA SADAO, *Tō-Sō jidai no kōtsū to chishi chizu no kenkyū* (A Study of the Communications Systems of T'ang and Sung China, and of the Development of Their Topographies and Maps) (Tokyo: 1963), p. 9.
2 Ibid., p. 47 n. 20.

3 Ibid., p. 177.
4 Ibid., p. 47 n. 21.
5 Ibid., p. 48 n. 26.
6 Ibid., p. 36.
7 Ibid., p. 114 n. 51.
8 CHIN FA-KEN (1964), p. 117.
9 SHIBA (1968), p. 52; Shiba/Elvin (1970), p. 4.
10 SHIBA (1968), p. 52; Shiba/Elvin (1970), p. 5.
11 D. TWITCHETT, 'Merchant, Trade and Government in Late T'ang', *Asia Major* XIV.i (1968), pp. 84, 85.
12 AOYAMA (1963), p. 284.
13 KUWABARA JITSUZŌ, trans. Ch'en Yü-ch'ing, *P'u Shou-keng k'ao* (A Study of P'u Shou-keng) (Peking: 1954 – reprint of Shanghai 1929 edition), p. 95.
14 SHIBA (1968), p. 61; Shiba/Elvin (1970), p. 9.
15 HOSHI/ELVIN (1969), p. 75.
16 LI CHIEN-NUNG (1957), p. 117.
17 HOSHI/ELVIN (1969), p. 7.
18 Ibid., p. 68.
29 SHIBA (1968), p. 65; Shiba/Elvin (1970), p. 11.
10 SHIBA (1968), p. 94; Shiba/Elvin (1970), p. 20.
21 SHIBA (1968), p. 94; Shiba/Elvin (1970), p. 20.
22 SHEN KUA, *Meng-ch'i pi-t'an* (Dream Pool Essays) (1086–91), ed. of Hu Tao-ching (Shanghai: 1956), I 432 (section 213).
23 SHIBA (1968), p. 64; Shiba/Elvin (1970), pp. 10–11.
24 Ibid., respectively, p. 67 and p. 12.
25 Ibid., respectively, p. 100 and p. 23.
26 Ibid., respectively, p. 64 and p. 11.
27 Ibid., respectively, p. 99 and pp. 21–2.
28 Ibid., respectively, p. 76 and p. 14.
29 Ibid., respectively, p. 110 and p. 27.
30 Ibid., respectively, p. 119 and p. 33.
31 R. LATHAM, trans. *The Travels of Marco Polo* (London: 1958), p. 180. Some versions give the number of ships as 15,000 rather than 5,000. Cp. A. C. Moule and P. Pelliot, *Marco Polo. The Description of the World* (London: 1938), I 320.

Chapter 11

1 CHIN FA-KEN (1964), p. 134.
2 E. BALAZS, 'Le traité économique du "Souei-chou" ', *T'oung pao* XLII (1954), p. 174.
3 Ibid., p. 175.

4 MIYAZAKI ICHISADA, *Godai Sōsho no tsūka mondai* (The Currency Problem in the Five Dynasties and the Early Sung) (Kyoto: 1943), p. 103.
5 D. C. TWITCHETT, *Financial Administration under the T'ang Dynasty* (Cambridge: 1963), pp. 165–6.
6 SHIBA (1968), p. 370; Shiba/Elvin (1970), p. 153.
7 Ibid., respectively, p. 201 and p. 85.
8 Ibid., respectively, p. 369 and p. 153.
9 MIYAZAKI (1943), p. 57.
10 Ibid., p. 51.
11 Ibid., p. 14.
12 Ibid., p. 60.
13 Ibid., p. 24.
14 Ibid., p. 28.
15 Ibid., p. 299.
16 Ibid., p. 57.
17 LI CHIEN-NUNG (1957), pp. 87–8.
18 KATŌ SHIGESHI, *Chung-kuo ching-chi-shih k'ao-cheng* (Studies in Chinese Economic History) (Peking: 1963), II 82. Chinese translation by Wu Chieh of Katō (1953–4), see note 23 below.
19 LI CHIEN-NUNG (1957), p. 95.
20 Ibid., p. 97.
21 Ibid., p. 99.
22 SUDŌ (1962), p. 355.
23 KATŌ SHIGESHI, *Shina keizai-shi kōshō* (Studies in Chinese Economic History) (Tokyo: 1953–4), II 223–4.

Chapter 12

1 *Han-shu, 24 shang.*
2 SATŌ TAKEHASHI (1962), p. 101.
3 D. C. TWITCHETT, 'The T'ang Market System', *Asia Major* XII.i (1966), p. 229.
4 SHIBA (1968), p. 341; Shiba/Elvin (1970), p. 142.
5 Ibid., respectively, p. 338 and p. 141.
6 AOYAMA (1963), p. 158 n. 44.
7 Ibid., p. 140.
8 SHIBA (1968), p. 297; Shiba/Elvin (1970), p. 123.
9 Ibid., respectively, p. 148 and p. 54.
10 Ibid., respectively, p. 284 and p. 116.
11 Ibid., respectively, p. 351 and pp. 144–5.
12 Ibid., respectively, pp. 357, 371, and pp. 147, 154.
13 Ibid., respectively, p. 161 and p. 61.

14 Ibid., respectively, p. 160 and p. 59.
15 Ibid., respectively, p. 165 and p. 64.
16 Ibid., respectively, p. 301 and p. 124.
17 Ibid., respectively, p. 138 and p. 48.
18 Ibid., respectively, p. 210 and p. 88.
19 Ibid., respectively, p. 442 and p. 191.
20 Ibid., respectively, p. 114 and p. 29.
21 SUDŌ (1962), p. 218.
22 SHIBA (1968), p. 333; Shiba/Elvin (1970), p. 139.
23 LATHAM (1958), p. 188. Cp. Moule and Pelliot (1938), I 324, which cites various texts giving the circumference as 9, 20, 40 and 60 miles.
24 PERKINS (1969), pp. 290–5.
25 J. JACOBS, The Economy of Cities (London: 1970).

Chapter 13

1 ISHIDA YOSHIHIKARI, 'Tō-Godai no chōin' (Printing under the T'ang and the Five Dynasties), Shūkan Tōyōgaku X (1963), p. 60.
2 SHEN KUA (1086–91), II 597–8. See also T. F. Carter, The Invention of Printing in China and Its Spread Westward (New York: 1925) second edition, rev. by L. C. Goodrich (New York: 1955), pp. 212–13.
3 MIYASHITA SABURŌ, 'Sō-Gen no iryō' (Medical Care in Sung and Yuan Times) in Yabuuchi (1967), p. 127.
4 Ibid., p. 128 n. 4.
5 Ibid., p. 128 n. 5.
6 Ibid., p. 131.
7 Ibid., p. 150.
8 CHU CHEN-HENG, Ko-wu yü-lun (A Further Discussion of the Investigation of Things) (1347), hsu.
9 SHIBA (1968), p. 414; Shiba/Elvin (1970), pp. 176–7.
10 YABUUCHI KIYOSHI (1967), p. 63.
11 WANG CHEN, Nung shu (Treatise on Agriculture) (1313), XIX 13a and XXII 4a.
12 D. DIDEROT, ed., Encyclopédie ou dictionnaire raisonné des Sciences, des Arts et des Metiers . . . (Neufchastel: 1765), VI 787–8.

Chapter 14

1 SHIBA (1968), p. 136; Shiba/Elvin (1970), pp. 46–7.
2 HIBINO TAKEO, 'Tō-Sō jidai ni okeru Fukken no kaihatsu' (The Development of Fukien in the T'ang and Sung Period), Tōyōshi kenkyū IV.iii (1939), p. 8. See also E. H. Schafer, The Empire of Min (Rutland: 1954), p. 79.

3 HIBINO (1939), p. 3.
4 SHIBA (1968), p. 425; Shiba/Elvin (1970), p. 183.
5 Ibid., respectively, p. 422 and p. 6.
6 HIBINO (1939), p. 24.
7 Ibid., p. 8.
8 SHIBA (1968), p. 424 n. 11; Shiba/Elvin (1970), p. 182.
9 Ibid., respectively, p. 423 and p. 182.
10 Ibid., respectively, p. 429 and p. 186.
11 Ibid., respectively, p. 430 and p. 185.
12 Ibid., respectively, p. 434 and p. 189.
13 Ibid., respectively, p. 159 and p. 58.
14 Ibid., respectively, p. 163 and p. 63.
15 FUJII HIROSHI, 'Shin-an shōnin no kenkyū' (A Study of the Merchants of Hsin-an) Tōyō gakuhō XXXVI.i–iv (1953–4): i, 26.
16 Ibid., i, 25.
17 WANG CHEN (1313), XXI 16b.
18 NISHIJIMA SADAO, Chūgoku keizai shi kenkyū (Studies in the Economic History of China) (Tokyo: 1966), p. 825.
19 KU YEN-WU, T'ien-hsia chün-kuo li-ping shu (Documents Relating to the Advantageous and Disadvantageous Characteristics of the Commanderies and Principates of the Empire) (1639–62; Ssu-k'u shan-pen ed. 1936), VI 29b.
20 NISHIJIMA SADAO, 'Shina shoki mengyō shijō no kōsatsu' (An Enquiry into the Early Chinese Cotton Market), Tōyō gakuhō XXX.ii (1947), p. 125.
21 Ibid., p. 126.
22 Ibid., p. 126.
23 Ibid., p. 128.
24 CHU HUA, Mu-mien p'u (Cotton Manual) (mid eighteenth century), in Shang-hai t'ung-she, ed., Shang-hai chang-ku ts'ung-shu (Shanghai: 1936), p. 11b.
25 NISHIJIMA SADAO, 'Mindai ni okeru kiwata no fukyū ni tsuite' (The Spread of the Cotton Plant during the Ming Dynasty), Shigaku zasshi LVII.iv and v (1948): v, 28.
26 Ibid., iv, 14.
27 KATŌ (1953–4), II 608.
28 YABUUCHI (1967), p. 26.
29 KUWABARA JITSUZŌ, 'On P'u Shou-keng, a Man of the Western Regions . . . together with a General Sketch of Trade of the Arabs in China during the T'ang and Sung Eras', Memoirs of the Research Department of the Toyo Bunko, II (1928) and VII (1935): I 24.
30 SHIBA (1968), p. 80; Shiba/Elvin (1970), p. 15.

31 SAKUMA SHIGEO, 'Minchō no kaigin seisaku' (The Maritime Inter-dict Policy of the Ming Dynasty), *Tōhōgaku* VI (1953), p. 45.

32 LI CHIEN-NUNG (1957), p. 161.

33 SAKUMA (1953), p. 48.

34 LI CHIEN-NUNG (1957), p. 162.

35 ISHIHARA MICHIHIRO, *Wakō* (The Japanese Pirates) (Tokyo: 1964), pp. 342–56.

36 HOSHI/ELVIN (1969), p. 8.

37 ABE TAKEO, 'Gen jidai no "pao-yin" seido no kōkyū' ('Pao-yin' or Taxes in Silver under the Yuan Dynasty), *Tōhō gakuhō* XXIV (1954), p. 243.

38 SAKUMA SHIGEO, 'Mindai ni okeru shōzei to zaisei to no kankei' (The Business Tax and Financial Administration in the Ming Period), *Shigaku zasshi* LX.i (1956), p. 12.

39 KATAYAMA SEIJIRŌ, 'Mindai kaijō mitsu-bōeki to enkai chihō gōshinzō' (Smuggling Trade in the Ming Dynasty and the Local Gentry in the Coastal Areas), *Rekishigaku kenkyū* CLXIV (1953), p. 26.

40 ISHIHARA (1964), p. 211.

41 HATANO YOSHIHIRO, *Chūgoku kindai kōgyō shi no kenkyū* (Studies on the Early Industrialization of China) (Kyoto: 1961), p. 58.

42 KATAYAMA (1953), p. 25.

43 E.g. the *Liang-chung hai-tao chen-ching* (Two Sailing Manuals with Compass Bearings) (Peking: 1960).

44 M. LOEHR, 'Some Fundamental Issues in the History of Chinese Painting', *Journal of Asian Studies* XXIII.ii (1964), pp. 192–3.

45 FANG I-CHIH, *Wu-li hsiao-shih* (A Brief Record of the Principles of Things) (1664; edition of 1884), VIII 13b–14a.

46 Ibid., I 5b.

47 Ibid., VIII 14a.

48 Ibid., *Tzu-hsu* 1a.

49 Ibid., II 33a.

50 SAKADE YOSHINOBU, 'Hō I-chi no shisō' (The Thought of Fang I-chih) in Yabuuchi Kiyoshi and Yoshida Mitsukuni, ed., *Min-Shin jidai no kagaku gijutsu shi* (A History of Science and Technology in the Ming and Ch'ing Periods) (Kyoto: 1970), p. 95.

51 FANG I-CHIH (1664), I 28b.

52 Ibid., I 3b–4a.

53 Ibid., I 4a.

54 SAKADE (1970), p. 121.

55 FANG I-CHIH (1664), *tsung-lun* 10b.

56 Ibid., II 32b–33a.

57 Ibid., I lab.
58 Ibid., *tsung-lun* 2a.
59 Ibid., II 4b.

Chapter 15

1 SHIMIZU TAIJI, *Mindai tochi seido shi kenkyū* (Studies in the History of Land Tenure in the Ming Dynasty) (Tokyo: 1968), esp. pp. 16–33, 64–71, 385–458.
2 Ibid., p. 386.
3 Ibid., pp. 407–8.
4 FU I-LING, *Ming-tai Chiang-nan shih-min ching-chi shih-t'an* (An Enquiry into the Economy of the Urban Population of Kiangnan during the Ming Dynasty) (Shanghai: 1963), p. 61.
5 Ibid., p. 33.
6 Ibid., p. 63.
7 HOSONO KŌJI, 'Minmatsu Shinsho Kōnan ni okeru jinushi doboku kankei' (Relations between Landowners and Their Serfs in Kiangnan in the Late Ming and the Early Ch'ing), *Tōyōgakuhō* L.iii (1967), p. 28.
8 Ibid., p. 11.
9 FU I-LING (1961), p. 91.
10 HOSONO (1967), p. 26.
11 FU I-LING (1961), p. 79.
12 HOSONO (1967), p. 27.
13 LU WANG-TA *et al.*, rev., Li Lin-sung *et al.*, ed., *Chia-ch'ing Shang-hai hsien-chih* (Gazetteer for Shang-hai County in the Chia-ch'ing Reign) (Shanghai: 1814), XIX 27b.
14 FU I-LING (1961), pp. 81–2.
15 SUDŌ (1954), pp. 119–20.
16 HOSONO (1967), p. 16.
17 Ibid., p. 16.
18 Ibid., p. 4.
19 FU I-LING (1963), p. 71; *Shen-shih nung-shu* (Mr Shen's Treatise on Agriculture) in *Hsueh-hai lei-pien* (Shanghai: 1920), vol. 104, pp. 19ab.
20 HOSONO (1967), p. 19.
21 Ibid., p. 20.
22 Ibid., p. 11.
23 FU I-LING (1963), p. 2.
24 FU I-LING (1961), p. 172.
25 Ibid., p. 109.
26 Ibid., p. 95.
27 YEH MENG-CHU, *Yueh-shih pien* (A Survey of the Age) (MS,

Shanghai: late seventeenth century), in *Shang-hai chang-ku ts'ung-shu*, I 10b.

28 FU I-LING (1961), p. 95.

29 Ibid., p. 102.

30 Ibid., p. 120.

31 KOYAMA MASAAKI, 'Minmatsu Shinsho no daitochi shoyū – toku ni Kōnan deruta chitai no chūshin ni shite –' (Large Landownership in the Late Ming and the Early Ch'ing – with especial reference to the Kiangnan delta), *Shigaku zasshi* LXVI.xii (1957) and LXVII.i (1958): xii,16.

32 TERADA TAKANOBU, 'Yōsei-tei no semmin kaihō-rei ni tsuite' (The Yung-cheng Emperor's Edicts Liberating Persons of Mean Status), *Tōyōshi kenkyū* XVIII.iii (1959), *passim*.

33 FU I-LING (1963), p. 44.

34 HATANO (1961), p. 1.

35 Ibid., pp. 16–17.

36 Ibid., pp. 67–8 n. 23.

37 FU I-LING (1961), p. 156.

38 KOYAMA (1957), xii, 1.

39 Ibid., xii, 1.

40 FU I-LING (1961), p. 179.

41 Ibid., p. 189.

42 IMABORI SEIJI, 'Shindai no kōso ni tsuite' (Resistance to Paying Rents during the Ch'ing Dynasty), *Shigaku zasshi* LXXVI.ix (1967), p. 41 n. 6.

43 T. C. SMITH, *The Agrarian Origins of Modern Japan* (Stanford: 1959), chapters VIII to IX.

44 FU I-LING (1963), p. 74; *Shen-shih nung-shu*, pp. 22ab.

45 KOYAMA (1958), i, 61.

46 Ibid., i, 59.

47 FU I-LING (1961), pp. 188–9.

48 IMABORI (1967), p. 39.

49 JOHN LOSSING BUCK, *Land Utilization in China* (Chicago: 1937), 3 vols; T. L. Hsiao, *The Land Revolution in China, 1930–1934. A Study of Documents* (Seattle: 1969). See also the review article on the latter book by M. Elvin, 'Early Communist Land Reform and the Kiangsi Rural Economy', *Modern Asian Studies* IV.ii (1970), pp. 165–9.

50 HOSONO (1967), p. 11.

51 Ibid., p. 26.

52 Ibid., p. 18.

53 Ibid., p. 18.

54 FU I-LING (1961), p. 83.

55 SHIBA (1968), p. 429; Shiba/Elvin (1970), p. 185.
56 SHIMIZU (1968), pp. 205–20.
57 This point is excellently brought out in an unpublished paper by C. M. Wiens, 'Bondservants and their Revolts during the Late Ming' (June, 1970).
58 O. B. VAN DER SPRENKEL, 'Population Statistics of Ming China', *Bulletin of the School of Oriental and African Studies* XV.ii (1953), p. 309, translation slightly modified.
59 HOSHI/ELVIN (1969), p. 30.
60 Ibid., pp. 30–1.
61 YEH MENG-CHU (late seventeenth century), VI 12b.
62 KU YEN-WU (1639–62), VIII 74b–76b.
63 YEH MENG-CHU (late seventeenth century), VI 18a.
64 See M. Elvin, 'Market Towns and Waterways. The County of Shanghai from 1480 to 1910', in G. W. Skinner, ed., *The City in Late Imperial China* (Stanford: forthcoming), for the sources of the following quotations.
65 *Hsin-hai ko-ming ch'ien shih-nien-chien shih-lun hsuan-chi* (A Selection of Discussions of Current Affairs in the Ten Years Before the 1911 Revolution) (Hong Kong: 1962), I 174 and 182.
66 YÜ CHIH, *Te-i lu* (Tei-i Records) (1869), XIV 18a–19b. I am indebted to Piet van der Loon for drawing this remarkable book to my attention.
67 NAKAHARA TERUO, 'Shindai ni okeru sōryō no shōhinka ni tsuite' (The Mercantilization of the Tribute Grain under the Ch'ing Dynasty), *Shigaku zasshi* LXX (1958), pp. 47 and 50.
68 Ibid., p. 51.

Chapter 16

1 FU I-LING (1963), p. 39.
2 HO PING-TI, *Chung-kuo hui-kuan shih-lun* (A Historical Survey of *Landmannschaften* in China) (Taipei: 1966), esp. pp. 38–64, 102–12.
3 SAKUMA SHIGEO, 'Mindai ni okeru shōzei to zaisei to no kenkyūi (The Business Tax and Financial Administration in the Ming Period), *Shigaku zasshi* LXV.i and ii (1956): ii, 23.
4 FU I-LING (1963), p. 17.
5 Ibid., p. 42.
6 LI WEN-YAO, ed., *Shang-hai hsien chih* (Shanghai County Gazetteer) (1750), I 21a.
7 NISHIJIMA (1966), p. 846.
8 LI WEN-YAO (1750), V 69b–70b.
9 Ibid., I 22b–23a.

10 HATANO (1961), pp. 42 and 80.

11 FU I-LING, *Ming Ch'ing shih-tai shang-jen chi shang-yeh tzu-pen* (Merchants and Mercantile Capital in the Ming and Ch'ing Periods) (Peking: 1956), p. 11.

12 FU I-LING (1963), pp. 46–7.

13 Ibid., pp. 89–90.

14 HATANO (1961), p. 74; Fujii (1953), i, 18.

15 FU I-LING (1963), p. 130; Terada Takanobu, 'So-Shō chihō ni okeru toshi no mengyō shōnin ni tsuite' (On the Cotton Merchants of the Cities in the Su-chou and Sung-chiang Region), *Shirin* XLI.vi (1958), pp. 66–7.

16 YOKOYAMA SUGURU, 'Shindai ni okeru tambugyō no keiei keitai' (The Management Structure of the Calendering Industry under the Ch'ing Dynasty), *Tōyōshi kenkyū* XIX.iii (1960) and iv (1961), iii, 337–8.

17 Ibid., iv, 460.

18 Ibid., iv, 460.

19 Ibid., iii, 339.

20 Ibid., iii, 342.

21 Ibid., iv, 463.

22 HATANO (1961), pp. 86 et seq.

23 YOKOYAMA SUGURU, 'Shindai no toshi kinu-orimono-gyō no seisan keitai' (The Organization of Production in the Urban Silk Manufacture in Ch'ing China), *Shigaku kenkyū* CIV and CV (1968), part ii, 54.

24 Ibid., part ii, 56.

25 HATANO (1961), p. 36.

Chapter 17

1 FU I-LING (1956), p. 13.

2 Ibid., p. 14.

3 Ibid., p. 6.

4 R. NURKSE, *Problems of Capital Formation in Underdeveloped Countries* (Oxford: 1953), pp. 5–6.

5 YEH MENG-CHU (late seventeenth century), VII 5a–6a.

6 FUJII (1953), ii, 33.

7 Ibid., iii, 76; Hatano (1961), p. 51.

8 FU I-LING (1956), p. 31.

9 FUJII (1953), ii, 41.

10 FU I-LING (1963), pp. 89–90.

11 NAKAHARA (1958), p. 45.

12 NAKAHARA TERUO, 'Shindai sōsen ni yoru shōhin ryūtsū ni tsuite' (The Flow of Commodities on Grain Transport Ships during the Ch'ing Dynasty), *Shigaku kenkyū* LXXII (1959), p. 69.

13 Ibid., p. 70.

14 Ibid., p. 71.

15 FUJII (1953), iii, 73.

16 YAMAGUCHI MICHIKO, 'Shindai no sōun to senshō' (The Tribute Grain Transport and the Shipping Merchants under the Ch'ing), *Tōyōshi kenkyū* XVII.ii (1958), p. 62.

17 IMABORI SEIJI, *Chūgoku hōken shakai no kikō – Kuei-sui (Hu-ho-hao-t'e) ni okeru shakai no jittai chōsa* (The Structure of Chinese Feudal Society – A Factual Investigation of Social Groups in Kuei-sui [Huhehot]) (Tokyo: 1955), ch. 3. I am grateful to Professor Ramon Myers for drawing this book to my attention.

18 NIIDA NOBORU, 'Shindai Konan no "Girudo Māchanto" ' (The Guild Merchant in Hunan in Ch'ing Times), *Tōyōshi kenkyū* XXI.iii (1962), pp. 71–92; Tou Chi-liang, *T'ung-hsiang tsu-chih chih yen-chiu* (Organizations of Fellow-Regionals) (Chungking: 1943), esp. ch. 2. I am grateful to Professor John Fincher for drawing this book to my attention.

19 YANG TUAN-LIN, *Ch'ing-tai huo-p'i chin-jung shih-kao* (A Draft History of Currency in the Ch'ing Dynasty) (Peking: 1962), p. 147.

20 KATŌ (1953–4), II 469.

21 FUJII (1953) iii, p. 80.

22 Ibid., iii, p. 66.

23 Ibid., iii, p. 81.

24 FU I-LING (1956), pp. 27–8.

25 FU I-LING (1963), p. 43.

26 KU YEN-WU, *T'ien-hsia chün-kuo li-ping shu* (Documents on the Strengths and Weaknesses of the Commanderies and Principates of the Empire) (1639–62), Ssu-k'u shan-pen edition, XXVI 36a–37b.

27 Ibid., XL 66b–67a.

28 Ibid., III 42b.

29 O-ERH-T'AI, *et al.*, ed., *Shou-shih t'ung-k'ao* (Comprehensive Examination of Seasonal Practices) (1742), XXXVIII 13b–22b.

30 *A Glance at the Interior of China, obtained during a journey through the silk and green tea districts* (Shanghai: 1847), no author (? Robert Fortune), pp. 27–9.

31 SHIGETA ATSUSUSHI, 'Shinsho ni okeru Konan kome shijō no ikkōsatsu' (An Enquiry into the Hunan Rice Market during the Early Ch'ing Period) in Tōkyō daigaku tōyō bunka kenkyūjo, ed., *Tochi shoyū no shiteki kenkyū* (A Historical Study of Land Tenure) (Tokyo: 1956), pp. 442–3.

32 Ibid., p. 444.

33 ADAM SMITH, *An Inquiry into the Nature and Causes of the Wealth of Nations* (1776), Everyman edition (1910), II 175–6.

34 KOIZUMI TEIZŌ, 'Shina minsen no keiei ni tsuite' (The Management of Junks in China), *Keizai ronsō* LVII (1943), pp. 70–2.

35 PERKINS (1969), pp. 16–17.

36 P. SCHRAN, *The Development of Chinese Agriculture 1950–1959* (Chicago: 1969), chapter IV.

37 LO ERH-KANG, 'T'ai-p'ing T'ien-kuo ko-ming ch'ien ti jen-k'ou ya-p'o wen-t'i' (The Question of Population Pressure before the Taiping Rebellion) (originally published in 1947; reprinted in Pao Tsun-p'eng, Wu Hsiang-hsiang and Li Ting-i, eds, *Chung-kuo chin-tai shih-lun ts'ung* (Collected Essays on Modern Chinese History) II.ii (Taipeh: 1958), p. 51.

38 Ibid., p. 44.

39 OTANI TOSHIO, 'Pao Shih-ch'en no jitsugaku shisō no tsuite' (The Practical Ideology of Pao Shih-ch'en), *Tōyōshi kenkyū* XXVIII.ii and iii (Dec. 1969), p. 49.

40 IMURA KŌZEN, 'Chihōshi ni kisaiseraretaru Chūgoku ekirei ryakkō' (An Outline Investigation of Chinese Epidemics Recorded in Local Gazetteers), *Chūgai iji shimpō* (1936 and 1937), 8 parts, esp. part 3.

41 PERKINS (1969), pp. 216 and 240.

42 South Manchurian Railway, *Third Report on Progress in Manchuria, 1907–1932* (Dairen: 1932), pp. 17, 140; *id.*, *Fifth Report on Progress in Manchuria, to 1936* (Dairen: 1936), pp. 163–4; A. Eckstein, 'The Economic Heritage', in A. Eckstein, W. Galenson and T. C. Liu, eds, *Economic Trends in Communist China* (Edinburgh: 1968), p. 62.

43 Research Office on the Shanghai Economy of the Chinese Academy of Sciences and the Economic Research Unit of the Shanghai Academy of the Social Sciences, ed., *Ta-lung chi-ch'i-ch'ang ti fa-sheng fa-chan yü kai-tsao* (The Genesis, Development and Reconstruction of the Ta-lung Machinery Factory) (Shanghai: 1959), chapters I and II.

44 SHIH MIN-HSIUNG, *Ch'ing-tai ssu-chih kung-yeh ti fa-chan* (The Development of the Silk Industry in the Ch'ing Period) (Taipeh: 1968), pp. 35–8, 65.

45 WU CHIH, *Gōson shokufu kōgyō no ichi kenkyū* (A Study of a Village Weaving Industry), Japanese translation by the East Asia Research Office of the Investigations Section of the Manchurian Railway (Tokyo: 1942).

Topical Index